MW00532514

A Whistleblower's Lament

The Perverted Pursuit of Justice
in the State of New York

JUDGE STUART NAMM (RET.)

HELLGATE PRESS   ASHLAND, OREGON

A WHISTLEBLOWER'S LAMENT
©2014 Stuart Namm

Published by Hellgate Press
(An imprint of L&R Publishing, LLC)

Hellgate Press
PO Box 3531
Ashland, OR 97520
email: sales@hellgatepress.com

Editor: Harley B. Patrick
Cover design: L. Redding
Cover photo courtesy of *Newsday*

Library of Congress Cataloging-in-Publication Data

Namm, Stuart, author.
 A whistleblower's lament : the perverted pursuit of justice in the state of New
York / Judge Stuart Namm (Ret.).
   p. cm.
 Includes bibliographical references.
 ISBN 978-1-55571-740-7
 1. Namm, Stuart. 2. Judges--New York (State)--Biography. 3. Whistle blowing--
New York (State) I. Title.
 KF373.N36N36 2014
 347.747'0234--dc23
 [B]
                    2014001034

Printed and bound in the United States of America
First edition 10 9 8 7 6 5 4 3 2 1

A Whistleblower's Lament

The Perverted Pursuit of Justice
in the State of New York

CONTENTS

Dedication

T HIS BOOK, WHICH TOOK OVER TWENTY-FIVE YEARS TO FINALLY publish,
is dedicated to the three wonderful women of my life, without whose
support it would never have happened!

Lenore Rhona Abelson Namm, my teenage sweetheart whom I met when
I was seventeen years old, and she was sixteen, and to whom I was married
for forty-one sometimes tumultuous years. She was born in Brooklyn, New
York, in 1934 to a family as poor as church mice, during the depths of the
Great Depression, at a time when a young woman, no matter how smart
(except for the fortunate few) could not pursue an education at a college, even
one without tuition like Brooklyn College or City College of New York. Her
lot in life was to go to work and contribute to the family. The mother of my
three very talented children, she never lost the desire to pursue an education.
Thus, when our youngest daughter Suzanne was signed up for kindergarten,
and we were living on Long Island, she decided to pursue that dream and was
accepted at the State University of Stony Brook where she earned both a
Bachelors and Masters degree in Sociology, with honors, going to school part
time, both in the daytime and evenings, but always there for our children
when they needed her. Upon graduation from Stony Brook, she was hired as
a Suffolk County Probation Officer after passing a civil service examination.
At that time, I was already a judge in Suffolk County, and she was assigned to
the Family Court to avoid any "conflict of interest." She loved her work, and
was very proud of what she had accomplished. Then came the evening that I
told her that I felt compelled to write to Gov. Mario Cuomo to "blow the
whistle" on a corrupt system of justice and that "our lives would never be the

same!" She never flinched or had a second thought when she responded, "Stuart, do whatever you feel you have to do!"

That was 1985, and Lenore continued her work as a probation officer until the decision was made by the powerful political bosses of Suffolk County, at the end of my ten year term in the County Court, to not nominate me for a second term. The "fix" was in, and we had to leave New York for our property in North Carolina for fear that if I stayed around, who knew what might have happened!

Just three years after we left Suffolk County, my very healthy wife of forty-one years, at the age of sixty-one, died of a sudden and massive heart attack in my arms on a Sunday morning in March, Palm Sunday, having never really been sick before.

The second woman to whom I dedicate this book is Nancy Parmenter Middleswarth Namm, my "angel," whom I met in March 1996 at Lenore's memorial service at Temple of Israel in Wilmington, North Carolina. She introduced herself to me saying, "I know what you are going through, and if you need someone to talk to, you have my number, and you can just give me a call." I knew that Nancy, who had been Lenore's water aerobics instructor, had lost her husband two months before after his six year bout with prostate cancer, but I had never met Nancy before. When you are in grief, you don't really see faces, but you remember words spoken with compassion. Six weeks later, after my children had gone back to their homes in Okinawa, Tennessee, and South Carolina, when I was alone with my pet dog "Laddie" who had become my only companion, I began to reach out to anyone I knew by telephone. I remembered that nice lady who had spoken to me at the memorial service, and after several telephone conversations I got up the nerve to ask her out for a late lunch, and she consented. When I went to her home, any woman could have answered that front door, because all I really remembered were those sweet words.

I had been married to my teenage sweetheart for forty-one years, and I had told my children before they left that I was not going to get married again. Nevertheless, just six days after we first had a late lunch together, I proposed marriage to Nancy, who was in shock, but after a private conversation with God, she accepted. She is a "born again" Christian, and

I am a Jew, but that has never been a hindrance to our life together. As I write this, we have been together as husband and wife for almost seventeen years, and my Nancy Ann, who is eleven years younger than me, has heard all of the stories over and over again, but she has always been the supportive and loving wife. We have traveled the world together, created two video documentaries, and she has never flinched in her support of whatever I chose to do, no matter how crazy—including the publication of this book after so many years.

The third woman to whom I dedicate this book is my only daughter, Suzanne Lizabeth Wolonick, mother of three special grandchildren, administrator of husband's Richard's medical practice, cellist and church organist, who each day since the untimely and devastating death of her mother in 1996 has communicated and supported me—sometimes more than once—either by email, telephone or face to face.

However, before closing this dedication, there must be a special shout-out to my son, Gary, our firstborn, who toils in public relations and who took time out of his personal life to promote his dad's book, much as he did as a seventeen-year old, in 1975, climbing telephone poles to place political posters, when I first ran for the District Court of Suffolk County and won against all odds as an unknown Democrat in a very conservative town.

Prologue

The cost of conscience: permanent anonymity...This says something...about our gut reaction to people, who for one reason or another, blow the whistle on former friends. Stool pigeons or heroes? Depending on the circumstances, there should be no doubt. Yet there frequently is doubt, if only because the courage to speak out against prevailing attitudes is something we honor far more often in theory than in fact. Courage of that sort is often inconvenient, at least in its own time. It's not easily understood in a society where conformity is king....

—Vincent Canby, *The New York Times*[1]

COURAGE, COURAGE, COURAGE! I'VE GROWN SICK OF THAT WORD. Too often I've heard it uttered behind the closed doors of my courthouse chamber, over the telephone, in the media, on a neighbor's front lawn or from a stranger on the street. It didn't take courage to expose a corrupt system of criminal justice. A judge is sworn to uphold the law and preserve the constitution.

Yet it did require a conscience and an aroused sense of decency. But where was the conscience and decency of those judges and attorneys who, out of complacency, greed or misplaced fear, were unwilling to speak out to preserve the integrity of the system which they too were sworn to preserve? It was not enough to goad me on in an impossible battle.

I expected no courage from anyone, but I was hurt and angered by the apparent lack of conscience and decency of persons unwilling to speak out publicly, though they privately agreed that the system was unjust and even corrupt.

By virtue of their uniform black robes and the anachronistic judicial canons of ethics, judges are generally comfortable with their cloak of anonymity. No one familiar with the criminal justice system in Long Island would dare say that I too had achieved such anonymity. In fact, there are some who would say that, in my role as a whistleblower, I achieved certain infamy in some quarters. Had I been able to arouse the collective conscience of the so-called decent people, I'd have willingly accepted anonymity without protest. However, conscience, decency and courage were in short supply in the justice system in Suffolk County, New York.

Preface

The belief that the ends justified the means was alive and well in the New York State county of more than one million men, women and children. Suffolk has been called a microcosm of middle America, where it seemed like "almost every day...somebody is murdered by somebody else, a friend, a neighbor, often a close relative." [1]

"PROUD OF OUR POLICE!" WERE THE WORDS ON a bumper sticker which began to appear on automobiles throughout the county in 1987. As a County Court judge, I too was proud of most of the men and women in blue. Still whenever I spotted one of those stickers, I couldn't help but feel personally responsible for the cloud that nestled over law enforcement in our county. It was a cloud that struck a defensive chord in those persons who simply could not believe that a police officer would ever lie or concoct evidence to make a case.

Most residents of Suffolk County left New York City to make a better life for themselves and their children—-to escape the crime and grime of the city. They reasoned that the sacrifice of a few rights which protected criminals was a small price to pay to keep their streets crime-free and safe. But how about the accused who was truly innocent? In the zeal to ensnare the criminal element in society, did the safety net of justice snag some innocent person as well?

"Guilty!" How often I've heard that response to the court clerk's request to a jury for its verdict. Countless times as a trial judge I instructed juries that the burden of proof in a criminal case is upon the people, represented by the prosecutor. The state's burden is to prove the guilt of the accused beyond a reasonable doubt. This burden is the very essence of the American system of justice. It is founded in the constitutional presumption of innocence. A defendant in a criminal case need never prove his or her innocence!

Over the years I've seen countless defendants profess their innocence. Some elected to remain silent and put the prosecution to its burden under the law. Most presented evidence in their defense and some even chose to take the witness stand. Despite some vigorous defenses presented on their behalf and the vehement protestations of innocence, most defendants on trial before me were convicted. Twelve persons "tried and true"—a jury of their peers—had been unanimously convinced of their guilt beyond a reasonable doubt.

So I was often called upon to punish persons who professed their innocence, even until the moment they were removed from the courtroom in handcuffs to begin what would be a very long term of imprisonment.

I've watched defendants like the teenager, Robert Brensic, convicted of the brutal murder of a young schoolmate, tears pouring down his cheeks, sobbingly profess that he couldn't hurt an animal, much less another human being. But the tears of a convicted murderer, even those of a trembling teen, rarely moved me.

More often than not I would dole out the maximum punishment allowable in New York—twenty-five-years-to-life.

Reasonable doubt? In the beginning of my tenure as a judge, reasonable doubt was not particularly troublesome to me since the question of guilt or innocence was the sole province of the jury. It is only when a judge believes, as a matter of law and conscience, that the people have failed to prove guilt beyond a reasonable doubt, will he or she intervene to set aside a jury verdict. Where one person, even a judge, interjects his or her own opinion to supersede the unanimous opinion of twelve jurors, that person should be absolutely certain that the law would permit no other verdict.

I had little cause for concern until I began to try cases where the ultimate penalty could involve many years of incarceration, and very often the balance of a person's natural life. I suppose that if I'd been sitting as a judge in a state like Florida or Texas where capital punishment is in force, these thoughts would have weighed even heavier upon my conscience. But two consecutive New York governors, Hugh Carey and Mario Cuomo, had for years successfully vetoed capital punishment legislation in New York State. Thus all New York judges had been relieved of this awesome responsibility.

Still, where a defendant, about to face a long term of imprisonment, continued to profess his innocence, it was sometimes difficult to free my mind of the thought that perhaps this might truly be an innocent person who was about to pay a high price for the mortal sin of another. This became more and more my concern as unexpected events involving certain members of the police homicide squad and the office of the district attorney began to unfold in my courtroom in the summer and fall of 1985. In a period of less than five years, I would become impaled upon a sword of cynicism, losing faith in a system in which I had always believed. This streak of skepticism sometimes threatened my ability to function as an impartial criminal court judge.

A number of troubling questions have remained, for me, unanswered. Why, for example, should it take more than three years for the State of New York Commission of Investigations (SIC), chaired by a former U.S. Attorney and dean of a prominent law school, to publish its report detailing the corruption of a system which it uncovered in little more than one year?

Why did the liberal governor of New York, and would-be president, Mario Cuomo, think it was more important to appoint a special prosecutor in the Howard Beach case, and to investigate the Tawana Brawley affair, than to appoint one to investigate the systemic corruption of a county's criminal justice system?

What kind of a system would spawn a detective or an assistant district attorney capable of scrawling obscene graffiti directed at a sitting judge on the walls of a public toilet, or who would stoop to hurling verbal epithets at a judge from the 5th floor window of a criminal courts building?

Why did the administrators of a court system conduct their business in a manner which would serve to enhance the less than honorable motives of a corrupt prosecutor's office?

And finally, why did two local bar associations sit silently by as the system in which they functioned each day crumbled from a lack of ethics and morality? What had happened to justice in Suffolk County?

As I look back upon those shocking events and attempt to answer these unhappy questions, with the benefit of hindsight, I've come to the sad realization that the corruption of the Suffolk County criminal justice system, as I saw it, can take place anywhere in America. The atmosphere of complacency which fostered the perversion of the system in Suffolk, unfortunately, is not unlike the climate which has slowly pervaded America as a whole. We Americans have come to expect easy answers to difficult problems. It is as if slogans like "Proud of Our Police" plastered on automobile bumpers can magically make police and prosecutorial corruption disappear. That is why this story needs to be told over and over again.

A very experienced and well meaning literary agent once suggested that this story should best be reduced to fiction. To do so, I believe, would be intellectually dishonest. It is important for all who read this book to know that these events, which often were more unnerving than fiction, really did take place. With the criminal justice system as it is, they may be doomed to happen again in Suffolk County or anywhere else in America.

Author's Notes

M OST NON-FICTION BOOKS THAT YOU WILL READ ARE COMPLETE with hundreds of footnotes for every quote or reference in the book. Without making any excuses, at some point, some twenty-five years ago, I got tired of footnoting every comment and every quote from a trial transcript and from my copious notes from which court reporters would often ask to see to ensure that the final transcript of the trial accurately reflected what was said under oath, or by the court during the course of the trial. As you, the reader, reads this book, it will become clear that the quotes which you are perusing come directly from the court record, or from my notes, or from a recorded telephone conversation (at some point I became paranoid and began recording all of my calls to my chambers telephone), or from official records of the Suffolk County Police Department, or from some relevant newspaper article on any given day. It would have been nice to footnote every item, but those transcripts and judicial notes, all of which we carried from New York state, have been buried in the musty crawl space of our North Carolina home on the coastal marsh for more than twenty years now, and with the ravages of lymphoma, even with a mask, it was impossible to access that crawl space and these documents without fear of serious infection which would end my ability to complete this book.

Moreover, you, the reader, should always remember that virtually all of these words were written almost twenty-five years ago, when the facts were fresh in my young mind, and when I was suffering the ignominy of almost seventeen years as a hard working judge who was trashed by a system which was more interested in its public reputation and political power than the truth as we now know it!

We have lived in a digital world for some time now. As I write this note, I am surrounded by three monitors, and four or more computers, in a small converted bedroom. When I left the bench in 1992, we did not even have access to a computer in my chambers, although most active attorneys were already immersed in their computers and word processors. Virtually everything that I have spoken of, other than my personal conversations, within the covers of this book can be found somewhere in that ever expanding universe of information now known as the Internet, or someone's "cloud." Thus, the concept of footnotes for research may even become obsolete some time in the not too distant future, although I do not offer this as an excuse for not have completely done so to support my conclusions and words.

Some time ago, I offered all of my massive collection of documents and transcripts to the Library of the State University of New York at Stony Brook as a sad part of the history of Long Island. It was turned down by the head librarian whom I first met by telephone when I turned over a portion of my huge political button collection relating to Suffolk County elections, in memory of my beloved Lenore, who had earned two degrees at that great institute of learning. Sadly, some new state or local regulation which I never understood prohibited her from accepting them on behalf of the state, although they are stocked with the papers of many others of historic interest. Perhaps, with the publication of this book, she or they will rethink that decision, and keep these important documents where they truly belong— for future historians, authors and the curious public who have a right to know!

Introduction

A S I SIT AT MY COMPUTER AT 3:30 AM, ON THE DARKENED, but beautiful, coastal marsh of North Carolina, in the eightieth year of life, having been diagnosed with the dreaded "Cancer," defined as "Type B Non Hodgkin Lymphoma," and having recently concluded the first session of the dreaded chemotherapy at Duke Cancer Center, I think that I could have gone sometime in the future quietly into the night with this story still buried, as it has been for more than twenty years. Why now? Why regurgitate for those who might have a simple curiosity the worst five years of my life when there is not much more of my life to give? Why not pass into eternity some unknown time in the future peaceably without digging up ancient history for an audience that is too young to have known this story, or too old to remember or care about the gory details of the life of the man whom they had laughingly dubbed "Maximum Stu," or "The Hanging Judge," much like in the "Wild West" of days of yore in this once great country of ours? Yet, there is still life in this old man that the *Hollywood Reporter* had once dubbed "The Serpico of Judges," and this story has to finally be told, for it is doomed to happen again and again unless we wake up to the dangers of a corrupt system which I had long since coined "Criminal Injustice!" So long as we allow politics, which has sunk to the deepest depths in many parts of this great country, to control what should be a fair and honest judicial system, most assuredly what I chronicle in this book will be repeated over and over, and some innocent person will pay the price with his or her life, or spend years in a prison built for profit to fill the pockets of some greedy person or persons with sufficient capital to compete with the state in the business of housing "criminals."

Born in Brooklyn, New York, in 1933, in the midst of the Great Depression, in the crowded tenements of Brownsville, then known as the home of "Murder Incorporated" and the infamous Louis "Lepke" Buchalter, I somehow managed to graduate from Brooklyn Technical High School, one of three special high schools in New York City, from where I entered City College of New York, one of a few free tuition colleges in New York City. There I discovered the sport of Lacrosse, and was a four year member of the varsity team under coach "Chief" Leon Miller, the Cherokee brother-in-law of Jim Thorpe, and one of the athletic stars of the Carlisle Indian College in Pennsylvania .

When I entered City College, the United States was engaged in the Korean War, so I chose to join the ROTC, and upon graduation in 1955, after marrying, during Christmas recess, my teenage sweetheart, Lenore Rhona Abelson, I was commissioned a 2nd lieutenant in the Infantry, and was immediately assigned to Fort Benning, Georgia, where I graduated from the U.S. Army Infantry School and volunteered to enter the U.S. Army Ranger school. Immediately thereafter, I was assigned to the 17th Infantry Regiment at Camp Kaiser, Korea, in the heart of the Chorwan Valley, and north of the 38th parallel. Almost immediately after commanding a rifle platoon, and having been successful in two successive Special Courts Martial, I was assigned as Regimental Asst. S-1, Courts and Boards officer, until I was discharged from the Army in 1957.

In 1957, although accepted to both Georgetown and George Washington University Law Schools, I chose to remain in New York City, where I attended Brooklyn Law School in the evening, while working as a contract analyst for the Equitable Life Assurance Society, which paid for half of my law school. Having entered the Army after the Korean War ended, I was not eligible for the G.I. Bill. While in law school, I was the winner of the school's annual moot court competition while attending the evening session, and selling some casualty insurance and a few early mutual funds.

In 1961, the year President John F. Kennedy was inaugurated, I graduated from Brooklyn Law School and was immediately employed as an attorney-examiner in the New York City office of the Federal Trade Commission (FTC) under President Kennedy's "Law Honor Graduate Program." I worked for the FTC for five years where I investigated such major companies as Timex, Decca Records, Johnson and Johnson and Bristol Laboratories for various anti-trust violations. While in law school, both of my sons were born. In 1966, after the birth of our daughter, and after moving from New York City to Suffolk County, Long Island, New York, I entered into the private practice of law with Dominic J. Baranello, the Suffolk County Democratic Chairman, who went on to become the New York State Democratic Chairman, and Frederic Block, who went on to become the president of the New York State Bar Association, and who is currently a United States District Court Judge after appointment to that office by President Clinton.

I was ostensibly the litigation member of the firm, spending most of my time in the various courts of Suffolk County. In 1969, the original firm of Baranello, Block & Namm was dissolved, and Dominic and I continued to practice law in Centereach, New York, under the firm name of Baranello and Namm.** In 1975, I was nominated by the Democratic party as candidate for Judge of the District Court of Suffolk County from the Town of Brookhaven. In November 1975, I was elected to that post, previously held by an incumbent Republican judge (largely as a result of the Watergate

---

**I believe that I was never satisfied as the junior partner of the firm of Baranello, Block & Namm, or even Baranello & Namm. Dominic Baranello was firmly established in politics, and rarely was in the office after lunch. Fred Block, now United States District Court Judge Frederic Block of the Eastern District of New York, was a brilliant workaholic. Virtually, every afternoon, it was just he and I and the secretaries in the office, and he always made me feel that I was simply the equal "junior partner"who never pulled his weight in terms of paying clients, so I was the "worker bee" as he now refers to me in his published biography. We never really got along! He worked well into the night and on weekends, and I, having been groomed at an insurance company and the federal government, was accustomed to a work day from 9:00 am to 5:00 pm. Often his work week would begin at Sunday dinner time when our home telephone would ring, and Fred would be on the other line wanting to discuss the next week's work. Wife and mother Lenore hated this habit of his so much that she convinced me to change our home telephone number to unlisted, and for years Fred never again knew our home number! At one point, I got so angry with some comments that he made about me, in the presence of Dominic, that I caught my fist as it approached his face in a moment of sheer anger. I had been a tough, well conditioned, Lacrosse player and a former Army Ranger, and Fred was always slightly built. It would have been a disaster, but things were never again the same between us, although, I must say, to his credit, that Fred was one of the only three Suffolk County lawyers to attend the meeting of the New York Association of Criminal Defense Attorneys at the Marriott Marquis Hotel in Manhattan, when I was the first recipient of the distinguished Justice Thurgood Marshall Award in January 1993. For that alone, I will never forget him, but he could really get under my nerves!

scandal and a local Republican scandal), by the slimmest of pluralities, fifty-eight votes out of a total of 68,000 votes cast. Thus, I was declared the winner after several recounts on December 30, 1975, long after most victorious candidates had celebrated their election.

In January 1976, I was sworn in as a District Court Judge. I had realized my childhood ambition of becoming a judge, having spent many cheap Saturday nights with my fiancee and future wife, Lenore Abelson, in New York City's Magistrate Court in Manhattan during my college years. I quickly developed a reputation as a no-nonsense, tough judge, in the administration of criminal justice, having heard complaints about "the revolving door system of justice" from potential voters, and I spent six years in the District Court. In 1981, when I ran for reelection against an unknown Republican candidate in Brookhaven, I was endorsed by every law enforcement organization in the county of Suffolk, save the New York State Trooper's Association, as they were unhappy with a traffic radar decision I had previously rendered. In short, I was the sweetheart of virtually every local law enforcement organization. This relationship would turn out to be short lived as I was defeated by an overwhelming plurality in an election when the town of Brookhaven had returned to its normal conservative Republican roots and since judicial candidates are virtually unknown to the voting public.

In May 1982, after returning to the private practice of law, I was nominated by Governor Hugh Carey to fill a vacancy on the Suffolk County Court bench. Quickly confirmed by the New York State Senate, I ascended to the court of highest criminal jurisdiction in a county of over 1,000,000 people. It was there that I would have the greatest impact upon the criminal justice system. In November 1982, after receiving the endorsement of both major political parties, I was elected to a ten year term on that court. Shortly thereafter, I was selected by the administrative judge, Thomas M. Stark, as one of three judges handling all of the homicide cases in the county. I quickly reestablished my reputation as a hard working, no nonsense, tough criminal court judge. In homicide cases, I was not reluctant to hand out the maximum twenty-five-year-to-life sentence (New York did not have the death penalty at that time) where it was, in my opinion, appropriate.

In 1985, I presided over two consecutive highly publicized murder trials, *People v. Peter Corso* and *People v. James Diaz*, when I began to notice a pattern of corruption in the investigation and prosecution of these cases by senior members of the district attorney's office and the elite, highly paid, Suffolk County Police Homicide Squad. Both of these defendants were acquitted by unanimous juries despite alleged confessions. These cases came on the heels of another homicide trial, *People v. Vincent Waters*, where I believed that senior members of the District Attorney's office had perjured themselves during the course of a hearing on alleged systematic exclusion of young blacks in the jury selection process. I believed I was witnessing the systemic corruption of the county's criminal justice system. In short, I believed, cases were being manufactured to obtain convictions in major homicide trials.

In November 1985, I took the extraordinary step of writing to Governor Mario Cuomo to request the appointment of a Special Prosecutor to investigate the county's criminal justice system in homicide cases. For more than three years, the New York State Commission of Investigations (SIC) conducted a sweeping investigation of the county's criminal justice system. They conducted two public hearings and wrote two reports. The commission corroborated the corruption discovered by me, and more, and I was the lead witness at these hearings. I became a pariah in the "old boy network" which permeated the county's system of justice. I was shunned by the establishment bar, both defense and prosecutorial. The police commissioner resigned and was replaced. The district attorney, who went on to become a Supreme Court Justice one year later, was directed not to seek reelection. Virtually, the entire homicide squad either resigned, retired or was transferred. The county's chief forensic pathologist, then Director of the Maryland Crime Laboratory, was convicted of perjury. The County Executive resigned from office. *Newsday*, the largest newspaper of general circulation, published an award-winning week-long series commencing December 7, 1986 (Pearl Harbor Day) entitled, "The Confession Takers," which documented the entire sordid affair.

As my reward, I was transferred out of the County Court to a civil part of the Supreme Court, the highest court of trial jurisdiction in the county, but despite this experience, I firmly believe I remained a tough, but fair jurist. In my last criminal case, prior to the transfer, I sentenced Scott Carrol, a notorious serial rapist, referred to in the media as the dreaded "South Shore Rapist," to the longest sentence ever handed out in New York State at that time—375 to 750 years in prison. For two years, I fought vigorously for my return to criminal court. In 1991, after much media and editorial pressure on the administrators of the judiciary, I was transferred back to the County Court and criminal jurisdiction. I remained on the bench as a trial judge until December 1992. Both major political parties, one of which was still led by my former law partner, conspired not to re-nominate me to the County Court. The Democratic Party, led by my former law partner, extracted three judgeships and mine in exchange for not re-nominating me. Although some asked me to run for district attorney in 1993, we, as a family, chose to move to our newly constructed home in the safe confines of the North Carolina coast.

In 1993, I completed the manuscript for this story, then entitled *Criminal Injustice* which documents the story of my involvement in uncovering the corruption of the criminal justice system of Suffolk County; corruption of the type which probably does occur elsewhere where judges are selected through the current political election system. In January 1993, I was shocked to learn that I was to be the recipient of three distinguished awards. Lenore and I were flown back to New York City, to the Grand Hyatt and Marriott Marquis Hotels, where on one day I was the first recipient of the Justice Thurgood Marshall Award of the New York State Association of Criminal Defense Attorneys as a "champion of individual rights and liberties, with a strong commitment to principle"; the David C. Michaels Award of the New York State Bar Association for "Courageous efforts in promoting integrity in the criminal justice system"; and a special award from the NAACP "to someone who stood up for what was right at great personal sacrifice....A man who practiced and lived what everyone else preached."

For years after dabbling in television with a British production company, I continued to be a hero to those who claimed that they were unjustly convicted in what they perceived to be a corrupt system of justice. I received hundreds of letters from all over the United States from prisoners with impassioned pleas for assistance in their plight, including some on death row in Texas and Mississippi. The closest I could come to helping them was un unsuccessful attempt at a TV series entitled "A Question of Guilt," where we published what would have been a pilot for the series on DVD, the story of Martin Tankleff who spent seventeen years in a New York State maximum security prison for the murder of both of his adoptive parents at age seventeen. After allegedly giving an oral confession, but refusing to sign a written confession prepared by the homicide detectives who are depicted in this book, he was released by the New York State Court of Appeals after his family hired two retired New York City homicide detectives who produced the real killers, but who were never tried by Suffolk County. To do so, would be an admission that they had tried the wrong man! As I write these notes, Martin Tankleff will have completed his third year at Hofstra University Law School, where he remains an advocate, as he was in prison, for those whom he believes were, like him, unjustly convicted.

Three weeks after my first wife, Lenore, who passed suddenly in 1996 of a massive heart attack in my arms, herself a Family Court Probation Officer, and I, a "retired County Court Judge,"—two poor kids from the tenements of Brooklyn—reluctantly left our Long Island home of twenty-five years and the birthplace of our three wonderful children, I received several calls from New York City about the aforesaid awards.

Less than one month later, after one of those telephone calls, Lenore and I found ourselves in a plush office across the street from the huge Warner Brothers studios in Hollywood, California, where we were told that a fictionalized version of my life as a judge, would be produced by the man who had produced the movie "Hoffa" with actor Danny Devito. Unfortunately, this never happened, as is the story of many a Hollywood project. Still, as soon as that option period expired, I signed another option on my life for one year with the Abby Mann, who had both an Oscar and an Emmy displayed in his opulent Hollywood home, that he referred to as his "bungalow," for creating the legendary television character known as "Kojak," and for writing the movie script for "Judgment at Nuremberg," the Academy Award winning motion picture about the infamous trials in the aftermath of WWII and the Holocaust.

XXVI A WHISTLEBLOWER'S LAMENT

At that point, after almost two years, despite the fact that actors like Al Pacino and Gene Hackman, although they probably never knew it, were being considered to play me, and hundreds of hours on the telephone and the fax machine, the Hollywood dream ended, and I was so disgusted that I vowed to bury my manuscript in an office drawer and get on with my life. My days in the law, however, were over and I wasn't about to resurrect the seven most unhappy years of my life.

Before long I became involved with a British television production company after being referred to them by someone I'd never met—Ronald DeFeo, the young man convicted of the brutal 1974 "Amityville Horror" murders of his parents and four siblings and now a prisoner for life. I was hired as their "judicial consultant" in a thirteen-part series entitled "The Serial Killers." It had its world premiere on Ruppert Murdoch's Sky Television network in the United Kingdom and elsewhere in Europe and Japan, and ultimately on The Learning Channel in the United States. Because the original creator of the series ran out of serial killers to comply with the contract requiring thirteen episodes, I was enlisted to find two additional serial killers in the United States. My search and personal interviews in Michigan and California resulted in the last two thirty-minute chapters entitled "The Lethal Lovers," a title which I had coined. It was the story of two lesbian lovers who worked as aides in a nursing home in Michigan, and who murdered Alzheimer's patients silently in their sleep with a washcloth held over the victims' mouths for their personal recreation when they were bored!

Three years after leaving New York, my teenage sweetheart and healthy wife of forty-one years, the mother of my three wonderful children, died suddenly of a massive heart attack in my arms on a Sunday morning in March. She had loved her job as a Suffolk County probation officer, after having gone back to afternoon and evening college at the State University of New York at Stony Brook when our daughter entered kindergarten, where she earned both her Bachelor's and Masters degrees, and passed a Civil Service exam to become a probation officer in the Suffolk County, New York, Office of Probation. Lenore never really wanted to leave the position which she loved so much, and had worked so hard to achieve. However, in 1992, during my final Christmas recess, it was time to take our leave and head south to our new home in North Carolina, because I, the classic whistleblower, had become "personna non grata" in Suffolk County and it was time to leave. I am convinced that this unhappiness lingered in Lenore's heart for three long years, and took its final toll on Sunday morning, March 31, 1996.

However, whether it was God's will or sheer luck that I met my sweet angel, Nancy Ann, herself a widow of two months and Lenore's water aerobics instructor, at Lenore's memorial service, I will never really know. We have been together as husband and wife ever since that fateful day some eight months later. She retired from her position working with senior citizens in New Hanover County, and we have traveled the world, on land and on sea, above the oceans and under, much as Lenore and I had done before her when we had earned enough money together to do so. I had been exposed to the television industry, and I readily continued my lifetime hobby shooting photos and video all over the world, including three photo safaris to Africa, the great reefs of the world, including the Great Barrier Reef of Australia, and beyond. We have authored two documentaries on video, with Nancy as nominal "Executive Producer," the first about Martin Tankleff entitled, "A Queston of Guilt," whose story will be recounted in this book, and "Men of 'Truth and Courage': The 17th Infantry Regiment in the Korean War," the unit which I served in for sixteen months north of the 38th parallel after the war had ended. We have had a great time doing so, and we have met so many wonderful and appreciative people over the past seventeen years of an incredible life.

ONE

The Hanging Judge

M Y LEGENDARY HERO, JUSTICE THURGOOD MARSHALL, was dead for three days. He hadn't yet reached his final resting place. Yet here I was, a "kid" from the tenements of Brooklyn, seated on a huge dais in a ballroom of the Grand Hyatt Hotel in New York City about to receive a prestigious award given in his name. They said only Marshall himself had been presented with that honor before me. It was mind boggling. Even more unbelievable—it was the third distinguished award that I received that day.

They couldn't be talking about me! In my eyes, I was no hero, and I was certainly not the courageous icon that was being depicted by one person after another. It didn't seem real. The former judge, whom many had mockingly called "Maximum Stu" or the "Hanging Judge" was about to be honored by the New York State Association of Criminal Defense Lawyers— a group of some of the most well known and high priced attorneys in the country. Wasn't I the same judge who'd sentenced Scott Carroll—the infamous "South Shore Rapist"—to two consecutive prison terms totaling 375-750 years? Hadn't I handed out the longest term ever imposed in New York state upon a drunk driver who'd taken the life of an innocent child?

Those who claimed to know me best, the most visible and vociferous members of the Suffolk County Criminal Bar Association, boycotted the annual dinner meeting because I was to be the honoree. I was no hero to the small but powerful group of Suffolk County lawyers who presided over the organized bar. I'd made too many waves! By instigating an investigation that should have started years before, somehow in their minds, I'd made them all look bad.

The words of praise rang like eulogies. I couldn't suppress the feeling that the awards seemed almost posthumous. Though I was very much alive, my spirit had been destroyed, and my controversial judicial career had suffered an early demise at the hands of ruthless and unprincipled politicians. How had I gotten to this point? I'd long since vowed to tell the members of the Suffolk County Criminal Bar Association to shove their "Judge of the Year" award up their collective asses, if they gave even a momentary thought to presenting me with an award for having shaken up the corrupt system of justice in which they toiled each day. But this was not the Suffolk County Bar.

Suffolk County. Only fifty miles away from this hotel in the heart of the city, but it seemed more like a million. I had spent sixteen and a half years on the bench in the county which had been our home for twenty-eight years—the place where Lenore and I raised three great kids. It was difficult to suppress the bitterness.

TWO

An Ungrateful Electorate

WHERE HAD THIS ROAD TO IGNOMINY AND FAME BEGUN? As I lightly squeezed Lenore's soothing hand, the din of the speakers' voices was smothered by thoughts of the life which we'd left behind. My life literally flashed through my wandering mind.

****

We were two poor kids from the tenements of Brooklyn who didn't have but a few dollars between us at any given time from our on and off part time jobs. However, when I finally settled into an inter-disciplinary major of "pre-law" at City College of New York, I began to get serious about our future. We were already engaged to be married, with a ring I had given her in September 1952, against my mother's wishes (although she helped me find a ring on the Bowery in Manhattan) from the earnings that I made as a busboy at Sunrise Manor in the summer of 1952. I had earned this money, something short of $1,000, at my mother's rich uncle Jack Kramer's hotel in Ellenville, one of the ghetto Jewish kosher escapes in the Catskill Mountains of New York State, known then as "the Borscht Circuit." For less than $1,000, believe it or not, at that time I was able to buy a .90 carat, almost perfect, diamond engagement ring mounted in platinum, with side baguettes—in Manhattan! But it could only have been with Lily Namm, my reluctant mom, doing the bargaining!

Lenore was now working at a rug manufacturing company, Bigelow Carpets, in Manhattan as a stenographer to help support her very poor family, and I was working part time, after school and City College of New York (CCNY) lacrosse practice, at Guide Systems and Supply Company which manufactured file folders for businesses in a loft off of Canal Street in Manhattan, one of the lofts now converted to plush condos for wealthy artists and actors.

We couldn't afford a ticket to one of the major movie theaters in downtown Brooklyn, like the Brooklyn Paramount or Fabian's Fox, and certainly not places like the Roxy or Radio City Hall in Manhattan, although we both loved movies, so I suggested that a cheap date on a Saturday night, and an educational experience, would be a trip to the Manhattan Magistrate's Court on Centre Street, where I could begin to learn what it meant to be a lawyer.

At that time, I didn't even know the function of a magistrate's court, so every time we went I had my trusty steno pad (from Lenore) and I began to take copious notes. My head was filled with the names of some of the well known judges of New York City, like Sam Liebowitz, but I wasn't going to see any of them at 100 Centre Street. Yet, cheap date it was! The New York City subway at that time cost five cents for the trip on the IRT from Pennsylvania Avenue, deep in the heart of Brooklyn, to lower Manhattan, Chambers Street station.

Two Hundred Centre Street was a very impressive edifice to two poor kids from Brooklyn, and we would spend hours watching the presumed innocent Saturday night drunks and hookers being dragged before the imperious man for arraignment and bail, who seemed to know many of them, on his huge seat behind the bench in his impressive black robes. When there was a recess in the proceedings, and we were getting tired of the repetition, we would return to the subway for another five cents each, and take the subway line to a ferry terminal in Brooklyn, where a Brooklyn ferry would travel from Brooklyn to Staten Island past the well lit Statue of Liberty and Governor's Island, and usually with the entertainment of an Italian organ grinder who worked for tips. On some nights, we would take the South Ferry from Battery Park to Staten Island past the same magnificent sites, including the well lit Manhattan and the Brooklyn waterfront. Incidentally, this was before the Verrazano bridge was built between Brooklyn and Staten Island, thereby removing the need for these great ferry lines.

For the same nickel, we would never exit the ferry; so for five cents, we had the cruise of a lifetime for two poor kids from Brooklyn, who never cruised again but for a one day cruise out of Fort Lauderdale, Florida many years later. Sometimes, we even got off the IRT train to Pennsylvania Avenue at the Fulton Street station in Brooklyn, and stopped in at our favorite all night ice cream parlor in the downtown commercial area of Brooklyn, which even featured, at that time, a "Namm's" department store, owned, according to my poor sometimes working class grandfather, by Col. Benjamin Namm, a cousin of his from "the rich part of the Namm family."

So for twenty-five cents each, on many a Saturday night, exclusive of the cost of the frappe or ice cream soda in Brooklyn, I began my education as a courtroom lawyer and a lower court trial judge!

****

As my mind returned to the ballroom and to the speaker's voice, the peaks and valleys of my judicial career meshed together in an entangled web, but one theme stuck out. This controversial, tough ex-judge, at age fifty-nine, was being bestowed a distinguished honor by members of the defense bar. It hadn't always been this way. I wasn't always seen as a hero to lawyers who represented criminal defendants. But that was before I was perceived by some as a whistleblower and a courageous, outspoken critic of a corrupt system of justice. Judging from the way that I'd ascended to the bench, it was almost predictable that this was not destined to be an ordinary experience.

Although I was admitted to the bar for twenty-two years, including seven as a judge, until 1983, I was never involved in a homicide trial, despite an active law practice which relied heavily upon criminal cases. Ever since my undergraduate days at City College of New York, when I'd spent many a Saturday night date with Lenore in the musty, overcrowded and overworked courtrooms of 200 Centre Street in Manhattan, my ambition had been to become involved in the excitement and drama of a homicide trial. Little did I know that I would, in my lifetime, realize this ambition—in spades!

In 1975, in the wake of Watergate, and a scandal in the local Brookhaven Republican Party, I, a Democrat, was elected a judge of the District Court of Suffolk County in a town that was overwhelmingly Republican in registration. I won by a plurality of fifty-eight votes out of a total of some 68,000 votes cast in 134 election districts—a margin of less than one half vote in each district. In that election every vote had really counted, especially since my plurality decreased with every official recount. That was the price I paid for defeating an incumbent Republican judge. The tortuous history of my election was a sure omen of things to come in my tumultuous judicial career.

The final certification of my narrow victory was withheld by a Everett McNab, the reluctant Republican Commissioner of Elections, until January 2, 1976, long after other candidates' victory celebration parties were faded memories. McNab stubbornly refused to put his signature on the certification until he was directed to do so by the county attorney's office.

Despite the thin margin of victory, a plurality of only one vote would have been enough to add the name of Stuart Namm to the twenty-three members of the District Court bench, and, thereafter, by fortuitous circumstance to the County Court bench where my real troubles began, and my judicial career would come to an ignominious conclusion.

It was in the District Court where I first established my reputation as a tough, no-nonsense, law-and-order judge. To some lawyers, according to my former law partner, Dominic Baranello, I was in the "district attorney's pocket," as I was the "sweetheart" of the law enforcement community.

How did they get such a perception? How did a poor Jewish kid from the crowded tenements of Brownsville, in the heart of Brooklyn, become the sweetheart of the predominantly Christian criminal justice establishment of suburban Suffolk County? Had those in law enforcement somehow miscalculated their assessment of me and my philosophy of justice, or were they correct?

The District Court handled both civil and criminal cases, but I spent most of my time in the criminal parts of the court. The criminal jurisdiction of the court only extended to misdemeanors- petty crimes such as shoplifting. While the court only tried minor crimes, it was responsible for the arraignment of all defendants charged with any crime committed in one of the five western towns of Huntington, Islip, Babylon, Smithtown or

Brookhaven, from where I had been elected. This gave me the opportunity to get involved in serious felony cases, to the limited extent of setting bail and conducting preliminary hearings to determine whether there was sufficient evidence to hold a defendant for the action of the grand jury. Despite this minimal exposure to heavy criminal cases, I was rapidly developing a reputation as a tough judge, one whose sentences in lesser criminal cases generally exceeded those handed out by most other judges of the court, and whose bail sometimes exceeded the amount requested by the young prosecutors assigned to my court.

I attributed this tough reputation to an attitude that I displayed on the bench which evolved from the manner in which I had ascended to the bench—a contested election. Most of the Suffolk judges were either the product of uncontested elections, or were Republicans who'd been elected from towns with an overwhelmingly Republican registration, where nomination to any public office was tantamount to election. They'd never have to answer to an increasingly frustrated electorate which had become disillusioned with what they perceived as a "revolving door system of criminal justice."

Perhaps it might have been viewed by some as pandering to public pressure, but I viewed this toughness on the bench as my responsibility as an elected judge. I had long since shed the mantle of liberal philosophy with which I became cloaked during my undergraduate days at New York's City College. That was a natural outgrowth of my working-class Jewish ghetto environment. It was now the 1970s. The "Father Knows Best" innocence of the '50s had given way to the violence and lawlessness of the '60s.

Yet those who live by the sword will often die by it. As fate would have it, after six years as a District Court Judge, a fickle electorate put me out of office in 1981, just as they had put me there in 1975. This time it wasn't even close! I was swept out of office by the tide of Brookhaven Republican sentiment which had gained renewed vigor with the 1980 election of Ronald Wilson Reagan, 40th president of the United States. It was difficult not to be bitter, since my reelection bid had been endorsed by every law enforcement association in the county, except the state police who were miffed about an opinion I'd authored on the subject of radar enforcement of speeding vehicles in moving police cars.

Editorially, I was endorsed by the most conservative weekly newspaper in the county, Suffolk Life. Moreover, I received the highest possible qualification rating by the Suffolk County Bar Association, whose membership was not only overwhelmingly Republican, but often beholden to the Republican leadership when it came to judicial ratings.

But endorsements and qualifications mean little to an electorate which is largely ignorant about the judiciary, and which is blind to any judicial candidate whose name does not appear on the ballot line preceded by the Republican eagle. I rationalized that if Mickey Mouse had been my opponent on the Republican line that year, I'd have been defeated just as handily.

So by public referendum, and not by personal choice, I was returned to the practice of law. I privately brooded and longed to return to the bench where I felt I now belonged, believing that I'd been cheated out of my seat by a less than intelligent electorate which put politics above competence. Fortunately, this chapter of my life proved to be very short. In April 1982, Hugh Carey, in the last year of his eight year tenure as Governor of New York, saw fit to appoint me to the bench of the County Court of Suffolk County to fill a vacancy in that court. It was no small irony that by being defeated for reelection to the District Court, I was elevated to the criminal court where I would finally be given the opportunity to try serious felonies and homicide cases. Suffolk County Court in Riverhead was light years away from City College of New York and the Saturday nights with Lenore at 200 Centre Street. But it mattered not, for I was about to realize my dream.

****

I had been found "well qualified" to sit on the County Court by the governor's non-partisan judicial screening committee, and many letters were written in support of my appointment to the governor's counsel. But the fact that my former law partner and friend, Dominic Baranello, was now the chairman of the New York State Democratic Committee must have played a large role in that appointment, or so he would have me believe. He took every opportunity to remind me that there was a "long line" of would-be Democratic County Court judges seeking that vacancy. According to him, he'd done me a great favor for which I was to be forever indebted to him and the party.

It was then that I learned what many had long since suspected—that my former partner had no concern for the quality of the judiciary. Cynically, he told me: "When you create a judge, the party loses a worker, and more important, a financial supporter." He was more concerned with filling tables at the semi-annual fundraiser with warm bodies, than he was with filling vacancies in the judiciary with qualified candidates. But I had never been a "financial supporter" of the party, or even a worker for the party. I had been Dominic Baranello's law partner for a full ten years, and if Lenore and I had ever even gone to a party function, which was rare, it was as Dominic's guests, not as financial contributors or party workers. So I guess that put me in a special category, one where Dominic could do as he pleased with me at any given moment. This, I supposed, must have been one of those moments!

By 1987, Dom had so forsaken the remaining Democratic members of the Suffolk county judiciary, who by then were a breed in danger of extinction, that his subordinates failed to file the names of designated Supreme Court candidates after completion of a judicial nominating convention, thereby depriving them from appearing on the election ballot as Democratic candidates. Not that they would have been elected in the light of the overwhelming odds against them, but they were entitled to the opportunity of running, and the electorate was entitled to a choice. Dom's public response was, "*Mea culpa.*" But I was certain that he felt no responsibility for what was described as a clerical oversight by the persons running the convention under Dom's leadership.

It was rumored that he had intentionally sacrificed the Democratic judicial candidates so that the name of Patrick Halpin, the Democratic candidate for county executive, would appear at the head of the Democratic line on the ballot, a slot which would have normally been filled by the candidates for Supreme Court. Could Dom have been that ruthless and that shrewd at the same time? It was difficult to believe that he would be, but in view of what I knew about him, this possibility couldn't be summarily dismissed. In any event, it was a good way to take public credit for doing whatever was necessary to elect a Democratic county executive against all the odds.

As for myself, I quickly took to my new position with a new found enthusiasm. Mentally ready, I was resigned to show an ungrateful electorate the mistake that

I was sure they had made. The chest and shoulder pains that began in the spring of 1981 and which lasted through the winter months, pains which drove me to the emergency rooms and intensive care unit of University Hospital, were now ancient history. Casting a dark shadow over my enthusiasm was the prospect of another contested election, and the very real possibility of an even more overwhelming defeat on the county level. But this time around lady luck smiled down upon me, and my fortune took an unusual turn for the better.

In the summer of 1982, after weeks of seemingly hopeless negotiations, and while the Democratic county chairman, Dom Baranello, was recuperating from open heart surgery, Jack Braslow, a lawyer and the Babylon Democratic chairman, reached an agreement with the Republican county leadership to seek several new judgeships from the state legislature. All were to be filled by cross-endorsement of the various candidates. There would be six Republicans and four Democrats, including the newly appointed County Court Judge—Stuart Namm! For the time being, I was safe from the sharp edge of the electoral sword. In November, I reaped the benefits of a Republican endorsement, and my future was secure for another ten years. And what a future it would turn out to be!

THREE

Robert Catone: Flying High on Drugs and Alcohol

I T WAS IN THE COUNTY COURT WHERE I SOLIDIFIED MY reputation as a tough judge, handing out long sentences. There I met the cast of characters who would play an important role in the events of the next ten years which shaped my future, and the future of Suffolk law enforcement.

Initially, I developed my closest relationship with Tom Stark, the hard-nosed administrative judge of the County Court. Thomas M. Stark was a graduate of Harvard Law School, the son of the former president of Riverhead Savings Bank. Not yet sixty, he was old before his years from the ravaging effects of a crippling physical ailment. When I first appeared before him as a young trial lawyer, his cold demeanor struck fear in my heart, and in the hearts of my clients who were charged with serious crimes. His personality was hardened by many years as a criminal court judge. Some wondered aloud whether Tom ever met a defendant whom he presumed was innocent. A chronic illness had softened his limbs and slowed down his gait, but one could discern little change in the outward toughness of his judicial demeanor.

Many years as one of only two County Court judges, trying virtually every major case in the county, including the infamous Amityville horror—the massacre of the DeFeo family—left its indelible mark on his persona. Yet there were few in the legal profession who'd dare to openly say that he was unjust or lacking proper judicial temperament. He was my early role model. We developed a close professional relationship which was short lived. But for the time being, I would call upon his long years of judicial experience and accumulated knowledge for advice and interesting conversation.

Events that began to unfold in 1985 seriously strained and ultimately changed our relationship, and the temporary bond of trust which we formed. I seemed to be the only one of the ten judges of the court who developed such a relationship with him. Most privately disliked him, although outwardly they expressed friendship. Perhaps that, and my reputation for long sentences, was why I was quickly moved to the trial of important homicide cases, passing over other senior judges and my contemporaries.

Tom had to be happy when it was reported in *Newsday* that I'd handed out the longest sentence ever given in the State of New York for the reckless manslaughter of a pedestrian in a drunk driving case.

Five to fifteen years in a state correctional facility didn't seem like excessive punishment for one who, in his own words, while "flying high on drugs and alcohol" took the life of an innocent fourteen-year-old girl. Yet that was the maximum term of incarceration in the state of New York for the crime of reckless manslaughter in cases of vehicular homicide. So it was a great surprise to me when I read in *Newsday*, after I sentenced Robert Catone to that term of imprisonment for recklessly causing the untimely death of Patricia Morisco, that this was the longest term of imprisonment ever meted out in the state for a conviction arising out of the drunken operation of an automobile.

Such an incident was not uncommon in New York. By 1981 the state's roadways were awash with the blood of countless innocent victims of intoxicated drivers. By that date an overburdened judiciary hadn't yet awakened to the pleas of an angry, aroused public which was crying out "Enough slaughter on the roads!" Groups such as MADD (Mothers Against Drunk Driving), SADD (Studentss Against Drunk Divers) and RID (Remove Intoxicated Drivers) were being formed all over the country. I was well aware of the tragic numbers which were mounting each week. I had resigned myself to do something, even if it was perceived as excessive by some, to help stem this unhappy tide. It troubled me that the legislature had so limited the maximum punishment for such a heinous crime, that I tacked on an additional one and one-third to four years for leaving the scene of the accident, which left a little girl dying on the side of the roadway.

Eventually, because of a technical quirk in the law, the Court of Appeals, while upholding the maximum term which I had imposed, reluctantly set aside the additional consecutive term of incarceration. Still, the highest court of the state recommended to the state legislature that the law be changed so that a judge could impose consecutive prison terms under those circumstances. At the next session of the legislature the law of New York was changed to support the sentence which I'd imposed upon Mr. Catone.

It was in the Catone case where I was introduced to the Suffolk County police homicide squad, the "interview room," and in particular to Detective K. James McCready and his method of extracting confessions from suspects.

Catone claimed that a confession was beaten out of him by McCready and four other detectives while handcuffed to a desk in the interview room of the homicide squad at police headquarters in Yaphank. He testified that it was only after being continuously punched, kicked in the chest, and having his hair pulled by a team of detectives, that he agreed to sign a written confession. But at that time, I was still in my "believe the police" mode, and I knew nothing about McCready, except that he came from a family of detectives, whose father had been a high ranking police official. I had not yet been jaded, and I accepted the police version that Catone had freely and voluntarily confessed after McCready appealed to the conscience of one who was "flying high on drugs and alcohol" when his speeding vehicle snuffed out the life of an innocent Pattie Marisco on the very day that she graduated from junior high school.

Police brutality was not a charge which was unknown to the Suffolk County Police Department in the early 1980s. The department was the subject of a scathing rebuke by a special committee of the Suffolk County Bar Association in the late 1970s, and it had been singled out for attack in the National Law Review. Despite these largely unsubstantiated charges, the department, especially its elite homicide squad, took great pride in the manner in which it maintained law and order in the county, and the fact that it was the highest paid police department in the nation. So it was no small irony that a formerly activist bar association stood silently by as the integrity of the Suffolk County criminal justice system was publicly shattered by one investigation after another in 1986 and 1987.

But that was far in the future. In 1982 I rationalized that defendants were reading the newspaper reports of alleged police brutality. The publicity alone, I reasoned, served as a self fulfilling prophecy, causing an ever increasing number of defendants to claim that they'd been physically abused by members of the homicide squad. So too did Robert Catone. Or so I believed at that time.

FOUR

Johnny Pius: A Microcosm of Middle America

ONE BY ONE, I WAS INTRODUCED TO THE CAST OF CHARACTERS that would influence my life and actions for the next ten years. From Catone, I graduated into some of the most heinous and highly publicized trials in the county. One which will long be remembered by this generation of adults was the brutal murder of a Smithtown boy by four teenage neighbors. It wasn't that the asphyxiation of little Johnny Pius was the most horrible crime ever recorded in the county. Certainly, Robert DeFeo's crazed slaughter of his family in the quiet community of Amityville will unlikely be exceeded for its stark demon-like brutality and horror.

But the pebbles that were shoved down the throat of Johnny Pius to silence him over a worthless mini-bike struck a discordant note with the populace. In 1979, Suffolk county, the microcosm of middle America, had come of age. Nine years later, many could still recall the details of the Pius case, and were still disturbed that such a crime could have been committed in the tranquility of eastern Smithtown by four otherwise average teenagers who had grown up in a nice, white middle class suburban community. The crimes of Ronald DeFeo in butchering his entire family, which achieved literary infamy as the "Amityville Horror," could easily be rationalized as the actions of an enraged and crazed mind. But how do you rationalize the senseless murder of an innocent thirteen year old by four normal teenagers?

The county reached its maturity by baptism under fire—the brutal death of one of its young. Johnny Pius could have been anyone's child. More frightening, perhaps, was the realization that any one of the perpetrators could have been your neighbor's child, or even one of your own. By casting suspicion upon numerous Smithtown teenagers before arresting anyone, the police made it frightfully clear that they believed that there were many youths capable of committing such an horrendous crime walking the halls of Smithtown East High School. The community was distressed over the question of how the clean streets of Suffolk had somehow become no different than the mean streets of the city from which most had fled!

The answer was no different in Smithtown than it was in countless other such communities throughout America of the 1970s—drugs, alcohol, broken families, self indulgent parents, unsupervised children and the breakdown of social institutions responsible for teaching respect for the law and the rights, person and property of others.

Two of the teens were already tried and convicted when I entered upon the scene. The juvenile brothers, Michael and Peter Quartararo, were serving life sentences when the cases of Robert Brensic and Thomas Ryan appeared on my trial calendar. They were the oldest of the four, and quite possibly the most culpable. An aroused community was crying out for their hides, although there are still many who believe in their innocence.

The assistant district attorney who inherited the Pius case from Thomas Spota, the former chief of the major offense bureau, was the flamboyant, boyish looking, overly nervous, self proclaimed reformed alcoholic and street fighter William Keahon. Known to friend and foe alike simply as "Billy," he developed a reputation for his ability to play to a jury, especially the female members. His bag of tricks included impassioned tirades, tearful summations and angry gesticulations directed at the accused. His actions sometimes bordered on prosecutorial misconduct, but he used them all successfully in both the Brensic and Ryan trials. In every case that he tried before me, Keahon appeared to have a deep emotional attachment to his cause and the victims, but never more than to the Pius family. He always seemed to be deeply moved by any testimony concerning the deceased, and he was forever in a state of nervous agitation. At times he appeared to be on the verge of a nervous breakdown as he consumed several quarts of water each day to soothe his frazzled nerves.

Bill Keahon became a friend of mine, professionally, but not socially, like many members of the district attorney's office. In the spring of 1985 such friendships and professional relationships gave way to the realities of the criminal justice system in the county of Suffolk. I quickly learned then that such "friends" have short memories when they or their associates are called to task for their actions. I learned that the old boy network in the law enforcement community was tied together by stronger bonds than professional relationships created by common involvement within the system. In fact, most such relationships apparently turned on opportunism—the belief, perhaps, that it might give you, or your case, an edge with the judge. Certainly, it became apparent to me, early in my tenure as a County Court judge, that the office of the district attorney, especially the major offense bureau, of which Keahon was chief, had a clear edge with the administrative judge, Tom Stark.

Since our chambers were adjacent to one another, I was well aware of the regular meetings which took place between him and representatives of that office, ostensibly to discuss cases which were pending in the felony criminal parts. Until the state investigation began in the winter of 1985, the most important purpose of those meetings was to decide which judge would handle which homicide case. It was not until 1986, well into the investigation, that judges were purportedly assigned from a rotating list, and the meetings suddenly ended. Then it was all judges, not just the select three. But even then, Tom played the assignment of judges in homicide cases close to the vest. He wasn't about to be replaced by a computer in the assignment of a judge to a highly publicized trial.

It was clearly a breach of ethics for the administrative judge and representatives of the district attorney's office to be involved in such discussions, but that was the nature of the criminal justice system in Suffolk county before it became the target of the state's investigators. With the aid of hindsight, I'm convinced that it was the district attorney's representatives who recommended that I be moved immediately into major homicide trials. I should have realized it then, but in 1983, I wasn't concerned with challenging the system which I was just then mastering. I was still wet behind the ears! My every concern was directed towards the important cases on my calendar, and the trials which resulted from them. It was more important to try the alleged murderers of young Johnny Pius, than to think about the ethics of what was taking place all around me, of which I was an integral, but a willingly naive part. There was much unfinished business to be accomplished between early 1983 and late 1985, not the least of which was the retrial of Robert Brensic and the trial of Tommy Ryan.

Besides the administrative judge, Suffolk prosecutors developed other relationships which were extremely useful in the prosecution of persons charged with murder. They were masterful in their use of "snitches" and jailhouse informants, probably the most unreliable and least credible of witnesses. Yet this didn't deter the defenders of law and order in the county.

Only one of the four defendants in the many Pius trials confessed to involvement in the murder, and he'd implicated the other three. But even young Peter Quartararo recanted his confession after the police allowed him to see his mother and brother. The others were uncharacteristically tight-lipped in their conversations with the police. So the homicide squad was forced to scour the streets of Smithtown and the corridors of the county jail for persons who claimed to have heard the perpetrators admit their guilt. As was so often the case, the search was successful.

They produced James Burke,** an eighteen-year-old admitted "pot head," who went on to become a Suffolk County police officer. He claimed that he heard Robert Brensic admit: "The pigs fucked it up. They'll never get me!" This was an obvious reference to the Pius investigation.

Brett Locke, a twenty-three-year-old convicted burglar and junkie, was discovered in the county jail. It was his claim that Brensic bared his soul to him when he'd saved him from other prisoners who were taunting him and calling him "pebbles," a cruel reference to the manner in which Johnny Pius met his untimely and unnatural death. Brensic, he said, was more than willing to confess to this good Samaritan who'd rescued him from jailhouse harassment and the code of the convict.

Yet Locke supposedly kept this damning confession to himself for more than one and a half years when he was arrested for burglary in 1981. It was

---

**James Burke, who was one of ADA Thomas Spota's chief prosecution witnesses in the first Pius murder trial, has gone on to become the Chief of Police of the Suffolk County Police Department. Former ADA Spota is currently the District Attorney of Suffolk County.

then that he made contact with Detective Jack Miller of the homicide squad to bargain for a misdemeanor conviction in exchange for his testimony. This wasn't going to be the last time that the name of Jack Miller was linked to a jailhouse informant, nor the cheapest bounty that would be accepted by a convict informant in exchange for very damaging testimony adverse to a defendant charged with murder. Miller was deeply involved in the testimony of Joseph Pistone—a jailhouse informant in the Diaz case in 1985- whom I'd label a "pathological liar" in open court, paving the way for the various investigations of law enforcement in the county. In 1983, to me, Miller was just another Suffolk homicide detective doing his duty- bringing a young killer to justice the best way he could!

In the trial of Tommy Ryan, Keahon didn't have to resort to the likes of Locke and Burke. To convict the most close-mouthed of the four, he could turn to a nineteen-year-old girl from New Bedford, Massachusetts, to seal Ryan's fate with the jury—Ryan's own girlfriend. (Initially, the case against Ryan was so weak, that the district attorney waited two years before presenting evidence against him to the grand jury.)

Anne was Tommy's girlfriend in the early part of 1981. She was introduced to him by the Quartararo brothers, and they had developed a very close relationship. They were in love! As they grew closer to one another, Tommy, she said, began to talk more and more about the Pius case, and about his fears of the future, and what was going to happen to his good friend, Peter. He admitted that he was scared, and that he didn't want her to end up like Peter's girlfriend—with a boyfriend serving a life sentence. In an indirect reference to the Pius case, he confessed: "You can't love someone who took someone else's life!"

Both of the Suffolk County juries heard enough to convict Brensic and Ryan of murder, and the "district attorney's judge" meted out two maximum sentences of twenty-five-years-to-life. The ends of justice were served—at least for the time being. Just ten years later, only one of the four continued to serve a prison sentence—Tommy Ryan. All four of the convictions were reversed by either the Court of Appeals or the United States District Court, and only Ryan, now a father, was again convicted of murder.

In reversing the conviction of Peter Quartararo after he served nine years of a life sentence as a juvenile, Federal District Court Judge Edward Korman, a former United States Attorney, blasted the homicide squad and its investigation:

> The Suffolk County Police here deliberately violated the Constitution of the United States and the laws of the State of New York to obtain a confession. They did not develop any significant additional evidence against petitioner. Because of the manner in which they conducted the investigation into the death of John Pius, which the SIC found was characteristic of conduct long tolerated by responsible officials of the Suffolk County Police Department and the District Attorney's Office, Peter Quartararo may go free after serving only nine years of a nine year to life sentence.

In September 1989, The Federal Circuit Court of Appeals unanimously affirmed the reversal of the Quartararo conviction by Judge Korman. In little more than three months, the Second Circuit heard, reviewed and decided a complex criminal case involving a multitude of legal issues. This must be some kind of a record, if records are kept of such things. I'm convinced that the reputation of the criminal justice system in Suffolk County now precedes every case on appeal to the federal courts. The Suffolk prosecutor now comes to the appeal with two strikes against him!

In May 1983, before I became the pen pal of all of the convicted Suffolk criminals and citizens with a grievance against the criminal justice system, I received a letter signed by both of the Quartararo brothers. It was written by Michael. He was writing me "...because I have heard from people that have been in your court during Thomas Ryans [sic] trial, that you have been most fair and impartial throughout these trials; that you yourself were amazed with some of the perjured testimony that you heard,..."

It's ironic that this letter was written on May 20, three days before I sentenced a weeping Robert Brensic to twenty-five-years-to-life, and little more than one month before I sentenced Thomas Ryan to the same term after both were found guilty of murder in the second degree. I wasn't privy to the source of Michael's information about my feelings, which at that time was grossly inaccurate. In 1983, my eyes had not been fully opened to the devious capabilities of those involved in Suffolk law enforcement. I had not yet developed the cynicism necessary to view the system in its proper perspective. That cynicism developed slowly, and blossomed to maturity in the spring, summer and fall of 1985. Even Robert Brensic's tearful plea that he "couldn't even hurt an animal," much less a human being, had fallen upon deaf ears.

Michael Quartararo's letter continued:**

> ...in a "work release program." [Where he gained an education into the world of business and where he now thrives, forever professing his innocence. It is with great irony that Michael Quartararo, now a very successful businessman, after his long periods of incarceration, and we have become good friends, although from a distance despite one dinner at our home several years later with his mother, who had moved to North Carolina, and wife. Perhaps it was because of our continuous course of communication by email, and our common belief in the injustices of the Suffolk County criminal justice system!]
> Sometimes, I get the feeling that this is one giant conspiracy.
> That there is no way to beat the system, even if you are in the right...who makes up for the years we spent in prison because of an over-zealous police department and a conviction-hungry District Attorney?
> Granted, John Pius was brutally murdered, he is gone and nothing can bring him back, but compounding the wrongfulness of his death by convicting 4 innocent boys is even more wrong. I feel terribly bad for the Pius family...Nobody thinks that innocent people go to prison, they do. we are living proof...[1]

**Ironically, Michael Quartararo, the youngest of the four, who was sentenced as a juvenile, was incarcerated from 1981 until 1988, again from 1990 until December 1998, and again from November 1999 until 2000, ultimately served the longest term of incarceration because he would never admit his guilt, always professing his innocence even until this date. Much of his incarceration was served in a "work release program," where he gained an education into the world of business, and where he now thrives, forever professing his innocence.

With the benefit of hindsight, I know now that this letter was both prophetic and insightful, but it, like Robert Brensic's impassioned plea to my humanity, was playing to the wrong audience. As I read the words again, even today, it doesn't move me confidently to the belief that four innocent boys were convicted, especially in the light of Brensic's later confession in a Brooklyn courtroom.

Yet I would feel more confident in my belief of their collective guilt if Robert Brensic had admitted his guilt to the Brooklyn judge under circumstances which would not have insured his almost immediate release into society. Even as he uttered his confession in Brooklyn Supreme Court, "In a barely audible voice and with a blank expression on his face...," his prematurely aging mother, who, together with his ever present, sad-faced father, in their own way had suffered terribly from the years of accusation and public humility, and his most recent attorney, law professor Frank Bress, refused to believe that Robert was involved. Said Bress: "I believe the entire prosecution's case was created."[2]

How can one feel confidence in a confession uttered in exchange for an agreement that Brensic wouldn't have to testify against any of the others; the prosecution wouldn't object to his parole; he could leave the state and be released on his own recognizance pending his new sentence; and he would only be sentenced to four to twelve years, the minimum of which he had already served? Perhaps I could have bought it in 1983, but certainly not through these cynical eyes, after so much polluted water has flowed over the dam. He was made an offer that could not be refused!

The Quartararos were never tried again. Brensic was allowed to plead to manslaughter in a Brooklyn courtroom when his case became entangled in the state investigation and the district attorney wanted the case removed from my courtroom. Only an over-confident Tommy Ryan chose to continue to profess his innocence.[3] For that, he has paid a very heavy price. He has taken the fall for all four! Justice has indeed been blind and cruel in the Pius case! The community will forever be divided as to whether it was the deceased and his parents or the four young defendants who were denied the justice to which all were entitled.

FIVE

Lai, Wang and Barbaran: "No Video, Please!"

I N MAY 1988, A UNANIMOUS APPELLATE DIVISION reversed the murder conviction of Phillip Wang, for which I had sentenced him, along with his two cohorts, to a maximum sentence of twenty-five-years-to-life. However, in 1983 it was not considered "devastating" under existing law to try codefendants jointly in one trial where their confessions were deemed to be mirror images of each other. A joint trial was my decision after the application to sever the joint indictment charging the three defendants with murder had been made on behalf of Wang, William Lai and Fabrizio Barbaran for the senseless killing of Richard Berger. Nonetheless, the "devastating" nature of a codefendant's confession had become the law of the land by 1988, and that law was applied retroactively, so that in 1988, Phillip Wang was granted a new trial by the Appellate Division.[1]

The judiciary in Suffolk County was the product of a one party dominated political system, but my relationship with the top Democrat in the county, together with a good deal of luck and some ability, had taken me, arguably, to the pinnacle of the legal profession. Yet I never considered myself to be a politician. I had been nothing more than a student of government and politics—a voyeur of the local political scene, if you will. The 1970s and Richard Nixon had given politics a bad name, but more important, I had always believed, perhaps somewhat too idealistically, that it was essential to remove sitting judges from their creators, the political movers and shakers in the person of county chairmen and local leaders. So, it was with some irony that the two New York city attorneys representing Lai and Wang should ask me to disqualify myself as trial judge because the father of the eighteen-year-old college student killed in a gas station robbery served as the Republican Deputy Commissioner of Elections.

I had never even met Gerald Berger, whose son had been fatally shot while visiting with his high school buddy at a Shell Oil gas station on Nesconset Highway in Smithtown in the early morning hours of March 20, 1982. Apparently, many of the county's judges had either attended his son's funeral or a subsequent memorial service held in his honor. Perhaps it was because Gerald Berger was a prominent Republican, or because I knew very few people in politics, that I had not even been aware of the tragic events of March 20. In any event, their application was summarily denied, and Lai, Wang, Barbaran and Berger would become deeply etched in my memory, whether because of the unusual nature of the case, or because it was one murder trial of many in which I would become involved as a judge, and murders have a way of etching themselves into one's memory.

It was 1983, and the state of New York did not have a clearly defined definition of murder. The jury in this case would have to decide, in addition to the question of guilt, whether Richard Berger had died from the bullet of William Lai's handgun which had pierced his brain, or whether death had been caused by his removal from a respirator which had kept his heart beating in a brain dead body at University Hospital in Stony Brook.

In the evening of March 19, 1982, four vehicles had left Chinatown on the south side of Manhattan. Their final destination was a party being sponsored by the Korean Club of the State University at Stony Brook. The occupants of the vehicles included the three defendants, all of whom were uninvited, and all of whom were of oriental ethnicity, except for one Hispanic, Fabrizio Barbaran. William Lai was armed with a .22 caliber handgun, and Barbaran was carrying a toy revolver with a blackened barrel to lend authenticity to the weapon. One of the vehicles was operated by Phillip Wang who protested his innocence throughout the trial, claiming ignorance of the events leading to the untimely death of Richard Berger. Each, however, according to the testimony of the investigating detectives, was a member of the Chinatown gang known as the "White Tigers," and none had any regard for the life of another human being, including the self-professed "innocent" Phillip Wang, who according to Michael Albanese, the gas attendant, had told him to give them the money. Innocent Phillip Wang, who would have you believe that he was completely unaware of the second robbery on Queens Boulevard in New York city later that morning, although he was seated in his car outside the gas station with his engine running, while the gas attendant had been shot by one of his cohorts, and who was still seated in his car with the engine running when the police arrived at the scene of a third robbery in progress on Astoria Boulevard, in the borough of Queens, falsely explaining that he was "waiting for his girlfriend" at 4:45 a.m., outside of an automobile rental office.[2]

Any murder trial is, by definition, dramatic, but this trial provided more drama than most, because of the overriding issue of whether Richard Berger's death had been caused by the gunshot wound, or his removal from the respirator which had kept his heart beating, even after he had been declared "brain dead." This issue was brought immediately into focus during opening statements when the attorney for William Lai surprisingly conceded that his client had shot Richard Berger; that his actions were unjustifiable; and that the jury would convict him for his action, but that his actions had not caused the death of Richard Berger! Furthermore, this was probably the first time that videotaped confessions were utilized by the police to procure convictions, videotapes not made by the Suffolk County detectives, but by the New York City Police Department in conjunction with the Queens District Attorney's office. In fact, Detective McCready of Suffolk County Homicide had specifically instructed that no questions be asked on tape concerning the robbery and shooting of Richard Berger. Apparently McCready, whose name would come up again and again in murder trials, did not trust modern day electronics to faithfully portray the interrogation and confession process. However, McCready's actions in later murder trials would bring into clear focus, in my mind at least, why he had given such instructions to the New York city investigators.

The trial would be a battle of medical and ethics "experts," each called to the stand in an effort to assist the jury in determining of the cause of death.

If death was caused by removal from the respirator, none of these defendants could be found guilty of any degree of homicide. It would match the testimony of attending neurosurgeons against he testimony of a Jesuit theologist from Loyola of Chicago and a neonatologist from Creighton University, called by William Lai, to convince the jury that Richard Berger was still a living being when his kidneys and spleen were removed for the purpose of transplantation in another human being, a twenty-two-year-old man in a Queens hospital.

The prosecution, once again represented by Assistant District Attorney Steven Wilutis, vigorously opposed Lai's attorney, Martin Stolar, a prominent New York defense attorney, in his application to permit the jury to hear the opinions of Father Paul Quay, the Jesuit priest from Loyola, as to the time and cause of death of Richard Berger. Thus, it became necessary to conduct a hearing out of the presence of the jury in order to hear his testimony, and to rule on whether or not to permit him to do so.

After several days of trial, on the morning of March 29, 1983, the jury was sent out for a lengthy recess while Father Quay was examined and cross-examined outside of their presence. While there might have been an initial tendency on my part to exclude the testimony of a theologian on what seemed to be a complex scientific question, one could not help but be impressed by his credentials, which included two Bachelor's degrees in the Classics and Physics, a Master's degree from Wiesbaden in Theology, a Ph.D. in Physics from M.I.T., and post-doctoral studies at Case Western University. He had been a teacher of Physics, Philosophy and Theology at St. Louis University, and the author of more than forty scholarly treatises, six of which were on the subject of moral theology, and had been published in the *Journal of the American Medical Association*, as well as the *Gonzaga Law Review* on the subject of "brain death." At the time of the trial, he was Associate Professor of Philosophy, Theology and Physics at Loyola of Chicago, and a lecturer in bio-medical ethics at Loyola University Medical School, having studied the subject of "brain death" since 1976. Therefore, he could not be passed off as a religious fanatic or zealot whose testimony had no place in a court of law.

Clearly theology, religion and morals played an important, if not an overriding, role in his opinions, and the fact was brought into clear focus when, on the witness stand, he asked the rhetorical question, "When did Christ die on the cross?"* While it was his belief that Richard Berger was "critically wounded" during the time he was on the respirator, and had been declared "brain dead," he was of the opinion that one was not, in fact, dead until there was a departure of the soul from the body, a total disintegration of the human person, a " loss of all power of living."*

However, he did admit that his opinions were not necessarily the opinions of the Catholic church, where persons are deemed dead after a declaration of "brain death." The opinions of Father Quay were supported, however, by Dr. Paul Byrne, a neonatologist and Clinical Professor of Pediatrics at Creighton University Medical School, who told the jury about an infant that had been on a respirator for a period of five weeks, with a flat EEG, meaning no brain activity, consistent with "cerebral death," and how in one week to ten days after the first flat line reading, he was off the respirator, breathing on his own, and in 1983, functioning normally in second grade. He, like Father Quay, was openly critical of all of the existing medical criteria for determining "brain death," and was of the opinion that there must be "total destruction" of the person for death to occur.

While the testimony of Drs. Byrnes and Quay proved fascinating, and provided much food for thought, the jury apparently bought into the conventional wisdom as provided by the attending neurologists at Smithtown General Hospital, where Richard's vital organs had been removed for transplantation. In the final analysis, in finding the defendants guilty of murder after two and one half days of deliberation, the jury had rejected the opinions of Byrnes and Quay, and had accepted the sober opinions of Drs. Pearl, Rosen, Kessler, Newman and Zippen, neurologists and neurosurgeons, that on March 21, 1982, at Smithtown General Hospital, Richard Berger was already medically dead. Thus, while the New York State Legislature had provided them with no statutory guidelines,

---

*Wherever in the book there is a quote from trial testimony, and there is no indication that it comes from the official transcript or some other such source, it comes from Judge Namm's personal trial notes and will be indicated by a single asterisk (*) rather than cited separately in the Chapter Notes section at the end of the book.

twelve lay persons had apparently unanimously accepted "brain death" as being synonymous with death itself, despite a beating heart and warm body.

****

The Criminal Courts building was located in Riverhead during my tenure as a judge, and was a modern, modular concrete structure consisting of six courtrooms. Mine was on the third floor of the building. Directly behind the courtrooms were my Riverhead chambers, and adjacent thereto, the jury deliberations room, an austere 8' x 20' chamber with a large window overlooking the county jail, a conference table and chairs, and two toilet facilities, one male and one female.

The courthouse, which had been designed by an architect who was the brother of a Republican political leader, was obsolete almost as soon as it opened, and was so poorly designed that it lacked a staircase to the secure areas behind the courtrooms, so that the only mode of transportation in the non-public areas was one elevator, which was always breaking down. The walls were so paper thin, that one without the desire to do so, could hear conversations from adjacent offices, especially if those conversations became heated and loud. Thus, since my chambers were directly adjacent to the jury deliberations room, if one was not in conversation, or in deep thought, it was possible, even though it was not your intention to do so, to overhear loud conversations in the jury room. Needless to say, the court officers assigned to the jury, who were seated outside the jury room, could hear, if they were so inclined, everything being said above hushed tones in the jury room.

This jury was not particularly quiet, so that I was aware early in the deliberations that the jury was not troubled with the issue of "cause of death," and had not spent much time on that, but were spending most of their time on the question of intent to cause death by William Lai. This would not be the last time that I would be secretly aware of the progress of deliberations during a criminal trial. This jury did not have to consider the question of intent to cause death with respect to Wang and Barbaran since I had already dismissed the intentional murder charges against them at the end of the People's case. Ultimately, the jury did not find Lai guilty of intentional murder, but they did find him guilty of manslaughter in the first degree, a lesser included offense, which required only an intent to commit serious physical injury, as opposed to the intent to cause death. They did find all defendants guilty of felony murder of an innocent person resulting from the commission of a felony, as well as attempted robbery in the first degree. After dismissing the jury, sentencing was scheduled for May 19, 1983, and once again I was faced with the decision of whether to sentence a human being to the highest sentence allowed by law in New York, twenty-five-years-to-life!

In the period between verdict and sentencing, I found myself often thinking about the very moving testimony of Gerald Berger as a witness for the prosecution; about the agony that he and his family had experienced and had to re-live each day of the trial; and about how he had vowed to "bring to justice the scum that had done this" to his son, of whom he had been so proud.

Gerald Berger, who with his ex-wife had made the difficult decision to disconnect the life support systems and donate his son's kidneys so that two others might live, now was possibly second guessing that decision in the light of the testimony of Father Quay and Dr. Byrnes. In addition, perhaps having to live with the guilt of somehow being involved in the death of his son, as irrational as that might seem.

As the trial judge, I saw my role as the person who was responsible for administering retribution on behalf of the victim, his family and friends, and society at large. In a state where the ultimate punishment had been declared unconstitutional, and had never been reinstated, it was important to fashion punishment which would not dishonor the memory of Richard Berger, and send a message to the streets that the court would not tolerate the senseless murder of an innocent human being resulting from the commission of a robbery.

On the day of sentencing, each of the three defense lawyers pleaded passionately that his client should be shown compassion and mercy, and that the sentence be limited to the minimum allowable by law—fifteen years to life. I was reminded that Lai had been high on cocaine; that he had not intended to kill Richard Berger; that he was the son of hard working immigrant parents who toiled many hours each day; that his brother was a community worker in Chinatown; that his sister had to leave the State University of Stony Brook because of this incident; that Wang's mother had suffered a nervous breakdown as a result of his arrest; that his father was a successful businessman; that he was in the top 5% of his class at Rutgers University; that he had "already been punished by his own conscience"; that Barbaran had come to the United States in 1976 from Lima, Peru; that he was the child of divorced parents living in an unstable environment; and that he had intended to enlist in the United States Army.*

Assistant District Attorney Wilutis, on the other hand, made a strong argument for imposition of the maximum sentence for each of the defendants, and it did not take much to convince me of the rightness of his cause.

Thus, once again as the trial judge, I imposed the maximum term of incarceration allowed by law, twenty-five-years-to-life on each of the defendants.[3] I carried out my role, as I saw it, to administer justice, retribution and punishment on behalf of the victim, his family and society.

This was something that I would do often in the next four years, and which would I would later learn would earn me the sobriquets of "The Hanging Judge" and "Maximum Stu," among others, and which would incur the wrath of some of my brethren on the bench who were not so philosophically inclined. I felt that the rap was a bum one, and it was not particularly troublesome to me until the sarcasm of some of my brethren on the bench gave me cause to resign from the Suffolk County Court Judges Association. It was difficult to enjoy your lunch at the same time that you found yourself deflecting verbal barbs intended to convey the thinly veiled message that some were not happy with my assignment handling major offense cases, and more important, the publicity which those cases were receiving in the news media.

SIX

Timothy O'Toole: "Bloody Forensics."

IN 1986, IRA DUBEY, CHIEF OF THE MARYLAND STATE POLICE Crime Laboratory, entered a plea of guilty before a Suffolk County judge to several counts of perjury. He was indicted for falsifying his credentials as a prosecution expert in several major felony cases. Dubey was the chief forensic serologist and deputy director of the county's Criminalistics Laboratory, and a hero of the law enforcement community, when he was eagerly snatched by the state of Maryland to supervise its crime lab. The authorities there, as did most in Suffolk county, believed they were hiring a bright, knowledgeable, articulate, well educated, forthright director, who would, through his scientific experience, education, laboratory analysis and expert testimony, strengthen the prosecution of important felony cases. What they got instead was someone who wasn't as educated as they were led to believe, and who was certainly not forthright in his dealings with them, as an expert witness, or in his dealings with his associates. As a consequence, by 1987, he was out of a job.

In 1983, Dubey was still a legend in the Suffolk County Criminalistics Laboratory, and the backbone of many of the county's most difficult homicide investigations. It was largely his testimony, and his widely acclaimed "expertise," coupled with a written confession, that led to the conviction of twenty-nine-year-old Timothy O'Toole for the brutal, bloody murder of Patricia Finn in her Sayville apartment. She died from multiple stab wounds which punctured both of her lungs and her aorta causing a massive loss of blood.

Detectives William Mahoney and K. James McCready—once again-partners, eighteen and fourteen year veterans, respectively, of the Suffolk County Police Department were accustomed to bloody crime scenes. Such is the lot of experienced homicide detectives. They were assigned by Det. Sgt. Richard Jensen to investigate the murder, along with the other members of their squad—Detectives Ryan, Cleary, Miller and Leonard. Mahoney was designated as the lead detective, which meant that he and McCready would do the bulk of the investigation.

The investigation, although it focused on several potential suspects, went nowhere until November 17, 1982 when Mahoney was asked to recover a bloodstained sweatshirt at the Police Property Bureau. The sweatshirt was the property of one Timothy Patrick O'Toole. It was taken from him when he was arrested at the Sayville office of a clinical psychologist during a robbery attempt. O'Toole told the doctor that he had already killed four people. He was, he said, capable of killing again. The doctor's office was, like Patricia Finn's apartment, located in the business district on Main Street.

From the crime scene, in addition to viewing the blood which covered the deceased, and the stains throughout the apartment, Dubey recovered a bloodstained towel for laboratory analysis. There was no murder weapon found, although the scene was thoroughly searched. Miller was dispatched to a sanitation yard to search three garbage dumpsters for a discarded weapon, but none was found by him. Under the victim's head was a bloodstained ballpoint pen, a Bic, which Dubey and the detectives theorized was used by her to fight off her attacker. Two of the stains on the towel weren't consistent with the blood of the victim, but, according to Dubey, were deposited by a person whose blood type was different than 99% of the general population.

At the trial Dubey not only offered very damaging expert opinion concerning blood type and genetic markers as to the various pieces of evidence offered by the people, but he also explained a blood spattering test which he'd performed using string to measure angles of blood spatter from which he offered an opinion as to the location of the source of the blood. His opinion was that each time the knife was physically removed from the body of the deceased and raised upwards, it left a specific pattern of spatter on the wall and floor. He testified that the intersecting points were over the bed, and in his opinion the attack took place in that bed, and the murder weapon, a knife, was raised to a height as high as 6' 10" each time that it was plunged into her helpless body.

Ira Dubey was a very effective witness. His presentation exuded extreme self-confidence, almost to the point of cockiness. His stated credentials were very impressive to judge and jury alike. He was unquestionably the key to the conviction of O'Toole. He was able to show that the genetic markers in the defendant's blood were consistent with the extremely rare blood found at the crime scene, on the ballpoint pen, and on the towel.

The case was assigned to ADA Steven Wilutis, a cold, methodical, unsmiling, extremely serious, professional prosecutor, whose future as an assistant district attorney became inextricably linked to Dubey's perjury. O'Toole, likewise, was represented by an extremely sober Suffolk county lawyer, Robert Quinlan. Quinlan unsuccessfully mounted an almost prophetic, relentless attack against the credentials, expertise and opinions of the prosecution's chief witness.

Of course, it had to be done. Dubey's testimony was extremely damaging to his client, and it corroborated the testimony of McCready and Mahoney concerning O'Toole's written confession which put the final nails into O'Toole's coffin. The defense attorney couldn't have known that he was cross-examining a perjurer. You would've needed a crystal ball to know that in 1983, or you would've needed to be privy to the deepest recesses of Dubey's mind. Even the members of the district attorney's office who were close to Dubey, both professionally and socially, like Wilutis and his cohort, Barry Feldman, who surfaced in the Dubey debacle and as one of my chief protagonists, didn't become aware of this chink in their star witness' armor until 1984. Even then, if they're to be believed, they couldn't accept that Ira Dubey was falsifying his credentials and his testimony in court. He had so mesmerized the persons who depended upon his expertise by technical scientific jargon, and his smug air of confidence, that it was almost three years later before his cover was publicly exposed by *Newsday's* investigative reporters.

Experienced court stenographers, who had recorded the testimony of countless witnesses, were so hypnotized by the rhythm of his testimony that even if they were unfamiliar with his scientific phraseology, they couldn't bring themselves to interrupt him. They had no reluctance to do that with other witnesses to insure an accurate record. With Dubey, they waited until he completed his recitation in order to have him correct or fill voids in the record. This was done at Dubey's direction. He made it abundantly clear that he didn't wish to have the rhythm of his testimony interrupted by the court reporter. Self confidence bordering on arrogance was his long suit, and that confidence inured to his benefit and to the benefit of the prosecution. It conveyed a clear impression to the jury that his outward arrogance was simply a natural derivative of the confidence he had in the correctness of his own expertise. How could someone who was so self confident be incorrect in his analysis?

It was one and a half years after the death of Patricia Finn before McCready and his team of detectives focused on Timothy O'Toole as the culprit, and almost two years before a written confession was extracted. McCready claimed that he read a newspaper article in connection with O'Toole's arrest for attempted robbery, and his boast that he'd already killed four people. Suffolk County homicide had six unsolved murders of females on their hands, all on the south shore from Patchogue to Bay Shore, including two in Sayville, between 1980 and 1982.

Playing a hunch, the detective retrieved a sweatshirt which was recovered at the Finn crime scene. He sent it to the crime lab for analysis, while he and his partner began an in-depth investigation of the suspect who was now a resident at St. Joseph's Rehabilitation Center for substance abusers in upstate New York. The noose was beginning to tighten around O'Toole's neck. The detectives believed they had a serial killer on their hands.

Nineteen-year-old Christine Kozma disappeared on September 8, 1982. A resident of Bay Shore, in the same town of Islip as the community of Sayville, her decomposed body was found one month later in the Brookhaven community of Coram. She was the victim of strangulation, and she was last seen with a man fitting the general physical description of O'Toole. The color of O'Toole's car matched the gold color of the car driven by the stranger. His estranged wife, Diane, whom he abused regularly, told the police that on one occasion he had attempted to strangle her.

Margaret Forbes was forty-six years old and a resident of Brightwaters, another south shore community in Islip. She disappeared in early 1982. Her decomposed body was found in November 1982, in the vicinity of a business where O'Toole had been employed. Both she and O'Toole attended meetings of Alcohol Anonymous in the Islip area.

The dismembered body of nineteen-year-old Brentwood (another Islip community) resident Tina Foglia was discovered along the Sagtikos Parkway, a north-south state parkway in the town of Islip on February 3, 1982. She often attended discotheques which were frequented by O'Toole.

Twenty-six-year-old Robin Wolcott, a Patchogue (a village very near to Sayville) school bus driver was found stabbed to death in a Bay Shore parking lot in November 1981. She had been stabbed thirty-two times, and she and Pat Finn had wounds in "identical" places on their bodies.

Eve Wilkowitz, a twenty-year-old resident of Bay Shore, was abducted from the Bay Shore station of the Long Island Railroad. She was found strangled on March 25, 1980.

All of these murders were under intense investigation by the homicide squad as Mahoney and McCready zeroed in on O'Toole as the prime suspect. To be sure, there were other suspects being considered, but for one reason or another each had now been eliminated. In O'Toole, the police knew that they had an alcoholic who became extremely violent when he was drunk. His wife had been afraid for her life. She thought that he was going to kill her. He had also been charged with sexual abuse, when it was alleged that he threatened a girl with a knife. His wife described scars on his hands, and a wound on his leg "about the size of a pen."

The trail was beginning to get warm, and hunches blossomed into genuine suspicion, suspicion not only as to the Finn murder, but in regard to the five other women as well. But probable cause to arrest did not come until February 7, 1983 when Ira Dubey confirmed a match between secretions found at the crime scene and O'Toole's bloody sweatshirt.

It was probably no coincidence that the detectives targeted O'Toole immediately after his sentencing. Before that, they couldn't talk to him without a lawyer present. They were now free to ensnare the perpetrator without having to deal with a meddlesome intruder. It was time to make the long trip to Poughkeepsie where O'Toole was living in a halfway house. Even though 1% of the male population of Suffolk County could have deposited the secretions found in the Finn apartment, they believed that they had enough to effect an arrest, but not nearly enough to convict, or even to indict! McCready would take care of that.

Two unmarked police vehicles were dispatched to Poughkeepsie to make the arrest. Consistent with a technique used in almost every Suffolk homicide case, the arrest was made when O'Toole was spotted alone in a Sears parking lot. Suffolk homicide detectives were not fond of arrests made in the presence of others.

During the three and a half hour automobile trip back to the Yaphank headquarters, according to McCready, Mahoney read the handcuffed O'Toole his constitutional rights and he agreed to talk to them without a lawyer, immediately protesting, "I didn't do nothing!"

"You ain't going nowhere," replied McCready, in an effort to flush him out. In his usual bravado style, spoken like the streetwise cop that he was, McCready boasted: "We have you—we got you good!" This was typical McCready style, which was repeated time and time again in other homicide cases. In fact, he knew quite well at that time that they had nothing, certainly not enough to indict, let alone to convict. They had barely enough probable cause to make a lawful arrest without a warrant. O'Toole continued to deny being involved, as he shifted the subject of the conversation to his alcoholism and the alcoholism of his father.

He claimed that he never frequented bars because of several bad experiences, mentioning a fight at a bar in Oakdale, the community adjacent to Sayville. He had been "rolled" by a girl in a motel after a pickup in a bar. "I ain't never heard of the Sayville Inn," he protested. Pat Finn had last been seen alive there.

His hand injuries, he said, were caused by a chainsaw accident. He was confronted with the fact that there was no record at the hospital of treatment for his chainsaw cuts. When asked about Diane's assertions, he denied that he'd ever beaten his wife, or that he'd ever said that he'd killed four people. The discussion kept returning to Pat Finn, whom he denied knowing, even after being given the details of the brutal stabbing. The usually soft spoken Mahoney boasted: "We got you on five different lies," but the conversation in the car went nowhere.

The "interview" which continued at headquarters proved to be more successful. After less than two hours in the 8'x 12' interview room with

McCready and Mahoney, O'Toole, no longer in handcuffs, broke down and confessed: "I did it, I did it!" All the "fatherly" McCready had to say, according to him, to get O'Toole to spill the secret he'd been carrying for two years were these magic words: "These things are gnawing at your guts and mind. You'll have peace of mind, if you get this off your chest."

Shades of Robert Catone! The "good guy-bad guy" team of Mahoney and McCready had succeeded once again in extracting a confession from a homicide suspect with almost no effort. They seemed to have perfected their form of police interrogation to an art form. In short order, not only did they have a complete oral confession, but they also succeeded in obtaining a complete written confession- written in the hand of Mahoney, but willingly signed and initialed by Timothy O'Toole, reformed alcoholic and murderer, and perhaps also a serial killer.

Suffolk county homicide detectives never allowed a suspect to write out his own confession. It was much more neat and efficient to conduct a question and answer session which resulted in a narrative statement derived from the suspect's answers. When the detective wrote out the statement himself, he could be certain that the suspect wouldn't interject anything which might be detrimental to the people's case. By the same token, when McCready requested that there be no videotaping by the New York City police of Lai, Wang or Barbaran in connection with the Berger murder, he was insuring that nothing would be said which might taint any future confession, or point to innocence rather than guilt. At that time, Suffolk homicide detectives never for one moment considered that their sworn testimony would ever be suspect, or that a videotaped confession, or a confession in the defendant's own hand, might serve to strengthen the people's case, rather than weaken it.

The story which O'Toole confessed to McCready and Mahoney was a sordid one of sex and violence, which culminated in the brutal slaying of a young woman in the prime of her life. O'Toole admitted that he'd met Pat Finn at a bar named "Backstreets" on a Saturday afternoon. They began talking and drinking together. She asked him, he said, to take her home to her apartment.

They drove to her apartment in his 1964 Mercury Comet, and they went to bed. After having sex, O'Toole said that he fell asleep until the next morning. Pat wanted sex again that morning, but he couldn't get a "hard-on." She began to laugh at him, and he got angry. His manhood was being challenged! He then pulled out his pocket knife and began stabbing her. In an effort to defend herself, she stabbed him in the left leg with a pen.

He put a pillow over her head to quiet her screams. The knife became slippery because of all the blood, and the blade cut him as well. Believing that she was dead, O'Toole washed his hands in the sink, cleaned the knife with a towel and threw it in a basket. He then went to his girlfriend's house where he disposed of his clothes, and went to sleep. He last saw his knife at his ex-wife's apartment.

Needless to say, O'Toole told a very different story about the interview at the homicide squad. According to him, there were more police involved in the interrogation than McCready and Mahoney. He described an interrogation which lasted more than seven hours, including a period of two to three hours when he was beaten mercilessly after being told to remove his clothes. He claimed to have been kicked in the groin and beaten with a fifteen inch rubber dildo, shaped like a man's penis, by McCready. He was beaten over the head with a telephone directory by a tall detective whom he couldn't identify. During each of the beatings, according to O'Toole, Mahoney—the good guy—was out of the room, returning only to attempt to convince him to confess to avoid further beatings.

Finally, O'Toole said, he agreed to confess to this one murder to Mahoney, who brought him papers and photographs to initial and sign. He said that he used the initials "TPO" on each occasion, although he always used the initials "TOT", to show that he "didn't want to sign the papers." Not only did he claim to have been beaten, but he said that McCready had threatened to drop him out a window and blow his brains out, and directed to draw a diagram of the crime scene which was described to him by McCready. That done, according to O'Toole, he was left alone in the room for about one hour, until the arrival of Ira Dubey who took pubic and head hair samples, as well as blood and saliva from him.

Until 3:00 a.m., O'Toole underwent intensive questioning about the remaining five unsolved murders, but the detectives were unable to obtain any other confessions. In a murder case, one confession is as good as five. You only have one life to give to the system.

After another wait of about thirty minutes, McCready, Mahoney, the tall detective and a fourth young member of the team escorted O'Toole out of the building, where, according to him, he was shoved to the ground, stomped on, and beaten for several minutes. "What are you trying to escape for?" he was asked tauntingly.

Once again, an accused murderer challenged a confession which was extracted by Detective K. James McCready and his partner in the windowless "interview room" off the squad room at police headquarters in Yaphank. Perhaps at that time I should have begun to see a pattern. But I still hadn't been exposed to enough homicide cases, and besides there were other members of the police department whose testimony was in direct conflict with the story told by O'Toole.

Detective Donald Froehlich of the Identification Section photographed the accused's palms and hands at about 12:30 a.m., at a time during which O'Toole claimed that he was being beaten and terrorized. He said that O'Toole was cooperative, and walking by himself.

Lieutenant Charles Meyer, the duty officer at the 5th precinct in Patchogue, where the accused was lodged for the night, stated that he interviewed O'Toole at 4:00 a.m. when he arrived. Although he appeared nervous, he made no complaints and claimed no injuries. Neither of these officers was affiliated with the homicide squad. I reasoned that they would have no motive to testify falsely.

However, Michael Cahill, a legal aid lawyer and distant relative of O'Toole by marriage, who had never met him before, visited him in the county jail after his arraignment. O'Toole complained to him of being attacked by "two animals," detectives—"one a big fat guy"—who took off his clothes, laid him on the floor, "spread-eagled" him, and "kicked him in the balls and head." He claimed to have been beaten from 11:00 p.m. to 2:00 a.m., during which time McCready attempted to shove a "lead filled dildo down his throat." Cahill noted that O'Toole had seven or eight lumps on the back of his head, purplish swollen testicles, a welt inside his left thigh, black and blue buttocks, a dark area on his left rib cage and a mark on his right shoulder.

But Cahill hadn't been there, and the detectives all testified that O'Toole attempted an escape as they left Yaphank headquarters to lodge him in Patchogue. They admitted that he was thrown to the ground, kicked in the groin, and punched and kicked, in an effort to thwart his attempted escape. In September 1983, I, like so many other judges, was still giving the benefit of the doubt to the police version of such a story. They still wore the white hats in my eyes. There were so many of them willing to swear to the official version of what took place. Like Catone before him, there were many inconsistencies in O'Toole's version of what transpired in Yaphank, and walls and furniture tell no tales. On the other hand, the police version was very consistent. Once again, I ruled that the people proved that an allegedly coerced confession was given voluntarily, and that a defendant's rights were not violated. His statements, both oral and written, could be used at trial. In a written opinion, at the conclusion of pre-trial hearings, I wrote the following:

> ...if this defendant had undergone the beatings for a period of two to three hours which he described at the hands of the investigating officers, it is inconceivable that he would have remained unbloodied, uncut, or that he could have survived same in a state of consciousness. In an effort to discredit the police, the defendant has woven a tale which could only be accepted by the gullible or uninitiated.

During the jury trial, the indelible pattern of Suffolk homicide prosecutions continued. At the eleventh hour of trial, after both sides rested, the prosecution sought to produce a very unusual witness, Alexis Louise Courtney. She'd never even met O'Toole until September 1983 when the hearings commenced.

I had to conduct a hearing out of the presence of the jury to determine whether she was a police agent, because if she was, anything O'Toole had said to her could not be used. This was the first of many hearings that I would be forced to conduct during a homicide trial resulting from the production of a surprise witness who was not revealed before the trial began. The testimony of Robert Pistone, a perjurious police informant, in the 1985 prosecution of James Diaz for the rape and murder of Maureen Negus, turned out to be the straw that broke this camel's back. But yet in 1983, when I was still somewhat inexperienced in the ways of wily police and prosecutors, I somehow instinctively and cynically noted the following in my trial book:

> I permitted her to testify in a limited fashion, even though I know she's a liar, and she's probably acting as a police agent.... Credibility is an issue of fact for the jury.

Despite my obvious misgivings, I ruled that the jury could hear her story. O'Toole's rights hadn't been violated. There was a vast difference between my human instincts and speculative thoughts, and real hard proof that she was an agent of the police. She proved to be almost as damaging as Dubey!

At the request of her brother-in-law, who was being held in the county jail, she visited a lonely Timothy O'Toole who wanted someone to correspond with. Although he had never seen or met her before, he told her that he was in jail for attempting to rob a convenience store in Westchester County. He was taken by the police to a deserted area where he was beaten for seven hours, and as a result he sustained a broken jaw and ribs. It took him nine months to recuperate in a Suffolk County hospital. He bragged that he was going to sue for $1,000,000.

She said that she visited O'Toole on two occasions. He wrote to her, but she destroyed his letters when she learned that he was being held on a murder charge. She had no contact with the police until she heard that he might get out of jail because of a mistrial. She then decided to call the local precinct to talk to the detective in charge.

They referred her to McCready and Mahoney who took a statement, but she was not asked to testify until the night before she took the stand. On cross-examination, she admitted that her brother had been in jail for three days, one month before, and that he had now been released. But she hadn't seen him for awhile. So the sister-in-law of an accused robber and the sister of a released prisoner who just happened to surface as the good Samaritan added some additional nails to O'Toole's coffin.

Good Samaritans were as plentiful in Suffolk homicide convictions as the gulls that hovered over its scenic beaches, and these informants scavenged upon unworthy defendants just as the seagulls scavenged upon the ever-present tidal debris. Although O'Toole did not confess his involvement in the crime to her, her testimony was significant. If the jury believed that he had been injured at the hands of the police, they could now place the blame on some unknown and unidentified upstate officers, or they could conclude that O'Toole was simply a liar. Judging from the verdict of guilty, the jury had reached one or the other of these conclusions.

Alexis Courtney was not the only unusual civilian witness to surface in the people's case. Averne Hall, a friend and landlady of Madeline Couch, O'Toole's girlfriend, was the ex-wife of a Suffolk County police officer. Although she didn't report the incident until almost two years later, she testified that on September 8, 1981, the defendant, whom she did not know at the time, entered her home in a "slightly intoxicated" condition. He identified himself as "Timmy's father," stood in her dining room crying and sobbing: "I killed a girl,I killed her...I did it, I did it!"

Yet she never reported this to the police until she was visited by McCready and Mahoney at the end of October 1983. Despite the fact that she said that she would always remember that incident, she gave no written statement to the police, and there were no notes taken by either detective of this conversation, a fact which I noted with three asterisks in my trial book.

On that note the people rested their direct case, an unusual combination of scientific, police and informant testimony. After about eight hours of deliberation, the jury found O'Toole guilty of both intentional and depraved indifference murder.

Justice cried out for the maximum sentence. So on January 18, 1984 a maximum sentence of twenty-five-years-to-life was the price a convicted killer would pay for a brutal and senseless murder. O'Toole's attorney argued that the concept that "the punishment fit the crime" was Gilbert and Sullivan law. I agreed! Never once did I honestly believe that the punishment fit the crime. The last two New York governors had seen to that!

On May 7, 1987 an appeals court reversed the conviction and ordered a new trial based upon a typically hyper-technical interpretation of the law. They didn't believe that O'Toole had anything less than a fair trial, or that he was not guilty of the murder of Patricia Finn. The case was returned because O'Toole was, in their opinion, over convicted, although he'd been sentenced to concurrent life terms. The two murder convictions were inconsistent and unlawful..."because guilt of one necessarily negates guilt of the other." According to the Court of Appeals, you can't intentionally kill someone while at the same time acting under circumstances evincing a depraved indifference to human life.[1]

I have read and reread their decision time and time again. I have concluded that my powers of reason and logic are obviously not keen enough to reach the same result "...by the application of simple logic and common sense..." as they said. I have always found it difficult to pick the hairs from a gnat. Most troubling to me was their ultimate conclusion that despite the convictions, a new trial was necessary, because "...the jury...failed to make the critical determination of defendant's mental state...," an omission that could not be cured by the courts. It was not enough for the appellate judges sitting in their cloistered tower that O'Toole was found guilty of murder beyond a reasonable doubt, or that the rules were changed after his conviction. That had not been the law when O'Toole was convicted!

O'Toole was returned from a state correctional facility, where he was serving his life sentence, to Suffolk County to be retried in my court. But I never envisioned the final unhappy result. I was divested of my criminal jurisdiction as a County Court judge before O'Toole's retrial could be reached, and it rested in the hands of another judge to mete out justice on behalf of a deceased innocent victim of a ruthless, bloody murder.

****

By January 5, 1989, I was mired in the civil part of the Supreme Court for eight months. I was paying penance in a civil purgatory for the investigation of the homicide squad and the district attorney's office, and for my public criticism of the manner in which the courts were being administered in Suffolk County by its chief administrative judge, Arthur M. Cromarty, former Republican supervisor of the Town of Babylon and close associate of Patrick Henry, the incumbent district attorney. After weeks of public comment by myself in the news media and before the Public Safety Committee of the county legislature, three of seven county court judges were returned from the Supreme Court where they'd been assigned to handle civil cases, to preside over felony criminal cases. Since I was the one who had brought public pressure to bear for their return, my punishment was to remain in a civil court, divested of criminal jurisdiction. I was an unhappy, bitter and angry judge when I was handed a copy of *Newsday* by my law secretary. A story on page twenty-five made me even angrier and more bitter. The anger and bitterness slowly coalesced into a form of revulsion. The caption of the story read: "Perjury Case Affects A Trial."[2]

Timothy Patrick O'Toole was afforded the opportunity to plead guilty to manslaughter in the first degree for the murder of Patricia Finn. The plea was taken by my successor. The man that I'd sentenced to concurrent terms of twenty-five-years-to-life, who'd already been convicted of two counts of murder, and who'd already served more than five years of his term of imprisonment, was allowed to bargain for a sentence of five to fifteen years for the cold blooded murder of an innocent young woman in the prime of her life. The sentence was no greater than the term of imprisonment which I'd imposed upon Robert Catone for vehicular manslaughter. This was justice, New York style! Such a result was encouraged by the Office of Court Administration, where numbers and the need to dispose of cases rather than try them, was becoming more important than the need to dispense proper justice.

The assistant district attorney, Timothy Mazzei, agreed to this plea bargain because "it would be difficult to retry the case without being able to have Dubey testify and that to do so would be putting a person on the stand who has been convicted of perjury and I don't think we can do things like that."

This was the same prosecutor who had allowed Robert Brensic to plead to manslaughter in a Brooklyn court for the murder of Johnny Pius. He had to be aware of the written confession. Was the credibility of McCready and his cohorts so suspect that Mazzei feared to call them to the witness stand? None of them were admitted perjurers, nor had any ever been charged with perjury!

What about Alexis Louise Courtney to counter O'Toole's anticipated claim of police brutality? Had she dropped from the face of the earth, or otherwise become unavailable to the prosecution? What happened to Averne Hall, the police officer's wife?

Why not try the case under these circumstances? At the very least, O'Toole already spent almost five years in jail. Under the worst case scenario, he'd spend almost as much time behind bars until acquittal, as he might spend with this plea. With a trial, he stood a good chance of conviction, Dubey or no Dubey. Was Mazzei privy to some fatal flaw in the people's case of which I was not aware? How could these people sleep nights? How did they face themselves in the mirror? These questions and more danced about my subconscious as I went through the monotonous, routine and simplistic motions of an acting Supreme Court justice in Suffolk County, more certain than ever that I'd never be returned to my elected office, unless something drastic occurred. I'd simply made too many waves, affected too many lives and overturned too many carpets!

On January 18, just two weeks after O'Toole was sentenced, I received an unexpected letter from the Division of Parole at Greenhaven Correctional Facility, a maximum security prison in Stormville, New York. O'Toole had already been transported to a state facility, and he was scheduled to appear before the Board of Parole on January 23. Theoretically, he could be paroled within one week, since he'd already served enough time on the original sentence to satisfy the minimum term of five years. The senior parole officer sent me the letter in error, believing that I was the sentencing judge. I was outraged by the contents. I'd been given up to thirty days to respond, but O'Toole would be before the parole board in five days. He could be on the streets of Suffolk before I could respond. I immediately called the parole office at Greenhaven to express my strong feelings about how this matter had been mishandled. I was assured that O'Toole's appearance before the parole board would be delayed until March so that I'd have the opportunity to make my feelings known.

Having no faith in such assurances, on the following day I drafted a four page letter to the Division of Parole. To assure that this wouldn't happen again, I sent a copy of the letter to Ramon J. Rodriguez, the chairman of the New York State Board of Parole and the district attorney. Copies were sent to the administrative judge to pique his conscience. Perhaps, but not likely, he'd be as disturbed as I had been when confronted with the facts of the O'Toole plea bargain. I hoped that this letter would be deeply troublesome to Tom Stark.

In the letter, I expressed, in the strongest terms, the opinion that O'Toole should never have been granted a manslaughter plea, attempting, in my frustration, to explain the background of the case so that the board might understand why I had such strong feelings that O'Toole "...never be paroled with respect to this matter, and...he not be considered for early release prior to his completion of a fifteen year term of imprisonment." I made this recommendation knowing full well that even if he weren't granted parole, he could still receive a reduction in sentence to ten years for good behavior. My goal was to keep O'Toole incarcerated for the longest possible time, under these unhappy circumstances.

Unfortunately, Timothy Mazzei and the sentencing judge, Tom Mallon, by this obscene plea bargain, had insured the return of Timothy O'Toole to the streets of Suffolk County while he was still a relatively young man. I continue to be haunted by this horrible thought!

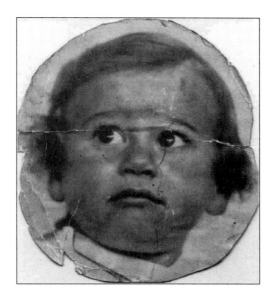

Top: Earliest known photo of Stuart Namm, 1934, age five to six months. *Left*: Stuart, age 18 months to 2 years, 1935, studio photo. *Right*: Age 3, 1937, acting as a Professional Page Boy (ring bearer) for Namm and Kramer families.

Parents Paul and Lillian Namm with Stuart, age 3, during the Hudson River Day Line annual excursion to Bear Mountain State Park, 1937.

Stuart's father, Paul Namm, sister Sandra and Stuart, on Sutter Ave., Brownsville, Brooklyn, New York, during the "Great Depression," 1939.

Stuart's Bar Mitzvah reception. His grandmother, Minnie Kramer, stands next to him with his grandfathers, Joseph "Pop" Namm (*left*) and Nathan Kramer (*right*), standing behind, Oct. 1946.

Stuart, age 16, Explorer Scout, on a camping trip to Lake George State Park, New York, Spring 1950.

Lenore Rhona Abelson, Stuart's future wife and mother of three children—
Gary, Keith and Suzanne. Highland Park, Brooklyn, New York, Spring 1949.

Stuart and fiancee Lenore at her senior prom, Thomas Jefferson High School, Brooklyn, New York, May 1952.

Stuart's graduation photo, Brooklyn Technical High School, June 1951.

City College of New York (CCNY) Varsity Lacrosse team, Spring 1953. Stuart (*middle of 2nd row*) wore No. 28 and was the goaltender. Coach Leon "Chief" Miller (*in light suit on top row, second from left*) was the brother-in-law of Jim Thorpe.

Coach "Chief" Leon Miller (*left*) briefing CCNY varsity attack Lacrosse players as Stuart, No. 28 (*standing, right*) looks on, Spring 1954. (Courtesy of *The New York Times*)

Wedding photo of Mr. & Mrs. Stuart Namm. Parkway Caterers, Brooklyn, New York, December 25, 1954.

Stuart graduates from City College of New York with a BA degree in pre-law, June 1955.

Upon graduation from City College of New York, Stuart is commissioned a 2nd Lt., Infantry, United States Army, June 1955.

2nd Lt. Stuart Namm, United States Army Infantry. Outside Fort Benning, Georgia, Fall 1955.

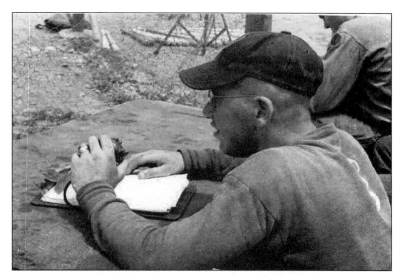

Lt. Stuart Namm announces 17th Infantry baseball games over Armed Forces Radio, "Radio Gypsy," Spring 1956.

As an Army Ranger, Camp Kaiser, Korea, Chorwan Valley, somewhere North of the 38th parallel, Spring 1956.

Stuart Namm, Esq., in the law offices of Baranello, Block & Namm, Port Jefferson, New York, 1967.

SEVEN

My Eye Opener

O N THE VERY NIGHT THAT I WAS BEING HONORED WITH the most prestigious award of the New York State Association of Criminal Defense Lawyers, the Thurgood Marshall Award, I was unexpectedly presented with a magnificent international clock by the members of the Long Island Region of the NAACP. It was mounted on a plaque with the following inscription:

To Someone Who Stood Up for What
Was Right at Great Personal Sacrifice
"Principle Was Ahead of Expediency"
A Man Who Practiced and
Lived What Everyone Else Has Preached
You'll Always be an Honorary Life Member
of the NAACP LI Region
Thanks

Looking back upon the turbulent years of 1985 through 1988, I frequently wondered, and members of the media would ask me, when it was that I first began to realize that there was a serious problem in the prosecution of Suffolk County homicide cases. With the benefit of hindsight it has become increasingly apparent that blind innocence became a skeptical, microscopic scrutiny of law enforcement with the trial of nineteen-year-old Vincent Waters for the attempted murder of a uniformed Suffolk County cop.

Peter Newman, an African-American attorney from the Town of Babylon, sat directly behind me during four years of night law school. We both graduated from Brooklyn Law School and were admitted to the bar in 1961, but we never developed a close personal relationship, although there was a certain undefined kinship. While in school, I was employed as a group life underwriter by the Equitable Life Assurance Society, which was paying for most of my education. Pete was employed by the Internal Revenue Service as an enforcement agent. We were both married with children, and immediately upon graduation from law school, I also entered federal government service as a staff attorney in the New York office of the Federal Trade Commission.

President Kennedy made government service extremely attractive to young, idealistic lawyers like Pete and myself in the early '60s. Upon graduation we parted ways, and I didn't see Pete Newman again until I started practicing law in Suffolk County in 1966. By that time, both he and I had moved our families to the suburbs where we were engaged in the private practice of law. He was practicing in the predominantly black community of North Babylon, and I was in partnership with Dom Baranello and Fred Block in the predominantly white middle class communities of Centereach and Port Jefferson. We sometimes ran into each other in court. I developed great respect for his abilities as an attorney, but more important, for the maturity and humanity which he displayed in his relationship with others.

When Harry O'Brien, the much maligned Democratic District Attorney, first took office, he asked for my opinion about Pete. He was being considered for the position of District Court Bureau Chief. I could give nothing but the highest recommendation since, in my opinion, he would certainly be an asset to any government position. Pete served in that capacity for the four years of O'Brien's administration, returning to private practice when O'Brien was defeated by his chief assistant, Patrick Henry. By that time, I was a District Court Judge. In 1983, I appointed Peter Newman to represent Vincent Waters who was indigent and unable to afford private counsel. He was charged with a very serious violent felony. I felt that Waters, a black youth, could best relate to a black lawyer, of which there were less than a handful in Suffolk. But there was none more qualified than Pete. He would provide Waters with the defense to which he was entitled under the law. It was the first of many homicide cases that I'd ultimately assign to Peter Newman.

In New York State, the attempted murder of a police officer is as serious a crime under the law as the murder of a civilian. In fact, until New York's last death penalty statute was declared unconstitutional, a person could theoretically still be executed for the murder of a police officer, while the maximum penalty for the murder of someone else was twenty-five-years-to-life. Absent a New York death penalty statute, today both presently provide for a maximum sentence of twenty-five-years-to-life. Waters faced a possible maximum penalty equivalent to the punishment which I'd handed out to Brensic, Ryan, Lai, Wang, Barbaran and O'Toole for murder.

Because of the serious nature of the charge, the case was assigned to the major offense bureau of the district attorney's office. The people were represented by deputy bureau chief Barry Feldman. He'd been recruited some years earlier from the Kings County district attorney's office. It was my first real encounter with Feldman, although the reputation which preceded him acted as a caution light in my dealings with him. In the ensuing months, Feldman handled several homicide cases in my court, culminating in the trial of James Diaz, the ultimate catalyst in my request for a state investigation.

In 1983 and 1984, to my uninitiated eyes and ears, Feldman was simply a somewhat overly zealous prosecutor, complete with an unevenly thick, dark mustache and an irritatingly whining voice. Still he could be quite gracious and friendly, and our mutual love of Chinese food, probably a product of our common Jewish heritage, became the centerpiece of a somewhat limited friendship which blossomed into mutual animosity in the summer of 1985. But for the time being, Feldman was a great source of excellent eastern Long Island Chinese restaurants. He was a veritable oriental gourmet!

It wouldn't be long into the Waters case before I became suspicious of Feldman's trial tactics, and if Pete Newman hadn't been such a gentleman, at some point, he might have openly accused Feldman of the type of prosecutorial misconduct which became evident in the later Diaz trial. His alleged misconduct became a centerpiece of the first public hearing conducted by the State Commission of Investigations in January 1987. At that hearing a subpoenaed Feldman, with counsel at his side, underwent an intense period of heated cross-examination by the entire commission and its counsel. Feldman found his name inextricably linked with Joseph Pistone, an admitted perjurer, and with Ira Dubey, Suffolk's chief forensic serologist who was convicted of perjury. Ultimately, in 1988, after a transfer to the east end bureau which was, in effect, a demotion in the hierarchy of the district attorney's office, Feldman quietly resigned to enter private practice with a former associate, Billy Keahon, the volatile prosecutor in the Brensic and Ryan trials.

There was a close bond formed in the office of the Suffolk County district attorney. Many former high ranking prosecutors left the office to enter private practice as partners. Long after they left, most retained a close kinship with their former associates still in government service, and perhaps, more importantly, with key members of the police department.

There was the partnership of Gerald Sullivan and Thomas Spota, both former chiefs of the major offense bureau, who represented various police associations and police officers. They represented Feldman before the State Commission of Investigations. Two other partners in the firm were James O'Rourke, a former deputy bureau chief, and Vincent Malito, former chief of the appeals bureau. There would be a period of time in the early 1980s when Timothy Mazzei, the final prosecutor in the Brensic and O'Toole pleas, left the District Attorney's office to work for them.

Another prominent local law partnership was that of David Clayton and the enigmatic Peter Mayer, both former deputy bureau chiefs. Peter Mayer was involved in the Peter Corso trial. In 1989, Peter Mayer was represented by Bill Keahon, the former prosecutor, after being charged with driving while intoxicated for a second time. In May, 1993, Bill Keahon, the reformed alcoholic, was himself charged with driving while intoxicated. His attorney was David Clayton. He'd been driving his '93 Mercedes Benz "for a period of time" on the wrong side of a median in the vicinity of police headquarters. A prominent doctor who was driving home from work was seriously injured when his vehicle was hit head-on by Keahon. The former prosecutor was also charged with driving with a suspended license. The arrest came on a day when he was co-counsel with Tom Spota in the defense of ex-detective K. James McCready on charges of felony assault.[1]

Ethical questions were raised by Newsday as to the manner in which the trial judge, Justice Kenneth Rohl, was assigned by the administrative judge of the District Court, Peter Dounias, to handle the Mayer DWI case. It was reported that Keahon and Clayton, Mayer's partner, suggested that the misdemeanor case be assigned to Justice Rohl, whose jurisdiction encompassed the trial of felony cases, and who, under normal circumstances, had no involvement with a District Court case, although his courtroom was in the Dennison building, where the District Court was physically located.

After three days of a nonjury trial (Mayer waived his constitutional right to trial by jury as did McCready in 1993), Rohl, a former president of the Suffolk County Criminal Bar Association, whose membership included many present and former prosecutors, suddenly chose to disqualify himself because of an "appearance of impropriety." The case was then transferred to Nassau County for trial, where it should have been sent in the first place, since many District Court judges, who probably had lesser links with Mayer than Rohl, appropriately disqualified themselves to avoid that very appearance.

Only Steve Wilutis, in a long line of major offense bureau chiefs, left the office in 1988 to practice alone in Hauppauge. After a long period of reflection, I've concluded that perhaps the most tragic fallout of the investigations and Newsday revelations was the resignation of Wilutis, and the resultant loss to the people of a dedicated, diligent and successful prosecutor. In 1988, the office of the district attorney could ill afford such a loss. The burden of important murder cases fell upon the likes of Timothy Mazzei and others who were not yet equipped to shoulder such a heavy responsibility.

Several of these prosecutors, who were still in the office in 1984, were called by Feldman to testify in a pre-trial hearing which had to be conducted in the Waters case. In preliminary motion papers, Pete Newman alleged that his client's constitutional right to a fair trial was being violated by the systematic exclusion of black youths between the ages of eighteen to twenty-one from the county's jury pool. The trial jury that would determine Waters' guilt or innocence would ultimately be selected from this source.

Suffolk County, like so many other suburban counties, was predominantly white middle class, with pockets of poorer minority communities, like Brentwood, Central Islip, North Amityville, Wyandanch, North Bellport and Flanders interspersed throughout the county. Most of the black youths were educated in high schools which were predominantly black and Hispanic, while most white youths obtained their education in high schools with a very low black student population.

During the course of the hearing, we learned through the testimony of Roy Fedelm, a senior planner for the Long Island Regional Board, that 1 out of every 149 persons, or .67% of the general population, between the ages of 18 and 76 in Suffolk County was a black youth between the ages of 18 and 21. This was according to statistics provided by the 1980 census. We also learned that in the communities of North Amityville, Wyandanch, Central Islip and Brentwood, each of which had its own high school, the percentage of black youths between the ages of 18-21 was 83.5%, 64.5%, 21.5% and 7.2%, respectively.

By contrast, in the wealthier white communities of Smithtown and Stony Brook, for example, the percentages were .19% and 1.41%, respectively. In other words, North Amityville had 400 times more black youths in that age group than Smithtown.

In his moving papers, Newman presented a copy of a letter allegedly sent to predominantly white school districts by the commissioner of jurors soliciting the names of the graduating seniors for jury service. He also provided an affidavit from the principal of Brentwood High School stating that his school never received such a letter. So it was necessary to conduct the hearing to determine whether the constitutional rights of young black defendants, such as Waters, were being violated by a jury pool which didn't reflect a fair cross-section of the Suffolk County community.

During the course of the hearing, which began on April 4, 1984, the principals of Central Islip High School and Wyandanch High School testified that their schools never received any letter soliciting the names of graduating seniors. Mysteriously, during the testimony of Carmine Puleo, the white principal of Brentwood High School, a copy of a letter was retrieved from the files of that school, dated September 22, 1983, by a detective-investigator from the district attorney's office. The letter seemed to be a response to a letter of request from Albert J. Cavagnaro, the former commissioner of jurors, for a list of graduating seniors.

Puleo appeared to be visibly shaken by its production, since, as he testified, he'd caused a search of all of the school records in all of its three buildings for the past three years, and no such letter was found.

He was recalled to the stand on April 11 by the prosecution, although he'd initially been a defense witness. On this occasion he said that he checked his files since he first testified, and that he'd now found the original of the September 22, 1983 letter. He also said that he found a copy of a 1983 letter from the commissioner of jurors. On cross-examination by Newman, who'd been taken aback by this revelation, Puleo referred to his discovery as "human error" and an "honest mistake." What he couldn't explain was why his files contained the "original" letter to the commissioner of jurors and a "copy" of the letter of request from the commissioner. His files should have contained a copy of the former, and an original of the latter. He originally testified that he made the initial search of his files, but now, still under oath, he said that his secretary conducted the first search, and he the most recent "successful" search.

The secretary, Lois Birkel, was called by Newman in rebuttal. She said that she'd made a "thorough search" of the general correspondence file, and that she'd "flipped through the letters one by one," but that she couldn't find any such letter. Yet, when Puleo went into the file in her presence, he found the letters, stapled together, within five minutes. She couldn't recall ever receiving such a letter in the summer of 1983, when she was working, and when very little correspondence came from outside the school district.

Unfortunately, the mystery of the disappearing and reappearing letters was never solved during the hearing, which would be decided on more important and clearly definable issues. Suffice it to say for the moment, Feldman prosecutions seemed to always create such insoluble problems for me. I was merely a judge, not a detective, and it would've taken extensive investigation to solve this particular mystery.

Easier to detect, however, was a pattern of deception which I noted in the testimony of several prosecutors called as witnesses for the prosecution during the course of the hearing which lasted for several days. This didn't require sophisticated detective work, only the use of one's common sense.

Newman called several prominent defense lawyers whom he simply found in the corridors of the courthouse. One of them was Harry O'Brien, the last

Democrat district attorney. All testified that in their years of experience selecting juries in criminal cases in Suffolk County, none had ever seen a black youth between the ages of eighteen and twenty-one in a jury panel. The fact was, that after eight years as a judge, I couldn't recall ever having seen a black youth in that age group summoned to my court for jury service.

Yet after Fedelm, the regional planner, testified, Feldman called four assistant district attorneys from his office to testify, including Keahon, Wilutis, Edward Jablonski, who was involved in the Corso case, and William Kearon, who later became a deputy police commissioner under commissioner DeWitt Treader (Treader resigned during the SIC investigation, after the indictment of his chief of detectives). Fedelm testified that one out of every 149 persons in Suffolk County in 1980 was a black youth between the ages of eighteen and twenty-one.

Keahon then testified that out of every three jury panels of about sixty persons, one or two was a black person in this age group. Jablonski, likewise, said that he'd seen one or two out of every three jury panels; Kearon, one out of every two panels; and Wilutis, one in every one, two or three panels. Yet when asked to do so, none could produce trial notes of the jury selection process to corroborate their testimony. Not even Jablonski, who kept meticulous notes in a bound looseleaf book of every case he tried.

My eyes were now literally wide open! I'd never again permit them to close during my tenure as a criminal court judge. Having heard this absolutely incredible testimony by four prosecutors, sworn to uphold the law, it didn't take a great intellectual leap to realize that in the major offense bureau of the district attorney's office, as it was then constituted, the conviction of a defendant justified whatever means was necessary to insure that result, including manufactured testimony to fit the situation at hand.

Despite my very strong feelings about what I'd observed at that time, in a written opinion published after the hearing, I couldn't bring myself to openly accuse four prosecutors of perjury, and the assistant handling the case, Barry Feldman, of prosecutorial misconduct—subornation of perjury. I buried these thoughts within the deepest recesses of my mind, and simply noted in my decision that their testimony comported with the statistical data that Feldman provided, although seven defense lawyers testified that they'd seen none.

I did, however, reach the legal conclusion that there had been a systematic exclusion of black youths in that age group from the Suffolk County jury pool, and that the fault for that lay with the office of the former Commissioner of Jurors, which kept no records of the source material used in the random selection of persons for jury service. I wrote that I could not "...ignore the facts discovered during the course of the hearing which shocked the conscience of the court," a de facto exclusion of black youths from jury service "...by reason of either malfeasance (fostering a system which was susceptible of abuse) or invidious discriminatory practices..."[2]

On May 2, 1984, *Newsday*, which had obtained a copy of the decision from the court, published the following headline on its front page: JUDGE: JURY POOLS EXCLUDED BLACKS SAYS SUFFOLK IGNORES THOSE 18 to 21.

Nevertheless, this decision and the subsequent headline gave little comfort to Vincent Waters, since I also concluded that there'd been no violation of his constitutional right to trial by a jury representing a true cross-section of the Suffolk County community.

The Supreme Court of the United States held some years earlier that in order to establish a violation by the state in its failure to guarantee that juries represent a fair cross-section of the community, a defendant must show that the group alleged to be excluded was a "distinctive group" in the community. Judicial precedent did not favor Peter Newman's argument on behalf of his client. Several appeals courts, both federal and state, previously uniformly held that eighteen to twenty-one year olds did not constitute a recognizable, or distinctive, group within the community. So Vincent Waters had been unable to meet his heavy burden of proving a violation of his constitutional rights. Nevertheless his attorney had succeeded in convincing me that a segment of the Suffolk County populace was being systematically excluded from jury service, whether or not his client's constitutional rights were violated.

This theme was instantly adopted by the Suffolk County chapter of the New York Civil Liberties Union which made plans to periodically monitor a new system of filling the jury pool which was being developed by the new Commissioner of Jurors in conjunction with the computers of the Office of Court Administration. This burgeoning bureaucracy was created when a unified state court system had its genesis the New York State constitution.

But I needed to know whether I had witnessed perjury by four prosecutors, or whether I and the members of the defense bar who testified were mistaken in what we'd seen over the years. I decided to begin an unofficial study of future jury panels to determine whether, in fact, there were black youths between the ages of eighteen and twenty-one in the master jury pool, and if not, whether the new system would bring them into the mainstream of jury selection. That study began with the impaneling of the Waters jury, and continued into the spring of 1988.

The study required a joint effort involving Bob Meguin, my law secretary, the court clerk, and one or more court officers. Bob transcribed the birth dates of prospective jurors from computer cards, while the clerk, the court officers and I studied the faces of prospective jurors for racial ethnicity. The survey would probably not pass muster as a true scientific study, but for my purposes it sufficed to provide the information I was seeking.

The results were startling, but to the newly born skeptic, somewhat predictable. In four years, I didn't see one black youth in that age group brought into my trial part for prospective jury service. From the spring of 1984 until the spring of 1988, 2,534 prospective jurors were impanelled for service in my courtroom in twenty-four separate jury trials.

Not only did I not find even one black youth in that age group, there were virtually no young people at all between the ages of eighteen and twenty-one. Either the four prosecutors had been uniformly mistaken, had perjured themselves under oath in a court of law or the master jury pool had changed drastically after 1984.[3]

There was no basis upon which to draw the last conclusion, and it was highly unlikely that all four could be so mistaken. There was only one logical conclusion to derive from the indisputable facts. Henceforth, their statements and actions would be suspect and subject to extremely close scrutiny by me. But it is safe to say that I didn't reach that inescapable conclusion until the statistics began to mount, and by that time I was in the thick of the morass created by the Corso and Diaz trials. Those cases only corroborated in my mind what I had already so unhappily discovered.

More important was the finding that during the four year period only seventy-nine black persons were sent up from the central jury room, or 3.1% of all those impaneled. Blacks represented approximately 5.6% of the entire

Suffolk County population eligible for jury service. In other words, not only were there no black youths in the master jury pool, but blacks of all ages were under represented by almost 100%. There was no question in my mind but that the master jury pool did not represent a true cross-section of the Suffolk County community.

Yet, unless an intentional systematic exclusion of a recognizable group—in this case all blacks—could be shown, this did not represent a violation of anyone's constitutional right to a fair trial. But this did not mean that the system in Suffolk County was fair, especially in the light of what I witnessed in the Waters hearing.

As only one County Court judge with very limited jurisdiction, in 1984 I didn't have the power nor the authority to order a change in the manner of selection of the master jury pool in Suffolk County, despite its obvious perpetuation of inequality. However, I attempted to place immediate pressure upon the new Commissioner of Jurors, Thomas Hennessey. He had recently been installed in his position by the Republican dominated county board of judges—all of the judges of the Supreme and County Courts. With no experience in the courts, his most recent employment had been in another political patronage position with Suffolk County Off-Track Betting.

On May 10, 1984 I wrote to him to remind him of the Waters decision which had received extensive coverage in the press. I asked him to respond within thirty days as to what actions he would take to insure that the questionable practices were corrected immediately. Although I did not mention this finding in the Waters case, I pointed out that there was an "...apparent imbalance in the numbers of prospective jurors from black communities such as North Amityville and Wyandanch..."[4]

When I received no response from him, other than that Judge Cromarty, the county's Administrative Judge, would reply to me at a later date, I wrote again on June 19, 1984. This time I sent a copy of my letter to the district attorney, the presidents of the two local bar associations, the executive director of the Suffolk County Human Rights Commission and the chairman of the Brookhaven Chapter of the NAACP. I wasn't going to let this issue die without a challenge![5]

Sending copies of the letter to all of these officials was apparently what it took to flush out some response to my correspondence. On June 27, I received an "off the record" telephone call from Arthur Cromarty. He was

extremely apologetic that the Commissioner of Jurors hadn't responded to
me. According to Cromarty, both he and the commissioner were now
working with the Office of Court Administration to create a source of
prospective jurors in the county that would account for approximately 90%
of the county population.

He carried the conversation into areas that I would never have expected
him to discuss. In his opinion, the present commissioner was a complete
change from his predecessor, whom he was trying to get rid of for years
because he wouldn't do anything he told him to do.[6]

I was positively flabbergasted. Why was he telling me these things? Did
he think that I'd be sympathetic? Here was the Administrative Judge of an
entire court system, servicing a county of more than 1,000,000 people,
admitting that he'd been inept for years. If he wanted to rid the system of a
worthless administrator who served at the pleasure of the Board of Judges
over which Cromarty presided, why hadn't he suggested that they do so?
Was politics so much in control that an administrative judge couldn't carry
out a fundamental administrative task? The answer to that question was a
resounding "yes!", and the new commissioner was appointed under that
same system of patronage.

I had attended the meeting of the Board of Judges at which Hennessey
had been selected. It was a farce, an excuse for the county's judges to partake
of a free buffet lunch. It was readily apparent that the choice had been made
by the Republican leadership, and that the judges were merely rubber
stamping their choice, a man with zero experience in the judicial system.

"Frankly, your decision said it all," Cromarty stated in a patronizing tone.
He said that in the future it was their intention to work like the Board of
Elections—to go directly to the high schools to qualify eighteen year olds
for jury service. I learned later that this method was vetoed by the
bureaucrats of the Office of Court Administration.

In even more patronizing words he uttered: "I certainly agree with
everything you said in your opinion. You were absolutely right on the law."
He said that there was to be a greater effort to have a more random selection
of jurors. "Believe me, it's not being overlooked. I want to be sure of myself
before I tell you anything."[7]

In the ensuing months and years, I learned that Arthur Cromarty, former county Republican chairman and former chairman of the now defunct County Board of Supervisors, was capable of saying anything in an attempt to avoid confrontation and criticism. The few conversations that we had in the future became more and more contentious, culminating in his actions which removed me from the County Court bench to serve as an Acting Supreme Court Justice handling only civil litigation. But in 1984, Arthur was playing the role he thrived on, that of the concerned father figure.

The ball was immediately picked up by Ricardo Montano, Executive Director of the Suffolk Human Rights Commission, who, in a series of letters to Hennesey, demanded speedy action in the implementation of a "new computerized system" to eliminate the concerns which had been raised in the Waters decision. On July 18, Cromarty responded to Montano by letter, with copies to all concerned parties, including myself. He indicated that they were then in the process of revising jury questionnaires utilizing the computers of the Office of Court Administration to "...get a greater representation or cross section of our overall county population." The system which, according to Cromarty, would commence on or before September 15, 1984, and would involve computer random selection from voter registration lists, lists of licensed drivers and lists of high school graduates.

District Attorney Patrick Henry wrote that "...we wholeheartedly endorse and encourage the selection of all potentially qualified jurors from every walk of life, regardless of ethnic or religious background." Everyone was now on record as opposed to discrimination in the jury selection process.

On July 27, Ron Sussman, a lawyer and former assistant district attorney, who was an active member of the Suffolk Academy of Law, the educational arm of the Suffolk County Bar Association, attempted to publish a short article in the *Suffolk County Bar Association's Academy News* entitled "NEW JURIES COME TO SUFFOLK." He wrote:

> But for Judge Namm's initiative with the Commissioner of Jurors, the Office of Court Administration and the Suffolk Human Rights Commission, Suffolk County's jury pools would continue to exclude those who comprise a fair cross section of

our community...Lawyers and litigants alike should be grateful
for the opportunity to have their cases heard before a jury truly
representative of the population of Suffolk County.

The article was summarily rejected by the editor, David Besso, who also
practiced criminal law in Suffolk. I had apparently made too many defense
lawyers unhappy with my prior decisions. Nothing complimentary about
Judge Namm, even if true, was to appear in the Academy News. This pattern
emerged early, and continued through my tenure as a judge. There were to
be no kudos for one who was not part of the old boy network in the county,
which included both defense and prosecution lawyers.

Each year the Suffolk County Criminal Bar Association awards a plaque
at its annual dinner to the Suffolk County "Judge of the Year." Even in years
when the association was literally scraping the bottom of the barrel to find
someone deserving of the award, the judge who caused a radical change in
the selection of jurors; who was responsible for revealing abuses in the
investigation and trial of homicide cases; who was responsible for a
restructuring of the district attorney's office in order to deal with those
abuses; and who was responsible for raising public awareness of the problems
within the system, was never seriously considered.

I longed for the unlikely day that I might receive the telephone call
advising me that I'd been selected, so that I might enjoy telling the caller
and all whom he represented to shove the award up their collective asses.
But this was pure fantasy, since I knew that this day would never come.

Even more outrageous was the reaction of the president of the Suffolk
County Bar Association, a prominent civil lawyer. He was interviewed by a
Newsday reporter about the issue of discrimination in jury selection. The good
president was not interested in the fact that a segment of the black community
was being systematically excluded from the master jury pool, but he was very
concerned that the master jury pool, from which civil juries were also selected,
did not contain enough wealthy residents of the affluent communities in the
Hamptons. This resulted, he said, in money verdicts which were too low in
Suffolk County. Of course, this resulted in lower legal fees.

So much for equality and justice in Suffolk County, as far as the Bar

Association was concerned! Not one public word was ever uttered on the subject by any member of the organized bar. That pattern never changed even as the county's criminal justice system literally came apart at the seams during the state investigation of the police department and the district attorney's office between 1986 and 1988. In 1992, the Bar Association grudgingly commissioned a study of minority representation in jury pools. It was too little, too late!

On August 9, 1984, Judge Cromarty, in a memorandum to all county judges, proudly announced the development of an automated jury system installation in conjunction with the Office of Programs and Planning of the state's Office of Court Administration. The plan was to develop a master jury list, utilizing the state computers, merging the lists of registered voters, licensed drivers and state taxpayers. The expectation was that an additional 30,000 jurors would be qualified each year, thereby enhancing minority group representation in the jury pools. It was an acknowledgment, but not an admission, that there was something seriously wrong with the old system. He emphasized, however, that any increase in the number of minorities would "occur gradually."

And gradual, it certainly was. In 1984, with a smaller general population and a smaller minority population, there were 103,029 persons on the Suffolk County master jury list. In July 1988, that number had only increased to 210,863 of a total eligible population of approximately 875,000—less than 25%. My study, which continued into April 1988, revealed that there had been little, if any, change in the number of prospective black jurors being impaneled. In fact, minority representation decreased slightly.

In the summer of 1988, a report was published by a team of citizen volunteers known as the Suffolk County Court Monitors. The independent monitors spent twelve weeks in the fall and winter of 1987-1988 observing criminal court sessions in the Supreme and County Courts. They were sponsored by the Fund for Modern Courts based in New York City. Among their findings was the following:

> The monitors were...bothered by the lack of minority members in jury pools when so many defendants were black."Their

recommendation: "The Commissioner of Jurors should institute outreach programs and consider enforcement measures to increase the participation of the minority community in jury duty."

That finding and those recommendations have fallen on deaf ears in Suffolk County!

In January 1988, the Chief Judge of the Court of Appeals created the New York State Commission on Minorities, chaired by Franklin H. Williams, a former Ambassador to Ghana, to study and report on the treatment of minorities within the judicial system. The commission consisted of several prominent lawmakers, jurists, attorneys and members of the academic community. Its executive director was a young black attorney, Edna Wells Handy. As is usually the case, the commission commenced its study in New York City.

On August 19, 1988, a meeting was scheduled with all of the judges of Suffolk County to discuss the commission's goals. About thirty judges were in attendance on a hot Friday afternoon. We were introduced to the workings of the commission by James C. Goodale, its vice chairman, an attorney for *The New York Times*. After he completed his presentation, and the introduction of Ms. Handy, a heated discussion ensued involving the then only black judge in Suffolk County, Marquette C. Floyd, a Republican who had been mired in the District Court, watching both his Republican and Democratic brethren pass him by for more than eighteen years, and several white conservative judges who vociferously defended the fairness of the system in the county.

Although I had not intended to do so, I openly referred to the study which I'd been conducting for four years. I had never publicly revealed my findings or the fact of my survey before, and this was certainly not the forum in which I had intended to do so. But I became so enraged by some of the comments that I heard about equality and justice in Suffolk County that I simply couldn't remain silent. At the conclusion of the meeting, Ms. Handy asked if I would meet with her privately in the future to discuss my findings. I agreed to do so, since it had been my intention to request such a meeting. We exchanged business cards, and I awaited her communication. After several weeks, she finally called me, and I agreed to meet with her representative, a junior counsel to the commission. Months passed. Several scheduled meetings were cancelled by counsel, until I finally met with her representative.

I was sent a questionnaire to complete, which apparently was being used throughout the state to survey all judges as to their observations. The lack of follow-through by persons, especially a black woman, who had a license to study this very problem simply added to the disappointment. But by that time, disappointment was commonplace, and I probably would have been surprised if anyone even remotely related to the criminal justice system would conscientiously fulfill his or her mission. When their report was finally issued, no mention was made of my findings although the statistics were given to them, and the commission came to the same conclusion without any hard statistical data.

The issue of whether Suffolk County had engaged in invidious discriminatory practices in filling its master jury pool became so paramount in my mind that the actual trial of Vincent Waters for the attempted murder of Police Officer Thomas Spreer almost seemed anticlimactic. On April 17, 1984, jury selection began after I ruled once again that there had been sufficient probable cause to arrest the defendant, and that his written confession had been given voluntarily. It was somewhat of a change to preside over this case, since it was one of the few times that the prosecution witnesses were not members of the homicide squad. For the most part, the police witnesses, including the victim who had been shot with his own weapon at point blank range, were from the 1st precinct, which was located in the Town of Babylon.

As the people's case came to a close, I came face-to-face with District Attorney Patrick Henry for the last time. Our future confrontations would be through the media and third party representatives like Arthur Cromarty, the County Administrative Judge. Henry was the last witness called by Feldman. It was very unusual for the District Attorney to appear as a witness, but he was at Officer Spreer's bedside on the day that he was shot. He was accompanied by Chief Inspector Caples who would later become the temporary Commissioner of Police while the county sought a new commissioner after the resignation of Commissioner Treader.

Henry had little to add to the case, but it gave him an opportunity to publicly display his concern for a police officer shot in the line of duty, and to volunteer on cross-examination for the benefit of the jury and the media the statement "Conviction will send out a message to the community." This was a widely publicized trial, and such a statement certainly wouldn't hurt the public image that he sought to convey as a tough, concerned prosecutor, and 1985 would be an election year. Nor, for that matter, would it hurt the verdict! Immediately after the People rested, the defendant, Vincent Waters, took the stand as the only defense witness. While he admitted to participation in the commission of the robbery, he attempted to minimize his involvement by placing the greatest blame upon Eddie Mike, whom he said masterminded the "snatch" at the Wheatley Heights Shopping Center.

It is safe to say that the all white male jury was not impressed with Waters' defense, which treated them to a short sociological study of the roots of crime in our society. Waters testified that he never knew his natural parents, and that he lived with his grandmother until he was nine years of age, when he was placed in a foster home by the Louise Wise Agency. From there he was moved from place to place like St. Mary's and Little Flower, shelters for children without homes. At age sixteen, he left Little Flower on his own, living on the streets, "hustling and stealing." In 1981, he was arrested for stealing a safe from Little Flower. In 1982, he was arrested for burglarizing four homes, stealing a pocketbook and trying to steal a Dodge Dart.[30]

If he didn't take the stand, the jury would never have heard of his prior record, but the stakes were high and Waters needed to deny that he intended to kill a police officer. In what may well be record time, Vincent Waters was convicted of attempted murder in the first degree, robbery in the first degree, and two other lesser felonies. It took the jury of twelve white men, all over the age of thirty four, only fifty minutes to reach its unanimous verdict. Through the paper-thin walls, I heard one juror who thought he couldn't be heard probably utter the group's feelings: "Can you imagine if we came in and said 'not guilty?' They'd really shit, wouldn't they?"

The entire jury panel had consisted of ninety-five persons, 40% of whom had been women, most of whom either asked to be excused or were challenged by the prosecutor. Only one woman was challenged by the defense. Of the ninety-five, there were two black men, one who asked to be excused, while the other was peremptorily challenged by Feldman. So much for trial by a fair cross-section of the Suffolk County community. Nevertheless, under the law, Waters had received a fair trial.

On May 31, 1984, I imposed a sentence of twenty-two and a half years to life for the attempted murder of a police officer. For the robbery of Officer Spreer, I sentenced him to eight and one-third to twenty-five years concurrent with the life sentence. For the robbery which started the incident, he received consecutive time of two and a half to seven and a half years. It will be twenty-five years before he can even be considered for parole.

On December 22, 1986, Waters got no Christmas present from the Appellate Division. His conviction and sentence was unanimously affirmed in a short three paragraph opinion stating, in part, as follows:

> The defendant's constitutional and statutory right to have a petit jury 'selected at random from a fair cross-section of the community' was not violated. At his pretrial hearing, the defendant failed to show that blacks between the ages of 18 and 21 years old constituted a recognizable group in the community, or that their under-representation in the jury pool was caused by systematic exclusion. While the county's practice of soliciting the names and addresses of recent high school graduates was concededly "poorly administered," the hearing record also indicates that many high schools declined to respond to the solicitation, a factor which rebuts the appearance of intentional discrimination. We have examined the defendant's remaining contentions and find them to be without merit.[8]

It wouldn't be the last time that the Appellate Division disagreed with my finding of official misconduct, whether it was in the selection of jurors, or in the actions of certain police and prosecutors. They made their judgments, based upon a cold, typewritten record. I made my judgments in a courtroom filled with human beings whom I could see and smell, and, all too often, with perjurious witnesses and somewhat less than honest and overzealous prosecutors. The good justices of the Appellate Division were in Brooklyn, and my courtroom was a distant ninety miles away in Riverhead, and rarely did we see eye to eye in cases of police and prosecutorial misconduct.

In my years as a judge, I never mastered the art of avoiding the obvious which would prove controversial and harmful to the political status quo, while reaching the same or similar result without rocking the establishment boat. Perhaps if I did, there would have been no investigation, this book would never have been written, and I would still be the sweetheart of an unchanged District Attorney's office and police homicide squad. But only in Hollywood movies is one blessed with the opportunity to go "Back to the Future."

EIGHT

"Was She...Sh...?

—William Patterson

In August 1979 Captain Jeffrey MacDonald, United States Army Medical Corps, Green Beret, the "most popular and most likely to succeed"[1] graduate of the class of June 1961, Patchogue High School, Suffolk County, New York, was convicted of the 1970 brutal slayings of his pregnant wife and two young daughters at Fort Bragg, North Carolina. MacDonald, who is serving three consecutive life terms of imprisonment, continues to profess his innocence. However, he's failed to convince even an otherwise objective biographer, Joe McGuinness, author of *Fatal Vision*, who wanted to believe that four unknown persons were responsible for the slaughter of the MacDonald family. Fortunately for society, few high school graduating classes can lay claim to such an infamous graduate.

On that same June day in 1961, William Patterson, an extremely shy and quiet individual, with somewhat below average grades, far from the most popular member of his class, also graduated from Patchogue High School. He didn't have the intellectual or financial ability to go on to Princeton and Northwestern University Medical School, or even to college, like his infamous classmate, but he was blessed with enough ability and ambition to become a junior level executive in the air freight business. He successfully served four years in the United States Air Force, but unlike MacDonald, he didn't volunteer to jump out of airplanes. He served as a meteorologist, and, according to Patterson, he'd never even learned to fire a rifle.[2]

While the two were certainly not intellectual or social equals, they had something in common—the love of sports and a deep involvement in high school athletics. Jeffrey MacDonald was the quarterback of the high school football team, and a member of the boxing team at Fort Bragg. Even while on trial for murder, he'd still run five miles a day. Bill Patterson was also a member of the football team in his freshman and sophomore years, and a four year member of the track and cross-country teams. He was so much into running that his senior class would thus describe him for posterity: "Ah, what a weary race my feet have run!"[3]

How prophetic! Patterson's feet, especially his choice of footwear, helped to ensnare him in a web of circumstances which caused him, like his infamous classmate, to spend the rest of his life in prison. Twenty-one years after his graduation, Patterson became a key suspect in the June 27, 1982 murder of his estranged wife, Frances. Like Jeffrey McDonald, he will forever profess his innocence. Like so many convicted murderers, he too has acquired a professional biographer, but the entire story has yet to be published.

Frances Patterson was shot with a high powered rifle through the basement window of their former marital residence in East Northport, New York. She was watching television with their two young children, Frank and Laura. Bill Patterson was not indicted for the murder, however, until October 1983. The indictment was the culmination of sixteen months of intensive investigation, some excellent detective work and a certain amount of good fortune from the police point of view. But even the good luck was the result of relentless investigative police work which dug deeper and deeper into the murky facts of the case.

Exactly two years to the day that he witnessed the horrible death of his mother, on June 27, 1984, thirteen-year-old Frank Patterson sobbingly described the "firecracker" explosion that he heard as he, his mother and his eight-year-old sister watched the television sitcom "Alice" on television. I was practically moved to tears as he told about the untimely, violent death of his mom. As the father of two sons and a daughter, I found myself wishing that he would not have been called to the stand. I had to consciously repress thoughts that this event must have had upon his young, fragile psyche. What emotional scars were being reopened by dragging him into court to recount this terribly traumatic event? I had to suppress my feelings of anger towards Patterson's assigned attorney, Robert Gottlieb, for whom I gradually developed the greatest respect as a professional. But somehow I could feel no compassion for Bill Patterson who sat at counsel table, visibly shaken and sobbing openly, as he listened to his confused son reluctantly describe the events of that gruesome nightmare.

The Patterson case is important to me because it was my first real introduction to Robert Gottlieb, the attorney. He was a former assistant district attorney in the Manhattan office of Robert Morgenthau. He had recently entered into a law partnership with Ron Sussman, a long-time friend. I was introduced to Gottlieb by Ron at a social gathering at Ron's home in Port Jefferson. Although Ron was not much older than my oldest son, we developed a friendship when, as an assistant DA, he was assigned to my part in the District Court. My wife, Lenore, and I grew very fond of him and his very pleasant wife, Karen, the daughter of two Nazi concentration camp survivors. We occasionally went to a movie or had dinner together, and we developed a special closeness to the young Sussmans. When Ron Sussman and Bob Gottlieb opened a law office in Hauppauge, we happily accepted an invitation to the celebration.

Some months after that, I learned through Sussman that Gotlieb was approved by the Bar Association for the assignment of homicide cases. So when William Patterson was found eligible for legal assistance because he couldn't afford an attorney, I was more than happy to assign an experienced, capable, highly articulate lawyer who'd never before been assigned a homicide case in Suffolk County.

Patterson got a better defense than he ever bargained for, and the people, represented by Steve Wilutis, had their work cut out for them. How could I have known that in less than two years, largely as a result of the favorable publicity he got in two Patterson trials, Robert Gottlieb would emerge as the Democratic candidate for District Attorney, and I would become unwittingly embroiled in his election battle with the incumbent, Patrick Henry?

In the summer of 1985, between the Corso and Diaz murder trials, and in the heat of the District Attorney's race, *Newsday* erroneously reported that

Robert Gottlieb had been my campaign manager. In that same article, there were several quotes attributed to the District Attorney. I remain firmly convinced that someone in the District Attorney's office planted that blatantly false information in the newspaper to convey the impression that my actions in the Corso case, which received almost daily coverage in the media, were politically motivated to help elect Gottlieb, a Democrat, to the District Attorney's office.

Newsday should have known better! In 1982, I had no campaign, and in 1981, the year of my unsuccessful bid for reelection, I didn't even know Gottlieb. The names of the few contributors to my campaign were a matter of public record at the Board of Elections, but no one from the newspaper even bothered to verify this information. *Newsday* was being used! From their point of view, this story involved dirty politics and controversy. Newspapers love that kind of story. Violence, controversy, sex, sports and the comics sell newspapers, and Long Island's only daily newspaper was no different than any other daily tabloid in the New York area, though *Newsday* had an excellent reputation for investigative reporting, with more than one Pulitzer Prize under its belt.

Frances Patterson had been mortally wounded by one bullet fired from a high powered rifle which passed through the upper part of her neck and severed her jugular vein, a major artery and her cervical spine. She was pronounced dead at her home at 8 Atlas Way, a modest single family residence in a typical middle class community of Suffolk County. At the time of her death, William Patterson was separated from his wife and living with his paramour, Patricia Martin, in Riverdale, Georgia. He was working at Atlanta's Hartsdale Airport as a mechanic for an air freight company. Patterson was previously employed as the regional manager of an air freight company at Kennedy Airport in New York City before transferring to its new office in Atlanta. It was there that he met Ms. Martin who was working for the company as an export agent. It was a large economic step down to the position of mechanic when the Atlanta office was subsequently phased out and all employees, including Patterson and Martin, were laid off.

In June 1982, William and Frances Patterson had virtually reached agreement on a matrimonial settlement which was being negotiated by two Long Island lawyers, Herbert Kotler and Robert Yonkers. Because of numerous marital debts they agreed to file a joint petition in bankruptcy. On June 28, 1982, they were scheduled to meet Kotler at the Bankruptcy Court at Westbury in Nassau County. Frances Patterson never lived to see that day. June 28 was a Monday. On Sunday evening, June 27, she was dead, the victim of an unknown assailant armed with a high powered .35 caliber Marlin rifle.

On June 26, 1982, Bill Patterson and Patricia Martin were on an all day rafting trip on the Nantahala River in North Carolina. I t was a four hour trip to the river in Bill's car. They were accompanied by two friends. After spending three and a half fun filled hours on the river, they were soaked to the skin. They spent more time in the water than on the raft. Fill was dressed in shorts, a tee shirt and his blue and white tennis shoes.

When they got back, at about 9:00 p.m., she went to her mother's where her child from a previous marriage had been staying. Bill went back home to change clothes and rest up before his scheduled automobile trip to New York to meet his wife. He enjoyed the long drive to New York from Georgia, and he made the trip quite often— alone. At about 10:00 p.m., Bill called Tricia to say that he was going straight to New York. According to her, he seemed even quieter than usual that day, like he was deep in thought. When asked about it by Tricia, he said that nothing was bothering him.

Only William Patterson could describe what he did after calling Tricia. Before leaving Georgia, he showered, shaved, changed his shirt, shorts and underwear, and donned his highly shined wing-tip leather dress shoes. Although he couldn't remember where he stopped along the way, he drove directly to his former home in Suffolk County, arriving in East Northport at about 7:00 or 7:30 p.m. on Sunday.*

The house at 8 Atlas Way was adjacent to a ball field on Cedar Road, and, according to him, he parked his red and white Chevrolet Citation next to a basketball court some distance from the family home. He parked there because he didn't want his daughter, Laura, to know that he was in New York. She had suffered most traumatically from the marital discord and he didn't want to upset her with a short visit. Since he didn't want to be seen by his children, but he did want to see them, he decided to climb over a six foot chain link fence in back of the house to peer through a rear window.

He could see his wife on the basement couch through an opening in the rear shutters. His children, who were in the basement with her, seemed to be walking towards him. Fearing that he would be seen, he decided to leave immediately, after being in the backyard "less than one minute."*

He then spent the night sleeping in his Chevrolet in a rest area of the Long Island Expressway, which had no restaurant or rest rooms. He chose that location because his first choice on a road near a dairy farm in the adjacent community of Deer Park was too noisy. At 7:45 a.m., he tried to call Frances. He wanted to arrange to pick her up, but no one answered the phone. He assumed that she was in the shower. At about 8:20 a.m., he drove to her home.[4]

From that point, it is possible to look to the collective testimony of police officers Jeff Rubin, James Connell and John Byrnes who were assigned to preserve the crime scene at 8 Atlas Way, which was outlined and isolated with yellow tape. Each, in turn, was responsible for maintaining a chronological log of persons arriving at the scene. At 8:23 a.m., they spotted a small white vehicle coming towards them. The car stopped abruptly in the middle of the road near the Patterson house. A tall male subject exited the vehicle advising them that he had just returned from Georgia. They all immediately concluded that it was the husband of the deceased. They had been advised to expect his possible arrival.

He appeared to be in an agitated state as he asked nervously: "What happened to my wife—what happened to my wife?" But none of the police had said anything, let alone anything about his wife. He was told nothing other than an incident had occurred at the house. As if on cue, Bill fell to the ground twice. To officer Connell "it seemed theatrical." Still he was assisted into the police vehicle to await the arrival of their uniformed supervisor.

In just a few short minutes, Sgt. Lauer was on the scene. Again Patterson asked what happened, and again he was told only that there had been an accident. While the sergeant put a call into the detective bureau, Bill uttered a broken phrase which he will probably forever regret. Turning to Officer Rubin he asked again: "What happened? Is she okay? Please tell me what happened." When he was again given the meaningless answer that an incident had occurred, Bill, in a fit of frustration, stuttered: "Was she...

sh...?"* Whether he was, in fact, stammering out of excitement, or whether he was about to ask whether his wife had been shot became a matter of great debate and speculation at trial.

Only officer Rubin heard this question. He claimed that he noted this conversation in his memo book and on separate pieces of paper after being instructed to do so by one of the homicide detectives who arrived at the scene. But two and a half years after the incident, according to him, many months of memo book pages which he stored in his personal vehicle were stolen and never recovered. There was no way to corroborate his testimony. Yet he seemed to be a very credible witness, and Bob Gottlieb, even with a painstakingly methodical cross-examination, couldn't break his story. As a uniformed officer not involved in the homicide investigation, and not necessarily interested in the outcome of the case, the jury could assume that he didn't have a motive to fabricate this story.

On the other hand, detective Robert Amato was a twenty-year veteran of the Suffolk County Police Department. He was a detective for seventeen years. Sgt. Robert Misegades, his team supervisor, had assigned him as the lead detective in the Patterson murder. It was his persistent investigation which ultimately cracked the case. On the day after the murder he came face to face with Bill Patterson for the first time in the interview room of the homicide squad. Amato was almost immediately suspicious of the tall, bespectacled, estranged, "bereaved" husband, who was curiously dressed in a white tee shirt, khaki shorts, light brown socks and "highly polished wing-tip shoes."[5]

"Nobody's told me a thing. What's going on?" asked a troubled Patterson.

"Your wife was watching television last night. Somebody shot her through a window. She's dead," responded Amato.

Upon hearing Amato's response, Bill threw himself to the floor.

"Get up," said the detective, handing Patterson a cigarette to calm his nerves.

"Who killed my wife?"

"We don't know."

At that point, Patterson, who was a "technical suspect," was given his rights. He said that he understood his rights, and, according to the police, he didn't seek to have a lawyer present during the questioning. "Of course, I'll be only too glad to help you guys out, if I can," was the response of the cooperative suspect.*

Detectives Walter Warkenthien, Thomas Cavanaugh and four other detectives of the Misegades team were also involved in the interview which lasted from sometime after 9:00 a.m. until about 9:00 p.m. that evening with periodic breaks for coffee and lunch provided by the police. The twelve hours also included a short visit to the crime scene. Only Amato made notes of the interview during the various intermissions, and Amato's notes became a prime source of controversy in this case. All of the detective's original notes were destroyed by him, he said, after transferring the information to more formal reports. Patterson continues to accuse Amato of perjury and the intentional destruction of his original notes to hide the true facts of what had taken place at that first meeting and subsequent meetings between Amato and Patterson.

On July 20, 1984, in an opinion written after the completion of pre-trial hearings, when I was still giving great credence to police testimony, I came to the following conclusion about Amato's original notes:

> The testimony given by Detective Amato concerning the destruction of his original notes was credible and uncontroverted by the defendant. The court finds that the original handwritten notes totaling ten pages written by Detective Amato as and after the defendant answered questions of the police consisted of abbreviations, shorthand notations and scratch notes barely discernible by the detective himself. These original notes were written by him hastily without regard to legibility, comprehensive thought or chronological order. Later that day, while flying to Atlanta to continue the investigation, Detective Amato reviewed his original notes and transposed them into a thirty-four page memorandum, while the events of the day were still clear in his mind.
>
> The detective's explanation as to why he did so is fully worthy of belief and reasonable under the circumstances, i.e., the original scrap notes would have been incomprehensible to him or anyone

else in the future unless transposed into a more legible, understandable form and complete as to original content. Accordingly, the court concludes that Detective Amato acted in good faith in failing to retain his original notes and was not, as the defendant urges, motivated by a pernicious scheme to thwart the ability of the defendant to effectively cross examine him at trial by using his notes for such purpose. The court has no reason to believe the second draft was anything more or less than a duplicate equivalent of the detective's original notes.

A complete copy of the second draft consisting of thirty-four pages of notes written by Detective Amato was furnished to defense counsel at the hearing. They contained statements attributed to the defendant by Detective Amato which were both inculpatory and exculpatory in nature depending upon one's subjective interpretation. The defendant has not demonstrated to the court that the second draft of Amato's notes failed to include additional exculpatory comments of the defendant which might have appeared in the original notes, or that Detective Amato fabricated or embellished events and statements made by the defendant during his interview by the police on June 28, 1982.[6]

In the spring of 1985, I was still giving full credibility to the testimony of a police officer which was not contradicted in the record. Although there was extensive cross-examination by Gottlieb on this issue, William Patterson did not testify at the hearings, and there was absolutely no reason to believe that the detective was being anything less than candid on this very critical issue. This was unlike the Corso case, as I would later learn, where there were virtually no notes and no reports prepared by anyone during or after a lengthy period of investigation. Yet I wrote a cautionary note in the opinion, in the hope that the police would get a message for the future.

"In hindsight," I wrote, "the better practice would have been to retain the original scratch notes as a supplement to his 'final' notes, so that this question would not have arisen."*

Obviously, I was beginning to become skeptical, but this was not enough for Bill Patterson. After reading about my Corso and Diaz decisions in the news media and, presumably, in the official court reports of published decisions, he latched onto this issue in an application, dated February 18, 1986, for a new trial. In a well written and well researched memorandum of law sent from Sing Sing Correctional Facility, without the assistance of legal counsel, he wrote:

> The defendant maintains that both Det. Amato and the prosecutor knew that he was not telling the truth on May 31, 1984, and that the judgment obtained against him, was done with misrepresentation and fraud on the part of the prosecutor.
>
> Defense counsel asked that the prosecution provide a copy of any rules and regulations that would pertain to the taking of notes by the Suffolk County Police during an investigation, but the Court denied this request. In refusing this request, the Court aided and abetted the prosecutor in the misrepresentation and fraud....
>
> It has been discovered and shown that the actions and methods of the Suffolk County Police and Prosecutor's office, dating from 1979 till present are ver(y) suspect, to say the least. They have been shown to be unable to retain evidence taken during an investigation (Peter Corso case); the(y) have been shown not to take notes during an investigation, claiming that as Homicide Detectives, they were 'exempt' from doing so (Peter Corso Case); they have been shown to not follow up on leads presented to them during an investigation (Peter Corso case); and it has been shown that the prosecutor's office has tried to enter perjured testimony against a defendant (James Diaz case). It has further been shown that there are definite rules and regulations pertaining to the taking and retaining of notes during their investigations....
>
> Judge Stuart Namm, the Justice that sat at both trials of the defendant, upon the conviction of the defendant, called the above actions and methods of the Suffolk County Police 'good

police work.' From Judge Namm's rulings, actions and comments over the past two years, it would appear that there is a lack of fairness and equality under the law here....[7]

It was during the first interview of Patterson that the detectives learned the details of his marital problems, his employment history, his relationship with Tricia, the rafting trip to North Carolina, the overnight automobile ride to Long Island and his military experience.

"Did you ever own any guns?" he was asked.

"No, I never owned, shot or held a rifle. In the Air Force I trained with a Daisy air rifle. I never owned a pistol or ammunition," Patterson volunteered. "I hate guns and violence. I won't even go hunting!"

These words would come back to haunt him, just as the first words of his classmate, Captain Jeffrey MacDonald, had come back to haunt him. Later that day, Amato flew to Atlanta, Georgia. On June 29, in Georgia, he met with Tricia Martin at her home in Jonesboro in an attempt to corroborate Patterson's story. She turned over two live rounds of Remington .35 caliber ammunition that she'd found in a box in the garage containing some of Bill's personal belongings. By then the police had learned from the ballistics laboratory that Frances Patterson was killed with a .35 caliber Marlin rifle.

Within an hour of the start of the first interview, Amato asked coldly and to the point: "Did you kill your wife?"

"You're crazy!" Patterson responded. "I'm tired of being treated like a criminal. I've been honest with you guys."

"You can leave at any time," he was told.

"I don't care what you think. I've never owned a rifle or fired one in my entire life," stated an obviously agitated Patterson who was growing weary of the questions.*

With his own words Bill Patterson was digging his own grave. At that point, the police only knew that Frances had died of a gunshot wound. It hadn't yet been established whether the wound was caused by a handgun or a rifle.

"I think you killed your wife in front of your two kids," accused Amato.

"Yeah, you prove that!" Patterson angrily snapped back. "I think you're trying to set me up."

"If I want to set you up, I would go out and tell my sergeant that you confessed," Amato responded cockily.

Apparently, the detective was aware of a Suffolk County homicide investigative technique which many felt was prevalent, but which did not become a matter of public concern until 1985.

Patterson was then asked for permission to search his Chevrolet Citation. With an air of confidence, he stated, "I want you guys to look, because you're not going to find anything." He was right. The search turned up some NoDoz tablets, a box with clean underwear, a camera, a change of clothing, an attache case with business papers, personal letters, model airplane equipment and some hand tools. There was nothing to connect Patterson to the cold, brutal slaying of his wife.

The questioning continued with an almost continuous rotation of detectives involved in the "interview." At times the conversation would become heated as one or another of the detectives, intent upon wearing Patterson down, with a detective leaning up close, eyeball to eyeball. Like Amato, detective Thomas Cavanaugh was by now convinced that Patterson was their man.

"Bill, I think you killed your wife," Cavanaugh said.

"NO!" Patterson yelled.

"You know we're going to find the gun."

According to Cavanaugh, Bill twice responded: "You'll never find the gun!"

In an appeal for sympathy, and in an effort to reach his conscience, Cavanaugh said, "Look, Bill, you have to think about the kids. They just lost their mother. It would be better for them if it was over with now. Why don't you tell us about it now. You'll feel better." According to Cavanaugh, with his head lowered Patterson answered softly, "I'd like to, but I can't."

William Patterson, who took the stand in both of his trials, gave an entirely different version of the "interview." In his version, the police were not quite so fatherly and gentle. In his version, when he fell to the floor after being told of his wife's death, Amato picked him up, shoved him in a chair, and shouted: "You bastard, you killed her! You've shot her and killed her!"

""You're crazy, Patterson responded. "I want to call my lawyer, Mr. Kotler.

Don't I have a right to a phone call?" According to Patterson, Amato shoved him into the chair again and shouted, "You have no fuckin' rights!"

However, police and defendant were all in agreement that Bill was asked to submit to a Firearms Discharge Residue test to determine whether he had recently fired a weapon. The testifying detectives all agreed that he refused to do so, but Patterson said that he wanted to take the test with his attorney present. No attorney was ever called, and no test was ever performed.

According to Patterson, he was never left alone, and there were always at least two detectives in the room, sometimes as many as eight. He also denied ever saying, "Was she sh...sh...?" to Officer Rubin. He might have been saying, "Was she hurt?", but the word "hurt" never came out. Though he finally did have to admit, for the first time, on the witness stand that he purchased a Marlin .35 caliber rifle in May 1982, because, as he said, "Everybody in Georgia hunted," and the guys at work were planning a hunting trip. He never told Amato that he owned a rifle because "he was scared of Amato." He was accused of murder and he was "frightened, terrified." He denied saying that they would never find the gun. Visibly shaken during an intensive cross-examination by Wilutis, he conceded that he said to Cavanaugh, "You'll never find the gun if you continue to talk to me, and not look for someone else."*

Patterson had no choice but to admit to the jury that he had owned the very type of rifle that had been involved in the death of Frances Patterson. The prosecution had the goods on him in the persons of two critical witnesses, Herman Gerald Morris and his wife, Cathy, who were flown to Suffolk from Riverdale, Georgia. It was the discovery of these two witnesses by Detective Amato which virtually clinched the circumstantial evidence case against William Patterson. His hands were caught in the cookie jar, and he knew that he couldn't deny their testimony—that he was the man in the baseball cap with a northern accent who purchased a Marlin .35 caliber rifle with a four power scope from Herman on June 22, 1982, just days before the fatal shooting.

Upon his arrival in Georgia, Amato spoke by telephone to Sgt. Misegades who filled him in on the latest findings in the case, the most important of which was the ballistics conclusion that Frances Patterson had been killed by one bullet from a .35 caliber Marlin rifle. This finding had been made by Detective Sgt. Alfred DellaPenna, a twenty-three year veteran of Suffolk County P.D., and a sixteen year veteran of the criminalistics laboratory. He was a senior firearms examiner and crime scene investigator—an established and well recognized expert in the field of ballistics. He had test fired so many weapons over the years that when he testified in court he would often have to cup his hand over one ear in order to hear the questions. Countless gunpowder explosions had taken their toll on his auditory senses.

Four bullet fragments were found on the scene at 8 Atlas Way, all of which were placed under microscopic examination. From the nature of the striations, or scratch marks, on the fragments which had been caused by the rifling grooves in the barrel of the murder weapon, he was able to conclude that the weapon was a .35 caliber Marlin. It would be no mere coincidence that Bill Patterson had bought that very weapon type only one week before the death of his wife. Still, Sgt. DellaPenna had no weapon to assist him in reaching his conclusion. To this date, and to my knowledge, the actual murder weapon has never been found. Armed with the rifle description, Detective Amato and his partner, Detective William Schwabach, visited every gun shop and pawn shop in Clayton County, Georgia, to search for the recent seller of a Marlin .35. However, their search proved fruitless. On August 2, after returning to New York, Amato played a hunch. He called Tricia Martin to ask whether there was a newspaper in the Atlanta area like the Long Island paper called *Buy Lines*, where private persons advertised automobiles, appliances and guns for sale. The hunch paid off! She told him of the *Atlanta Advertiser*. On August 10, armed with this information, he returned to Atlanta.

On August 11, he went through all of the back issues of the *Atlanta Advertiser,* from January through June 1982. That type of Marlin rifle was very popular for hunting, and he obtained a list of about 75-100 persons whom he had to call by telephone. Within twenty-four hours, he hit pay dirt in the person of Herman Gerald Morris who had advertised just such a rifle for sale on May 13 and 27. Morris told Amato about a man from out of state, a "Yankee," at least six feet tall, dressed in a blue uniform, a baseball cap, tennis shoes and wearing eyeglasses, who paid him $140 in cash, because he was looking for a "varmint gun." The man had volunteered that he worked at the Atlanta airport.

Morris testified that a .35 caliber rifle with a 4X telescope was certainly no varmint gun. Agreeing with him, Sgt. DellaPenna described a varmint gun as a small caliber, high velocity rifle used to shoot woodchucks or farm varmints, such as rodents. "A .35 caliber is not a varmint gun," he told the jury.

Unfortunately, Morris had never really looked at the buyer. He had not paid much attention to him, even though he had returned two days later to purchase a box of shells-200 grain Remington shells. Frances Patterson had been shot with a .35 caliber Remington bullet. Yet, Morris could say that the man had been driving a small white automobile. Cathy Morris, who had been home when the shells were bought, and who had been home on the day before when the man had returned to ask about the purchase, could make an identification. She said that he wore a dark blue uniform, A V-neck tee shirt, wire rim glasses, blue and white tennis shoes, and that he was bald. Bill Patterson had very little hair atop his head. He was driving a Chevrolet Citation with a white top and a maroon bottom. In a dramatic moment in the courtroom, in her deep southern Georgia drawl she pointed out William Patterson as the man who had bought Herman's rifle. The noose was slowly tightening around Bill Patterson's neck!

In June 1983, in an effort to get a more positive description of the perpetrator, both Herman and Cathy Morris were subjected to hypnotic suggestion attempts by John Connelly, a psychotherapist/hypnotherapist on the faculty of both Suffolk and Nassau County Community Colleges, who had been enlisted by the police. Both attempts had been largely unsuccessful. At a Holiday Inn near the Atlanta airport, in the presence of Detective Amato, after several hours of attempting hypnosis, it was decided that Herman could not relax because of a chronic back problem. At their home, Cathy had undergone hypnosis for about fifteen minutes, when a concerned neighbor came barging in and aborted the session. She did, however, remember the name "Bill" for the first time, and she recalled a telephone conversation with the man about the shells. They were attempting to have her recall a license plate number, but the effort had to be terminated when they were disturbed by the inquisitive neighbor. Hypnosis or not, both Morrises proved to be very damaging witnesses for the prosecution.

Still, if Patterson had admitted purchasing the Marlin .35 from Herman Morris for the first time at the trial, where was it and why wasn't it produced for examination by ballistics to exclude it as the murder weapon? For that, Bill Patterson had a tailor made explanation. He testified that because Tricia "hated and detested" guns, he decided to sell the rifle within two or three days after he bought it. He said that he sold it to one John Finley, whom he had known for about one month, for $110.00. The sale included the ammunition and loose shells which he had also purchased from Morris, but he apparently missed the two shells which were found by his paramour. When pressed by Wilutis, on cross-examination, about the mysterious John Finley who has never been heard from since, Patterson said that the sale had taken place in the parking lot of a bar called the "Scotch Inn," and that no one else had witnessed the sale. When pressed further, he said that he had gone back to the bar on one or two occasions after that, but he had never seen Finley again. He remembered that Finley had been a carpenter, who worked in home construction. After the murder, and before his arrest in Georgia, he claimed he went to the bar to look for Finley, but someone who knew Finley told him that he might have gone back to Alabama. To this day, John Finley remains a mystery man—a probable phantom created by William Patterson, not unlike the four "hippie" cultists apparently created by his Patchogue classmate to account for the murder of his family.

Patterson's would-be biographer, Jeb Ladouceur, the publisher of a small weekly in Suffolk County entitled the *Fire News*, truly wanted to believe his story. After Patterson's conviction, he flew to Georgia making appearances on radio talk shows in an effort to flush out the mystery man. His efforts were in vain, and he returned somewhat less a believer in Patterson's innocence. Shades of Joe McGinniss' "Fatal Vision."

However, the police did not have to look as far as Georgia to obtain witnesses for the prosecution. Two witnesses, father and son, Joseph and Peter Levinsohn, surfaced right in the vicinity of 8 Atlas Way. Joseph, the father, was a TV executive and the president of the Commack North Little League which played its baseball games at the Cedar Road Park immediately adjacent to the Patterson residence. On the day of the murder, at about 9:20 p.m., he and his wife became concerned that their oldest son was not yet home. He and Peter then drove to the Cedar Road park, a local hangout for the kids in the neighborhood. When they pulled into the parking lot, they saw a car inside the gate that should have been closed for the night. The car was a small white Chevrolet Citation with only a driver inside. They observed the car drive across the field and park between some trees. Its lights were then turned off. They could see nothing after that. Although Levinsohn was concerned about the car, he was more concerned about his son. So, he left. They returned after about ten minutes, locked the gate and returned home. Shortly thereafter, Joseph Levinson heard sirens in the distance.

According to young Frank Patterson, his mother had been shot about 9:30 p.m. Bill Patterson testified that he had climbed the chain link fence at about 7:00-7:30 p.m., some two hours before Frank heard the "firecracker." It was still light out, Bill said, and the sun was still shining. Yet, the Levinsohns put a vehicle matching his at the scene, in the dark, almost at the very moment of the shooting. Under the trees, the vehicle would have been in close proximity to the Patterson backyard. Patterson's story was coming apart one piece at a time. The prosecution's circumstantial case was growing stronger with each prosecution witness.

While the People's case, which was almost entirely circumstantial, was indeed a strong on, with all the evidence pointing to the estranged husband, there was one very troubling aspect of the case that could have created the "reasonable doubt" which might result in an acquittal. There seemed to be no motive for the crime. Why had Bill Patterson suddenly decided to murder his estranged wife after they had apparently settled all of their matrimonial differences? It made no sense, but in New York state, the prosecution does not have to prove a motive in a homicide case.

Nevertheless, in an effort to display a motive and strengthen the People's case, Wilutis called one of Patterson's fellow employees to the stand. Ronald Hopping of Ipswich, Massachusetts, had worked with him at Inter-Continental Air Freight, and they had been "drinking buddies." He testified that at a Hilton hotel in May 1982, Bill had said, "If my wife does not grant me the divorce, I'll kill her!" However, on cross-examination, he admitted that he didn't think Bill was being serious. However, Tricia Martin testified that on four or five occasions, Bill had said that he wished he could have custody of his children. Had custody of the children been Patterson's motive?

Attorney Herbert Kotler, testifying for the defense, stated that the negotiations over the separation were "business-like, amiable and unemotional." The separation agreement had been signed on June 10, 1982, and "the defendant seemed to be glad that it was over—he could continue with his life." He said that Frances Patterson seemed to feel the same way. In fact, she had agreed to the commencement of a divorce action where she would be served with a summons in an uncontested divorce. The grounds for the divorce was to be "constructive abandonment." She would not deny that she had withheld sexual intercourse from her husband for more than one year. She even agreed to file a joint petition for bankruptcy because of their numerous marital debts. On the surface, there did not seem to be any rational reason why Bill Patterson would decide to bring Frances Patterson to a violent and untimely death on June 27, 1982. By the same token, no one has yet been able to determine, with a reasonable degree of certainty, why Capt. Jeffrey MacDonald had brutally murdered his pregnant wife and two beautiful daughters. One is left to speculate and wonder what terrible thoughts possess a person who is capable of committing such unthinkable and heinous acts. That is precisely why the prosecution does not bear the sometimes impossible burden of proving motive. In the law, defendants are presumed to be innocent, but they are not presumed to be smart!

What was the significance of the highly polished wing-tip shoes which Bill Patterson was wearing on June 28 while dressed in a tee shirt and khaki shorts? According to Tricia Martin, Patterson, the former high school runner, wore blue and white tennis shoes almost all of the time. He wore them on the June 26 rafting trip. The only footwear she could remember him owning were the tennis shoes, a pair of dress shoes and a pair of cowboy boots. Their relationship ended immediately after she learned of the murder. But she saw Bill again two weeks after he left for New York on June 26. At that time, he was wearing a short sleeved shirt, pants and wing-tip shoes. She'd never seen him dressed like that before.*

Patterson testified that he was wearing his "blue and white sneakers" on the rafting trip, and that he had changed to his dress shoes to drive to New York. He said that he next saw his sneakers, blue and white Pumas which were produced at trial, when he picked up a box of his clothing which had been packed by Tricia in Georgia. He said that he had left them in a bag with his other wet clothing after returning from the rafting trip. However, Detective Amato had testified that the defendant had told him that he had worn the wing-tip shoes on the rafting trip.

"Bill, you went rafting like that?" an incredulous Amato asked.

"Yes, in fact when I went back to Tricia, I plopped in bed just like that. Then, I drove to New York."

"In those shoes?" There was no response.

"They look like you just polished them."

Patterson angrily retorted, "What are you trying to do anyway? What have shoes got to do with all this? The shoes are not a story! I drove all the way up in the shoes."

"Do you own any others?

Patterson said that he also owned a pair of cowboy boots and work boots, and no others. But, according to the detective, he was becoming more and more puzzled and nervous by the interrogation.*

The detective's interest in shoes had been piqued by Patterson's story that he climbed a tree and a six foot chain link fence, but the highly polished shoes showed no scuff marks. Patterson testified that he had been over this fence "100 times." The inference which the prosecution wished the jury to draw from this was that Patterson had been wearing his tennis shoes at the time of the murder, and that he disposed of them in the event that any footwear impressions had been found at the scene. In fact, none had been recovered.

Before leaving for Georgia, Amato had examined the fence. He noted that the top of the cyclone fence was a line of wire "x" crosses and that the fence was rusty. When he ran his hand over the fence, rust and dirt came off on his hand. Moreover, in the opinion of Robert Genna, the supervising criminalist of the crime lab, the shot had been fired through a front window since there was a hole in a screened front window, and there were glass and metal fragments on the floor of the den. The perpetrator had apparently accomplished his dastardly deed, then quickly and quietly evacuated the crime scene undetected by anyone, without so much as causing the family dog, a gray Weimaraner, which had been bought by Bill as a watchdog, to bark. "Ah what a weary race my feet have run!"

Physical sports involving athletic prowess, like football and running, were not the only sports that Bill Patterson and Jeffrey MacDonald had in common. Each had initially professed to the police that he had been a devoted husband and father, and each, when confronted with the truth, had to admit his involvement with other women. Of course, Patterson was no longer living with his wife, and had not done so for some time. Although he said that his marital problems had begun as early as 1979, he did not move out of his home until January 1982 when he moved to Atlanta "to try to save the Atlanta office." Prior to that time, his job had involved quite a bit of travel which his wife did not care for. He had told Detective Amato that "he never fooled around until he met Tricia." That, the police knew, was after he moved to the Atlanta office.

Once again, Patterson had been caught in a lie which he had to admit when confronted with the true facts by Wilutis on cross-examination. The intensive police investigation had uncovered female companions, like Kathie Mulholland whom he met in 1981, a woman known only as "Heidi" whom he had met in Switzerland and Gora Raniforas, a woman he had met in Sweden. He was also asked about his listing with "VIP Escort Service" in Atlanta, but he had no recollection of this.

Bill, despite eyeglasses and a balding head, much like the handsome Green Beret Doctor MacDonald, never seemed to be lacking female companionship, and always seemed to be on the prowl. Even after breaking up with Patricia Martin, and while the investigation of the murder was pointing more and more in his direction, in January 1983, Bill remarried in Georgia to one Bette Moore. That marriage did not last long after his conviction. Perhaps it was the Patchogue water on which they had been weaned that made these men so attractive to women; or perhaps, as is more likely, there was a similar need in both of their personalities to continually prove their manhood in sexual exploits as well as in sports.

In any event, in the case of Bill Patterson, his relationship with other women, in particular Patricia Martin, did seem to have a profound effect upon his children. Although Bill spoke of a loving relationship with his children even after he had moved to Georgia, Mother's Day cards which were hand made by Frank and Laura in 1982 for Frances' last Mother's Day spoke volumes of their contempt for their father and his "girlfriend." Frank sadly depicted "Dad" as a monster with gutteral sounds coming from his mouth, being struck by lightning and hanging with a rope around his neck. The girlfriend is depicted with six daggers in her body, one directed at her genital area. This card read: "*To The Best MOM There ever was. I'm glad Dad ain't here. PS: Aren't you?*"

Apparently fearing that they were going to be taken by their father, both cards read: "This is from a kid you will have every day."

Laura's card also showed "Dad" hanging from a rope and being struck by lightning. But her card depicted her father with long donkey-like ears and walking hand in hand with a nude "Girlfriend." Either Bill Patterson was fabricating his relationship with his children in 1982, or he was so far removed from them by that time that he could not discern what unhappiness he had brought into their young lives.

You could feel the sadness in Frank's heart, and hear the sadness in his voice, when he was asked about these cards on cross-examination by a cold, seemingly heartless Wilutis, who was obviously thinking more about a conviction than the feelings of an innocent child. Frank said that he had made it "when he was little." He was mad at his father then because he had left. He had just been carried away because he "was mad at him." It was obvious that in two short years he had forgiven and wished to forget this unhappy episode in his young life. That unhappiness had to pale by comparison with the loss of his mother, and he seemed to believe deeply in his father's innocence—a father he might lose forever if he were convicted. What normal thirteen year old would want to believe that his father had murdered his mother? And, young Frank seemed, at least outwardly, to be a normal, well adjusted and intelligent child, despite the horrible trauma to which he and his baby sister had been subjected.

In a further effort to cast the worst possible light upon Bill Patterson's relationship with the ill fated Frances Patterson, the prosecution called Richard Marconi to the stand. He was her brother and the defendant's brother-in-law. But it was obvious from the outset that there had been no love lost between Richard and Bill, even though they knew each other at work before Patterson married his sister. When the marital problems had come to a head, Marconi arranged for Frances to see an attorney.

He was asked to describe Bill's conduct at Frances' funeral, a funeral which he said, had not yet been paid for, more than two years after her death, although Bill had made the down payment. He said that Bill was very upset by the treatment he had received from the police. He complained that he was being "crucified," just as they had crucified "a friend," Jefferey MacDonald. Wilutus was planting a seed in the jury's collective mind!

Marconi testified that in 1982 he would have to bring food to his sister's house because there was no money for food. He would, he said, sometimes even give her money for food for the family. In contrast, the defendant said that he had taken care of all the bills, even after he was out of the house. He said that he would send and bring money to Frances, and that he gave her more than $500 cash in May of 1982, and $600 to $700 the month before. Yet, this did not sound like the actions of someone who was about to seek a dissolution of his debts through a bankruptcy proceeding. As far as Bill's relationship with his children was concerned, Wilutis sought to have Marconi tell about a voodoo doll made in the image of Bill by eight-year- old Laura. It had pins stuck in it, and he had seen it in the house on one of the days that had brought food for the family. However, I sustained a defense objection, the story was stricken from the record and the jury instructed to disregard that testimony. Nevertheless, the same goal was accomplished by the prosecution in the cross-examination of Frank about the Mother's Day cards.

On December 16, 1986, in a motion for a new trial, Bill Patterson had this to say about Richard Marconi's testimony:

> On December 19, 1984, Mr. Richard Marconi, the brother of the deceased, testified at the defendant's trial as follows:
> Page 133, Cross-examination by Mr. Gottlieb
> Q. Now, in addition to the money that was in the bank, do you recall money being found in the house?
> A. No.
> Q. Are you aware that in addition to the bank accounts there was $1462 in cash and coin found inside your sister's house at the time of her death?
> A: No, this is news to me.

The fact that Mr. Marconi committed perjury and that his answer to the above question was false can now be shown by his statements made in an affidavit he prepared as the Administrator of his sister's estate in August 1985, and of which the defendant just received a copy of in November 1986....

The following is a statement made by Mr. Marconi in his sworn affidavit prepared on August 1, 1985: "Immediately following my sister's death, I conducted a search of the premises where she resided and which she owned in her own name, to wit, 8 Atlas Way, East Northport, New York....At which time I discovered cash totaling $1462 which was deposited in a special account of my attorneys, Zinman & Chetkof.

In June 1982, Mr. Marconi finds and turns over to his attorneys, $1,462 in cash that he found in his sister's house immediately following her death, but on October 19, 1984, while under oath, Mr. Marconi perjures himself by testifying during defendant's trial that he did not know of this money being found in his sister's house, much less that he discovered it himself. It is clear that Mr. Marconi could not tell the truth about finding this money, for it would have destroyed his contrived testimony that the defendant had left Mr. Marconi's sister without money and that he (Mr. Marconi) was forced to give his sister money and food. This testimony was contrived with the prosecutor in an attempt to put forth an image to the jury of the defendant that was not true.[8]

Although, Patterson requested that his application be heard by another judge, under New York law, a motion for a new trial is referred to the trial judge for consideration, unless he is no longer available or he decides to disqualify himself. He argued in his motion papers that:

...Justice Namm allowed prosecution witnesses to lie in his court during defendant's hearings and trials. Justice Namm maintained that he was neutral during defendant's hearings and trials, however, at defendant's sentencing on February 26, 1985, Justice Namm stated, "I have to admit that at this very moment I am not a neutral person when it comes to you," in referring to defendant. Defendant maintains that this feeling towards defendant by Justice Namm should preclude Justice Namm from hearing defendant's Motion...Further, it would appear that Justice Namm holds to a double standard in defendant's case because it brought about a conviction against defendant, the other being that Justice Namm calls for a State investigation into perjury by prosecution witnesses when it helps to bring about an acquittal before him. For these reasons it is asked that a Justice other than Justice Namm be assigned to hear defendant's Motion to Vacate Judgment.*

Not only did I deny Patterson's application for a new judge, but on April 10, 1986, in the heat of the investigation, I denied his application for a new trial and to set aside his conviction. I wrote: "...these issues were raised at the original trial. Under these circumstances, it cannot be said that such events constitute newly discovered 'evidence' within the meaning of the statute...An appeal...is presently pending and sufficient facts are contained in the record to permit an adequate review of the legal issues now raised by the defendant upon such appeal."[9]

What I would see in the Corso and Diaz trials, which followed in 1985, would not be enough to raise doubts in my view that William Patterson had received two fair, if not perfect, trials, and that the jury had been absolutely correct in its guilty verdict. The law does not give the defendant a right to a perfect trial. Rarely, is any trial perfect. Still, Bill Patterson certainly had the right to a fair one—and before it was over, he ended up having two!

The last weak link in Bill Patterson's story was his testimony that he could see his wife and children through a "crack" in the shutters covering a rear window in the basement after climbing over the chain link fence. In order to get over the fence, he said that he had climbed a large tree alongside the fence. After Amato had turned Patterson over to Sgt. Misegades and Detective Cavanaugh to continue the June 28 interview, and before the flight to Atlanta, during his investigation of the crime scene, he attempted to peer through the crack in the shutters. No one had touched the shutters since the murder. He testified that "the crack between the shutters was less than 1/8 inch," and he could not observe anything.

Before terminating a full day of questioning, Detective Cavanaugh asked Bill if he would going to the scene of the crime with them to show them what he had done the evening before. Bill readily agreed. Anything to get out of the interview room! Cavanaugh and Schmidt drove Bill to the 4th precinct to get his car. They arrived at 8 Atlas Way at about the same time as Patterson. It was still light out. Dusk was settling in and the sun was low in the sky, but directly behind them. Patterson said that the windows in the back were the same as the day before-the day of the murder.

"Look through them and tell me what you can see," Cavanagh directed. "No!" Bill snapped back. Cavanaugh testified that he could see nothing through the shutters.

The last conversation that Detective Amato had with Bill Patterson took place in a jet plane sitting on the runway of Atlanta's Hartsdale Airport on October 27, 1983 awaiting traffic control clearance for take-off. Patterson was handcuffed. He was arrested earlier at his new marital home in Jonesboro. Detectives Amato and Warkenthien were taking him back to Suffolk County under an extradition order.

"Amato, I know you're not supposed to talk to me, but what kind of chance do you think I have?" Patterson asked.

"What kind of chance would anyone have who shot his wife in front of his kids?"

According to Amato, but vehemently denied by Patterson, Bill responded: "Do you think I would have shot her if I knew my kids were there?"

Patterson said that they only talked about the Air Force and flying. But Amato said that he would get twenty-five-years-to-life and that he would go to Sing Sing where Bill would "become a white whore, a piece of meat." If Patterson was telling the truth, Amato must have had a crystal ball. If not, Bill Patterson had a vivid imagination which portended his future. To this day, he pounds out volumes of paper on a Sing Sing typewriter protesting his innocence to anyone willing or obliged to read what he has to say.

Although Steve Wilutis had seemingly fit together all the pieces of the jigsaw puzzle, except motive, into a complete picture that appeared to point in only one direction, this classic circumstantial case, absent the murder weapon, was not enough to convince two members of the first jury. Summations were completed on June 29, 1984, exactly two years and one day from the day that the Suffolk County Police Department was first introduced to William Patterson. For more than three hours, Bob Gottlieb pleaded on behalf of his client, who, in his opinion, had not been proven guilty beyond a reasonable doubt. During the middle of his impassioned and very eloquent summation, as if on cue, Richard Marconi and his mother, the mother of Frances Patterson, made a dramatic entrance into the spectator section of the courtroom which did not go unnoticed by the jury. As she listened to defense counsel, the elderly Mrs. Marconi began to sob and cry out causing an obvious distraction. At a recess in the summation, Gottlieb, sensing conviction, made an application for a mistrial which I summarily denied. However, when the jury returned I felt compelled to instruct them to ignore the outbursts of persons for whom we all felt sympathy, and to remind them that their verdict was to be based solely upon the law as I would instruct them, and the facts as they found them, without consideration of sympathy.

Wilutis, in a very workmanlike and organized manner, took the jury, step by step, through the web of evidence that the people had presented. As he argued the People's case late in the afternoon for little more than one hour, Bill Patterson, seated at counsel table, eyes fixed on the jury, would keep nodding "no," as if to give the message once again that the people's case had been fabricated. However, you could tell that he was extremely nervous as he would alternately stroke his chin and the lower part of his cheeks, as though he was smoothing the hair of an imaginary beard.

On July 2, after a long holiday weekend, I charged the jury on the law and the twelve jurors were sent out to deliberate a verdict. There would be no down charge to a lesser offense such as manslaughter. Both sides agreed that Bill Patterson was either guilty of murder or he was not guilty at all. The defense was shooting craps and the stakes were extremely high. Bill was betting many years of his life that he would be acquitted. He and Gottlieb were not looking for a compromise verdict!

The deliberations lasted for more than two full days, and the jury was sequestered in a local hotel. During this period I received a total of thirteen separate notes from the jury, the first five requesting read-backs of portions of the trial testimony. By lunchtime of July 3, I received a note from the jury giving me an unsolicited count of the jury's vote on the question of guilt. The note read as follows:

> *Your Honor:*
> *Jurors stand at this time,*
> *7/3 12:30 p(m), 10 Guilty 2 Not Guilty*
> *How much further do you advise us to go at this time? It seems unlikely that this vote will change toward unanimous.*
> *This is the third poll,*
> *7/2 4:24p(m) 3 Not Guilty 7 Guilty 2 No Opinion*
> *7/3 9:12a(m) 6 Not Guilty 6 Guilty*
> *The two jurors voting not guilty feel that there is insufficient evidence to support a guilty verdict*
> *1:26 pm* [10]

I had never instructed the jury to advise me of their vote count since deliberations thereon were done in secret. I now knew where they stood, but I was not about to advise the parties. I simply advised them that I was aware of the count, and that I was instructing the jury to continue their deliberations. The jury then requested some further explanation of "reasonable doubt," which I gave them from the bench. Nevertheless, at 3:22 p.m., I received another note, wherein the jury foreman had written the magic words: "The Jurors are hopelessly deadlocked."*

This was a murder trial which had taken about three weeks since the commencement of jury selection, and I was not about to declare a mistrial. I brought them back into the courtroom, and, over objection of defense counsel, gave them what is known in New York state as an "Allen charge." The charge simply, in uncoercive terms, asks them to continue their deliberations, to go back over the evidence and the law in an attempt to reach a unanimous verdict if they can do so without surrendering their individual conscience to the will of the majority. They did so, and they continued to send out notes requesting additional testimony.

At 5:02 p.m., the jury requested to visit the Cedar Road Park because "the identification of the car seen by the Levinsohns seems to be critical." They wanted to "visit the site with both a light colored car and a white car situated between 75' and 100' from the gate at 9:30 p.m."

They were brought back into the courtroom, at which time I advised them that I could not honor such a request during jury deliberations since they were bound to reach their verdict only upon the evidence presented at trial. The jury was sent back to continue deliberations. On July 4, at 1:43 p.m., I received the following note:

> *Your Honor*
> *The Jurors have reviewed all evidence again, the minority have had every opportunity to review their opinions with reference to reasonable doubt as have the majority. Both the minority and the majority have made every possible attempt to review their positions by a conscientious and thorough exposition of their views based on the evidence and to the elimination of surmise and speculation. I must state without equivocation that our deliberations have been fair and based on the evidence, and that no force in any way has been part of our deliberations. We have taken a fourth poll the result of which is: 10 Guilty 2 Not Guilty. It is our unanimous decision that further deliberation will be to no avail in that no change in vote is possible. 7/4/84 1:43 P (sic)**

By 2:30 p.m., I would declare a mistrial. We were all convinced that we had a "hung jury." As they said the day before, they were "hopelessly deadlocked," and nothing short of unlawful coercion would change that vote. The ten men and two women, all white, average age forty-nine, were discharged with the thanks of the court. Bill Patterson had won a Pyrrhic victory. Robert Gottlieb had done his job well. It was a downtrodden and unhappy Steve Wilutis that left the courtroom with the entourage of assistant district attorneys, secretaries and detectives that afternoon. He had neither won nor lost the battle, but he was convinced that he would win the war.

On their flight back from Georgia, Bill Patterson had asked Detective Amato, "Do you think Vitale is a good lawyer?", referring to Kotler's law partner, Joseph Vitale. To that, Amato responded,"Yes!" Obviously feeling sorry for himself, Bill sadly stated, "I can't afford him. I'll probably be stuck with a court appointed lawyer."* Stuck, he was not! He received much more of a defense than he could ever have hope for. Bob Gottlieb could not have done more had Patterson been a paying client, and paying clients, charged with murder, have been known to put forth an entire life's savings to less talented lawyers.

An exhausted Gottlieb left the courtroom with mixed emotions, not certain whether he could afford to accept the assignment for the anticipated second trial. He had battled all of the unlimited resources of the Suffolk County district attorney's office and police homicide squad, but yet they had been unable to convince twelve jurors in an almost airtight circumstantial case of the guilt of William Patterson. While Gottlieb was not victorious, he certainly could take pride in the result. Several days later, he notified me that he had discussed the matter with his partner, Ron Sussman. He would accept the assignment once again. I sensed that Bob might have believed that Bill Patterson was innocent and that he owed this to him. I certainly did not! But, fortunately, I didn't have to make that difficult decision.

The second trial, which commenced on December 6, 1984, would be a virtual replay of the first trial, except that it would last some two weeks longer taking us through the Christmas recess. At this trial both counsel were armed with transcripts of testimony from the earlier trial. And each witness would be cross-examined methodically and painstakingly with reference to prior testimony where there appeared to be an inconsistency. Each side was now well aware of the other's case, both its strengths and weaknesses. The lawyers would slowly feel each witness out, not unlike two boxers who had fought to a draw once before, dancing and weaving, feigning and jabbing, feeling out one another in an effort to penetrate any discernible weakness in the other's case.

Between trials, Patterson continued to be held, in lieu of $250,000 cash bail. At the conclusion of the first trial, Gottlieb made application to reduce the bail to $25,000, which I denied. I genuinely believed that William Patterson was capable of fleeing the jurisdiction and that he was guilty of cold-blooded, premeditated murder.

During jury selection, we would learn from the prosecutor that the police had acquired a "jailhouse informant"—a snitch—to whom, it was now alleged, William Patterson had confessed that he had murdered his wife. Upon hearing this, my mind could not help but drift back to the sudden emergence of Alexis Louise Courtney as an informant in the trial of Timothy Patrick O'Toole.

Ralph Anthony was black, tough, and a street-wise resident of the Suffolk County Correctional Facility. He had been arrested on May 10, 1984 for a violation of parole. Between May 11 and November 21, 1983, he had been a "tier rep" (an inmate designated as the leader of all gang members on a specific tier in a housing facility) in the jail before being sent to Sing Sing for six months, from where he had been paroled. It was during the first week of November, 1983 that he claimed he had met and spoken to Bill Patterson for the first time in the county jail. He so testified at a pre-trial hearing, which was conducted immediately upon completion of jury selection. He had originally been arrested on a violent felony charge of armed robbery and he had a lengthy criminal record. Although he claimed to have had his first conversation with Patterson in November 1983, he did not speak to the authorities until September 21, 1984. According to him, at a meeting at the district attorney's office with Wilutis, Norman Novick, a detective investigator in Wilutis' office, and Bill Nash, another assistant district attorney, was arranged without his knowledge, although he had agreed to talk to them.

Novick, a fourteen-year veteran of the Major Offense Bureau, testified that he had received a telephone call from an unnamed inmate at the jail who told him that Anthony might have information about Patterson. They had been seen together at the jail. Novick then contacted Nash who was prosecuting Anthony's pending robbery charge. Nash, in turn, spoke to Robert O'Leary, a legal aid lawyer representing Anthony, who conveyed their interest to Anthony. He supposedly agreed to talk to them because he feared that he was about to be sent upstate.

The prisoner was produced in Wilutis' office and they met for about one and a half hours, during which time they discussed the quid pro quo. Anthony would be willing to testify if they would guarantee consecutive one year terms in the county jail. Although they claim that no promises were made to Anthony, he somehow agreed to talk to them. The district attorney's office had miraculously discovered another good Samaritan with a social conscience. Anthony, the tough habitual criminal, testified that he had decided to cooperate because "he [Patterson] was a man about to walk," who had left "his children "motherless" to benefit himself. He apparently had a personal moral code which transcended his criminality, or so they would have me believe.

He said that he had originally approached Patterson because he heard through the grapevine that Bill was a child molester, Anthony, the tier rep, felt that the other inmates might be uncomfortable with Patterson's presence, and that there might be violence. Like Anthony, inmates have a well documented, but unwritten, moral code that abhors woman and child abusers. He suggested to Patterson that he ask to be moved. Bill denied that he was a child molester, telling him that he had been confined for shooting his wife. He then proceeded to admit, according to Anthony, that he had shot his wife. Three or four days later, he claimed that he had another conversation with Bill Patterson. This time it was about the possibility of an escape. Bill had asked, "I'd like to find a way to get out of here. Which way do you think it would be best?" The conversation then turned to the murder.

"Pat, you actually shot your wife? What was the cause?" asked Anthony. At that point, Bill Patterson, who until then had confessed nothing to anyone, chooses to tell an almost perfect stranger the entire story—including motive. If Anthony was to be believed, Bill shot his wife as he was "frustrated because she wouldn't grant custody."*

In the spring of 1984 they met again near the elevator shaft. Anthony asked, "How are you coming along?" To which Bill confidently responded, "Things are looking good for me right now!" In another conversation later that summer, Anthony asked his "friend" again: "How are you coming along?" Bill told him that he had a "hung jury."* It was obvious to me that any of this information that Ralph said he got from Patterson could just as easily been acquired by reading *Newsday*, which gave extensive, continuous coverage to the hearings and trial.

My function, however, was simply to determine whether or not he had been an agent of the police when he spoke to the defendant. It was clear that he had not been, and I so ruled. His testimony would be permitted at trial even though I did not believe a word he uttered. I was convinced that any jury would see him for what he was—an opportunistic perjurer. Obviously, Wilutis would come to the same conclusion. Despite the fact that Ralph Anthony could provide the missing motive and very damaging oral admissions of guilt, and he was announced as a prospective witness to the jury, he would never surface as a witness during the second trial, and I would never learn what happened to the people's mystery witness. Nevertheless, I would never forget him and other good samaritans who would surface on the eve of a trial when Barry Feldman would, at the last moment, produce his star witness, Joseph Pistone, another alleged jailhouse informant, in the trial of James Diaz for the rape and murder of Maureen Negus. That presentation would be the straw that broke this camel's back, and I would no longer sit back and wait for a lay jury to decide whether the people's witness was a liar.

In the summer of 1984, after declaring a mistrial in the first Patterson trial, I would preside over the trial of one James Moore for murder, a trial where Feldman would once again be the prosecutor. Once again, a jailhouse informant would come forward, this time in the person of one Leno Gee, a multiple felony offender, who would be used more than once by a prosecutor until he would be finally shipped upstate for a long term of imprisonment. Moore would be convicted of murder and Leno Gee would play an important role in that conviction. For years, James Moore, like William Patterson, continued to protest his innocence.

The straws were in the wind, and they were beginning to pile up like dung on a heap of manure, but the moment had not yet arrived when I could speak out with certainty about what was taking place in my courtroom. In the summer of 1984, that moment was still months away.

On December 5, 1985, after selecting a jury of four women and eleven men, all white, average age fifty, the second trial of William Patterson began with opening statements by counsel. After telling the jury that he'd call twenty to twenty-five witnesses, an outwardly confident Steve Wilutis stated that he'd present "a wealth of evidence which will prove the defendant's guilt beyond a reasonable doubt."

"It will be a case," he said, "which will be proved through circumstantial evidence." William Patterson was "the man who knew too much," the man who knew only what the murderer could have known.* As he gazed at the deeply interested faces of fifteen strangers, he had to be wondering whether in this group, like in the first jury, there might also be one or two persons who might never be convinced.

Bob Gottlieb, seemingly convinced of the rightness of his cause and the innocence of his client retorted: "No matter what you just heard, no matter how convincing that side of the story sounded...Mr. Patterson is not guilty of the charge of murder in the second degree...He did not kill his wife, or cause the terrible, terrible tragedy which has befallen his family."*

A stone-faced Bill Patterson stared intently at the fifteen persons in whose hands his fate had landed, as the lines of conflict were once again drawn by the two courtroom gladiators.

This time, however, Bill Patterson's luck had run its course. As the case moved slowly through the Christmas recess into a new year, 1985, a year which for some meant renewed hope, the stress of two trials was beginning to etch its indelible marks upon his countenance. Three days of direct examination and grueling cross-examination by Wilutis would take its toll upon his veneer of confidence as his story began to fray at the edges. He appeared calm at one moment, would lash out in anger at another, sometimes shedding tears, and resort, in his testimony, to phrases like "to be honest...," "to tell you the truth, Mr. Wilutis...," "as I sit here, Mr. Wilutis, I don't honestly remember..." and "as I sit here today, I don't recall...."* From a witness who was under oath to tell the truth and anxious to tell his version of the story, those responses fell like lead balloons upon the jurors' ears. Piece by piece, once again, the parts of the puzzle logically pointed only towards one culprit, and he was seated at counsel table with Bob Gottlieb. Even his ebullience and extensive legal talent could not insulate Bill Patterson from the fate which awaited him on January 9, 1985.

Not taking any chances, however, a cautious Wilutis paraded ten rebuttal witnesses before the jury, including Amato, Cavanaugh, Warkenthien and Misegades, all from the homicide squad, for a second time around. This trial became a crusade, and he was not about to allow Patterson to have the last word before this jury. This was a tactic he had not used in the first trial, but he had been once burned and he did not want to lose his prey. He would leave no stone unturned in his quest to bring justice to the memory of Frances Patterson.

In summation, he told the jury that there was a motive. "He hated his wife," he said, "not just dislike." He implored the jury not to be taken in by Bill Patterson. Sneering at the defendant he pleaded, "I ask you ladies and gentlemen not to be conned by the Dale Carnegie man." Bill Patterson had testified, in response to a question by Wilutis, that he had taken a Dale Carnegie course some fifteen years before. Dale Carnegie had taught self confidence and the ability to "win friends and influence people." Bill Patterson had learned his lessons well. Once again Wilutis reiterated, in an effort to drive the point home: "He was the man who knew too much!*

In a summation which lasted about two hours, Bob Gottlieb, who was beginning to show the strain of two long trials and defending a person against very long odds, attempted to convince the jury that "The lack of evidence is powerful and overwhelming." Gottlieb was too smart to really believe that, but somehow he needed to get that across to an incredulous jury. He argued that "Mrs. Patterson was killed by a marksman—by a sharpshooter," and Bill Patterson never even learned to fire a rifle. Almost begging the jury for compassion, he urged, "It's a nightmare that only you can end!"*

For William Patterson, the nightmare had only just begun. In less than four hours, including a recess for lunch, after hearing about four weeks of testimony in a very complex murder trial, at 3:50 p.m., the jury of ten men and two women returned a unanimous verdict of guilty. An unbelieving and visibly shaken Bill Patterson slumped slowly backwards into his seat as the homicide detectives, seated in the rear of the courtroom, offered quiet congratulations to one another. The long journey was almost over. Patterson was remanded to the custody of the sheriff and sentencing was scheduled for February 27.

On February 27, the courtroom was again filled with police, prosecutors and curious onlookers. The trial received a good deal of attention in the media at a time when New York courts still did not allow cameras in the courtroom. It was an angry and impassioned Wilutis that addressed the court as he recommended the maximum sentence of twenty-five-years-to-life.

> Simply put, Your Honor, this was an execution, an execution of Frances Patterson...Through his testimony and the way he changed his testimony, I think he was proven to be a dissembler. He was an actor. Shaking his head, trying to influence the jury. Crying inappropriately at times...the police department discovered that this defendant had many girlfriends and many affairs with women prior to his separation..He was not the loving husband that he intended to portray on the witness stand. He physically abused his wife...She had a feeling before she died that she thought she was going to die...that something was going to happen to her...Mr. Patterson...tried to portray himself as a loving father...However, this man shot and killed the mother of his children in front of his children...He has left these children without a mother, and they have to live with the realization...that their mother was shot by their father...this was a most premeditated murder. This defendant purchased a gun...with the intent in mind to kill his wife, to kill a varmint...It was well thought out. It was a well conceived idea and plan...he drove approximately a thousand miles to New York...It's a long ride...imagine Mr. Patterson driving that approximate thousand miles with the...rifle in the car, and the bullets, with one objective in mind, to kill Frances Patterson...he took one shot and killed his wife. He gave her the death sentence...and...perhaps, ruined the lives of his children...Frances Patterson was young...She had, perhaps, 30 or 40 years to live, God willing. But she was shot down that day.

The people ask, because of the gruesome nature of this crime, because of the premeditation involved, that the Court sentence this defendant to the maximum term of 25 years to life...If there were a lengthier sentence, the People would recommend that....*

Turning to a visibly hostile William Patterson, standing alongside Bob Gottlieb and surrounded by armed, uniformed court officers, I asked if he had anything to say. Of course, he wished to say his piece:

...I am not guilty of this crime. I did not kill my wife. Regardless of what the jury of my supposed peers at this time came into a verdict with, the status of this Court, even with your own demeanor, Your Honor has shown that it is not neutral and it is not based upon the law. Basically, you made a comment during the second trial that you wished you were not on this trial, and based upon that, perhaps you should not have been on the trial to enter into your own demeanor into the trial. When the court system and the law system are allowed to do what they did with the lies that the police have put into this trial, it is no longer a fair and just system, and I only hope that the upper courts will look at this and correct the injustice that has been done in this court. I did not commit this crime, Your Honor.*

Bob Gottlieb was drained. He had given everything to the defense of a guilty man. The case had been time consuming. His cause was an unpopular one and he could never be adequately compensated for his time and human effort. The trials of William Patterson took their toll on his professional career, but he never once complained, accepting the challenge like a true professional.

Your Honor, I don't know what more I could possibly say than what I have already said through so many long hours in this courtroom...through two trials, through two summations...I have exhausted every conceivable legal argument...we tried very hard to present all of the evidence before this jury. I am not going to review Mr. Patterson's life...It's already been done. You have the probation report. The jury has spoken.

...The issue of doubt from what we perceived to be the lack of evidence was an issue which we tried very hard to have this jury consider...The only thing that on behalf of my client I could possibly raise before you...is that when the issue becomes doubt, when a defendant continues to protest his innocence, who among us as fallible human beings can be so sure, so certain, that indeed Mr. Patterson pulled that trigger? We believe that there were gaps in the People's case because of the fallibility of the system, because of the fallibility of human beings. "I just ask that you consider that possibility that, in fact, in this case the wrong person was arrested and the wrong person was convicted.

...I ask only that whatever mercy you can find within yourself in sentencing Mr. Patterson, that it be found today, and with that, I believe justice will be done.*

Despite Bob Gottlieb's quietly eloquent plea on behalf of his client, I had no mercy or compassion in my heart for William Patterson that day. I sentenced Bill Patterson to the maximum term of incarceration, twenty-five-years-to-life.

"I have been trying to say to myself," I said to him, "what is good about William Patterson? What can I do by way of compassion to compensate for the good in you? And I don't see anything good, because I believe that you're going to go to your grave without any remorse; that in your mind, you have absolutely rationalized that you had an absolute right to take the life of Frances...."*

I told him that it was my intention to write to the Board of Parole to ensure that he never be paroled because of the trauma which he heaped upon his children, and most important, because of the heinous, premeditated murder of their mother before their very eyes. Patterson had accused me of being prejudiced against him—a theme which he would repeat often—and he said that I should have disqualified myself from sitting on the second trial. Once again, he had protested his innocence, but his pleas fell upon deaf ears. I wondered to myself whether Bob Gottlieb still believed in the innocence of William Patterson. With that, he was remanded to the Commissioner of Corrections to be dealt with in accordance with the sentence and the law.

On March 26, 1985, just as I had promised Patterson, I wrote to Thomas A. Coughlin, III, Commissioner of the New York State Department of Correctional Services. After identifying myself as the sentencing judge, the letter reads in part as follows:

> The purpose of this letter is to transmit a copy of the sentencing minutes so that they may be kept in the defendant's records for perusal by any Board of Parole or other body considering parole or early release of this inmate. In addition, by way of this communication I wish to underscore my feelings as the sentencing judge at this time, since I will not be available for recommendation at the time of any such appearance by William Patterson.
>
> The victim in this case, Frances Patterson, was shot to death through a basement window by a Marlin .35 caliber rifle, with a 4X scope, in the presence of her two children, in a clearly premeditated, cold and calculating manner, by William Patterson. To this date, the defendant has shown no remorse for his actions, nor in the opinion of the writer will he ever show remorse or admit his actions in any way, although the evidence of his guilt which was circumstantial in nature, was overwhelming at trial. Nor was there any evidence presented at trial which could even remotely be considered justification for his actions—even if viewed through the eyes of the defendant. On the contrary, whatever marital discord existed in the past had been resolved by way of a separation agreement, and Frances Patterson had every right to live out the balance of her natural life at peace with herself and her children.
>
> It is for these reasons that I am recommending, at this time, that William Patterson never be granted parole or early release, and that he spend the remainder of his natural life in a state correctional facility. To do otherwise, would be to inflict a grave injustice upon the memory of the deceased and upon her children whose emotional scars can never entirely be healed.

On April 5, 1985, the commissioner acknowledged receipt of my correspondence and the information was forwarded to the Division of Classification and Movement. Other than a decision on his appeal, I thought that would be the last I would hear of Bill Patterson. I knew that Jeb Ladouceur, who believed strongly in his innocence, would be writing a book about the trials of William Patterson, and I looked forward with great interest to its publication. However, I never in my wildest dreams expected that I would become the addressee of reams of mail written by Patterson over the years, and that his views about the prejudiced judge would so change that he would write letters in support of my later actions. Nevertheless, he has never forgiven me for misjudging his "innocence."

On December 16, 1986, William Patterson made another lengthy application for a new trial. He claimed that his rights to a fair trial and due process of law were violated by the alleged perjury of Amato and Marconi. It was basically a rehash of his earlier application, except that then he claimed that the judgment was procured by fraud on the part of the prosecutor. He previously claimed that the prosecutor knew that material evidence adduced at the trial, specifically the testimony of Amato, Rubin and Marconi, was perjurious. Now he claimed that his constitutional right to due process was violated. Again he asked that the motion be heard by another judge. In that regard, he wrote the following:

> ...Justice (sic) Namm is not neutral in defendant's case and...Justice Namm allowed prosecution witnesses to lie in his court during defendant's hearings and trials, however, at defendant's sentencing on February 26, 1985, Justice Namm stated, "I have to admit that at this very moment I am not a neutral person when it comes to you," in referring to defendant...it would appear that Justice Namm holds to a double standard in defendant's case; one that condoned perjury in defendant's case because it brought about a conviction against defendant, the other being that Justice Namm calls for a State investigation into perjury by prosecution witnesses when it helps to bring about an acquittal before him....*

In William Patterson's mind, I was the devil incarnate. He probably believed that I was part of a larger conspiracy designed to insure his conviction. Little did he know how much I had hoped that, for the sake of his children, who were now de facto orphans, the police had been wrong and someone else would come forward—Perry Mason style—as the murderer of Frances Patterson. But this was cold, hard reality and not fiction. This tale was conceived, written and published by Bill Patterson himself. So, on July 15, 1987, I once again denied his application to disqualify me, and his motion to set aside the judgment was denied.

By January 29, 1988, three days after his appeal was argued in the Appellate Division in Brooklyn, William Patterson had changed his tune. In his opinion I was no longer the embodiment of all that was evil in the criminal justice system. By that time, *Newsday* had published a lengthy feature story detailing my involvement in the investigation of the District Attorney's office and the homicide squad, and *Newsday* had completed its week long feature story entitled "The Confession Takers."* Patterson seemed to be favorably impressed by what he read. Thus, he addressed his first informal letter to me:

> *Your Honor:*
> *I never thought I'd see the day that I would be writing this type letter to you, but we all can err in our judgment of others, and I erred in my judgment of you. I now find that I must take this time to compliment you on your efforts to bring fairness to the criminal justice system of Suffolk County...*
> *I now believe that you are indeed concerned...and I pray that you will continue to be.*
> *I'm seeing this criminal justice system from this side right now, and I've been trying to learn through college* [3.78 index after 50 credits of law and related subjects] *about the other side. I intend to continue in my efforts to bring to the attention of various people and officials what really goes on behind the scenes of the S.C.H.D.* [apparently Suffolk County Homicide Department], *and I intend to continue this as long as there is breath in my body.*
> *Your Honor, I'm sure my words mean nothing to you at this time,*

but I hope that they will have a meaning to you sometime during our lifetimes. Whatever you do, please continue to wonder—'Now I wonder if there's a convicted person who was really innocent'—for you will find that there is. I also ask you to wonder about the suffering of the family of the innocent person.

—*William S. Patterson, 85A1484**

Bill Patterson's kept his word. He has sent a battery of letters to various public officials in state and county government, to *Newsday*, to me and to Jeb Ladouceur. He has kept abreast of affairs in the county and in the state's investigation by means of a subscription to *Newsday* which is bought on his behalf each year by Jeb Ladouceur. According to Ladouceur, Bill uses the outdated copies of the newspaper to make prison friends and to barter for cigarettes and other institutional necessities.

On February 16, 1988, four judges of the Appellate Division of the Supreme Court unanimously agreed that William Patterson had been given a fair trial and that, accordingly, the judgment should be affirmed. Through his court appointed appeal lawyer, Bennett L. Gershman of White Plains, a city far removed from Suffolk County, Patterson had raised a multitude of issues, not the least of which had been the question of prosecutorial misconduct, perjury and the destruction of evidence. Nevertheless, not one word was uttered by the justices in a short, tersely written opinion. Bill Patterson had been dealt a mortal blow by a higher court in which he had expressed great confidence at sentencing. It was almost as if the court did not want to delve into the issues which had created the greatest controversy in the Patterson trial. The hearing court did not err in denying the defendant's motion to suppress the statements made by him to the police. The defendant was represented by an attorney in a bankruptcy proceeding that was unrelated to the homicide the police were investigating. The right to counsel based on an individual's representation in a pending proceeding does not extend to unrelated proceedings of a wholly civil nature. "Upon our examination of the record herein," the justices wrote, "we find that the evidence, viewed in the light most favorable to the prosecution....was legally sufficient to establish defendant's guilt beyond a reasonable doubt. Upon the exercise of our factual review power, we are satisfied that the verdict of guilt (sic) was not against the weight of evidence...We have considered the defendant's remaining contentions and find them to be either unpreserved for appellate review or without merit."

A disconsolate Patterson had to feel cheated as he read this opinion in the loneliness of his Sing Sing cell utterly oblivious to the ambient prison noises which surrounded him. In a sense, I, as the trial judge, also felt cheated by an appellate decision which had chosen only one legal issue to discuss out of the many which had been raised during the several weeks of hearings and trial. Every judge looks forward to being affirmed after appellate review, and no one enjoys reading that a legal decision which he has rendered has been reversed on appeal. So in that vein, I certainly felt good about the affirmance. Nonetheless, a trial judge also looks to an appellate opinion for guidance and education in the disposition of future cases. The opinion of the Appellate Division had been devoid of either. As I read the less than one page of written opinion, I could not help but look back to the two decisions I had rendered after Patterson's applications to set aside the verdict. I had written that an adequate review of the issues that he had raised would be had in the appellate court. I now wondered whether that had been the case.

I was also well aware, by that time, that the justices of the Appellate Division, although cloistered some eighty miles away in Brooklyn, were well informed of the events which had taken place over the past three years in Suffolk County. I sincerely hoped that these events, and the desire to stay out of the fray, had dictated the need for an innocuous, noncontroversial decision in a case which was complex and spilling over with controversial issues.

In any event, I braced myself for a barrage of Patterson correspondence and applications to the courts, both federal and state, as I commenced pretrial hearings in a major serial rape trial of the infamous "South Shore Rapist" involving a sixty-eight count indictment. Little did I know then that this was to be my last criminal trial before being "temporarily elevated" to the illustrious position of Acting Supreme Court Justice, hearing only civil cases, in April 1988.

As for Patterson, some years later, after I had received a mountain of correspondence from his latest spouse and from him still proclaiming his innocence, Nancy and I decided to produce a thirteen part TV series entitled "A Question of Guilt," which was to be about prisoners who claimed to be innocent. It would be based upon the hundreds of letters from prisons and death rows all over the country I had involuntarily amassed after leaving the bench. We had intended to use the Martin Tankleff case as the pilot for the series, but when we were advised by him that his appellate attorneys thought it was ill advised, we then scrambled to find another subject for the pilot, and I immediately thought of Patterson.

However, things had changed by the time we did a scheduled "recce" at Clinton Correctional Facility, where Tankleff was then confined, with our British producer, Fraser Ashford. After Patterson agreed to have his story used for the pilot, Tankleff decided to do the pilot. Thus, on our trip back from the Plattsburgh prison where Tankleff was then still confined, I felt obliged stop at Sing Sing Correctional Facility, not far from the New York Thruway, for a Saturday visit to Patterson to advise him that Tankleff had decided to do the pilot after all, but that his story would ultimately be told as part of the series.

The last I ever saw or heard from Patterson was the image of a disconsolate soul who prostrated himself in the small side room of the Sing Sing visitor's area in front of me saying, "I didn't think I would ever see you again," with tears rolling down his cheeks as I told him that Marty Tankleff's case was to be the pilot for the series.

As luck would have it, like most things in my life, the television series never happened, with Court TV backing out of doing a thirteen part series at the last minute. We did ultimately produce the Martin Tankleff story in "A Question of Guilt" on DVD, in which I interviewed the then retired Det. K. James McCready in a North Carolina courtroom about his role in the Tankleff case.

NINE

"They Got the Fly, Then They Spun the Web Around Him."

—Peter Corso

Peter Corso, alias Peter Carbone, alias Pedro Corro, like Samuel Beckett's mythical Godot, was forever keeping people waiting and guessing.

In late 1971, "The Prince of the City," detective Robert Leuci, and two of his partners from the New York City Police Department's Special Investigations Unit, waited for days in an unmarked police vehicle surveilling the Brooklyn home of Peter Corso, someone who "regularly moved big packages." In the language of the streets, this meant that he was a dealer in large quantities of narcotics.

After six days of staking out a Brooklyn brownstone, their target arrived on the scene carrying what looked like a box of Italian pastries. Later that day, they followed him to an apartment building on East 7th Street across the East River in Manhattan. Leuci checked the lobby mailboxes and noted the name "Peter Carbone," the closest he could come to the name Peter Corso. The experienced narcotics detective correctly surmised that Peter Corso and Peter Carbone were one and the same. Despite their successful illegal wiretap that revealed the movement of three kilos of heroin, they lost their collar to the federally funded Joint Narcotics Task Force of federal agents and local detectives which was also on to Corso's activities.[1]

Almost eight years later, on Saturday June 15, 1979, at 9:00 am, Archimedes Cervera, a prominent Suffolk County lawyer, called "Archie" by his friends and family, and known to some in the Hispanic community as the "unofficial mayor of Brentwood," was seated at the desk of his Brentwood law office. He was chewing on a large cigar awaiting the arrival of a prospective criminal client, Pedro Corro. By late that afternoon Archie was dead, the victim of a "gangland" style killing. It was literally an execution. He died from five gunshot wounds, one in his right temple, one in his left temple, two in his lower lip and one in his chest which penetrated his right lung and heart. The mysterious Pedro Corro, who placed several telephone calls to Archie earlier that week, was Peter Corso of Shirley, Long Island, formerly of Brooklyn and Manhattan.

Since late 1979, when veteran Detective Edward Halverson of the homicide squad was supplied the name of Peter Corso as the murderer of Cervera by Special Agent Lawrence Sweeney of The F.B.I., the police and the district attorney's office were waiting for a confession of guilt by Peter Corso. Corso was fingered by Michael Orlando, a former Suffolk County school teacher turned contract assassin for the mob. He spilled his guts to the feds in exchange for a lifetime of protection and anonymity. This same Orlando also fingered the United States Secretary of Labor, Raymond Donovan, in an alleged bribery and racketeering scheme. Donovan was later acquitted by a Bronx jury.

Suffolk County police and prosecutors continued to seek that confession long after Corso was acquitted of the Cervera murder by a Suffolk County jury on July 2, 1985. An admission of guilt, in their view, would be the long sought vindication of a prosecution team which many believed had bungled an investigation which should have resulted in the conviction of a person who was guilty of a contract murder. It helped strengthen the disingenuous belief that somehow I was responsible for the acquittal, a belief which was uttered often and loud in the media, as if repetition itself would make it so.

For years, confession was the name of the game in Suffolk County murder investigations. The homicide squad was so obsessed with obtaining a murder confession that all other forms of investigation and proof were relegated to the back burner. This was an investigative technique which ultimately came back to haunt the once highly touted elite squad of highly paid detectives.

I have often asked myself how a tough criminal court judge ended up in the unlikely position of being defended and supported by a convicted wife-killer and a suspected contract murderer and cocaine dealer, while a disinterested public and the entire organized bar sat silently by? I know now that it was destined to begin with the bloody assassination of Archie Cervera in 1979 when I was still a fledgling judge in the District Court.

Nellie and Archie Cervera married in October 1976. She worked as his secretary from 1965 until 1971 when he hired Denise Malleta, his secretary right up until his early demise. Before their marriage, Nellie and Archie lived together for three years in a meretricious relationship.

In the summer of 1976, Nellie saw Henry Medina and Benjamin Rodriguez in Cervera's Brentwood law office. Medina and Cervera both served on the board of a privately held corporation called Tele-Signal. Their visit to the Cervera law office lasted about three hours. After they departed, Archie gave Nellie an Eastern Airlines flight bag which they brought with them. He told her to hide it explaining that there was $10,000 cash in small bills in the bag. From time to time, she would give him money from the bag in currency denominations of no more than $20.

In May 1979, Archie and Nellie flew to the south Florida office of an attorney to discuss the business of Tele-Signal. Both Medina and Rodriguez were present at the meeting. After returning to New York Archie became "despondent and restless." He couldn't sleep and he suffered from headaches. Archie told Nellie that Rodriguez wanted the $10,000 back. Angrily, Archie shouted: "This is ridiculous! I'm not going to return the money, I didn't guarantee that Rodriguez would not go to jail."

After an intense telephone conversation between Archie and Medina, a concerned Nellie inquired of her outwardly distressed husband, "Why don't you give them what they want? Aren't you afraid of them?"

"No, they can't hurt me," he responded with typical Cervera bravado and machismo.*

Two weeks before the murder, the Cerveras went to dinner with the Medinas at the Seascape Restaurant in Smithtown not far from Archie's law office. According to Nellie, it was not a pleasant meal. Again Archie and Medina argued about the $10,000. Archie was livid. "Henry, I told you, I don't want to discuss this. I'm not returning the money. I didn't guarantee anything. When you pay somebody for a job, you don't ask for your money back."

There was probably little likelihood that Archie could have returned the money at that time, even if he had wanted to. At that point, Archie had debts and judgments against him amounting to about $1,866,000, but he was still "working on business deals," according to Nellie. He was losing no sleep over his debts, or the fact that he did not intend to pay federal or state tax on the $10,000 which was hidden away, and though he was "taking money from clients' escrow accounts." But he was concerned about his license to practice law which he felt was in jeopardy, and he was experiencing episodes of high blood pressure over the Medina-Rodriguez affair.*

On June 6, 1979, ten days before the murder, Archie's secretary, Denise, received a telephone call at the law office from a man with an Italian accent, named Corro, who wanted to talk to Archie about a narcotics matter. She described him as "very unpleasant," because he persisted in calling her "sweetie" or "honey" and insisted upon calling again despite the fact that she had explained that Archie did not handle narcotics matters. Not to be denied, Corro called again the next morning.

"Hello, sweetie, this is Mr. Corro. Is Mr. Cervera in?" "No," the annoyed secretary replied. Saying that it was urgent, Corro insisted upon speaking to Archie who was not in. She told him to call at 1:00 p.m., since she knew that she would be out to lunch between 12:00 and 12:30. She felt repulsed by the irrepressible Mr. Corro who would not be thwarted in his desire to speak to her boss.

Upon returning from lunch, she talked to Cervera about Corro for the first time. Archie told her to call his long-time friend and associate, Fred Reuss, to handle the criminal matter. Denise scheduled a meeting between Corro and Reuss for June 9 at 10:00 a.m. She noted it in the office diary, and she gave the information to Corro when he called again. The meeting was rescheduled to June 16 because Reuss' son was being confirmed on June 9. The meeting was to be between Cervera, Corro and Reuss, according to Reuss. But Reuss never attended the meeting because earlier that week, according to Reuss, Cervera decided to meet with Corro alone. Reuss testified that in discussing the Corro meeting, "he (Archie) was not his usual outgoing self. He was nervous and morose." Archie Cervera was dead by the afternoon of June 16, the day of the rescheduled meeting.

On June 13, Denise became aware that at some point Archie apparently met Corro for lunch. Cervera directed her to cross out the name of Corro from the appointment book as he angrily slammed the office door behind him. "Corro is bad news," shouted Archie. Being the good secretary that she was, she dutifully scribbled out the name "Corro" that she had noted on the June 9 and June 16 pages in Archie's diary. Yet he told her to expect a "coded" call from Corro.

On the last morning of his life, as he sat alone in his Brentwood law office, Archie called Denise twice by telephone, to ask about Corro. But, she said, to her knowledge, Corro never called the office again.*

On June 15, Rebecca Kane, Archie's daughter, then a Bay Shore chiropractor who lived alternately between a rooming house and Archie's home, answered a telephone call at the Cervera residence from "Pedro Corro" for her father. The caller said that it was imperative that she convey his message, which she repeated several times, exactly as he gave it. Corro told her that he had an appointment at 11:00 a.m. the next day. The message was that he "would not be hungry tomorrow," and so he "would meet him [Archie] at the other place, not at the eating place." She gave the coded message to Archie at 9:00 a.m. before he left for his office. Undoubtedly, this was the message which Cervera had been anxiously awaiting.

****

Rebecca Kane ate me alive in the print and television media after Peter Corso, according to the District Attorney, publicly, but silently, confessed to the murder of her father in the courtroom of Justice McInerney some nine years later. On television, on two separate occasions, she blamed me for the acquittal of her father's murderer. In her opinion, I had manipulated the jury by my "facial expressions" and control of the courtroom dialogue.[2] Although I would have been justified in doing so, I couldn't feel anger towards her for her public flogging of me. She was the daughter of a murder victim. She had suffered a trauma which few people can survive without permanent emotional scars, but there was no doubt in my mind that her comments were inspired by representatives of the police or district attorney's office who were using her in their campaign to embarrass and humiliate me so as to "vindicate" themselves. In her frustration she had allowed herself to be used by my self appointed enemies. My hostility was directed towards them. As a witness in the hearings and trial, Ms. Kane had hardly been in the courtroom during the testimony of other witnesses. Whatever she knew, she was getting second-hand. When the SIC finally issued its report in April 1988, she surfaced once again on television to blame me for the acquittal. She characterized the SIC's report as a "sham" and praised the police and prosecutors who had worked on the case despite the severe criticism by the jurors, the media and the various investigations.[3]

But on June 24, 1985, Rebecca Kane was just another prosecution witness whom I was seeing for the first time in the trial of Peter Corso, albeit the bereaved daughter of the deceased. She came close to causing a mistrial by blurting out to the jury, in response to a prosecution question, "I told Nellie, I know who did it. Pedro Corro murdered Archie!"* By that point in the trial, Pedro Corro was assumed by all, including the jury, to be the silent, bearded, grey-haired defendant, Peter Corso, seated at counsel table.

Corso was represented by the law firm of Clayton and Mayer—David Clayton and Thomas Mayer—former Suffolk County assistant district attorneys who had risen to positions of authority within the hierarchy. Clayton had been chief of the Rackets Bureau involved in important racketeering and narcotics prosecutions and Mayer had been a deputy bureau chief responsible for the trial of violent felonies, such as murder and rape. Their former positions within the bureaucracy helped them to develop a lucrative law practice which involved many important criminal cases while at the same time maintaining a close, friendly relationship with their former associates in the police department and district attorney's office.

Clayton handled the heavy questions of law, while Mayer had a reputation for being very smooth with a jury. Dave Clayton was short and paunchy, while Pete Mayer was tall and dark haired, with an innocent boyish expression behind horn rimmed glasses. They both appeared to be in their late thirties or early forties, and they worked the pre-trial hearings as a team. Apparently, they were being well paid by someone for their services to Peter Corso.

The People were represented by an equally young Ed Jablonski, an outwardly dedicated prosecutor, with mannerisms similar to Steve Wilutis, who had appeared so many times before me. But unlike Wilutis, Jablonski, who didn't seem to be as sure of himself, habitually maintained a very explicit trial book in which he listed all of his prospective witnesses, kept copies of documentary evidence to be presented and listed areas for direct and cross-examination of witnesses. He rarely asked a question or offered a piece of evidence without referring to the large looseleaf book laid out in front of him. Nevertheless, when he testified in the Waters case for the prosecution in the hearing about black jurors, only one year earlier, he had no notes of the jury selections at which he claimed he saw young blacks between the ages of eighteen and twenty-one. Knowing Jablonski's trial habits as I did, his failure to retain such notes was a major consideration in my suspicious evaluation of the credibility of his testimony, and the testimony of his cohorts.

Michael Orlando, a graduate of St. Johns University and a former Suffolk County elementary school teacher, fingered Peter Corso as Archie Cervera's assassin. Orlando was also an admitted hijacker, burglar, handgun toting robber and contract killer. He was recruited by special agent Lawrence Sweeney of the F.B.I. as an informant in 1976. In 1982, even after murdering one Salvatore Frascone in the Bronx in 1978 in exchange for a new car, he was permitted to enter the government's Witness Protection Program. Despite his close working relationship with the F.B.I. in the late '70s and early '80s, he had never testified in a court of law until May 8, 1985 when he was subpoenaed by the defense, over the strenuous objection of the Justice Department and the Bronx District Attorney's office, to testify in the Corso pretrial hearings.

It was Jablonski's intention not to produce Orlando until trial. The prosecutor did not relish having his star witness tested by the defense before he was slated to testify before a Suffolk jury. Nor did the Justice Department want to see its protected witness under the gun before his anticipated legal coming out in the upcoming trial of a big fish, Secretary of Labor Raymond Donovan, which was being tried in the Bronx. The department did all that it could legally do to delay or obstruct his appearance in the Corso case. They were unsuccessful, but even so, it cost the Corso defense about $6,000 for the transportation and housing of him and his entourage of federal protectors.

Edward Halverson was retired from the Suffolk County Police Department since February 1982. Before his retirement, he was the lead homicide detective in the Cervera murder, and he'd been succeeded by his partner, Detective Dennis Rafferty. Halverson was a large man, glib of tongue, who was now a successful entrepreneur, the owner of a local private security business. He was the senior homicide detective at the time of his retirement, and he displayed a smug attitude of assured self confidence nurtured no doubt by an "illustrious" career in the elite homicide squad. The commanding officer of the squad described him to the State Investigations Commission as an "extraordinary" detective and "excellent." Nevertheless, both he and Rafferty were among those officers who were singled out and severely criticized for their lack of professionalism by the commission. But their first findings were no less than twenty months away, and in 1985 Halverson was still a local police legend. There were many legends in the Suffolk County police department.

Jablonski had no intention of calling Halverson, Orlando or Orlando's F.B.I. contact, Special Agent Lawrence Sweeney, at the pretrial hearings. Good prosecutors, like good card players, hold their aces and trump cards in the hole until the opportune moment—the jury trial. Instead, they were subpoenaed by the defense in an effort, they claimed, to show that the police had violated Corso's rights in delaying his arrest until long after they had legal probable cause to do so. To get his star witnesses off the stand with the least damage, Jablonski never cross examined any of them. He didn't have to do so. He knew what they would say, and Clayton and Mayer were unsuccessful in displaying a violation of their client's rights. But they developed a wealth of startling information which proved invaluable to the defense at trial. They had gone on a successful fishing expedition.

It was an absolute revelation to hear Sweeney admit that Orlando, a criminal who was recruited in 1976 as an F.B.I. informant, continued to commit crimes while he was paid as much as $53,000 in taxpayer funds by the federal government. A court ordered wiretap in the F.B.I. probe—code name TUMCON—had been set up by the feds in a Bronx establishment referred to as the Masselli-Pellegrino Meat Market. William Masselli was a reputed member of the Genovese crime family.

Sweeney learned through the tap that his informant, Orlando, was involved in the hijacking of a truckload of batteries. He had also driven the get-a-way car in the armed robbery of a Staten Island home. Sweeney also had reason to believe that Orlando was either involved, or had knowledge of, no less than ten murders. On November 14, 1979, less than five months after the ruthless murder of Archie Cervera, Orlando told Sweeney that he possessed information about the murder of a Long Island attorney, Archimedes Cervera. He claimed that Peter Corso, a former associate in crime, told him that he killed Cervera for a contract fee of over $10,000.

Corso said that he had used a .32 caliber handgun equipped with a silencer, and that he shot Archie several times in the chest and face, and at least once in the eye. The lawyer, he said, was seated behind his office desk with a cigar gripped in his hand. His last words, as he quizzically faced Corso, were simply: "What are you doing?" In response to which Corso allegedly uttered the last words ever spoken to Archie: "If you don't know now, you'll soon know!"* Within seconds, Archimedes Cervera was slumped over dead.

Sweeney gave this information about Peter Corso to Halverson and District Attorney Patrick Henry within one week of his receipt of Orlando's revelation. But he was not about to give over the name of his confidential informant who refused to testify in court and was too valuable to be compromised, not even to the district attorney of Suffolk County. Orlando told Sweeney that his life wouldn't be worth a "plug nickel" if his name was known—even to the police.

From that day forward, for all intents and purposes, the Suffolk homicide squad discontinued its search for any other perpetrator despite the existence of numerous suspects, some connected to organized crime and with well established motive to do away with Archie Cervera. The police rationalized that only the real murderer would know the details of the crime, and the informant had been given the details by Corso—or so he said.

No notes or reports were generated by any of the investigating detectives for a period of six months. From a few short days after the murder until they began a surveillance of Corso's activities in December the record of police activity is silent. As for Halverson, he retired "without the name of the informant," and despite having lead a major homicide investigation, he took no notes and wrote no reports of the results of his extensive investigatory work. Yet he was certain that Corso was their man, even though he first learned the name of Michael Orlando when he read it in a newspaper long after his retirement. This twelve year veteran of the homicide squad had honed his intuition, investigative instincts and gut feelings into an investigative art form.

The manual for Suffolk police investigative procedures required the regular preparation of Supplementary Reports to maintain a record of the progress of felony investigations. The homicide squad in general, and Halverson in particular, had carved out a large exemption for itself. This meant that the preparation of a report, or the taking of notes, was purely a matter of individual judgment. Between June and December 1979, Halverson met with representatives of the F.B.I., interviewed countless witnesses and considered numerous suspects because of Cervera's questionable business dealings which, in the detective's opinion, involved "fraudulent S.B.A. loans."

He learned of other murders of individuals who had been involved with a prime suspect, Benjamin Rodriguez. As the detective testified: "There were some other bodies dropped along the way," and "If you have an argument with Benjamin Rodriguez, it's a possibility that you might get murdered." He was told about the telephone calls of Pedro Corro, and he discovered that the F.B.I. also was interested in the facts and circumstances surrounding Cervera's murder since the feds felt that it (the murder) might have been intended to obstruct an ongoing government investigation.

During that same period the F.B.I. was investigating Henry Medina, Benjamin Rodriguez, George Franco, Rigoberto Borrerro, all business associates of Cervera at one time or another, and the corporate entities with which they were associated. They too were interested in the slaying of Cervera as it related to its fraud investigation, and as a possible predicate crime to a RICO (Racketeer Influenced and Corrupt Organizations) investigation. Yet the police files were totally devoid of the requisite

Supplementary Reports, and any notes of Halverson's in-depth investigation and briefings were non-existent. The examination of Halverson at both the hearings and trial and the subsequent cross-examination proved to be an embarrassment to the prosecution and particularly damaging to the people's case against Peter Corso.

****

In its final report, the SIC commented upon Halverson's reputation as a detective and work habits in regards to the Corso case:

> In addition, although the Commanding officer of the Homicide Division described Detective Halverson to the Commission as an "extraordinary" detective and "excellent"...Halverson's partner stated that Halverson "didn't write things down" and that he "wrote very little." Such a favorable judgment by Homicide's Commanding Officer of a detective who did not take notes is indicative of unprofessional standards of police supervision. Homicide investigations, like other police work, require meticulous note-taking and documentation...Without a complete and well documented file, detectives, their supervisors and prosecutors could not adequately investigate, manage and prosecute any case.[4]

****

No less damaging to the people's case was Halverson's apparent failure to follow up leads concerning one Salvatore Avellino, then a reputed member of the Lucchese crime family, and an associate of Cervera in the garbage carting business. In Suffolk County garbage collection was linked often to organized crime in New York. In later years, Avellino was charged with conspiracy and racketeering in the carting business. On January 15, 1987, he entered a plea of guilty to two counts of conspiracy and one count of bribery. The sentence meted out by one of my brethren, County Court Judge John Vaughn, was a fine of $2,000, three years probation and community service—service which, under certain circumstances, could be served by an employee in lieu of Avellino, an admitted briber and criminal conspirator.[5]

In June 1989, federal prosecutors from the Eastern District office of United States Attorney, Andrew J. Maloney, filed civil racketeering charges under the RICO act against Avellino and sixty-three other persons, forty-four Long Island carting companies, the carters' trade association and two alleged organized crime families. It was charged that they had conspired together to form an illegal cartel which exercised virtual control over the entire garbage industry in Long Island. Avellino was described in court papers by the prosecutors as a member of the Lucchese crime family and as the acting head of the cartel.

It was also alleged that he was the overseer of a longstanding illegal system in which carters allocated customers and routes amongst themselves. It was also claimed that they would rig bids for sanitation contracts so that the chosen carter would submit the winning bid, and bribe or curry favor with Long Island town officials involved with municipal carting contracts. In exchange for protecting the routes and interests of cartel members, the charges said, cartel members made regular payments that Mr. Avellino then divided between the Lucchese and Gambino crime families.[6]

James J. Corrigan, Jr., a public relations consultant in Central Islip, now deceased, was the executive director of the Private Sanitation Industry Association of Nassau-Suffolk, Inc. He was described as the public cover of the organization which was run behind the scenes by Avellino. In September 1987, Corrigan was sentenced to six months in the county jail after being convicted in connection with the same bribery and conspiracy charges for which Avellino was sentenced to do community service.[7]

****

In January 1987, during the height of the state investigation, I received a letter from Corrigan, whom I'd never met. It was on the stationery of Corrigan Associates, Inc., his public relations business which operated out of the same address as the carting association. It was written after I was the lead witness before the State Commission of Investigations at public hearings conducted in Hauppauge, the county seat.

A portion of the letter read as follows:

It is indeed comforting to learn that men such as you possess the courage of your own convictions and do what must be done to oppose those who have been apparent proponents of prosecutorial misconduct in the County of Suffolk. It is indeed refreshing that, because of your expressed concern in the interest of justice, corrupt practice employed by both the Police Department and the Suffolk County District Attorney will, because of the State Investigation Commission's investigation, be brought to a screeching halt...

My primary concern is that other jurists have failed to bring to the attention of the investigative authorities similar problems that they too unfortunately have experienced in their respective courtrooms...[8]

At that time, bribery and conspiracy charges were already pending against Corrigan, Avellino** and their associates in the carting association. Some of the charges against the defendants related to the alleged use of grand larceny and coercion to drive two independent sanitation carters out of business between 1981 and 1983. The two had attempted to obtain the garbage business at the Cold Spring Harbor School District and the county complex in Hauppauge.

In 1982, Robert Kubecka, one of the independents agreed to do covert undercover work for the State Organized Crime Task Force which ultimately brought these indictments. He wore a body wire and recorded various conversations with several carters who were later convicted. He also recorded various telephone conversations which provided the necessary legal foundation for wiretaps which led to the later convictions.[9]

On August 10, 1989, Kubecka and his brother-in-law, Donald Barstow, who also was in the family carting business, were gunned down by unknown assailants in their East Northport office. An investigator who was familiar with the carting industry investigation expressed his belief to a *Newsday* reporter that the murders were "mob-related." "The message is, reinforce control...step out of line and we deal with you, permanently."

**According to *Wikipedia*, in February 1994 Avellino pleaded guilty to helping plan the two murders and was sentenced to ten years in federal prison. In 2004, Frank "Frankie the Pearl" Federico was sentenced to fifteen years for the 1989 murders. Fed. Dist. Ct. Judge Frederic Block, my former partner, said it was unfortunate he had even a glimmer of hope of freedom someday.

By this time, Edward Jablonski, Corso's prosecutor, was the chief of the district attorney's homicide bureau. He wasn't so sure that the crimes were mob-related—Suffolk prosecutors and police do not always jump to conclusions. Said Jablonski: "Quite frankly, it's a possibility. But, it's not something we're centering on. It's very early in the investigation and we are pursuing many avenues." To date, to my knowledge, nobody has ever been prosecuted in Suffolk County for the murders of Kubecka or Barstow.[10]

This was not the first time that a Suffolk carter who cooperated with the authorities was murdered. In 1957, John Montesano, the owner of a Sayville waste disposal business testified before a Senate labor rackets committee which was investigating the connection between organized crime and the New York carting industry. In 1978, he also cooperated with *Newsday* in an investigative report about the carting industry. At that time, he talked about mob control of the industry and predicted his own brutal demise. He was shot to death in front of his home on April 13, 1981.

Neither Avellino nor Corrigan could be reached by *Newsday* for comment on the east Northport murders of Kubecka and Barstow. But Corrigan's secretary said that his only comment was, "It's a terrible tragedy." Avellino's attorney, Samuel Dawson, was quoted also as saying, "It's terrible, horrible."[11]

In April 1993, Salvatore Avellino and an associate, Anthony Casso, were accused in a federal indictment of a conspiracy to murder in the furtherance of a racketeering enterprise in the 1989 shootings of Kubecka and Barstow. Both faced mandatory life sentences if found guilty of this charge. Avellino was listed in the indictment as one of four "capos" (Mafia boss) in the Lucchese crime family

In a controversial special hearing which I conducted after Corso's acquittal, Michael Grant, a former Suffolk County legislator and a friend of Cervera, testified that he told the Suffolk homicide investigators in 1979 that Avellino had threatened "to break Cervera's legs" because he'd welched on an indebtedness to Avellino.** Armed with this information, Corso's attorneys subjected Halverson to a relentless cross-examination at trial on the subject of Salvatore Avellino. The detective was forced to concede that he never investigated Avellino in connection with the homicide. He and Rafferty spoke to him as a former associate of Cervera for a total of "ten minutes," and he kept no notes and filed no reports. He accepted Avellino's representation that Archie owed him no money, and he never interviewed Michael Grant, although they had some friendly "light conversation," again with no notes taken.

****

There was a Sanyo answering machine in the outer office of Cervera's law offices which was monitoring unanswered calls to the law office as Archie spent his last hours puffing a cigar in the executive chair behind his desk. The recorder was recovered and invoiced by the police investigators, but they claim that they never listened to its contents. Both the answering machine and Archie's dictaphone, which was also recovered as evidence, were mysteriously auctioned in May 1984 by the police Property Bureau. On the answering machine tape were the voices of Salvatore Avellino and Henry Medina, both of whom were considered by some as suspects with motive to kill Archie Cervera, and both of whom apparently left messages on the answering machine on the very morning of his assassination. Yet nobody in the police department could explain how an important piece of evidence could be auctioned.

I did not learn of the answering machine until it was brought to my attention in the earliest days of the trial by Corso's defense team. Miraculously, the answering machine was somehow recovered from its purchaser, but one year later the contents of the tape were no longer intact. A tape which could have provided police investigators with a priceless source of information proved valueless as a piece of evidence. Its loss and later recovery served to seriously weaken the credibility of the police and the strength of the People's case in the eyes of judge and jury.

The preliminary hearings, although vital to the defense and despite the testimony of Orlando, were largely uneventful. The real fireworks didn't begin until almost immediately after jury selection. Every one of my rulings at the conclusion of the hearings were favorable to the People. I denied Corso's application to suppress the oral admission allegedly made to Michael Orlando where he supposedly confessed to murder. I also permitted the People to use certain oral statements which he allegedly gave to the investigating detectives.

It was claimed through the testimony of the detectives that Corso admitted that he'd been "blowing coke for forty years"; that he'd been in the law office of Archimedes Cervera on two different occasions on the day of the murder; that he spent some fifteen or twenty minutes with Archie before noon of that day; that he'd been referred to Cervera in connection with a narcotics charge; and that Cervera wanted a fee of $50,000, which Corso considered to be too high.

They also said that he admitted that he and "Pedro Corro" were one and the same. Yet he never confessed to the murder, although they claimed that he stated to the police: "I didn't hit the lawyer. I was there—but nobody could say they saw me do the murder!" He then boastfully added: "You cops don't like stoolies anymore than I do. I'm a businessman. I couldn't in good conscience tell you anything. You do what you got to do, and I got to do what I got to do!"* These alleged admissions might have proven extremely damaging to Corso at trial but for the intervening events which couldn't have been predicted at the conclusion of the hearings. They constituted strong corroboration of Orlando's testimony, and circumstantial evidence of guilt. But it didn't work out that way.

Significantly, I also reached the conclusion that the police had probable cause to arrest Corso on April 3, 1984. In a decision published on June 4, 1985, I agreed "...that the police possessed the requisite 'reasonable cause' to believe that the defendant had committed the murder of Archimedes Cervera on June 16, 1979." I was by then still a firm believer in the credibility of unimpeachable police witnesses. Thus I wrote:

> ...the court gives full credence to the uncontroverted testimony of several police officers who were called by the people or the defendant. The defendant chose not to avail himself of the opportunity to testify in his own behalf to contradict the police version of the events in question, and the police testimony was sufficiently consistent to support their credibility.[12]

At the conclusion of the hearings, the score was People-9, Defense-0, and it looked like the results of the trial were a foregone conclusion despite the seeming incredibility of Orlando's testimony. I had no idea that in just two short weeks I was to begin a public battle with the office of the District

Attorney which would last for years, and which resulted in the political demise of an appointed county executive, an appointed police commissioner, the elected district attorney, as well as countless associates and subordinates within the ranks of their offices, and finally in the demise of my judicial career.

In the eyes of many my role suddenly changed from that of law enforcement apostle to informer, whistleblower and Judas-like pariah. This role change began quietly on June 14, 1985 with the statement of David Clayton that he believed that his client's constitutional rights were violated by the improper withholding of certain material which was demanded from the prosecutor pursuant to existing law—commonly known as "Brady material." This is information in the prosecution file which might tend to show that a defendant is not guilty of the crime charged.

For the first time, the name of Salvatore Avellino was uttered in the case. In a report dated June 25, 1979, Detective Thomas Mongan, a member of Halverson's team, described an interview of county legislator Michael Grant during which he developed important leads involving persons with possible motives to be involved in the murder of Cervera.

...LEGISLATOR MICHAEL GRANT...stated that the subject, ARCHIMEDES CERVERA, also owed him money; that he was paid certain amounts over a period of time. That there was still an outstanding debt with he and ARCHIMEDES CERVERA. That the subject was well liked by all parties concerned and that he did owe money to all his friends, good mutual friends. Unfortunately, he never paid too many of them back at any time. MR. GRANT was contacted in reference to subjects he may suspect of either participating in or being involved in the murder of ARCHIMEDES CERVERA. It was ascertained that the following subjects were listed as suspects: SAL AVELLINO of Salem Carting, and JOE GALLO, a relative of SAL AVELLINO. It was further ascertained that monies were owed to SAL AVELLINO by ARCHIMEDES CERVERA. That he and other subjects have been known to be involved possibly in the murder of APONTE and GONZALEZ, who were murdered in Kennedy Airport a few years ago. These subjects, APONTE and GONZALEZ, were also involved in the sanitation field, along with SAL AVELLINO. They also created problems and had to be removed, because of the disruptance (sic) of the sanitation field. When GALLO was questioned at the funeral of ARCHIMEDES CERVERA by LEG. GRANT, he advised MR. GRANT that his bill was still outstanding. That he hadn't been paid of (sic) ARCHIMEDES CERVERA.

There are several other subjects who were suspected of possibly killing or having something to do with the killing of ARCHIMEDES CERVERA, and they are as follows:

FRANK LOREN, a former associate of Cervera.

ANGEL RODRIGUEZ, recently released from jail, in unknown location. That he had served recently in jail for a period of 30 days for unknown charges. This subject frequents the office of ARCHIMEDES CERVERA, and is known to the secretary of MICHAEL GRANT and the secretary of CERVERA.

Additional information will be developed by this detective in conversations with MR. MICHAEL GRANT, and should be made a part of this report.

Investigation continuing.[13]

Not another report or memorandum was ever generated by any of the investigating homicide detectives on the subject of Avellino or any of the other listed "suspects," although there was an entire team of detectives following leads and interviewing prospective witnesses in a major, highly publicized, professional hit. Although it was the prosecution's theory that Corso was hired to eliminate Cervera, to my knowledge, not another soul was ever targeted in the extensive homicide investigation, and no one else was ever indicted as a co-conspirator.

The next report written by anyone was on December 16, 1979 on the subject of a trip to Florida by Halverson, which he took with District Attorney Patrick Henry and Detective Lieutenant Robert Dunn, who later became commanding officer of the homicide squad, but who at that time was assigned to the D.A.'s office in connection with a corruption investigation involving the infamous southwest sewer district. According to Halverson, he went to speak to a criminal defense attorney named Al Krieger about a Memorial Day meeting in 1979 between Medina, Borrero and others. Although he had nothing to do with the Cervera murder investigation, Dunn sat in at the meeting with Krieger.*

Dunn was seated in the back of the courtroom during Halverson's testimony. It was almost necessary to exclude him from the courtroom since I had no idea where the questioning would lead us, and he might have become a witness. As it turned out, the cross-examination went nowhere. Halverson had no notes, and he professed a very limited recollection of what had transpired during the Florida trip.

****

On July 24, 1985, Lieutenant Dunn took it upon himself to address a nine page memorandum to Deputy Inspector Joseph Farnitano, Commanding Officer of the Major Crimes Bureau. It was, Dunn said, a response to a decision which I rendered on July 19 about an outstanding drug possession charge against Peter Corso. In his memo, written as the C.O. of the homicide squad, he accused me of an "attack at the conduct of the police." Contrary to my findings, and the subsequent findings of the State Commission of Investigations, he "found extraordinary quantities of handwritten investigative notes (hundreds of pages by recollection)...and numbers of Supplementary Reports, some exceeding five pages in length." He justified Halverson's failure to document his investigation as a "desire to protect the federal agents who were cooperating 'unofficially.'" It is referred to as a "judgment call." Dunn, likewise, defended the credibility of Michael Orlando as a witness upon whom the "Federal Bureau of Investigation...spent six years, millions of dollars...." He must have been credible, according to Dunn, since he had "a complete task force of agents acting on information provided by MICHAEL ORLANDO." "....several Organized Crime figures, and Secretary of Labor of the United States RAYMOND DONOVAN have been indicted and are awaiting trial in

Bronx County on the weight of information provided by the very same (using my words), questionable confidential informant...."[14] Although Lt. Dunn certainly could not predict the outcome of any of these indictments, every person accused by Michael Orlando was subsequently acquitted, in Suffolk and the Bronx.

While the memorandum was addressed to a deputy inspector, its addressee was clearly intended to be Judge Stuart Namm who was never sent a copy, but who fortuitously obtained one by means of a subpoena served in a subsequent criminal proceeding. This enlightening document continues:

> JUSTICE NAMM states in several instances that there were other persons who had "equal" or "more motive to kill..." MR. CERVERA. This is not so, but at the very least is an extremely speculative statement. Who had more reason to kill MR. CERVERA, JUSTICE NAMM, and how and upon what impervious source does this startling, seemingly unequivocal statement emanate?[15]

Michael Grant and his alleged sources are disposed of in one terse, but rambling, paragraph which contained more written information on the Grant connection than the entire homicide investigation file.

> The information provided by LEGISLATOR MICHAEL GRANT who is referred to as not having "an axe to grind," in which MR. GRANT speculated that several persons who MR. CERVERA owed money wanted to "break his legs" is just that, pure rhetoric on the part of MR. GRANT. Investigators who have interviewed MR. GRANT on other occasions regarding other matters are accustomed to his colorful speculations. To state that MR. GRANT had no axe to grind is to completely ignore the fact that one of the possible co-conspirators in this Murder (sic), HENRY MEDINA, was acquainted with MR. GRANT and, in fact, his nephew GUS MEDINA was a friend of MR. GRANT and manager of MR. GRANT's restaurant, the Fife and Drum.

The statement of an "independent witness with no apparent axe to grind" is not necessarily so, and certainly the description "independent witness" is not true based upon MR. GRANT's own admissions of CERVERA's indebtedness to him (subject of a five-page Supplementary Report). JUDGE NAMM again, on page 11, refers to MR. GRANT as "reasonably reliable source." In who's [sic] opinion? MR. GRANT was not "independent" of CERVERA's associations, was certainly not fond of CERVERA, and, in fact, was not fond of several of the persons he suggested as suspects, two of whom, GALLO and AVELLINO, by his own admission, had thwarted his ambition to form a garbage unit for the Brentwood School District.[16]

Newsday, and its daily reporting of the Corso trial, in Lt. Dunn's opinion, was jointly responsible with Judge Namm for the acquittal of Peter Corso.

Too, *Newsday's* daily portrayal of the proceedings were so sensationalized and so rife with extemporaneous statements as to create an impression that the Police Department was on trial and not MR. CORSO. A very sad tale indeed. I must wonder at the confusion in the minds of the jurors who witnessed the proceedings and could not help but sense the not-even-subtle disembowelment of the People's case within the Courthouse and prominently depicted on Long Island's only daily paper. What other conclusion was available to them?[17]

In Lt. Dunn's opinion: "...fairness and impartiality..." in this case "...have been muddied, clearly by other motivations." However, my alleged motivations remain undefined to this date. But, Detective Lt. Dunn's motivation for writing this memorandum was clearly defined in the final paragraph:

> I now believe, when re-reading my notes, that JUDGE NAMM and I have something in common. Both memorandums reveal two angry men. I submit, sir, subjective or objective?[18]

Even as I read this document over and over again in an attempt to understand its contents, I consciously suppressed feelings of hostility towards Lt. Dunn. His tenure as commanding officer of the Homicide Squad was short-lived. In 1986, he was relieved of his command. But this action like so many others, according to the police department, was simply a routine transfer and bore no relation to the state's investigation by the SIC.[19]

****

Six months elapsed, suspects were targeted and ruled out, leads were discounted, meetings were held with representatives of the F.B.I., but police files were devoid of any information in this regard. The public battles between Judge Namm and the prosecution began.

> THE COURT:...I find it incredible that a county legislator would give the name of a prospective suspect who is connected with two murders and it goes nowhere, but there is no report. That's hard to swallow, frankly.
>
> MR. JABLONSKI: Judge, I can only tell you what's there.
>
> THE COURT: ...between June 25th, 1979 and December 16th, 1979, the Suffolk County Police Department doesn't even have one Supplementary Report concerning the investigation of the death of Archimedes Cervera. I find that absolutely incredible as a matter of law, and I cannot believe it, and I'm going to have to conduct a hearing...I cannot believe that this...that this police department, the Homicide Squad, would allow six months to go by without any reports being filed...I'm not pointing fingers. I'm not accusing anybody, but I think I have to get to the bottom...
>
> MR. JABLONSKI: Well, Judge, you say you're not pointing fingers but you've already found certain things incredible as a matter of law, so you are pointing fingers and you have made decisions. You're putting yourself in a position of an investigation, what you might have done, what you're saying other people should have done. You're not a police officer. You're not in the Homicide Squad. You're doing what Judge Stuart Namm would do in that situation.[20]

The lines were drawn, and I had a serious problem on my hands, a problem which could have been alleviated if Jablonski had seen fit to turn over these reports to the defense at the appropriate time. I was forced to conduct another hearing out of the presence of the jury with the risk attendant that the jury would read about these proceedings in the daily newspaper despite my well meaning admonition not to read or listen to anything in the media about the case.

This was not the last time that a prosecutor forced me into the unhappy position where I would have to suspend a jury trial in order to conduct an evidentiary hearing outside the presence of the jury. In a few short months, history repeated itself in the trial of James Diaz for the brutal rape and murder of Maureen Negus, the Port Jefferson Station mother and Stony Brook University Hospital nurse.

Although I now had more pending homicide cases on my calendar than any other judge of the court, this was my very first experience with the homicide team supervised by Det. Sgt. Kenneth McGuire and the legendary duo of detectives Halverson and Rafferty. The encounter was enlightening since it gave me some real insight into the cavalier manner in which the elite homicide squad conducted its business. To their credit, they were brutally frank in describing the way in which the squad went about the investigation of what can only be described as a major homicide involving the gangland style death of a prominent attorney.

As the following trial excerpt shows, their approach may have been brutally frank, but yet shocking to the uninitiated listener:

> MR. CLAYTON: You say you have Avellino as a suspect in other murders, sir?
> DET. RAFFERTY: Yes.
> MR. CLAYTON: And you say that you have communicated with members of the Rackets Bureau...
> DET. RAFFERTY: Yes.
> MR. CLAYTON: Regarding Salvatore Avellino.
> DET. RAFFERTY: Yes, I have.
> MR. CLAYTON: Did you file any reports or make any

written reports or memoranda regarding your conversations or investigations?

DET. RAFFERTY: When I talked to other detectives you mean?

MR. CLAYTON: When you were in the process of eliminating, as you said, Salvatore Avellino as a suspect in this homicide, did you file any reports in written form with regard to that elimination?

DET. RAFFERTY: No, I did not.

MR. CLAYTON: Did you make any written notes whatsoever of the conversations that you had with individuals in reaching that determination?

DET. RAFFERTY: No, I did not...

MR. CLAYTON: Did you interview any other individuals other than Rackets Bureau detectives with regard to eliminating Salvatore Avellino as a suspect in the murder of Archie Cervera...?

DET. RAFFERTY: I talked to an informant, a confidential informant about him, also.

MR. CLAYTON: Did you make any reports concerning the results of that interview?

DET. RAFFERTY: Absolutely not.

MR. CLAYTON: None?

DET. RAFFERTY: No.

MR. CLAYTON: Is that a registered confidential informant?

DET. RAFFERTY: No, I don't believe he is.

MR. CLAYTON: Is he your confidential informant?

DET. RAFFERTY: Certainly is. He's mine.

MR. CLAYTON: Okay. Did you notify your superiors of the results of this conversation with the confidential informant?

DET. RAFFERTY: I may have.

MR. CLAYTON: You may have?

DET. RAFFERTY: I may have and I may have not.

MR. CLAYTON: You don't know?

DET. RAFFERTY: I don't recall specifically.

MR. CLAYTON: What did the confidential informant tell you, sir?

DET. RAFFERTY: Based on what he had, that Avellino was not involved in this.

MR. CLAYTON: But my question, sir, is what did the informant tell you in the summer of 1979?

DET. RAFFERTY: Specifically, I don't recall, but after my conversation with him I came away with the feeling and the knowledge that it was his opinion that Avellino was not involved in the homicide with Cervera.

MR. CLAYTON: Is there any indicia in the official records of the Homicide Squad...which would point to and verify the existence of this so-called confidential informant?

DET. RAFFERTY: Oh, there are things that-nothing in the Homicide Squad but there are things that would-I would tell the Judge who it is in Chambers or in camera or whatever you want. I have no objection to that.

MR. CLAYTON: That's very nice of you to volunteer that, sir, but I'd like to inquire further if I might. I asked you the question, sir, is there anything in either of the Homicide Squad or the Suffolk County Police Department which would verify the existence of this confidential informant?

DET. RAFFERTY: Not in the department, no. There is nothing in the police department.

MR. CLAYTON: So that we're absolutely certain, sir, from the period of the latter part of June, 1979 and the end of...June 25th, 1979 up to and including December 16th, 1979 with respect to the homicide of Archimedes Cervera, a killing which has been described as a gangland execution, there is not a single, solitary official police report made and filed in the Suffolk County Homicide Squad files concerning the investigation?

DET. RAFFERTY: That's correct.

THE COURT: Isn't it his function in a homicide investigation as the lead detective to file the reports?

DET. RAFFERTY: No.

THE COURT: That's not the function of the lead detective?

DET. RAFFERTY: Not necessarily no, sir. Detective Halverson didn't file many reports probably in his whole career and in this case when I was working with him I was covering the reports.

THE COURT: You were filing the reports here, not Halverson as the lead detective?

DET. RAFFERTY: That's true, yes.

THE COURT: That was—his practice was not to file reports, is that it? You say he didn't file very many.

DET. RAFFERTY: He wasn't big into writing reports.

THE COURT: He wasn't report oriented?

DET. RAFFERTY: That's exactly correct."[21]

It was during the course of Rafferty's examination at the special hearing that I learned of the existence of Cervera's telephone answering machine and the dictating machine which were operating on the date of the murder. The discovery arose from an almost innocuous entry in one of Rafferty's notes which read: "Recording Sal Avellino 567-6670."

THE COURT: Okay. And what did that mean when you put the notation in there?

DET. RAFFERTY: I may have gotten that off his recording, Cervera's answering machine.

THE COURT: Does that recording still exist?

DET. RAFFERTY: I don't know.[22]

Incredibly, Jablonski, who was responsible for the prosecution, professed to have no knowledge of the existence of either the answering machine or its contents. He accepted the responsibility of conducting a hasty investigation to determine their whereabouts. His investigation revealed that both the machine and its recorded cassette were publicly auctioned by the Property Bureau in March 1984 to an unsuspecting innocent purchaser who had no idea of the value of what he bought. The recorder and its contents were auctioned by the police despite the fact that the recorder was tagged as "evidence" in a murder case which was still pending.

On June 24, during the course of the hearing, we finally listened to the recorded contents of the cassette. Some of its contents were apparently intact despite the passage of time. According to Jablonski, the purchaser was not certain whether he had used the tape for a day or two before replacing it with "a better quality tape."*

Among other things were three recorded messages from persons who might have been considered suspects at the earliest stages of the investigation, each with a possible motive to hurt Archie Cervera. There were three separate messages:

> Hello, Denise. This is Sal Avellino. Would you please call me back? 567-6670. Thank you.
>
> Archie, this is Henry Medina. This is Saturday, 11 o'clock. Please call me. I'm at my home. Thank you.
>
> This is Henry Medina. I missed your call, and I was trying to reach you during the day or this evening. Okay. Thank you.*

Representatives of the Suffolk County Police Department involved in the investigation were also present on the tape. The murder was of such importance that the Commissioner himself was on the wire.

> Captain Holdorf there? Yes. Detective Cassidy. Is Captain Holdorf there? Who's calling? The Commissioner. Hang on, sir.*

Although this call was apparently being recorded for no apparent reason, the recovered cassette tape was devoid of any further conversation between the police commissioner and Capt. Holdorf, or anyone else. Either the machine was turned off before Holdorf responded, or this conversation was obliterated by an unknown person or persons for reasons known only to them.

One can only speculate why persons who should have been under suspicion would be calling Archie within hours of his death, and on the very day of his murder. Such a call could certainly serve as an alibi for one who might become the target of an intensive homicide investigation. It could provide the perfect cover. It served to place a suspect at some other place than the scene of the crime. But in the case of Avellino and Medina, there was no evidence of any such intensive investigation by the homicide squad. Once Corso was fingered by Orlando, they were above suspicion as far as Halverson and Rafferty were concerned. Despite the fact that they believed that Corso was hired to eliminate Cervera, no co-conspirator was ever targeted or arrested!

Moreover, Sgt. McGuire and Halverson, in response to very pointed cross-examination about Halverson's failure to keep notes or make reports, insisted that this was just another homicide out of many pending that had gone cold in the summer and fall of 1979.*

Would the Commissioner of Police have been personally interested in just another homicide? One can only conclude that this was a very important investigation which called for the investigative talents of the most experienced homicide detective and his partner, who himself became a living legend until the trial of James Diaz.

In the case of Halverson, there were admittedly no notes taken. But another member of the team, detective Mongan, who was suffering the ravages of cancer in the summer of 1979, was a horse of another color. It was clear from the lengthy report of his conversation with county legislator Michael Grant that he was not adverse to filing reports or taking notes.

Grant was called as a witness by Clayton to give his version of his meeting with Mongan and to discuss the suspicions which he had conveyed to him at the very inception of the investigation.

THE COURT: Was there ever any conversation between you and Detective Mongan about any involvement of Archimedes Cervera in the Sanitation business?

GRANT: Yes. There was another person that had a business in Brentwood, Joe Campanella, and he got involved in the carting business in Florida, and I don't know what Mr. Cervera's involvement was, whether he was representing Mr. Campanella as an attorney or if he was a partner. I don't know that. But, I know that Mr. Campanella—the business went bad and Mr. Cervera owed Mr. Campanella quite a sum of money.

THE COURT: Did you give this information to Detective Mongan? The Witness: Yes, I did.

THE COURT: By the way, this first meeting that you had with Detective Mongan, how long would you say that lasted?

GRANT: A couple of hours.

THE COURT: By the way, the first time you met with Detective Mongan, did you notice whether he was taking notes?

GRANT: Yes, he was.

THE COURT: How about the second time you met with him, was he taking notes?

GRANT: Yes, he was.

THE COURT: Do you remember what he was taking notes on?

GRANT: Yeah, a yellow pad. In fact, I believe the first time he wrote out a statement and I signed the statement.[23]

Because of Mongan's serious physical condition, the preliminary hearing was adjourned until the trial. It was convened on July 11 in the detective's home at his bedside. In attendance were plainclothes representatives of the police department who, for some unknown reason, were clearly stationed at his home. During the course of the questioning, which I conducted myself as delicately as possible under the circumstances, the plainclothes guards were always in attendance. Since his residence had now become, for all intents and purposes, a public courtroom, a representative of *Newsday* was allowed in, over police protest, to cover the proceedings.

Mongan claimed to have no recollection of taking any notes although he had authored a very detailed report. He also denied that he ever took a written statement from Michael Grant. Clayton, who had worked with Mongan when he was a prosecutor, as a singular act of human kindness out of sympathy for his sick friend, declined to cross-examine this very important witness. It was clear that it would have been a fruitless gesture under the circumstances. Mongan wasn't going to change his story.

Unfortunately, no notes ever surfaced and no written statement was ever produced by the people.*

****

For the time being, the Michael Grant incident was a dead issue. My attention was diverted back to the question before the jury, the guilt or innocence of Peter Corso. While the testimony of Detectives Halverson and Rafferty provided a colorful backdrop against which police conduct and credibility were to be judged, there was no doubt that the People's case would sink or float with the testimony of the admitted murderer and career criminal, schoolteacher Michael Orlando. All else seemed inconsequential when the People's star witness took his place upstage center escorted by members of the FBI.

The jury, representatives of the news media, and criminal defense lawyers for the Bronx "Tumcon" defendants, all with pencil and pad in hand, silently greeted the bearded Orlando with an air of great expectation. The drama and impact of his incredible testimony in an unforgettable five hours in the witness box disappointed no one.

Under direct examination by Jablonski, this BBA graduate of St. John's University admitted to bookmaking, loansharking, armed robbery, arson, burglary, hijacking, receiving stolen property and murder in much the same way that a carpenter might describe the business of cutting boards and nailing walls. His testimony provided much greater detail under the friendly questioning of the prosecutor than when he was previously called at the hearing as a hostile witness by the defense.

He and Corso were friends since 1975. Both came from the Williamsburgh section of Brooklyn, a neighborhood of working class tenement residents. They socialized together both in Suffolk County and lower Manhattan where Corso lived on Avenue A within the confines of an Italian ghetto. It was on Avenue A between East 3rd and East 4th Streets, in November 1979, when Corso allegedly told him about his contract killing of a lawyer in Suffolk County.

He recalled that a mutual friend, Patsy Fucco, had just driven by in a car, when Corso volunteered that Fucco was still a "slob." He lived, Pete said, like a "slob" in prison. To that he gratuitously added that he had accepted a "contract." Their "paison" Patsy went along with him on the kill. The payment, he said, was made in a brown paper bag. When it came to split the money, the "slob" couldn't find the bag or the money. The contract originated with a guy known as "Spanish Raymond" Marquez. The lawyer, he said, was being paid back for not returning a legal fee after someone went to jail because of him.*

Corso said that he made an appointment to see the lawyer, but when he arrived in the lawyer's office, there were other persons present in the waiting room and he had been seen. He left the office and asked Patsy or "Moe," another associate, who was also along for the ride, to execute the contract. But it was to be Corso's kill. He waited downstairs for a while, returned to the office, and sat down to discuss the case with Archie. He removed a .32 from his attache case, attached a silencer, and shot the lawyer once in the chest, twice in the eyes and once in the mouth.*

Orlando related Corso's alleged admissions of a cold-blooded contract murder of a stranger in just as cold, matter-of-fact tones. Why not? He had once been a licensed embalmer, and he, Orlando, admittedly murdered one Salvatore Frascone with a .32 provided by his boss, a Bronx meat-dealer named Masselli, for whom he was simply doing a favor.

The execution of Frascone was accomplished with only three shots from a distance of six inches—one to the back of the head, one to the back of the neck and one in the back. The favor was requested at 7:00 pm for a murder which was committed at 11:00 pm that same night. This was while Orlando was on the payroll of the F.B.I. as a paid informant. It was a murder for which he was never prosecuted, although his agents in the F.B.I. were aware of his involvement when he listed his lifetime of criminality.* But they weren't interested in murder. They were interested in netting political figures like Secretary of Labor Raymond Donovan, and State Senator Joseph Galiber, an extremely successful African-American politico.

Orlando was well-paid for the execution—immunity from prosecution by his law enforcement protectors, and a light blue Oldsmobile "98" from his mob connected benefactor. He lived in the best of all possible worlds. He was being paid by the taxpayers and the "wise guys."

While Orlando exuded great confidence throughout Jablonski's direct examination, his value as a witness seemed to diminish right before our eyes under the relentless cross-examination of Pete Mayer. It didn't hurt to have confronted Orlando once before during the preliminary hearings. The obvious strategy was to avoid any discussion of the Cervera murder—to divert the jury's attention from the guilt of Corso to the credibility of the People's star witness. As Orlando would go, so would go the People's case against Peter Corso. Mayer slowly took him step by step through his "life of crime." Painstakingly, he was asked to describe all of the gory details of the murders of two other mob victims, Salvatore "Sallie" Frascone and Samuel Feinberg.

Unlike the Frascone murder, he couldn't get Orlando to admit to the murder of Feinberg, who was shot twice in the back of the head from the back seat of his own automobile with Orlando, his friend, seated alongside in the front passenger's seat. But he did admit that the .32 used in the murder by Tony "T" Turano and Joe "The Cat" Sylvestri was then given to him. He claimed that he emptied the remaining rounds and took the weapon home.*

The jury was being asked to consider whether it was mere coincidence that a .32 was used in the assassination of Archie Cervera. Mayer took every opportunity to create the inference that Orlando was as capable as Corso of committing the Cervera murder. No felonious stone was left unturned in the effort to paint a vivid picture of a ruthless, opportunistic, habitual criminal whom the jury was being asked to rely upon in their judgment of the criminality of Peter Corso—a ruthless criminal who was subsidized by taxpayer dollars, and who was granted a cloak of immunity from prosecution in exchange for his cooperative testimony.

The cross-examination was not as lengthy as it might have been considering the wealth of information which Orlando claimed to possess. Yet it was extremely effective and ended on a very damaging note for the prosecution. Orlando was forced to admit that his crimes were too numerous to recall in detail. Nevertheless, he took great pride in admitting that he always possessed a weapon and that he "committed more than one burglary a month" over a period of twenty years.* Perhaps it wasn't good enough for the *Guinness Book of World Records*, but it painted a sordid picture of a sorry human being.

Jablonski's attempt to rehabilitate his star witness in a twenty minute redirect examination seemed futile at best. The People's case was in shambles. The testimony of the remaining witnesses, which included Rafferty and Halverson and a civilian witness, who attempted to put Corso in Cervera's office on the morning of his murder, was largely anti-climactic. However, it gave Mayer the opportunity to cast further serious doubt upon the homicide investigation and the manner in which it was carried out by Halverson and his successor, Dennis Rafferty, and their cohorts.

At the conclusion of the People's case, the die was cast, and an acquittal seemed to be the only logical result, whether Corso was truly guilty or not. The prosecution had obviously not met its burden of proving guilt beyond a reasonable doubt. The defense team seemed so confident of this result that they chose not to put in a case. They rested upon the People's evidence. So certain was I that Corso would be acquitted that I decided to reserve decision on a defense motion to dismiss the indictment because of prosecutorial misconduct until after verdict. If I granted that application, there would be a prosecution right to appeal with a possible second trial. If the jury acquitted, there could be no appeal. There would be finality.

On July 2, 1985, at 6:05 pm, after less than six hours of deliberations, the foreman of the jury announced the verdict of "not guilty." The books could now be closed on the first chapter of the trials of Peter Corso. But, the story was far from over.

Before they left the courthouse, some of the jurors were merciless in their condemnation of the police's handling of the Corso case. One, a sixty-five-year-old operating engineer, was quoted by *Newsday* as saying, "I'm not a bleeding heart. This guy may have been this or that, but to hang this charge on him, it stinks. I think they should take the Suffolk police and teach them how to conduct surveillance and do reports...This guy Orlando, he talks to the federal program as an informant, and yet he murders and he kills. I don't understand it."

Another juror who was critical of the police investigation commented to the press: "It wasn't much for a murder case." Two jurors were observed shaking hands with Corso's brother, while another hugged Corso's wife and a fourth drove away honking his car horn and signaling a "V-for-victory" to Corso's relatives.[24] It was not the last time that Suffolk jurors would criticize the police investigation of a Suffolk County homicide. The trial and acquittal of James Diaz for the rape-murder of Maureen Negus followed on the heels of the Corso trial. In the interim between the two trials, I was involuntarily drawn into the thick of the 1985 District Attorney's race between Patrick Henry and Robert Gottlieb. The homicide squad and the District Attorney's office would not rest until there was vindication for their handling of the Corso case.

****

March 22,1988. Courtroom of Suffolk County Supreme Court Justice George F.X. McInerney. (The following occurred in chambers.)

THE COURT: What's your situation with him? Who do you represent?

MR. GUCCIARDO: I only came in as far as the plea negotiations were concerned with him, not with Mr. McGuiness, no, through Mr. Corso and his brother, Mr. Corso asked me to get involved in the plea negotiations. I've discussed it with Mr. McGuiness.

THE COURT: Who do you represent?

MR. GUCCIARDO: Peter Corso.

THE COURT: Fine.

MR. PERINI (Chief Assistant District Attorney): He came in as a consultant on the plea.

MR. MCGUINESS: First of all, I think that if you made certain agreements with Ray, these ought to be spelled out to Pete in toto and tell him what he's got to do and what he doesn't have to do because right now he's in the dark as to what he's got to do.

MR. PERINI: I'm going to put on the record, Judge—Peter Corso is not in here, I think whatever is said in here is going to be published in front of him, and very simply there were three prerequisites to my offers on the package deal.

He had to [one] admit to Archie Cervera's murder, which he did. He told that he received $15,000 for killing Archie Cervera.

Two, he had to fully admit to the cocaine distribution ring. He did that.

Three, he had to waive all rights to appeal which he did. In exchange for those three items his brother was getting probation, his wife was getting probation, his son was getting a misdemeanor and a conditional discharge. He was to get 12 to life. He was to die in jail. That was the plea bargain. I'm going to put that on the record and publish that in court today.

If he has any objection to any one of those items, then there is no deal and we will litigate the pulling of the pleas as to the other defendants because if he wants to go to trial, I want to try everybody.

THE COURT: You can't pull the plea on a defendant I've sentenced already unless it's on the record.

MR. PERINI: No one else has been sentenced judge, that's why Peter has to go first.

THE COURT: I thought I sentenced...

MR. PERINI: Carlos Herrera, that's it, maybe his girlfriend, and we're going to have to litigate whether that can be pulled or not. I don't think it can.

THE COURT: Unless it's on the record.

MR. PERINI: We'll have to check the record. I will have to order it.

THE COURT: I'll tell you gentlemen my situation. I do not enter into plea bargains. I take it with all things waived and everything else. So you're talking to the wrong guy when you tell me in effect that I have some concern with anything that goes on here.

MR. MCGUINESS: I have to understand something. I made that statement based on my information as to what was going on. My information admittedly was very sketchy because I wasn't privy to these negotiations that were carried on. My client has been in the dark.

THE COURT: I'm trying to tell you this has nothing to do with me. I don't enter into it. What I'm bound by is what's on the record, by your client's waiving all of the things that I asked, that's where you are. Whatever you work out with him, that's something else. That's not my bailiwick. I know I have sentenced two women, I think one or two.

MR. PERINI: You sentenced Herrera's girlfriend, I forget her name, his girlfriend, the gal he was living with at the time of the arrest.

THE COURT: He took the rap for her.

MR. PERINI: Michelle Kirchner. I don't think you've sentenced any other women that were part of this. Michelle was, Carmella who's out there awaiting sentencing was, I'm not sure...I'm not sure and I don't think anyone is sure what Corso is going to do.

MR. MCGUINESS: He's taking the plea.

THE COURT: What plea?

MR. MCGUINESS: The 12 to life.

MR. PERINI: I'm going to put all the conditions on the record and if he has a problem with any one of them, there is no plea.

MR. MCGUINESS: I have to understand, make this very clear in my mind. You're putting the conditions, you're not asking him to stand up in open court and say he whacked Archie?

MR. PERINI: I'm going to put that on the record.

MR. MCGUINESS: Okay, you're going to say it.

MR. PERINI: I'm going to say it and I'm going to say that he told the world, he said that to six different people that I know, all law enforcement. If he denies he did it, there is no deal because he had to admit truthfully to doing it.

MR. MCGUINESS: He's going to stand there with his mouth shut.

MR. PERINI: And accept the plea, fine.

MR. GUCCIARDO: This I didn't understand before. You're not asking him to come in now and admit to Archie Cervera's murder.

MR. MCGUINESS: He will say it, not Peter.

MR. PERINI: I'm going to rely on the facts as to what Peter told myself and several federal agents and he was supposed to give truthful testimony concerning the Archie Cervera's murder and he admitted to doing it, he admitted to getting $15,000, and he admitted it happened the way the trial testimony came in.

MR. GUCCIARDO: Okay.

MR. PERINI: If that is not truthful, then we will not go

forward with the pleas and that's that.

MR. MCGUINESS: Okay.

THE COURT: Wait a minute. If he stands quiet, does that satisfy you?

MR. PERINI: Yes."

(*The following occurred in open court*):

MR. MCGUINESS: Judge, at this time my client will withdraw his objection to having a camera in the courtroom.

THE COURT: All right, are you ready for sentencing, sir?

MR. MCGUINESS: Yes, judge.

MR. PERINI: Your Honor, before we go forward with the sentence there were certain prerequisites to the taking of this disposition and there were other defendants tied into the ultimate sentencing of Peter Corso. I want to put them on the record so that it's very clear and there is no misunderstanding at some future date concerning this plea. The first condition of the plea was that Peter Corso was to admit fully his guilt and his involvement in a cocaine distribution ring with one Carlos Herrera that included the importation of cocaine via the mails into Suffolk County for distribution, and he did that.

Secondly he was to admit or tell the truth, not admit, but give us a truthful recounting of what he knew about the murder of Archie Cervera.

MR. WALLER: I'm sorry to interrupt..."

MR. PERINI: Your Honor, he's not involved with Peter Corso at this point..."

(*The following occurred in chambers*):

THE COURT: Before we go any further. No one here as far as I'm concerned has a plea, you know this.

MR. WALLER: I know your policy, Judge. I just don't want to have you think that I'm going to get actively involved in this.

MR. WALLER:...there came a point in time when an understanding was reached, and I might say that I may have been the architect of that understanding in some ways with the district attorney's office. We came into chambers your Honor, and it was off the record, most of it because of very sensitive things...

THE COURT: Who do you represent?

MR. WALLER: Joseph Corso, the brother. The arrangements that Mr. McGuiness and Ray made or Mr. Gucciardo, I have nothing to do with at this stage other than that I hope it all works out, and we resolve the matter. One of the things that I have a problem with is security for my client's safety and his family. We have already received a number of threats...obviously Ray knows, Mr. Perini knows that the things that Mr. Corso indicated could be very serious things whether or not they're going to go further, whether the district attorney needs him for certain purposes...The problem is security for my clients, and I understand what Ray wants out of it and I'm opposing the things, what are we doing about my people?

MR. PERINI: You don't understand what's going to be said. You weren't privy. There is no statement concerning...there's one person's role in the Archie Cervera murder that will be published today and that is what he said about his involvement in that murder. There is no indication...

MR. WALLER: What about the other guy?

MR. PERINI: Nothing.

THE COURT: Just a minute. If I understand this, only Peter will be quoted.

MR. PERINI: Absolutely, and only as to his involvement.

MR. WALLER: They can get into my people, they can get to my people.

THE COURT: What is your problem?

MR. PERINI: I'm not going to say anything about your client. I'm not going to say anything what Peter did to kill Archie Cervera, nothing about who hired him other than the money he was paid.

MR. WALLER: Why didn't you let us know? I have to protect my client.

MR. PERINI: I have to talk to his lawyers.

THE COURT: They're not going to mention his client.

MR. PERINI: No, his client had nothing to do with it.

THE COURT: Does that solve it?

MR. PERINI: I'm going to put Peter Corso—his concern is that I'm going to put that Peter Corso cooperated with the federal government. Peter Corso did not cooperate with the federal government. I'll publish that if you like.

MR. MCGUINESS: Would you?

MR. KASE: I'd like that.

MR. PERINI: What he did was admit to his own role.

MR. WALLER: What happens, my people are at risk. They already know they're at risk. They're moving out of the jurisdiction.

MR. PERINI: Excuse me. What I will do, I will indicate that he was spoken to by the federal government. That he could be interviewed and if he cooperated, there may have been a recommendation of less than 12. He did not cooperate.

MR. MCGUINESS: They didn't even talk to him...

(*The following occurred in open court*):

THE COURT: Yes, sir.

MR. MCGUINESS: Judge, after first discussions and conferences in this case between myself and the court and the district attorney, my client at this time stands ready to proceed with his sentencing, and I believe the district attorney was in the middle of an allocution statement.

MR. PERINI: Before we go forward with the sentencing and the sentencing recommendation I am going to try and outline exactly what the plea bargain was because we have had two meetings in chambers now, we have had an intervention by co-defendants in this sentencing, and I want it very clear on the record so that there is no future attack on the sentence. As I stated earlier, the defendant, one of the conditions of the plea was the defendant was to admit truthfully his involvement in a cocaine distribution ring with one Carlos Herrera. He did that, and it had to do with the importation of a kilo a week of cocaine via the mails to Peter Corso and then its distribution. I will get into that at the actual sentencing statement.

Secondly he was to admit to his involvement if it was truthful, concerning the murder of one Archie Cervera, a matter in which he was the subject of a trial several years ago. Peter Corso in detail outlined his involvement in that murder stating that in fact he murdered Archie Cervera in Archie Cervera's office and received a sum of $15,000 for murder. That he did. Now if either of those statements are untrue, he should speak now and we will not go forward with this disposition.

MR. MCGUINESS: Judge, my client stands mute.

MR. PERINI: The third condition was he was to waive all rights to appeal. There was lengthy litigation on the court-authorized eavesdropping warrant. There is a recommendation of 12 to life sentence in this matter. They cannot be the subject of any appellate review. He has waived those rights. Those were the prerequisites to the plea.

In return for that the people are recommending a sentence of 12 years to life...Also his brother, Joseph Corso, received a probationary sentence, his wife, Carmella Cervone, is receiving a probationary sentence and his son is receiving a misdemeanor and a probationary sentence or a conditional discharge. That is the package. If there is any problems with any of that, I want it clear on the record now, and we'll withdraw our consent to this disposition.

MR. MCGUINESS: Judge, it is our understanding that this is the disposition.

MR. PERINI: At this time Your Honor, the people will file with the court a predicate felony statement....

THE COURT: Mr. Peter Corso, I have presented to me an instrument submitted by the people submitting that you are a predicate felon in that they recite that you were previously convicted in the United States District Court for the Southern District of New York on the 14th day of January, 1982, convicted of the crime of use of a telephone or facility to facilitate a conspiracy to distribute cocaine and that you were thereafter on the 24th day of June 1983 sentenced to two years incarceration.

If this is true, you must be treated as a predicate felon which means that the minimum of any sentence imposed on you must be at least half of the maximum instead of a third as is normal. This is the time for you to contest the truthfulness and accuracy of any one of these allegations in which case we'll have a hearing to determine whether or not they are true, and this is also the time to enter on the record any objections you may have to the constitutionality of this prior conviction.

THE DEFENDANT: It's true.

MR. MCGUINESS: It's true, judge.

MR. PERINI: He admits to being a predicate felon.

THE COURT: I adjudge you to be a predicate felon. Mr. McGuiness, do you have anything further to say?

MR. MCGUINESS: No, judge, I don't.

MR. PERINI: If I can just be heard, I would like to make a record before the defendant is sentenced. The people are recommending 12 years to life, a minimum of 12 with life as the maximum. This defendant is 66 years of age, he will not be eligible for parole until he is 78 years of age. We do this because of the defendant's background. The only time he has not committed crimes against society has been when he's been incarcerated. I stated earlier that he admitted to the very cold blooded act of assassination for $15,000. He tells us in great detail of opening an attache case, of screwing on a silencer and in his own words, of banging out Archie Cervera.

MR. MCGUINESS: I object to the district attorney going into certain details which have absolutely no relevancy to this plea. My client, as he says, admitted to him that he killed this attorney and that's the end of it.

THE COURT: Counsel, there's no plea here unless I sentence him, and normally one goes into the negatives of the other fellow's position.

MR. MCGUINESS: That's right. The negatives of this disposition on this case, not on a case that was settled years gone by.

THE COURT: Objection is overruled. Go ahead, sir.

MR. PERINI: While in jail awaiting trial for the killing of Archie Cervera, Peter Corso meets Carlos Herrera. Carlos Herrera was awaiting trial before your Honor in which I was the prosecutor. Herrera was ultimately convicted of importing and distributing of 54 pounds of cocaine, and you sentenced him to 25 years to life. While sitting in jail in Riverhead these men concocted a scheme to continue the sale of cocaine. Peter Corso being the outside man. Peter Corso receiving the cocaine that Carlos Herrera could arrange to be shipped to him, and in fact once he is acquitted of the murder, he comes out and starts dealing approximately a kilo of cocaine a week via the mails.

Carlos Herrera is doing an additional 10 years now. He is sentenced to 35 years to life for that crime.

Peter Corso now stands before you to be sentenced on the sale of cocaine. Peter Corso has engaged in crimes of greed, premeditated crimes against society's laws, against God's laws. Murder and distribution of drugs are the two most grievous crimes a person can commit in this state, in this world, and we think 12 years to life is a very reasonable sentence even in view of his age, your Honor. Thank you.

Counsel has stated that, and I want this very clear, so that there's no future attack on this plea also, that the 12 year to life could have been modified had there been meaningful cooperation by Peter Corso with federal authorities. In fact he admitted in detail to the killing of Archie Cervera but that was it, his role in it, to federal authorities. He did not meaningfully cooperate with anyone, so we are making no recommendation less than 12 years to life.

THE COURT: Mr. Corso, do you wish to be heard?

THE DEFENDANT: No, sir.

THE COURT: Peter Corso, for the crime of criminal possession of a controlled substance in the 2nd degree in satisfaction of indictment 1061-87, it is the judgment of this court that you be delivered to the custody of the New York State Department of Correction to serve an indeterminate period of incarceration therein. The minimum of such period not to be less than 12 years and the maximum thereof life.

I must say I cannot understand why not only you but your friends, never learn. I'm talking about Carlos Herrera. He's sent away 25 to life and then runs an operation from jail. It's incredible. Defendant is remanded...[25]

Peter Corso uttered a total of four words during that entire proceeding which must have lasted no less than one half hour. He never once admitted in open court to the murder of Archimedes Cervera, nor did the assistant district attorney present any written or recorded confession taken when Corso allegedly detailed his complete involvement in the Cervera murder to "federal authorities" and the district attorney's office. Yet on the following day, *Newsday* was emblazoned with bold headlines pronouncing that Corso confessed to the Cervera murder, together with a full color courtroom photo of Peter Corso in handcuffs with Archie Cervera's daughter, Dr. Rebecca Kane, seated in the front row of the courtroom. The headline read: "CORSO CONFESSES: Four Years After Acquittal, Admits He Killed Prominent Brentwood Lawyer in '79."[26]

The Suffolk County homicide squad and the district attorney's office now believed that they'd been vindicated. The *Newsday* story reported:

> ...Suffolk prosecutors and police hailed the plea as a vindication in their handling of a murder prosecution, which County Court Judge Stuart Namm blasted and held up as an example of shoddy police work. Officials yesterday said that it was Namm's bias against Suffolk police and prosecutors—rather than the case itself—that led the jury to acquit...

"We're never really vindicated," said Suffolk Det. Dennis
Rafferty, who ran the homicide investigation of the Cervera case
and was re-assigned from the homicide squad in the aftermath
of the acquittal. "He should be doing 25 years to life."

Newsday went on to report: "Namm described yesterday's events as 'too
incredible to comment on.'"[27]

You didn't have to be a legal expert to know that the events played out in
that courtroom, as described in the news media, were so bizarre as to defy
description within available legal precedent. Such an admission of guilt, if
that was what it was meant to be, could never withstand appellate scrutiny.
Corso actually plead guilty to the drug charge in January, but that plea
would have been struck if Corso was not willing to engage in the prosecutor's
charade in an obvious attempt to discredit the Corso verdict and the
presiding judge—Stuart Namm. It was an insult to the justice system, and
the only way he could be denied a reversal of the conviction was if the
appeals court sustained the "waiver" of appeal which Justice McInerney so
steadfastly required. Since that date, the Appellate Division has concluded
that there can be no appeal from such a waiver. Peter Corso is a cooked
goose. He will die in prison!

On the following day, March 24, 1988, a *Newsday* reporter, Joshua
Quittner, met with a usually close-mouthed Peter Corso for ninety minutes
in the Suffolk County Correctional Facility. Corso was far from close-
mouthed at this meeting. He took the opportunity to lash out at the Suffolk
police and district attorney's office. *Newsday* reported that Corso,

> ...neither admitted nor denied shooting Cervera. But he
> faulted the Suffolk police and district attorney's office for what
> he called shoddy police work that led to acquittal during the
> 1985 murder trial..."They got the fly, then they spun the web
> around him. The normal way is to spin the web and catch the
> fly," he said.
>
> "If anyone's to blame [for the acquittal], it's them, not
> Namm," he added, dismissing law-enforcement officials'

contention that the judge turned the jurors in the murder case against police and prosecutors....

"The people of Suffolk should wake up to what's going on. They're paying a lot of money for nothing," Corso said....

Asked why he thought prosecutors made the Cervera case a part of the plea bargain to the unrelated drug case, Corso replied: "Because they want Namm. They're knocking the hell out of Namm, which is what they wanted all along. You know, they have a feud."[28]

Newsday accurately reported that "Namm would not comment yesterday." When I was contacted by Quittner for my reaction to Corso's comments, my feeling was that Corso had said it all. There was no reason for me to discuss this in the press.

According to *Newsday*: "Raymond Perini, narcotics bureau chief of the Suffolk district attorney's office, called that assertion 'absolute nonsense...I've never even been in Namm's courtroom.'" True enough, he'd probably never been in my courtroom. But in 1988, Raymond Perini was the target of the state's investigation into illegal wiretapping by the narcotics squad of the police department, wiretapping, which the commission said, was sanctioned by Perini. It was I who was responsible for bringing the state's investigators into Suffolk County. Perini's response was disingenuous at best.

"We wanted to close the book on the homicide," Perini told *Newsday*. "Doesn't the victim's family have a right to know that the guy who committed the murder is behind bars?"[29]

In 1989, in its final report, the S.I.C., as a basis for its request for the appointment of a special prosecutor by Governor Cuomo, was not very kind to Perini and his accomplishments as a senior assistant district attorney:

> Based on the results of its investigation, the Commission is forced to conclude that Perini knowingly allowed, and indeed condoned, illegal wiretapping by the Interdiction Unit...the Commission believes that even in his role as prosecutor, Perini was irresponsible and grossly unprofessional....What this investigation

has revealed concerning Mr. Perini presents the startling, but thankfully rare, example of what can occur through the misuse and abuse of the tremendous power of a prosecutor....[30]

****

On March 22, 1988, the courtroom of the most senior judge handling criminal matters in Suffolk County was transformed into a Kafkaesque scene in an Alice in Wonderland world, where standing mute and choosing to remain silent represented an admission of guilt to murder; where the "publication" of a litany of criminality by a prosecutor represented, in his mind, vindication of a police department and district attorney's office which were under a dark cloud after being discredited by the State Commission of Investigations; and where a senior judge sat silently by as the prosecutor, who himself was under investigation by the Commission, controlled the dialogue in the courtroom because the judge didn't want to get "actively involved."

Did the judge believe that he could not be criticized or that his conscience could remain clear if he absolved himself of the whole bloody mess?

The subtlety of the bizarre events which took place in Justice McInerney's courtroom that day were not lost upon William Patterson who followed the proceedings from his dingy Sing Sing cell in the copy of *Newsday* paid for by Jeb Ladouceur, his would-be biographer. On March 26, Patterson addressed a two page letter to *Newsday*'s Carolyn Colwell who covered the Suffolk County courts. Copies were sent to me, the United States Attorney for the Eastern District of New York, the Governor's Criminal Justice Coordinator, the State Investigations Commission, the Suffolk County Executive, the majority and minority leaders of the Suffolk County Legislature and the executive editor of *Newsday*. To my knowledge, nobody responded to Patterson, whose letters were by then being simply taken as the ramblings of a disgruntled convicted murderer. Yet, although he was somewhat incorrect in his assessment of the nature of the legal proceeding which took place on March 22, he was perceptive enough to see through the charade. Thus, he wrote:

Dear Ms. Colwell:

I received an article that appeared in Newsday *on March 23, 1988, concerning the Corso case. Patrick Henry must have one hell of a hangover from his celebration, and his sides must hurt like hell from laughing over the fraud he has presented to the public. One stroke and he has undone all the good done by* Newsday, *the S.I.C., and Judge Namm.*

To show what a fraud this whole thing is I must cite a Section of law from the Criminal Procedure Law of New York. Under Section 220.50 it states 'Plea; entry of plea. (1) a plea to an indictment, other than one against a corporation, must be entered orally by the defendant in person…(3) If a defendant who is required to enter a plea to an indictment refuses to do so or remains mute, the court must enter a plea of not guilty to the indictment in his behalf.

Mr. Corso did not enter his plea orally but stood mute before Judge McInerney! By law, Judge McInerney could not accept this plea, but he did! Why? A judge of his time behind the bench surely must know how a plea must be accepted, so why did he allow this invalid plea to take place in order to discredit Judge Namm and the findings of the S.I.C., in collusion with Patrick Henry and the homicide department?

It must be noted that the only words spoken concerning Mr. Corso's plea were spoken by A.D.A. Perini. Mr. Perini is himself the subject of some question within the various investigations, so it is self-serving for him to discredit the S.I.C. and Judge Namm in any manner that he can come up with. What better method could he use than to promise Mr. Corso that nothing would be done to his family, all who faced major sentences, if Mr. Corso would just mouth the words of the District Attorney's office? Mr. Perini claimed this is what Mr. Corso did, but Mr. Corso did not do this in court, hence the plea is invalid but the District Attorney and homicide department reap the benefits of the publicity. Mr. Corso has said nothing, only the District Attorney's office has spoken, but the damage has been done to the efforts to clean up the corruption within Suffolk County! [31]

Bill Patterson, untrained in the law, did not recognize the nature of the procedure which had been used. But even an expert in criminal procedure could have been confused by the hybrid nature of this unprecedented sentencing. It took me several readings of the official transcript to fully grasp what had taken place. Peter Corso couldn't plead guilty because he'd already been acquitted of the murder. Yet the public perception would be the same as a guilty plea, and as Perini and Detective Rafferty said, it could serve to publicly vindicate the prosecution team in the Cervera murder. Justice McInerney should never have allowed such a charade to be orchestrated in his courtroom. His presence served as a judicial sanction to a meaningless quasi-judicial fiasco which had no recognition in existing law, but which was intended to serve as a media aided public relations show, TV cameras and all.

At long last, in April 1989, in a 199 page scathing final report which blasted the District Attorney, Patrick Henry, and many of his immediate subordinates, past and present, including Perini, the S.I.C. likewise described the procedure as "bizarre":[32]

> Finally, what can only be characterized as a most bizarre judicial proceeding occurred on March 22, 1988, in the case of People v. Corso, Indictment No. 1061-87, concerning a new and unrelated narcotics charge against Corso. On that day, a guilty plea was taken from Corso in a proceeding before Justice George F. X. McInerney on a narcotics charge. At that proceeding Corso stood mute after he was asked by the prosecutor, Raymond Perini, Chief of the Suffolk County District Attorney's Office Narcotics Bureau, whether he had murdered Cervera, with Perini stating on the record that Corso had described in detail how he was paid $15,000 to murder Cervera...In exchange for this "admission," which, even if Corso had assented, was legally useless in prosecuting Corso for murder due to his prior acquittal, the court approved Perini's "package" of recommendations, including that Corso's brother, son and ex-

wife be given probationary sentences for their roles in Corso's drug ring, and that Corso, then 66 years old, be sentenced to 12-years-to-life...The net result of this "bargain" was that in order to engineer what the District Attorney no doubt believed would somehow "vindicate" the Corso prosecutors, Perini and the District Attorney gave away far too much, and again allowed the guilty to escape imprisonment.[33]

Attached to the copy of William Patterson's letter was a short personal note on adhesive yellow memo paper:

Your Honor
For Your Info
Please Keep
Fighting!

TEN

Between Corso and Diaz

THE UNPREDICTABLE AND EXTREMELY UPSETTING occurrences in the Corso case forced me to make a very drastic decision which had far reaching consequences for myself and Suffolk County law enforcement. I had long since concluded that there had been probable cause to arrest Peter Corso for the murder of Archimedes Cervera, but what I had seen and heard in the spring and summer of 1985 gave me cause to question that conclusion. I was no longer convinced that there had, in fact, been sufficient probable cause. The only way that I could put my doubts to rest was to re-open the hearing. So I announced to the prosecutor and the defense team that before Corso could be tried on the pending drug charge, the prosecution would have to prove, once again, in the light of all that occurred, that the police were within their rights in arresting Peter Corso for murder. Little did I know then that this knee-jerk decision would cause the full wrath of the District Attorney's office to fall upon me.

The Corso jury reached its verdict in the early evening of July 2. I was so impressed by that verdict and the events which had preceded it that I took the unusual step of publicly informing the jury that despite their verdict, "I have heard things as a judge, I am not going to walk away from...like what happened to the recorder, why was it auctioned off, why there were so few police notes? Despite the trial and its ending now, these issues won't be settled until I issue a ruling...."*

Fortunately for all concerned, especially myself, it was the eve of a long holiday weekend. Lenore, and I couldn't wait to escape Long Island to visit our son, Gary, in Arlington, Virginia. We were leaving the verbal fireworks of Suffolk County for the visual fireworks on the Capitol Mall. The great Leonard Bernstein was conducting the National Symphony Orchestra, and the Beach Boys were slated to perform, despite the objection of James Watt, Ronald Reagan's very conservative Secretary of the Interior. We spent a peaceful weekend with our son and his future bride whom we met for the first time. Though I was in Washington, D.C., there was a hotly contested political campaign in Suffolk County and Patrick Henry was seething. Apparently, in his mind, I had besmirched the image of the police department, whose support he took for granted, and the reputation of the district attorney's office by my decision to re-open the Corso hearing.

On July 4, *Newsday* reported that the district attorney questioned whether I had jurisdiction to reopen the hearing. "I have to determine whether he has jurisdiction first," Henry said. "In fact, I don't think he has jurisdiction. And if there's no jurisdiction, we are not going to cooperate."[1] Despite his public protestations, he had to know there was jurisdiction to conduct the hearing. The drug charge was still pending on my calendar for trial. Yet that disingenuous comment was not the most disturbing aspect of the *Newsday* report which was given prominent play in all of its editions.

Robert Gottlieb, the Democratic candidate for District Attorney, saw this as an opportunity to make some political hay. He was quoted in *Newsday* as saying: "This is not just a police matter. The district attorney is in fact responsible to make sure at the beginning of a murder case that the detectives investigating the case are doing so professionally and thoroughly. This has not been done."[2]

Right then and there I was drawn into the fray. *Newsday* erroneously added that "...Gottlieb...was Namm's campaign manager when Namm was elected to his present post." Not only was Robert Gottlieb not my campaign manager when I became a County Court Judge, but since I was cross-endorsed by both major political parties, I conducted no campaign, raised no money and had no campaign manager. In fact, I wasn't certain whether I even knew Robert Gottlieb in 1982. But the inference to be had was clear. I was using the Corso case pulpit to foster the political ambitions of Robert Gottlieb!

I was convinced that Patrick Henry, or one of his cohorts, had planted that defamatory seed in the mind of a reporter who was probably too lazy or too busy to research the truth. It was no mere coincidence, I reasoned, that the article was full of Henry quotes: "We have an excellent homicide squad...Their work record speaks for itself. The fact that we didn't win this case was no big surprise, we can't manufacture evidence...But just because you don't have a sure winner is not a reason not to go to trial...When we have a prima facie case and a chance of prevailing, we have an obligation to go to trial."[3]

I was told after the fact that the reporter had attempted to reach me for comment and verification before writing the story but that I was unavailable to the press. Of course, I was unavailable. We were in Washington. We were enjoying a much needed respite in our nation's capital. Suffolk County, its police department, Peter Corso and Patrick Henry were the furthest things from my mind that weekend. We wanted out of that place. We needed a change of scenery and the company of our family. But there were forces at work in Suffolk, and they had apparently not forgotten about me.

The fireworks above the Capitol mall were no match for the human fireworks I would experience during the next several years on the bench. My courtroom would come to be known as the "combat zone" by many an experienced court officer. It was a standing joke that working in Judge Namm's court entitled one to "hazardous duty" pay. But to me, the target of the combat, it was no joke, and humor was in short supply as I plodded through my daily calendar for the next few years.

My Centereach law office was situated above the local branch of The Bank of Smithtown. After I left the practice, Dominic Baranello, my former partner and county chairman, continued to practice law in our former office, and I continued to do business with the bank.

Upon my return from an enjoyable holiday weekend, I had to visit the bank on the following Monday. I ran into Dominic who was returning from lunch. After a brief exchange of pleasantries, Dominic told me that he had heard from sources at the Suffolk County Board of Elections that certain persons were searching through my election campaign records.

These records are public documents which are required to be filed with the local election board by every candidate for public office. The records include names of campaign contributors, the amounts of campaign contributions and members of a campaign committee. In my case there were very few contributors and committee members, and the amounts of campaign contributions were miniscule.

The Board of Elections is established by New York State law. It is required to be bi-partisan in nature, so it is led by both a Republican and Democratic commissioner of elections. Each is generally beholden to the respective county chairmen. It is the legal responsibility of each of the commissioners to sign off on the official results of every primary and general election, and to approve the filing of election petitions of prospective candidates for public office. The board is staffed by numerous clerks and secretaries selected under a patronage system divided between the party faithful of the two major political parties. Under such a system, it was not unusual for the county chairman to be aware of everything taking place at the local board. In fact, it would be unusual if he was not in close contact with the members of his own party appointed by his largesse. Thus Dominic Baranello remained very close to the appointed party faithful. It was a means of control, and he had rarely been accused of "political malpractice."

While the commissioners are the nominal chiefs of the bureaucracy, each has a deputy commissioner who functions as the day-to-day supervisor of operations. My only real contact with the board of elections was in 1975 when I was deeply involved in the various re-counts of my District Court election results. At that time I was still in partnership with Dominic, and I was somewhat familiar with the Democratic Commissioner of Elections. I met him at various political functions which I attended gratis through the courtesy of my law partner. However, by 1985, there was a new commissioner and I knew virtually no one at the board of elections. But because I had presided over the trial of the murderers of his son, I had come to know Gerald Berger who was the Republican deputy commissioner. He'd been so impressed and so moved by the maximum sentences that I'd imposed upon his son's killers that he'd send a Jewish New Year's card to my family and me each year to wish us "good health and happiness."

It was common knowledge that Gerald Berger, a loyal Republican with many years of experience, was the de facto leader of the Suffolk County Board of Elections. He was the one person who knew about everything which went on in that complex bureaucracy. I decided to call him to find out what he knew about the persons who were reportedly examining my records. I wanted to know what it was that they were looking for. It was my feeling that he would set political loyalties aside to help the judge who had been responsible for sending his son's murderers away with maximum life sentences. I was wrong!

Gerald Berger, former schoolteacher and master bureaucrat, apparently suffered a lapse in memory. Yes, he could confirm that certain persons had been studying my election campaign records, but he had no recollection of who they were, and there was no way that he could find out at this juncture. He seemed to recall that they were representatives of an "east end newspaper," so he said. Yet he couldn't recall the name of the newspaper. Apparently, the realities of Suffolk County politics were far stronger and more important than the respect of a bereaved father for a judge who had done justice to the memory of his son. I never did learn the identity of the anonymous investigators or the goal of their mission. I could only surmise that it somehow related to the false tip to *Newsday* that Robert Gottlieb had been my campaign manager.

There was certainly no problem with anyone studying my records, such as they were, since all such documents are a matter of public record. But the real question which remained unanswered was why they had been doing so at that time-a time when my actions were being attacked by the district attorney in the news media. Was this mere coincidence? I didn't think so. There was too much at stake in 1985.

The remaining charge against Corso was scheduled for conference on July 9. I was still fuming about the *Newsday* article and the Board of Elections affair when I took the bench that morning, and I'd already decided what I was going to do to stop the Corso case from being used as a political football during the course of the district attorney's race. I decided to impose a "gag order" upon the DA, his staff, and all others directly involved in the case. I said,

> What is outrageous is that there is another trial which I have to conduct, and the district attorney of this county is questioning the jurisdiction of this court in a newspaper. From here on out, and this is a direct order of this court, nobody—neither you,

neither the district attorney, neither the representative of the
district attorney nor anybody else in the district attorney's
office—will speak to any news media, outside this courtroom,
about this case, about any matter pending in this court,
involving the defendant Peter Corso. If anybody does, they will
be subject to contempt of this court.[4]

I became more emotional under the circumstances than I should have. I
went so far as to accuse Patrick Henry of responsibility for the blatantly false
information contained in the *Newsday* article. I'd spoken to a *Newsday*
reporter, Thomas Maier, by telephone, and he left me with the clear
inference that such information had been planted by the district attorney's
office. My blood was boiling and my language was being dictated by
emotion:

> I will say something else, because I said it yesterday and I will
> get some of this that is boiling inside me, outside of me. I spent
> an entire life building a reputation as a person and as a judge,
> and the district attorney of this county, in one sentence planted
> in Newsday yesterday, can destroy my reputation as a judge.
>
> The irony of it is, I walk around this court and I'm pointed
> out as a hanging judge. That is what the defense bar calls me,
> and now the inference is, that in a homicide case, a major case,
> that I would allow politics to interfere with my judgment in this
> case. "That is so outrageous that it isn't worth quoting. But it's
> my life and I have to deal with it, and today in Newsday, there
> is a one sentence correction buried in page two in the index, that
> nobody reads, that says they were incorrect, and that comes from
> the district attorney of this county. Nobody else.[5]

With that I ordered that the hearing to determine whether there had been
probable cause to arrest Peter Corso for the murder of Archimedes Cervera
should begin. Ultimately I concluded that there had been insufficient
probable cause to do so and I dismissed the last charge pending against

Corso. But the results of the hearing were being upstaged by the drama which was being played outside of the courtroom.

Apparently, Robert Gottlieb also had a pipeline to the Board of Elections. He had also heard about the investigation of my financial records. He decided to make this a matter of public knowledge in a press conference which he held at his law office on July 11, one day after the hearing was re-opened. I was not certain whether he did so because he was outraged by what had taken place or because he saw this as an opportunity to criticize the actions of the district attorney, but I was certain that his possibly well-intentioned words had served to exacerbate a situation which was threatening to get out of hand. I needed to do something or I would be in the unhappy position of having gagged one candidate, a Republican, while his opponent, a Democrat, was free to speak out as he pleased. It was my belief that I was now vulnerable to possible legitimate public criticism for my actions which could be seen as interference in the election for district attorney.

Gottlieb told the gathered members of the local press that persons were inspecting my financial records at the Board of Elections in an effort to intimidate me. The ultimate goal, he said, was to deter me from a continuation of the hearing in the Corso case, which, he said, threatened my independence as a judge in an important criminal matter. I, too, had intuitively reached the same conclusion, but I wasn't about to make a public accusation unless it could be proven, and the proof was just not there. There was no smoking gun! Whoever they were, they'd covered their tracks well, especially in the light of Gerald Berger's convenient lapse of memory.

Judges do not usually hold press conferences, and judges usually stay out of the limelight, making their opinions known within the protected confines of the courtroom. Judges are also governed by a strict Code of Ethics which forbids conduct which will bring discredit to the judiciary or, which creates an appearance of impropriety or partiality. New York judges are also forbidden from getting involved in partisan politics. I had never conducted a press conference, and I was only aware of one prior press conference by a judge not running for public office. This unusual vehicle for getting the public's attention was used by New York City Supreme Court Justice Bruce Wright who had been given the undeserved nickname of "Turn 'em Loose Bruce" in the media because of his reputation for setting low bail in criminal cases involving black defendants. Wright, a professional poet and author, was a champion for justice for poor black defendants. He had been the target of a campaign of vilification by none other than the Mayor of the City of New York, Edward Koch.

On at least one occasion he had taken to the courthouse steps to conduct a press conference to make the case for black justice. In later years, while still on the bench, he would write "Black Robes, White Justice," a criticism of the way blacks are treated by the criminal justice system. To my knowledge, he had never been censured or otherwise punished for his outspoken ways. Armed with that knowledge, I decided to take the drastic step of conducting a press conference in the judge's lounge of the Criminal Courts building. I felt that it was necessary to get the Corso case out of the District Attorney's race and the news media and back into the courtroom where it belonged

Before meeting with the television, radio and print media, I called the law offices of Robert Gottlieb to slap a "gag order" upon him as I had done previously to the office of the District Attorney. As an attorney and officer of the court, he was directed to refrain from publicly discussing the Corso case until the pending narcotics charge was concluded.

> I've called this press conference today because of certain events which have transpired in the last several days over which I have had no control and which threaten my independence and integrity as a jurist, and more important, if permitted to persist, would threaten the very fiber of our judicial system. "1985 is an election year in Suffolk County...and for some reason the trial of Peter Corso and his acquittal by a jury of twelve Suffolk County citizens has been interjected as an issue in that race....In the last several days, however, I have seen that independence attacked by innuendo and unfortunate statements to the media by both candidates for District Attorney....The appropriate forum for the District Attorney to challenge my jurisdiction to conduct hearings in this case is within the confines of the public

courtroom, and not within the pages of a newspaper, or on the radio or television...every judge must ensure that politics never become a consideration in the administration of justice...The clear inference of that story [in *Newsday*]...was that this court was continuing a hearing into alleged prosecutorial and police misconduct in the Corso trial in an effort to assist the Democratic candidate in his campaign....I felt I had extinguished the fire by imposing the gag order on Tuesday, until I was made aware of statements made by the Democratic candidate to the press yesterday that efforts were being made to intimidate me....I know of no such efforts...but apparently there are responsible people who feel that such is the case, when they report that in recent days there have been inquiries made to the Board of Elections about my financial records. If such has been the case, I do not feel intimidated....However, if ever I had reason to believe that there was any attempt being made to intimidate me as a judge, in an effort to deter me in any way, or to challenge my independence as a jurist, I would not hesitate to request the appointment of a special prosecutor by Governor Cuomo...this morning I enlarged the [gag] order to include the Democratic candidate for District Attorney....[6]

The cat was out of the bag! The seed was now firmly planted in my psyche. If things got too far out of hand, I wouldn't hesitate to look to Governor Cuomo. Nevertheless, in July 1985, that action was never really seriously contemplated by me. Nothing had yet happened to consider the imposition of such a drastic remedy, although I was very disturbed by what was taking place around me. Involuntarily, I was being sucked into the eye of a hurricane. It was particularly troublesome that my conscience dictated that I needed to take steps to silence Robert Gottlieb who was speaking out in my defense and who was not responsible for the reprehensible conduct of others.

The hearings continued but the issue of the gag order overshadowed what was being disclosed each day in the courtroom. The revelations ultimately resulted in my dismissal of the remaining drug charge on July 22nd. It was no small irony that as this scenario was being played out in a Suffolk County courtroom, hearings were being conducted in the Bronx in the criminal conspiracy case against Secretary of Labor Raymond J. Donovan. On July 31, Michael Orlando, the key prosecution witness, invoked his Fifth Amendment right not to incriminate himself no less than 146 times. The star prosecution witness in People v. Peter Corso was suddenly transformed into the reluctant prosecution witness in People v. Raymond J. Donovan and others. It would have been naive to think that his unsuccessful performance in Corso had not played a significant role in his sudden change of heart. But my concern was no longer Michael Orlando and his unending criminal saga. He was now only another name in the daily newspaper. My concerns were directed towards Detectives Halverson, Rafferty and Mongan; the ramifications that my actions were having upon the heated race for District Attorney; and the public perception that I'd somehow violated candidate Gottlieb's constitutional right to free speech.

Arthur Eisenberg, chief counsel to the New York Civil Liberties Union, who would take up my cause to be returned to the County Court in 1989, was quoted in *Newsday*: "There are a number of extraordinary things about this gag order. Before violating a candidate's freedom of speech," he said, "a judge should sequester a jury or move the trial to another jurisdiction."

But I saw this as a balancing of the candidate's right to free speech with a defendant's right to a fair trial, and I knew something that he didn't know-that I would shortly issue an opinion which would render the entire matter academic. So contemporaneously with my decision dismissing the drug charge, I lifted the gag order and rendered Gottlieb's threatened federal lawsuit and an Appellate Division temporary injunction moot.

In dismissing the remaining charge against Corso, I used some of the strongest language I had ever used as a judge in a criminal case. This language was the result of the deep revulsion which I felt for the cavalier manner and shoddy investigation of the detectives involved in the Cervera murder case. It was this language and my subsequent rulings in Diaz which would incur the wrath of homicide detectives and prosecutors who, for the first time, felt the sting of an open judicial chastisement and the resulting public indignation which they believed was undeserved under the circumstances. In any event, they were unaccustomed to being on the receiving end in Suffolk County. They were the "law" in the county. In the habit of handing it out, they naturally resented criticism from any quarter, especially criticism which, they felt, hung them and their questionable tactics out to dry in full public view.

The decision which I rendered on July 19, 1985 received prominent attention in *Newsday* and was the front page lead story in *The New York Law Journal*, which is read by attorneys all over the country. I am certain that this publicity is what provoked the angry memorandum of Lt. Dunn. By this time, the media was following every word emanating from my courtroom about the Suffolk County Police Department. To their chagrin I'd written:

> This court finds it difficult to accept, and virtually incredible as a matter of law, that experienced police officers engaged in a major homicide investigation would permit a period of approximately six months to elapse, commencing nine days after the murder, during which time the investigation was continuing apace: prospective witnesses were being interviewed; likely suspects were being targeted; leads were being discounted; meetings were being held with representatives of other law enforcement agencies and other bureaus of the same police agency; without any supplementary report, as required by local police regulations, or any other report being written. This court reaches such conclusion, especially in the light of the disturbing testimony of the "lead" detective [Halverson]...in response to questions put by the court and defense counsel. This witness, who testified about events which were almost six years old without the benefit of any written notes or reports.....consistently asked to be shown the apparently non-existent reports or memoranda to refresh my memory...there is an aura which permeates the facts of this case which make it difficult—indeed impossible—to give credence to the testimony of the police officers involved. The explanations which have been offered for the non-existence of routine reports and memoranda

fly in the face of this court's experience as a trial judge who has
heard the testimony of many experienced police officers....Based
upon the totality of the evidence presented: the non-existence of
reports and memoranda; the evasive nature of the testimony of
the investigating detectives; the patent inconsistencies between the
testimony of an independent witness with no apparent axe to
grind and the testimony of the officers involved; and the almost
cavalier attitude of the police in their testimony before this court;
this court cannot, as a matter of law, conclude that there existed
sufficient probable cause to arrest Peter Corso on April 3, 1984. [7]

The reaction from the District Attorney was swift and predictably
defensive. He announced that he would appeal the dismissal to the Appellate
Division. He also said that I "...was unduly critical of the police during the
trial and overacted by dismissing the remaining charge. We feel the judge is
incorrect with his findings of fact and with the implications of the law. If a
detective violated police procedure, then chastise him. But don't throw out
the charge against Corso."[8]

The official police reaction was more muted. Chief Inspector James
Caples, who later became interim commissioner, announced that the
department would have no comment, "...but would study the judge's
findings as part of an internal investigation of the police handling the case."[9]
Now I am certain it was that internal investigation which prompted the
inter-office memorandum of Lt. Dunn placing the entire blame for the
Corso fiasco squarely on my shoulders.

The results of the so-called "internal investigation" were never made
public, but one can reasonably presume that the various changes in homicide
squad personnel by transfer, resignation and retirement was the direct result
thereof. These changes occurred quietly over a respectable period of time so
as to ensure that the public perception of misconduct in the Suffolk County
Police Department could never be confirmed by the department's own
actions. Yet on August 18, 1985, just one month after the publication of
the Corso dismissal, in a front page story, *Newsday* reported that Police
Commissioner DeWitt C. Treder "plans to impose tighter controls that will
change the way murders are investigated."[10] The article went on to say:

Commissioner DeWitt Treder says his proposed changes, spurred by last month's jury acquittal of a man accused of the 1979 murder of a Brentwood lawyer, will "tighten up" report filing and the preservation of evidence...As a result of a continuing police review of the case, Treder said he is studying possible "punitive action" against two police officers, whom he did not identify, and Det. Sgt. Kenneth McGuire, whose squad handled the Cervera murder case.... "It's got to change. Notes are the lifeblood of any department and you're dead without them," Treder said. "There'll be more changes as a result of the judge's admonishments." District Attorney Patrick Henry and Treder's own homicide chief, Lt. Robert Dunn, differ on Treder's assessment of the murder case. Henry and Dunn defend the Cervera probe and blame its outcome on Judge Namm. Says Henry: "We had detectives who wound up being ridiculed by the judge, but I think they did an admirable job."....Such practices violate the department's written rules and procedures. All notes are to be kept, and supplementary reports filed "as new information is developed and investigated," according to the Suffolk manual. And evidence—such as the telephone answering machine—will be properly preserved to maintain its integrity for possible court presentation," it further states. These investigative guidelines are also reflected in national standards published by the Commission on Accreditation for Law Enforcement Agencies. These rules are also followed by homicide squads in Nassau, and New York City, and by the state police....[11] On September 9, 1985, Det. Lt. Robert Dunn was replaced by Det. Capt. Robert Savarese as chief of the Homicide Squad. But the commissioner announced that Dunn would remain as head of investigations. "I think homicide investigations have been excellent," Treder said. "It's court preparations that we have to improve." Treder called Dunn one of the "best bosses" on the force and said, "To give him his due, he was wearing two hats there. Heading investigations and doing all the paperwork was too much."[12]

DeWitt C. Treder, a police commissioner, who had risen through the ranks of the department, for obvious reasons, couldn't bring himself to do the right thing. His latest statement was a step back from his pronouncement in August. In this case, the appropriate action would have been to immediately purge the homicide squad of those persons who had shown that they could not, or would not, abide by existing rules and regulations, and their superiors who had not enforced those regulations. This was necessary to restore public confidence in the department. Treder must have been convinced that a cosmetic change would placate those who by now were looking for meaningful changes. He was wrong, and in future months he'd pay dearly for his mistakes in judgment, and his failure to assert meaningful leadership, by the loss of his job. But much water was to flow under the bridge before these changes would occur.

After forty-three months of tenure as police commissioner, and thirty-one years of public service, on April 1, 1987, DeWitt Treder tendered his resignation to acting county executive Michael LoGrande, who felt that a change was necessary in the image of the Suffolk County Police Department, wilting under the heat of multiple investigations, which were having a detrimental effect upon his ability to be elected to the office of county executive in his own right. Treder became the sacrificial lamb.

The experience of the Corso hearings and trial were insufficient, in the opinion of the district attorney and police commissioner, to generate the kind of changes necessary to ensure that the Suffolk County Police Department, especially its homicide squad, would fall into step with law enforcement in other communities, like Nassau County and New York City. There was a pervasive chauvinistic spirit amongst county law enforcement that this was the finest police force in the nation. Suffolk would alternate, from contract to contract, with the New York City Police Department as the highest paid group of policemen. They obviously equated quality of investigatory work with the amount of base salary received. In terms of total salary, including overtime, the members of the homicide squad, prior to 1986, were, unquestionably, the highest paid members of the department.

By August 1985, however, my own attention was already directed to the trial of James Diaz, a twenty-one-year-old "drifter" from Port Jefferson Station, who was being held without bail for the rape and murder of

Maureen Negus, a thirty-five-year-old mother and registered nurse in her home on June 8, 1984. The misconduct which I had seen in the Corso case largely involved the actions of certain homicide detectives. What I had observed then paled by comparison to what would be revealed in the Diaz trial. The misconduct in Diaz involved the district attorney's office as well as members of the homicide squad, and it precipitated my October letter to Governor Mario Cuomo requesting the appointment of a Special Prosecutor.

ELEVEN

James Diaz: The Twenty-Year-Old Drifter

KATHLEEN FARMER WAS SUN-BATHING IN THE BACKYARD of her Port Jefferson Station home, on June 8, 1984, at about noontime. She couldn't help but notice her neighbor Maureen's son, five-year-old Billie Negus, crying to the point of hysteria. He had come home from school and found his mother lying motionless in a pool of red liquid in the basement of their home on Market Street.

Police Officer David Kopycinski was operating Sector Car 626, at 12:25 p.m., out of the 6th Precinct in the vicinity of the Fox Theater on Nesconset Highway when he responded to a 10-9, an aided case call, over his police radio. A female was reported to be unconscious in her basement. In the vicinity of 51 Davis Avenue, Port Jefferson Station, he heard screams on an adjoining street—Market Street. He ran through a backyard and observed a woman, with a boy crying at her side, screaming and pointing to a house on the east side of the street. Another uniformed officer was already at a doorway to the house, but Kopycinski entered first.

He wasn't prepared for the grisly scene which he'd encounter. Uniformed police officers, unlike homicide detectives, aren't accustomed to happening upon homicide scenes, if one can ever become accustomed to gruesome scenes of violent death. As he passed through the kitchen to the hallway, he noted reddish-brown markings running from the kitchen floor to the hallway floor. In the stairway to the basement, he noted similar stains on the basement wall. The reddish-brown substance appeared, to him, like dried paint.

At the foot of the stairs, he observed a nude female laying in a "star shape" in "spread eagle fashion." Her eyes were open, and they had a glazed look about them. Her skin was "very cold" to the touch. He could find no pulse inside her right elbow. Convinced that she'd expired, he didn't touch her again. By that time, another officer was on the steps—service revolver partly drawn. The Terryville Fire Department's Rescue Squad was also in the house. Emergency Medical Technician Judy Cahill, stethoscope in hand, confirmed his worst fears. Maureen Negus was dead.

At 6:45 p.m., he responded to the Office of the Medical Examiner, in Hauppauge, to identify the deceased. By now, a full blown homicide investigation was under way at 33 Market Street, a typical one-family Cape Cod house in the white working middle class community of Port Jefferson Station. Detective Sergeant Kenneth McGuire of the homicide squad had taken charge of the investigation. He immediately assigned Detective Dennis Rafferty as lead detective.

Rafferty arrived on the scene at 1:40 p.m. The deceased had not yet been removed from the basement. The detective observed fluid in her vaginal area, a large wound in her chest which was oozing blood, and abrasion patterns around her neck. Out of respect for the deceased, Rafferty covered the body with a towel and continued to observe the crime scene.

The senior homicide detective, Dennis Rafferty, was on the job once again. In June 8, 1984, I hadn't yet started the preliminary hearings in the Corso case. Although fate had apparently willed that our paths would cross in the spring of 1985, Dennis Rafferty was still totally unknown to me when I was assigned to the Diaz case. Though his investigative talents were legendary in the district attorney's office and the homicide squad, his was just another name that I had heard mentioned in casual conversation. But by the summer of 1985, the name of Dennis Rafferty was indelibly printed in my memory.

Dr. Sigmund Menschel, forensic pathologist, Suffolk County Medical Examiner's Office, arrived on the scene at about 2:45 pm. He made a quick visual inspection of the deceased, who was clad only in a "white terry housedress," which was pulled up to her chest. He noted a stab wound to her chest and a "pattern abrasion around her neck," which was in close proximity to a gold chain which was still on her neck. From the degree of rigor mortis which had set in, the temperature of the body and the room temperature, he concluded that she'd expired between some six to eight hours before his examination. He placed the time of death between 9:00 am and 12:00 noon of that day.

From the rigid, lifeless body he took fingernail clippings which might reveal invaluable hair or tissue attributable to her assailant. He removed her gold necklace for laboratory examination, and carefully collected some of her pubic hair which was mixed with, what appeared to his trained eye to be, male seminal fluid. All of this evidence was then bagged and marked for submission to the crime lab. Finally, the body was removed to the medical examiner's office for the performance of an autopsy to determine cause of death.

The post-mortem was conducted by Dr. Menschel that evening. After autopsy, he concluded that death was caused by "a stab wound to the chest causing injury to the aorta and right lung." The abrasions around the neck, he surmised, were consistent with considerable force having been exerted on the gold necklace. He noted no "petekial hemorrhages," which would be consistent with strangulation, despite the appearance of significant pressure to the neck. It was also significant that there were no visible signs of injury in the vicinity of the genitalia. This, he concluded, was "consistent with intercourse after stabbing."* The murderer, aside from being brutal and vicious, had indeed been vile and ghoulish in his actions. Maureen Negus, a mother and registered nurse—a people helper—had been spared no indignity, even in suffering a particularly violent and brutal death within, what should have been, the safe confines of her own home.

Police Officer Paul Dodorico worked with a very unusual partner. "Samson" was a large male German Shepherd assigned to the K-9 section of the Suffolk County police department. Samson, together with his handler, was capable of searching buildings and other areas for physical evidence, drugs and explosives. In the afternoon of June 8, 1984, the pair responded to the crime scene at 33 Market Street to conduct a search for evidence. They were partly successful in their joint endeavor. Although Samson picked up a strong scent along the back fence of the crime scene, after being ordered to "seek track" by Officer Dodorico, his find was limited to a pair of bloodstained ladies' white gloves. These gloves turned out to be important evidence in the case against James Diaz, the accused murderer. But the gloves and other very significant evidence was seemingly ignored by the jury in their ultimate decision to return a surprise verdict of "Not Guilty."

While a knife was also discovered in the woods, not far from the back of the house, Samson was not involved in its recovery. Officer Dodorico said that he had "never searched the area where the knife was located."* That knife, and a second knife, which was found several months later in the basement of the Negus home, became a matter of great controversy in the Diaz prosecution and the subsequent state investigation.

****

James Diaz was born on October 25, 1963 in Plainview, Nassau County, Long Island. He is the oldest of four children born out of the union of Peter and Joan Diaz, both of whom reside in Florida. He has two younger brothers and one sister, but James did not live with his family after he left their Port Jefferson Station home at age sixteen to wander the streets. Between September 1980 and May 1982, he was arrested for no less than ten burglaries, or attempted burglaries. His first arrest came at the age of sixteen. By the time he was eighteen, he had served three separate jail terms, including a sentence of one to three years which I imposed on him in 1982.

In 1982, a psychiatrist in the Nassau County Correctional Facility reported that James had "poor social judgment, a lack of conscience and a narcissistic, immature impulse control."[1] In the Suffolk County Correctional Facility, he had been housed under administrative segregation due to potential "suicidal ideation." He had displayed "high anxiety levels" and "periods of depression." He was an admitted substance abuser—admitting to the use of marijuana two or three times a week since age thirteen, the use of mescaline about twice a month in 1982, and the consumption of six bottles of beer at a sitting, two or three times a week.

He was reported to possess a "quick, violent temper" and to have "no internal controls over his actions." It was the opinion of an investigating probation officer that his "actions display an uncontrolled behavior that may indicate deep rooted psycho/sexual problems." In short, he possessed the classic profile of a sociopath who represented a clear and present danger to himself and to society.

But after being charged with the ruthless and brutal slaying of Maureen Negus, James Diaz insisted that he was a "changed man" since his release from state prison, and that he was being "framed" by the police because they knew that he was an "easy suspect" to prosecute. Whether James Diaz ever met Maureen Negus, or worse yet, whether he was responsible for her untimely and undeserved death, will always be cause for conjecture. Murderers and rapists do not easily confess their heinous deeds.

He too, like Peter Corso before him, was acquitted after trial by jury of the charge of murder. But there is no doubt that to this day the members of the homicide squad and the district attorney's office who were involved in the Diaz case are certain that he was the person who subjected an innocent victim to the ultimate form of degradation, violence and violation. Yet, they couldn't convince a Suffolk County jury that wanted to believe them of this fact. In the final analysis, it was they who were responsible for this failure—a failure which would overshadow the disastrous result of the Corso trial.

****

On June 19, 1984, Sgt. Joseph Adragna and Police Officer Frank Gennari were operating undercover in plain clothes, in an unmarked vehicle, out of the 6th Precinct. They were members of the Crime Control Squad. Their tour of duty took them to Old Town Road and Jayne Boulevard in Port Jefferson Station. They were looking for James Diaz in connection with an outstanding drug charge. He had escaped from Gennari on June 13th when they attempted to arrest him and two of his cohorts for the possession and sale of marijuana.

At about 4:20 pm, they observed Diaz walking towards them, bare chested, carrying tee-shirts over his shoulder. As they confronted him, he bolted once again, dropping the tee-shirts on the ground. A short foot chase proved unsuccessful, but they recovered the two shirts as evidence.* Diaz, they said, had been sweating profusely.

The following day an elderly woman was burglarized and assaulted by a shirtless young man in the vicinity of Bicycle Path, not far from Old Town

Road. Her assailant brandished a knife. Detective Rafferty was directed to respond to the crime scene because of the similarity to the Negus murder. At the 6th Precinct, the detective squad leader, Sgt. Adragna, filled him in on the details of the attempts to arrest Diaz. He also learned that Diaz was seen in the vicinity of the Bicycle Path burglary—just "two or three houses away," on the night of the 18th.* Rafferty was already informed by the crime lab that the Negus perpetrator had been a "type 'A' secretor." Playing a hunch, he suggested that Adragna turn over the recovered tee-shirts to the lab for blood type analysis of the residual perspiration. The art of forensic serology has become so sophisticated that it is possible to determine blood grouping and certain genetic markers from the various bodily fluids of 80% of the male population. These persons are classified as "secretors."

Officer Douglas Lotten, also of the 6th Precinct, and also working undercover in Crime Control, knew James Diaz and his habits well. He was aware that Diaz hung out in the vicinity of the Port Jefferson railroad station, the last stop of the North Shore branch of the Long Island Railroad. It was there that many of the commuter cars were stored overnight.

At about 11:15 pm on June 20th, Lotten spotted Diaz watching the bowlers in the local bowling alley, a few short blocks from the railroad yard. He immediately called for backup as he placed Diaz under arrest, handcuffed him, walked him out of the bowling alley into a police vehicle where he was read his Miranda rights. "You have the right to remain silent. Anything you say can and will be used against you...." In an attempt to calm his agitated prisoner, he shifted to a fatherly dialogue: "Jimmy, we've been looking for you. You'll be alright. I'm bringing you into the precinct."*

According to Doug Lotten, he didn't even become aware that Diaz was a suspect in the Negus murder until the following day. But his arrest of James was the beginning of a long and tiresome odyssey which would, for Jimmy Diaz and County Court Judge Stuart Namm, last for several years.

On June 5, 1984, Kim Lee, a young married woman who suffered from a slight emotional impairment, was assaulted and sexually abused in a wooded area of Port Jefferson Station, not far from the scene of the Negus murder and the Long Island Railroad station. The fingerprints of James Diaz were compared with latent prints recovered at the scene of that crime. There was a match! The noose was slowly tightening around the unknowing suspect.

In the early afternoon of June 21, lineups were conducted at the 6th Precinct in both the burglary and sex abuse cases. Diaz could not be identified by the elderly burglary victim, but Kim Lee identified him as the young man who'd assaulted and sexually abused her in his wooded hideaway.

It was then that Diaz was formally placed under arrest on the charge of sexual abuse, and he was again read his Miranda rights. Shortly thereafter, Sgt. McGuire of the homicide squad received a call from Ira Dubey, chief forensic serologist at the criminalistics laboratory. James Diaz' blood matched the blood of the person who had deposited semen at the scene of the Negus homicide. Like Diaz, the perpetrator was a "type 'A' secretor." That was the news they were waiting for!

Within ten minutes, Diaz was seated alone in the back seat of an unmarked police vehicle with detectives Rafferty and McGuire racing towards homicide headquarters in Yaphank to be questioned about the rape-murder in Port Jefferson Station. He, like so many before and so many after him, was about to be introduced to the Yaphank "interview room" of the homicide squad. According to the detectives, he, like so many other accused persons in Suffolk, agreed to speak to them "without a lawyer."*

The "interview"—never "interrogation"—began in earnest at 4:10 pm. Diaz was alone with detectives Rafferty and Cassidy in the windowless, sparsely furnished room behind a closed door. By 6:45 p.m., although he initially professed his innocence to the homicide, James Diaz supposedly gave a very detailed oral confession to the vilest of deeds. If they are to be believed, Suffolk County homicide had easily succeeded once again in eliciting a complete confession from the perpetrator of a terrible crime.

But there the confession story just begins. At 6:15 pm, the questioning was halted for a short sandwich break. Homicide detectives on the brink of cracking an important murder case do not usually partake of hearty meals, even if it is time for dinner. Suffolk detectives and accused alike suffer the same meager food portions. There seems to be a need to establish a camaraderie that can only be understood by experienced police professionals. It is a brotherhood of strange bedfellows, accuser and accused, temporarily suffering the same hardships and partaking of the same pack of cigarettes. The Diaz case was no exception.

Their appetites temporarily satisfied, the detectives pressed forward with the interview. Diaz was informed that his blood type was found at the Negus murder scene. Somewhat simplistically it was explained by Rafferty that blood type from sperm was like a fingerprint. To that he added that a witness had seen him go into the house. He was told that the detectives knew that he was doing burglaries in the Port Jefferson area and that he lived in the area. Most of what they were putting forth was either untrue or an exaggeration of the truth, but it mattered not. It was, they said, enough to convince Diaz that the jig was up. By his own words the innocent accused was instantly converted to a self-confessed rapist and murderer.

Diaz, they said, told them that he had planned to do a burglary when he saw a "very attractive woman" hanging clothes outside her house. He hadn't had sex for some time. He was hard-up. Aroused sexually, Diaz slipped into the kitchen through the open front door of the woman's home. He armed himself with a knife which was lying on a kitchen counter. The woman came up from the basement. He grabbed her around the neck and "stabbed her with his right hand." The detectives were aware from Diaz' pedigree that their suspect was right handed.

He carried the bleeding nurse into her basement, ripped her panties off, pulled up her blouse and, in his words, "fucked her" after covering the hole in her chest with a towel from the pile of clean laundry. As he "shot scum in her," he was wearing gloves. Diaz, they said, told them that he always wore ladies' gloves so that he wouldn't leave fingerprints when he committed a burglary. He hastily left the house through the rear door and threw the knife and the gloves in the woods behind the house. He said that he "had not wiped the knife."* The significance of the un-wiped knife in his alleged oral confession would not become apparent until the trial. It was revealed through the cross-examination of Rafferty and Cassidy that none of the supplementary reports which memorialized the alleged oral admissions contained the admission that he "did not wipe the knife."*

Although, according to the police, the crime scene was thoroughly searched on the day of the homicide by detectives and crime scene investigators, surprisingly the actual murder weapon was not discovered until Detective Cassidy responded to the Negus home on April 14, 1985, ten months after Maureen's death. In the basement, within a few feet of where the body was discovered, a carving knife with apparent bloodstains was spotted under a woodpile by David Negus, the deceased's estranged husband, while playing table tennis. He had moved back into the marital residence to live with his children.

Although Diaz' assigned attorney, Paul Gianelli, had long since been advised of the alleged oral admissions of his client, as required by law, he was not advised of the important "he did not wipe the knife" admission until May 1985 during the pre-trial hearings, and only after the discovery of the second knife. One could not help but wonder which knife the police believed to be the murder weapon, and whether they had tailored the alleged oral admissions of James Diaz about the murder weapon to the knife which was the suspected weapon at any given time.

At about 8:00 pm, Jimmy Diaz was shown the gruesome photographs of the victim, the gloves which were discovered by Samson in the woods and the Negus house. Again according to the detectives, he identified all of the photos and initialed them. Significantly, he was never shown the knife which was recovered from the back of the house. It was then, they say, that he agreed to give a written statement, which would be written by one of the detectives.

In Suffolk County, a homicide accused was never afforded the opportunity to write a confession in his own hand. The confession, which is written in the hand of one of the investigating detectives, is usually the product of a question and answer session that theoretically tracks the confessor's previous oral statement. Diaz, who had limited reading ability, supposedly asked Rafferty to read the written statement to him after it was completed. According to the detectives, he agreed that the statement, as written, was true. He proceeded to sign the Miranda rights portion of the confession on the first page, acknowledging that he had been advised of his constitutional rights, but for some unexplained reason he had a change of heart and refused to sign the confession.

"I don't think I'm going to do that. I don't think I'm going to sign it."

"It's the truth isn't it?" asked a frustrated Rafferty.

"Yes it is," replied a stubborn James Diaz.*

Diaz never signed the written confession. To this day he continues to profess his innocence, charging that he was framed by the investigating detectives.

****

On the following pages are excerpts for the final report of the State Commission of Investigations whose investigation dealt with the confession scenario in a manner which seriously questioned the detectives' collective credibility:

> At the Commission's public hearing on January 28 and 29, 1987, testimony demonstrated that at least five witnesses for the People in the Diaz case had presented incredible, false or perjurious testimony. In addition, evidence was presented demonstrating serious deficiencies with respect to police procedures for locating evidence at the crime scene, taking notes and documenting key events in investigations, and, following the trial, in investigating allegations of police and prosecutorial misconduct in that case.
>
> The principal evidence at trial consisted of a confession written in Detective Dennis Rafferty's handwriting and signed by Diaz only on the first page; testimony by a jailhouse informant named Joseph Pistone; and a knife, the alleged murder weapon, which was discovered at the basement site of the murder by the estranged husband of the deceased 10 months after the slaying—-approximately 15 feet from where the body was found. There was also a crucial oral admission by Diaz that he "never wiped the blood off the knife," which alleged statement by Diaz was not disclosed by Detective Raffery until a pre-trial hearing held shortly after the knife was discovered in the basement.
>
> Testimony regarding this knife played a significant role in undermining the credibility of police witnesses in the trial. The confession allegedly given to Detective Rafferty at Police

Headquarters during the first evening Diaz was questioned about the murder was three pages long. Rafferty testified at the Commission's hearing that Diaz signed the first page, containing innocuous identifying information, but refused to sign the other two pages. In this alleged confession, Diaz stated that "he threw the knife into the woods," despite the fact that the knife ultimately offered by the prosecution as the murder weapon was found in the basement (Public Hearing, 1987, Exhibit 12).

In fact, another knife had been found by the police, in the backyard of the deceased's house during the search immediately following the murder. However, despite the fact that several objects and photos were shown to Diaz on the night of his confession, such as a pair of white gloves allegedly used in the crime, and photos of the deceased's house, which Diaz initialed, neither the knife found in the yard nor even a picture of that knife was shown to Diaz—either to rule it in or out as the murder weapon. Detective Rafferty's explanation for his lapse in not showing the knife found in the yard was that Rafferty never believed that this knife was the murder weapon (Public Hearing, 1987, pp. 193-197).

Ten months after the murder, as the trial of Diaz approached, the estranged husband of the deceased, who had moved back into the deceased's house to care for his two children, discovered a knife, which was later offered in evidence by the People as the murder weapon, approximately 15 feet from where the body of the deceased had been found (Public Hearing, 1987, pp. 142-151).

At the Commission's public hearing, Robert Genna, the supervisor of the Suffolk County Crime Laboratory of the Medical Examiner's Office, who had responded to the crime scene on the day of the Negus murder, explained this glaring oversight, stating that he had conducted only a "cursory examination" of the room where the knife was found, consisting of "just visually looking around" (Public Hearing, 1987, p. 115).

After the discovery of this knife, which had blood residue on it, Detective Rafferty unexpectedly testified at a pre-trial hearing that at the time of Diaz's confession Diaz had said that "he never wiped the blood off the knife." This statement had not been included in the written confession, nor in police reports or notes, nor even previously been told by Rafferty to Barry Feldman, the assistant district attorney handling the case, despite several days of preparation prior to the hearing, and had thus not been previously provided to the defense (Public Hearing, 1987, pp. 197-199).

Feldman was astounded at this revelation, and the issue arose of whether this testimony would be considered a recent fabrication by Rafferty (Public Hearing, 1987, pp. 570-571 and Private Hearing, Feldman, 12/3/86, pp. 45-46). Detective Rafferty conveniently recalled that he had long before told two other assistant district attorneys of Diaz's statement that he had not wiped the blood off the knife. Assistant District Attorneys Steven Wilutis, Chief Trial Prosecutor, and William Keahon, Chief of the Major Offense Bureau, testified at a pre-trial hearing and at trial that Rafferty had told them of this statement nearly a year before Rafferty testified about it at the hearing (Public Hearing, 1987, pp. 571-572).

The purpose of this testimony was to answer the argument that Rafferty's trial testimony was a recent fabrication intended to counter the statement in Diaz's alleged confession that "he threw the knife in the woods." Judge Namm testified at the Commission's public hearing that the testimony of Wilutis and Keahon on this point was not "credible" (p. 44).

****

Standing right outside the interview room, within earshot and taking it all in, was none other than Detective K. James McCready, the self proclaimed master of eliciting confessions from reluctant homicide suspects. Rafferty and Cassidy left the room at 9:00 p.m. to report their progress to Sgt. McGuire.

"Do you mind if I talk to him?" asked an anxious McCready, obviously champing at the bit to ply his trade on the unwilling accused.

"No, go ahead. See if you can get him to sign it," replied a willing Rafferty.*

The detective entered the room and closed the door behind him. He was now alone, mano a mano, with what was described as a "sullen and calm" Diaz. McCready had never seen Diaz before that night, but according to the detective, "he never looked you in the eye." There was a Dictaphone in the room, but neither McCready nor anyone of the other detectives ever considered using it. It was taken as gospel in the Suffolk homicide squad that Dictaphones and similar recording devices hindered the free flow of oral admissions from untrusting criminals. The detective glanced over the unsigned confession.

"There's some heavy duty stuff in here," McCready said to Diaz.

"It's all true, but I'm not going to sign anything!" Diaz emphatically stated.

McCready says that he spent fifteen minutes alone in the room with Diaz. He made "no threats, no promises," and, most importantly, there was "no abuse" and "no violence."* Not even K. James McCready could succeed in breaking the steadfast Diaz. Yet, although he supposedly heard a prime suspect orally admit to rape and murder, he made no notes of this conversation and filed no written report. This was his first and last conversation with James Diaz, but he would surface as an important, but very questionable, prosecution witness at trial.

At 9:30 pm, a handcuffed Diaz was driven by Sergeant McGuire to the 6th Precinct to be lodged for the night. Rafferty wanted no part of this trip. He begged off because he'd lost his "rapport," as he said, with Diaz who now was "relaxed, calm and a little apprehensive."

"How you doing, Jimmy?" asked an outwardly sympathetic McGuire, putting on his most friendly face in an effort to create instant camaraderie.

"I'm glad it's over. I knew I'd be caught. I swear I just wanted to rip off the house. I raped her because she was good looking, and I got turned on."*

This time it was the supervising detective who was witness to the damning oral admissions of a confessed murderer. But once again, no formal report of this conversation was ever filed as required by police procedure. Eighteen months later, McGuire testified under oath as to the details of his informal conversation with whom he described as a "concerned" defendant from handwritten notes which he said he "completed at the 6th Precinct that night."*

TWELVE

Perjury and a Pathological Liar

T HE JUNE 1984 GRAND JURY WASTED NO TIME IN indicting Diaz on three counts of murder in the second degree for the death of Maureen Negus. The top count was the charge of intentional murder, while the 5th and 6th counts accused him of the crimes of felony murder, one connected to the burglary, and the other to the crime of rape. He was also charged with two counts of burglary in the first degree and one count of rape in the first degree.

The presentation before the Grand Jury was made by Deputy Bureau Chief Barry Feldman of the district attorney's office. He had been assigned the trial of this very important and highly publicized murder. This assignment came immediately upon the heels of the Waters pretrial hearing. Assistant DA Feldman was riding the crest of several successful prosecutions of high visibility major felony cases. His was a rising star within the ranks of Suffolk County prosecutors. He'd come a long way from his days as "just another assistant district attorney" in Brooklyn. But the Diaz case marked the beginning of the end for him as a supervising prosecutor, and ultimately as a prosecutor. *Mea culpa*! For that, I am sure, I will never be forgiven by him or his cohorts.

The constitutional hearings for Diaz began within days after the completion of the pre-trial hearings in Corso, and just a few short weeks before the Corso trial. For the prosecution, it couldn't have come at a more inopportune time. The district attorney's race was beginning to heat up. The stakes in a race for DA are always high. Patrick Henry had to be feeling Robert Gottlieb and the electorate breathing down his neck.

Once again, the prosecution sought to use the testimony of a "jailhouse informant" at trial. Again it was necessary to determine whether the informant, a tough talking, streetwise, petty criminal with a limited felony record, named Larry Middleton, had acted as an agent of law enforcement when Diaz allegedly confessed, "I killed a lady." The admission was supposed to have come at a time when Middleton was awaiting trial on a pending criminal charge in the Suffolk County Correctional Facility in June 1984. Not only did the usually close-mouthed Diaz admit his guilt to murder to a complete stranger, but allegedly he had also described every gory detail of this unspeakable and despicable crime.

Middleton said that Diaz told him that he had gone to her house to "burglarize it," but the woman took him by surprise. There had been a "tussle between him and the woman," and he "stabbed her, and raped her after he stabbed her." He found the knife in the house, he said, and he raped her in the basement.*

It would not have been difficult for any reasonably literate inmate in the county jail to have been aware of the details of the Negus homicide. A complete description of the facts was published regularly in the local news pages of *Newsday*, and admittedly Middleton had read the stories in *Newsday* and *The Daily News*. But, understandably, both police and prosecutor were convinced that he was legit. At least that was the impression they sought to convey during the hearings. For reasons known only to Feldman and his confidantes, Middleton was never called to the stand during the Diaz trial, although he was listed by Feldman as a prospective prosecution witness prior to jury selection. Perhaps it was the sudden emergence on the eve of trial of Joseph Pistone, Jr., the felonious son of a New York City detective, as a second "jailhouse informant," which moved Middleton to the back burner.

Pistone would ultimately play a key role in the public perception of the manner in which important homicide cases were being prosecuted in Suffolk County. But at the time of the preliminary hearings, Pistone hadn't yet surfaced, and even as he had in the summer of 1985, Feldman was careful to ensure that I, as the trial judge, would not become aware of his existence in relation to the prosecution of James Diaz until the absolute last possible moment. After my unpopular decision in Corso, it is fair to say that I was no longer the sweetheart of the Suffolk County district attorney's office or of their cohorts in the homicide squad. I was apparently not to be trusted with important prosecution secrets, and Joseph Pistone was a top secret weapon in the war against an accused rapist and murderer. Nor was I any longer the protégé of my former mentor, Hon. Thomas Stark, the prosecution-oriented administrative judge for the superior criminal courts in Suffolk County. I was now on his shit list!

Despite this new status, and my experiences in the Corso case which were still fresh in my memory, at the conclusion of the pre-trial hearings, I still managed to rule in favor of the prosecution. I held that none of Diaz's constitutional rights were violated by the police, and I permitted the introduction of all facets of his alleged oral confessions before the jury. Likewise, I ruled that there had been no illegal delay in his arraignment when he was held at the 6th Precinct to conduct the various lineups. The icing on the cake was my conclusion that Middleton, the only jailhouse informant of whom I was then aware, was not operating as an agent of the Suffolk County police. The so-called "jurisprudential philosophy" of Judge Stuart Namm seemed to be still firmly planted in the field of prosecutorial orientation. The Waters and Corso cases were apparently not sufficient to alter my overall view of criminal justice as it was then being practiced in the County of Suffolk. Yet, somewhere deep inside of me, I must have perceived that the clock was rapidly winding down towards a bleak midnight.

Somehow I sensed that Barry Feldman was going to drag his feet in bringing the Diaz case for trial. Perhaps, knowing the weaknesses in their case, the office of the district attorney had strategically concluded that the Diaz case should not be brought to trial before the November election. Another acquittal on the heels of the Corso case, and in the same year as the Troiano acquittal in the widely publicized Northport satanic ritual murder of a teen-ager (not one of my cases), in any place but Suffolk, might spell sure defeat for an incumbent district attorney. The powerful Suffolk County Republican organization could ill afford to lose the most powerful elected office in the county. It appeared to me that Diaz was intentionally being put on the back burner.

On August 5, I directed letters to Feldman and Paul Gianelli, the attorney that I had assigned to represent the indigent James Diaz. Both were formally directed "to appear and be ready to proceed to jury selection and trial" on September 3, 1985.[1] I can recall no other case in which I felt compelled to write such a letter. I was immediately contacted by Paul Gianelli by telephone to advise me that, upon hearing of my order, Justice George F.X. McInerney, whom we have already encountered in the "bizarre" court proceeding in Corso, directed that Gianelli proceed to trial on that same date in a multiple defendant drug case. But this case was only pending on his crowded trial calendar since March 1985. In contrast, Diaz had already been in custody for well over a year.

The battle lines were drawn! Right or wrong, I was seriously concerned that perhaps McInerney was cooperating with the office of the district attorney to insure a delay of the Diaz trial until after the election which was getting closer and more critical each day. Perhaps, paranoia was beginning to set in!

It was common knowledge amongst knowledgeable persons that Justice McInerney, the Republican senior criminal court judge, had an extremely close working relationship with the district attorney's office, and that his closest links were with David Freundlich, a former chief of the Rackets Bureau, and the person who was directly beneath Patrick Henry in the hierarchy of that office. It was Freundlich who literally ran the day-to-day operations of the Suffolk prosecutor's office. His fingers were somehow involved in every high visibility case in the county.

On August 15, I rushed off three letters, identical ones to Feldman and Gianelli and the third to Justice McInerney. I let it be known, in no uncertain terms, that I intended to proceed to the trial of the Diaz case on the day after Labor Day, September 3rd.

"I have been advised that the District Attorney would prefer to proceed in your multiple defendant case, however, it is not for the District Attorney's office to decide which case will proceed to trial, at what time," I wrote. "It is fundamental that a case which is more than one year old should take precedent over another, despite the number of defendants, which is no more than four or five months old."[2]

To Gianelli and Feldman, by certified mail I wrote: "This court has been available for the trial of this matter since the beginning of summer of 1985, and will tolerate no further adjournments, for whatever purpose, on the part of either side."[3]

On August 28, I received a disturbing telephone call at home from Tom Stark. He had never called me at home before, and I wasn't even at work that day. As a result of that call, I made a calculated decision to memorialize every subsequent event by dictating the details as soon as possible after its occurrence to my secretary. Those memoranda today number in the hundreds.

I had previously discussed my predicament with him in his capacity as administrative judge. He told me that he had discussed the matter with Gianelli on the previous day. He said that Gianelli told him that he had advised me as early as June or July of the conflict in the trials. That was simply not true! I told him that I had not even become aware of this situation until Gianelli called in August to advise me that he had been ordered to trial by Justice McInerney. Stark asked me to call McInerney who, he said, was offended because I hadn't called him in June or July. I repeated that I did not know of this problem at that time. I had no intention of calling McInerney.

But I did call Gianelli to confront him with what I had been told by Stark. Gianelli denied ever having told Stark any such thing. He said that he had told him that he only made me aware of the possible conflict after he had received my letter of August 5. He had called Stark because he received a telephone call from McInerney's law secretary advising him that if he did not appear in McInerney's courtroom on September 3rd, he would be held in contempt of court. Gianelli said that he had every intention of starting the Diaz trial on that date, but he felt that he was being cut to pieces by the conflicting judges.

I then called Stark and related my conversation with Gianelli. I revealed that I had previously discussed the problem with Arthur Cromarty, the chief administrative judge. Cromarty agreed that the Diaz trial should start on Tuesday. It was not my intention or desire to wait three months for the completion of McInerney's narcotics trial. With that, the conversation was terminated. As I clicked down the receiver, I wondered why Tom Stark had not accurately conveyed the essence of his conversation with Gianelli. His memory could not have been that impaired. I knew that he suffered from the effects of a serious debilitating physical ailment, but his mental faculties were as sharp as they had ever been. Unfortunately, with the events of the past several months flitting about my brain, I was beginning to conjure up conspiracies all around me.

I agreed to allow Gianelli to report to McInerney's courtroom in the morning of September 3rd. Knowing McInerney's reputation, I did not want to subject a decent person like Paul Gianelli, who had successfully represented the parents of "Baby Jane Doe," to possible contempt proceedings which could result in his imprisonment, the imposition of a fine, or both.

The entire episode was rendered academic when that morning the defendants in the drug prosecution agreed to plead guilty under a plea agreement with the prosecutor. I had been told previously that there was no possibility of any such plea. Thus, the entire episode was moot. Yet, I would not soon forget what had transpired. My relationship with Tom Stark was seriously jeopardized, and I now saw him in a completely different light. In the coming weeks and months the relationship would gradually deteriorate to one of mutual mistrust. The mentor became the accuser, and the protégé, the accused.

Jury selection in the Diaz case was to begin on the morning of the fourth, but Barry Feldman apparently had other plans. For the first time he announced that the People had discovered another informant who had allegedly spoken to Diaz in the county jail. His name—Joseph Pistone. Over one hundred prospective jurors were waiting in the wings, but instead I once again had to conduct a last minute hearing on the eve of trial.

****

Eighteen-year-old Pistone had been in trouble with the law since he was fourteen. His arrests covered the gamut of larcenous acts-burglary, unauthorized use of a motor vehicle, criminal trespass, grand larceny and criminal possession of stolen property. He had no recorded history of violence. Although he was described as "evasive and manipulative," by a Nassau County probation officer, the officer felt that he was "not a bad person, but...he is caught up in all sorts of illegal activities, and...he will go on to do 'big time.'"[4] His father, a "strict disciplinarian," was a New York City detective, who separated from his mother when Joseph was fourteen, not surprisingly the year that young Joseph had his first brush with the law. He had a poor relationship with his "step-father," and he was "seething with anger as a result of poor family relationships." He was the classic product of a broken home. He dropped out of school in the eleventh grade at Farmingdale High School. He was "disruptive, fighting, cutting classes, and running away."[5]

On August 28, 1984, he and a companion were arrested in Suffolk County after a high speed chase through the residential section of Farmingdale in a stolen 1981 Buick. They and the stolen vehicle were cornered in an apartment complex by several police cars which blocked the only available means of egress. Despite the presence of numerous uniformed police officers, Pistone, after being placed under arrest, attempted to flee the scene, displaying an air of arrogance and smug confidence not often seen in young suburban criminals. He displayed this same attitude as he plead guilty to criminal possession of stolen property before me in November 1984, and even as I sentenced him to one year in the county jail on March 6, 1985.

I did not see Joseph Pistone again until September 5, 1985. I had already forgotten about him. Petty criminals, even arrogant ones, are not generally memorable. They have a tendency to blend into one massive lump in one's memory. But the Pistone that I would encounter in the Diaz trial would be truly unforgettable.

****

Pistone was delivered by judicial order no less than six times between June and September 1985 from the custody of the jail warden to the homicide detectives and the Diaz prosecutor, Barry Feldman. These meetings were intended to prepare Pistone for his debut as a key prosecution witness in the Diaz trial. But not even one of the orders was requested of me, the trial judge, although that was the usual practice. Every order but one was signed by two judges, former law partners who had served as assistant district attorneys. Both were long-time buddies of the district attorney's office who were being used. It was a blatant attempt by the prosecutor to keep the existence of Pistone a deep secret from both the defense and the trial judge until the last possible moment. There were to be no questions asked until the last possible moment. Pistone was going to be Feldman's ace in the hole. Unfortunately for the prosecution, however, their "ace's" appearance sounded the death knell to the People's case and ultimately to Feldman's credibility and career as a prosecutor.

According to Pistone, he had met James Diaz in April when Pistone was serving the one year term of incarceration imposed by me. Pistone was lodged in tier "1 SE" of the Suffolk County Correctional Facility, under administrative segregation, or protective custody, which he claimed he requested. That placed him in the same area of the jail as Diaz. They'd "talk and play cards together." They quickly became friends and talked "about charges back and forth."*

He boasted that Diaz said that "he murdered the girl he is charged with." He had been walking down the street in Port Jefferson to burglarize a house when "he saw her ass as she was hanging clothes." This "got him all fired up." He entered the house through an unlocked door and waited for her in the kitchen. Defending herself, she hit him, so "he grabbed a knife and stabbed her." He dragged her into the basement of the house, put a towel over her face, and "had a good fucking with her."* He claimed that Diaz told him this story a couple of times. Under cross-examination by Gianelli he became more specific. Diaz, he said, had told him this story five times.

Pistone also told about an argument between Jimmy Diaz and another detainee, John Eulie, who was charged with murdering his wife. The argument took place across jail cells just one and a half weeks before the hearing, according to Pistone. Diaz and Eulie were supposedly exchanging newspaper clippings and bragging about their vile exploits. In a proud voice Eulie was said to have called out: "At least I didn't rape a girl!" To which, Diaz tauntingly responded: "At least I didn't kill my wife."*

It was Diaz' bragging that caused him to come forward as a witness, Pistone testified. Diaz bragged too much, and he wanted to teach him a lesson. It was claimed that he'd received no promises and nothing of value in exchange for his invaluable testimony. Once again the homicide squad and district attorney's office conveniently happened upon a critical informant in a major homicide prosecution, and once again the price was unbelievably inexpensive—nothing. In fact, assistant district attorney Timothy Mazzei, who in 1988 would become chief of the newly formed homicide bureau, testified that he'd told Pistone's lawyer, William Breuer, that "Pistone would gain nothing for his testimony."* There'd be no deal struck with this latest in a long line of felonious "Good Samaritans" in payment for his much needed assistance. Why then, I wondered, did Mazzei's file on Joseph Pistone contain the following notation: "Sentence according to original deal." That note certainly did nothing to assuage the skepticism which was building stronger within me each day, Mazzei's testimony and assurances notwithstanding. I remain firmly convinced that a deal was struck with Pistone, as with other police informants, but the exact terms were held in abeyance with a wink and a nod so that all could testify under oath that there had been no quid pro quo in exchange for their damaging cooperation.

The testimony of Pistone and Mazzei were not the only troubling aspects of this last minute hearing. The records of the Suffolk County Correctional Facility were subpoenaed to ascertain the whereabouts of Pistone during his various terms of incarceration when he claimed he'd spoken to Diaz. It was also important to determine who had visited him and how it was decided to confine him in the administrative segregation wing of the correctional facility where he was surely going to meet Jimmy Diaz and other accused murderers.

The official jail records proved to be in a state of utter disarray. Among other things, they contained white-out changes which couldn't be explained by anyone in authority. The records of outside visitation between April 1 and May 20 were missing, although Pistone testified that his father visited him on a weekly basis. During that same time he was being transported under the various writs, presumably by visiting district attorney detectives, to meetings with the investigating homicide detectives in the office of the prosecutor, Barry Feldman. None of these visits were contained in the records.

What records did exist indicated that on April 26 Pistone requested a transfer to administrative segregation, a request which was apparently granted by Capt. Thomas Leo who was in charge of jail security. Under intense questioning by defense counsel and myself, Capt. Leo volunteered that Pistone was a "frightened prisoner."* Yet there was no notation of the reason for his transfer in the file, and there was no logical reason given for his fright.

It is fair to say that I had grave suspicions that Joseph Pistone was acting as an agent of the homicide squad at a time when Jimmy Diaz was being represented by legal counsel, which would have violated his constitutional rights. But even with the benefit of an extensive fact finding hearing, neither Gianelli nor I could come up with a "smoking gun." I was constrained by law to conclude that Diaz's constitutional rights were not violated. It would be for the trial jury to decide whether Joseph Pistone was to be believed. I certainly didn't believe him. Yet in spite of my serious doubts as to his veracity, which I openly expressed at the conclusion of the hearing, the twelve trial jurors were given the opportunity to weigh the credibility of a person whom I later publicly labeled, in a fit of pique, a "pathological liar."

Had I been able to comfortably reach such a conclusion during the pre-trial hearing, Joseph Pistone would have been a non-issue in the trial of James Diaz for rape and murder, and the history of Suffolk County law enforcement might not have been rewritten. But fate is usually not that kind, and it was the "Jackie Miller" affair which insured Pistone's immortality in the annals of the county's system of justice.

Det. John Miller, a fifteen-year veteran detective of the Suffolk County homicide squad was a high ranking volunteer fireman. He, like so many of his brethren, was an expert in dealing with convicted felons who turned "jailhouse snitch." It was he who had met with Pistone in the district attorney's office on "four separate occasions." Pistone's story, according to Miller, "never changed." Pistone, he said, "never asked for anything...was to expect nothing, and nothing was being offered."

Pistone's attorney, he said, told him to "be a man," and to "get his life straightened out." These inspirational words and Pistone's own sense of decency and outrage were enough for him to come forward with very damaging testimony against a fellow felon—an accused murderer—for which "he had everything to lose, and nothing to gain," and despite the fact that he had been a "frightened prisoner."*

Miller had handwritten notes of his very important conversations with Pistone. These notes corroborated what the informant said he'd been told by Jimmy Diaz. The detective's testimony and notes had strongly influenced my decision to allow Pistone to testify at trial. But his conspicuous absence at another hearing which I was compelled to conduct during the course of the trial provoked my decision to strike a portion of Pistone's testimony from the record and to instruct the jury to disregard that testimony. This unhappy decision was underscored by my angry statement on the record, but out of the presence of the jury, that Pistone was a "pathological liar." The acrimonious exchange between the prosecutor and me was featured prominently in a *Newsday* article on the following day.[6] Trial judges don't usually label prosecution witnesses liars, nor do they usually infer that a prosecutor is involved in the subornation of perjury, and in October 1985 *Newsday* was closely monitoring everything being said in my courtroom. We were rapidly slipping into a quagmire in which my courtroom was becoming a battleground between judge and prosecutor.

Although Jimmy Diaz refused to sign the written confession, the police testified that he had agreed to sign the portion of the first page of the written confession which documented his constitutional rights—the Miranda warnings. They also said that he had initialed the various photographs which were shown to him during the interview at Yaphank headquarters. Paul Gianelli, Diaz' counsel, based upon what he'd been told by his client, believed that the signature and the initials were not genuine.

He retained the services of Jean Berrie, a New England handwriting expert, to examine these documents in an effort to determine whether the writings were, in fact, genuine. Feldman, as are all prosecutors, was entitled to her report in advance of her testimony, just as the defense was entitled to the scientific reports of prosecution experts. Barry Feldman was forever pressing Gianelli for the results of her handwriting analysis. He was entitled to prepare his cross-examination, and to have her findings reviewed by a prosecution expert.

Detective Rafferty was the first witness to describe the Diaz interview to the jury and to recount the alleged oral confession to the Negus murder. He was called to the witness stand on the morning of September 26, and he did not conclude his testimony until the afternoon of October 1. During the course of extensive direct and cross-examination he meticulously, and in great detail, described the events of September 21, 1984 when James Diaz, he said, admitted raping and murdering Maureen Negus to him and his partner. Never once did he mention whether Diaz, who was left-handed, had signed and initialed the documents with his right hand or his left hand. It seemed to have no significance at that time. Nor did his supplementary report mention this fact within its explicit contents. This did not become an issue in the trial until the cross-examination of Detective Cassidy on October 3. But there had been an intervening event which apparently precipitated testimony on this subject.

At the close of testimony on October 2, Feldman, Gianelli and I were engaged in an off-the-record conference in chambers to discuss the progress of the trial. The prosecutor asked again about the report of the defense handwriting expert. He insisted upon seeing the final report without any further delay. Gianelli said that he had not yet received a formal written report, but he had been informed that his expert was of the opinion that the initials on the backs of the photographs were not those of Jimmy Diaz. By the time of that revelation, Rafferty had concluded his testimony for the prosecution.

Rafferty's partner, Detective Cassidy, was called as a prosecution witness on the afternoon of October 3. During the course of direct examination by the prosecutor he largely corroborated the testimony of Rafferty concerning the Diaz oral confession. He identified the various photographs of the gloves, the Port Jefferson Station home of Maureen Negus, and the body of the deceased in the basement of her home. In painstaking detail he described how the accused initialed each of these photos. He even recalled Diaz saying: "That's the way she looked when I left." Once again, not one word was uttered about the manner in which the left-handed defendant initialed the photographs—with his right hand or his left.

It was Paul Gianelli's turn to cross-examine on the morning of October 4th. He nervously moved his barely five foot frame from counsel table to conduct what turned out to be something more than a routine cross. As smart as he was, and Paul Gianelli was as good as they came in Suffolk County, he could not have anticipated the answers he would get from

Cassidy just before the morning recess. It was enough to floor even the most experienced defense lawyer.

As the cross-examination returned to the Yaphank interrogation session Jim Cassidy repeated the police version that Diaz initialed the back of the photos of things with which only the perpetrator of the brutal murder could be familiar. But, like a bolt out of the blue, not in response to any question, he volunteered that he "saw him do it with his right hand." The detective "thought it was unusual, knowing that he was left handed." Despite the unusual occurrence, the impact that this might have upon the validity of the accused's confession, he'd made no notes of this, nor did it appear in any of the police reports.*

By that time, my experiences had me thinking about the possibility of a book. In my trial notes, I highlighted this piece of Cassidy's testimony in yellow with two asterisks. In the upper margin, I noted: "For the book." My trial notes now contain many such notations.

In an unusually brief redirect examination, Feldman made sure that he returned to the theme of initialing of the photographs. It was abundantly clear that Feldman fully intended that this testimony come out during cross-examination. He would now use the redirect examination to underscore this well planned and very damaging prosecution evidence. It would certainly serve to neutralize the anticipated expert testimony for the defense that the initials were a forgery. Like the chiming of a church parishioner to the minister's responsive reading Cassidy dutifully responded to Feldman's question: "It had struck me as peculiar that he initialed with his right hand and signed his signature with his left."* Jimmy Diaz's fate was being sealed by a chorus of rehearsed responses which could not be corroborated by even one line of notes or one notation on a police report. But the worst was yet to come.

As Detective Cassidy was leaving by the back door of the courtroom, being escorted from the lock-up area was Feldman's ace in the hole, the incarcerated Joseph Pistone, to help dig an even deeper grave for Diaz. He was now an involuntary guest of the Nassau County Correctional Facility. On the stand, Feldman walked him through his years of criminal activity since his sixteenth birthday. It was important for the prosecution to be open to the jury to soften the impact of an anticipated cross-examination intended to impeach his credibility as a critical prosecution witness by alluding to his life of crime. But only Feldman and his cohorts could know how critical his testimony would be. In little more than twenty minutes, I was left momentarily speechless and aghast by what I heard—for the first time.

After familiarizing the jury with his criminal pedigree, Feldman steered Pistone to his discussions with Jimmy Diaz in the confines of the protective security wing of the Suffolk County Correctional Facility. This testimony was very familiar since it tracked what he had told us during the pre-trial hearing. But then lightning struck. I had come to expect almost anything from a Suffolk County prosecutor, but with what was forthcoming, Barry Feldman would achieve a new low—even for Suffolk.

As Pistone passed by Diaz's cell just two weeks before the trial, he had seen his "friend" practicing the alphabet on a piece of paper with both hands. Being the inquisitive sort, Pistone asked Jimmy what he was doing. Jimmy, without hesitation, responded that "his lawyer told him to do it. It would help him with his case."* Pistone said that he had conveyed this information to Detective Jack Miller at one of their meetings.

We had suspended jury selection to conduct a hearing into the alleged admissions and confessions given to Joseph Pistone by Jimmy Diaz. He had been examined, cross-examined, reexamined and recross-examined. In his testimony, Jack Miller corroborated what had taken place at the four meetings. He had taken complete notes of what Pistone had allegedly told him. Yet, not one word on this subject was uttered by anyone during the course of the hearing. In my trial book I noted again in the margin: "incredible, incredible, incredible (the man is a pathological liar—being used by the prosecution)."

Visibly angered by this sleazy trial tactic and obvious piece of perjury, Gianelli chose to pursue his cross-examination, although he could have asked for, and I would surely have granted, a continuance in the trial. The circumstances certainly warranted an inquiry into what had just transpired. But that was left until the next morning when cooler heads would prevail.

Neither Paul Gianelli nor I are infallible, and we could have been grievously wrong in our independent assessments of what had taken place. Perhaps Pistone was telling the truth. Perhaps Feldman, in his zeal as a prosecutor, had not knowingly called a perjurer to the witness stand. It would have been simple to prove that we were wrong. Feldman need only have put Detective Miller on the stand again to produce the notes of his meetings with Pistone. Late that afternoon, Feldman said that he had every intention of calling Miller at a special hearing the next morning. He was incensed that his integrity was being openly questioned.

As a long afternoon and evening slowly turned to night and eventually to morning, we were once again in court out of the presence of the jury. Inexplicably and without any reason given, Feldman announced that he had decided not to call Jackie Miller after all. There was only one conclusion which could now be drawn. Pistone had perjured himself and the prosecutor who had to be aware of this perjury decided not to entangle Miller in the sticky mess. Joseph Pistone was an expendable tool, but a homicide detective was a horse of another color!

I was inwardly seething and rapidly losing control of my emotions. No conviction was important enough for any prosecutor to use the likes of a Joseph Pistone in a court of law, let alone in a trial where a person's life was on the line—even one like Jimmy Diaz. I decided to question Pistone myself. I was now even more convinced that he had intentionally falsified his testimony, and, even more disturbed that the prosecutor was probably a party to this entire charade. It was then that I totally lost my courtroom composure, whatever was left of it. I dug back into my knowledge of Pistone's history and referred to him as a "pathological liar."

A sanctimonious Feldman took immediate offense.

"Is this court alleging that we knowingly brought in perjured testimony?" snapped the angry prosecutor.

Taking charge of my emotions and fully understanding the possible ramifications of my words I elected to measure them very carefully to avoid any further courtroom confrontation. The middle of a murder trial was not the time or the place to publicly challenge the integrity of an assistant district attorney, even the likes of Barry Feldman.

"I am not accusing the district attorney's office of misconduct, but the defendant's rights have been seriously prejudiced."

But my blood was boiling and measuring my words only served to make me more angry as my voice boomed over the courtroom public address system.

"If this defendant is guilty, I want him convicted. But by God, if he is not guilty of this charge he should not be convicted, and it is not important enough to have perjurers come into this court to ensure that somebody is convicted of murder."[7]

That afternoon, the district attorney, Patrick Henry himself, was interviewed by a *Newsday* reporter about the events in the Diaz trial. "Our position is that there was no perjury," he told the paper. "Practically everything that [Pistone] testified to has been corroborated."

When a reporter asked about the testimony of the handwriting practice, Henry said, "Well, that's all been stricken. I can't comment on that."[8]

There is no question but when a large portion of Pistone's testimony was stricken from the record he was rendered absolutely ineffective as a witness for the prosecution. In fact, the events might very well have had an adverse affect upon the People's case. But the district attorney's office had much more than the testimony of Joseph Pistone. There was still the hidden trump card in the person of the other jailhouse snitch, Larry Middleton. His testimony might even corroborate a large portion of what Pistone told the jury about his various conversations with Jimmy Diaz. But once again, as in the case of Detective Miller, Feldman would inexplicably, and without any reason given, not play that card. Middleton never surfaced at the trial, and to this date, Barry Feldman and his cohorts may be the only people who can explain why he was never called. One can only speculate that even an overzealous prosecutor was not prepared to deal with another Pistone fiasco.

****

In its final report, the State Commission of Investigations corroborated my worst suspicions concerning Pistone and his role in the trial of James Diaz:

> The Commission believes that in the Diaz trial McCready, Dubey and Pistone all knowingly gave false testimony.
> ...a jailhouse informant named Joseph Pistone gave sworn

testimony before the Commission that he had perjured himself in the Diaz trial and that two Suffolk police detectives, John Miller and Leon McKenna, had suborned the perjury and coached him (Private Hearing, Pistone, 3/21/86, p. 10). Pistone testified before the Commission that Miller and McKenna had shown him the Diaz "confession" and said "this is how it happened.

Pistone...testified at the Diaz trial that Diaz had told him in extensive detail about his murder of Negus; however, before the Commission, Pistone recanted this testimony (Private Hearing, Pistone, 3/21/86, pp. 19-31).

Barry Feldman, the trial prosecutor, testified before the Commission that Pistone was one of five jailhouse informants who were anxious to testify about Diaz. Four were rejected, but Pistone was chosen because he had "built-in inherent credibility" because he did not ask for a deal (Private Hearing, Feldman, 12/3/86, p. 60). Despite the fact that a polygraph was given to one of the four rejected jailhouse informants, which he failed, no polygraph was requested by Feldman for Pistone (Public Hearing, 1987, pp. 525-530). Furthermore, there were no notes or reports prepared by the police or district attorney regarding the statements of any of the purported jailhouse informants except Pistone, regarding whom a few pages of notes were made by Detective McKenna, allegedly summarizing Pistone's statements about what Diaz had told him (Public Hearing, 1987, p.526).[9]

A polygraph administered to Pistone on February 17, 1986, by an independent polygraph expert at the request of the Commission indicated that Pistone lied at the Diaz trial and his testimony before the Commission containing his recantation was truthful (Public Hearing, 1987, Exhibit 6). Both Pistone and Miller had testified that Miller had been taking notes. (286)

****

The Commission concluded that Dubey and McCready, as well as Pistone, willfully gave false testimony. I would have needed a crystal ball to know that Dubey was falsifying his credentials, but K. James McCready was another story. His testimony for the prosecution served to both exacerbate and reinforce my feelings about what was taking place all around me in the midst of an important murder trial.

Detective McCready, successful accuser of Robert Catone and Timothy O'Toole, played a very limited role in the apprehension and accusation of James Diaz. As good a detective as he believed he was, he had been unsuccessful in eliciting a signed written confession from this accused. He had attempted to ply his art as an inquisitor, but he had gotten nowhere with this dull-witted drifter, and he could not have been happy with his failure to succeed where others had also failed. His statistics and reputation would certainly suffer. But as a trusted member of the team, he had a role to play.

Not long after the apprehension of Jimmy Diaz, he was assigned the task of interviewing Long Island Railroad workers at the Port Jefferson Station rail yard to determine whether they could identify Diaz as the person they had seen in the vicinity of the parked trains on June 8, 1984 where it was believed he sometimes made his home. There were always some empty railroad cars in the yard since the station was the easternmost terminus of the Port Jefferson line.

On June 26, 1984 McCready interviewed three railroad workers. Though McCready was called as a witness for the prosecution, Barry Feldman chose not to question him about his investigation at the rail yard. According to the detective, he had discussed this identification procedure with the prosecutor on September 13, 1985, about three weeks before his testimony, and they had agreed that the identification procedure was "tainted." He was told by Feldman that "If Gianelli wants to call them [the railroad workers], let him call them!"*

Gianelli was aware of McCready's conversations with the railroad workers. But he had been told by Feldman that there had been no photo identification procedure involved, and that Diaz was identified "based upon a photograph in the newspaper."* He had been set up by being told only half of the truth. A defense attorney in a criminal case has the absolute right to know about any identification procedure, such as a line-up or a photo identification, which has been used by the police, tainted or untainted.

The trap was set, and it was sprung upon an unprepared Gianelli during his cross-examination of McCready. Late in the afternoon of October 9, after an intense period of questioning, during which time the smug detective gratuitously blurted out to the jury, "I know this case will be successfully prosecuted...They said they had seen his picture in the paper...didn't know what paper."

When the detective checked to see if Diaz's picture had been in the *Daily News*, *Newsday* or the *Post*, he "couldn't find his picture in any paper." In fact, the first picture of Diaz appeared in the October 28, 1985 edition of a local paper, *The Port Jefferson Record*, two days after his interviews of the railroad workers. He testified that he returned in April 1985, at which time "they said it was a description, not a picture in the paper...they said they saw a sketch." He thought to himself: "What the hell is going on here?"*

Although under oath, McCready would not admit, until I released the jury for the day, that he had taken a mug shot of Diaz with him to display to the railroad workers in an effort to identify the perpetrator. He said that he had been told: "Yeah, that's him- that's the guy!" This photo display constituted an identification procedure about which Gianelli should have been informed. But McCready said that he "wasn't going to do a photo spread...[he was] not being identified as a perpetrator."*

Nothing could've been further from the truth. He knew that James Diaz was already accused of the Negus murder when he interviewed the railroad workers. According to the detective, Diaz had orally confessed to him and his cohorts less than one week before. Yet, he had the temerity to testify under oath that he was not being identified as a perpetrator. Gianelli immediately moved for a mistrial on the grounds that the assistant district attorney had not only withheld evidence, but that he had "manufactured" evidence. This application was neither granted nor denied. I took a calculated risk by deciding to "reserve decision."* By that time, right or wrong, I had concluded that even a lay jury was probably seeing through this charade and that they would return an acquittal. If I was right, I would be relieved of the burden of dismissing the indictment and creating the possibility of a new trial. One trial like this one was more than enough!

Before we left that evening, Feldman, Gianelli and I had an another off-the-record conversation about the case. The usually "cocky" prosecutor was visibly shaken by what had taken place. His face was ashen. But he assured us that McCready had probably assumed that the workers were referring to a photograph which they had seen in a newspaper. Feldman was directed not to discuss this case with McCready during the recess. I had given the same instruction to the detective. He was scheduled to return for a continuation of cross-examination in the morning.

Barry Feldman must have been possessed of super-human psychic powers. Virtually the first words uttered by the detective on the morning of October 10, as predicted on the evening before by Feldman, was that when Butch Schumel (one of the railroad workers) "said he saw Diaz in the paper...(he) assumed it was a picture of him." With an air of counterfeit innocence on his face, which was honed to perfection by McCready, he turned directly to the jury. In response to Gianelli's persistent questioning, he answered: "I did not discuss this case with Feldman or anyone else since yesterday...I went over this thing a thousand times in my mind...."*

I had heard enough. If there were any way to end the Diaz trial with any degree of finality at that time, I would have done so. But that was not within the realm of possibility. The charade would have to continue. There was too much at stake. Nevertheless, I denied Gianelli's application to strike all of McCready's testimony "as a matter of law." I had sufficient faith in the fifteen jurors to believe that they too were not being hoodwinked by this deadly game of double speak.

****

Detective McCready remained in the homicide squad long after all of his cohorts had resigned, retired or been transferred. He would continue even under a new police commissioner who had been hired by the county executive to clean house. But McCready was not ignored by the State Commission of Investigation in its final report:

> The final instance of false testimony in the Diaz case discussed at the Commission's public hearing concerned testimony by Detective James McCready regarding his interviews of three railroad workers who placed Diaz near the scene of the murder close to the day of its occurrence. In his police report McCready wrote that the railroad workers recognized Diaz from pictures

in the newspaper (Public Hearing, 1987, Exhibit 16). However, after it was demonstrated by the defense that there had not been any pictures of Diaz in the newspaper at the time of the McCready interviews, McCready changed his testimony and, contrary to his police report, said he actually had shown mug shots of Diaz to the railroad workers (Public Hearing, 1987, Exhibit 16).

Between the time of McCready's false testimony regarding the newspaper identification and his corrected testimony about the mug shots, Assistant District Attorney Feldman assured Judge Namm that there was no need for any identification hearing because McCready had not shown mug shots to the railroad workers (Public Hearing, 1987, Exhibit 16 at 532-536). After McCready admitted showing the mug shots, Feldman attempted to explain away his prior incorrect assurance to Judge Namm by claiming that the only discussion he had previously had with McCready on this issue consisted of a very brief conversation on the way to the courtroom when McCready answered, in response to a question by Feldman, that there were "no ID problems" in this case. Feldman's affirmative representation to Judge Namm was based upon McCready's brief comment, which later proved to be false (Public Hearing, 1987, p. 586). Even apart from false testimony, false representations or perjury, this was the second time in the trial that Feldman was taken by surprise by the testimony of his own police witnesses: McCready in this instance, and Rafferty in connection with the "wiping the blood off the knife" statement.*

****

The older and more experienced I get, the more I have come to recognize that life is full of unexpected irony. More often than not these ironies are the result of human shortcomings. It is written that we were all created in God's image. Unfortunately, however, we were not endowed by our creator with his qualities of perfection. Hubris, bred from arrogance and conceit, is too often the sire of irony. But to write of someone else's hubris, arrogance and conceit is to expose one's own flank to the same accusation. Nevertheless, there is no great risk in speaking of Suffolk's former chief forensic serologist, Ira Dubey, in the same breath that utters the word "hubris".

By the time of the Diaz trial, Dubey was firmly established in the state of Maryland as Director of the State Police Crime Laboratory. This rape-murder trial was his last major piece of business in Suffolk County. He spent almost two full days on the witness stand. In any other case, his testimony, coupled with the alleged oral admissions, would have been more than enough to bring in a quick conviction. But this was not any other case. This was "The People of the State of New York v. James Diaz" in 1985 in the County of Suffolk.

It was Dubey who had examined the sweat on the tee-shirts and concluded that its owner fell within the same blood grouping as the Negus perpetrator. Just as in the O'Toole case, he had given great impetus to the police investigation and interrogation of Jimmy Diaz. Yet there was more. From his tests, he concluded that the defendant's various genetic markers contained in his blood sample were consistent with the genetic markers found in the seminal fluid left by the murderer. It was his opinion that there was a "high degree of probability" that the two unknown pubic hairs found at the brutal crime scene came from the same source as the defendant's known pubic hair.

James Diaz was a dark skinned Caucasian of apparent Hispanic ancestry, or of possible black origin. Dubey concluded that if Diaz were Caucasian, he'd fall within 7.2% of the male population with the same genetic markers. If he were black, the probability would be reduced to 4.7%, but if he was truly of Hispanic ancestry, the number was as low as 2.7%. But, being the careful and fair forensic scientist that he was, Dubey assumed that Diaz was Caucasian, thus within the highest group—7.2%.* Diaz had been given the benefit of every reasonable doubt.

Upon hearing this testimony for the first time, Paul Gianelli became visibly livid. He claimed that he was being "repeatedly led down the garden path by the people [Barry Feldman]." It was, he said, a "vicious attempt to conduct this trial in anything but a fair" manner. He claimed that he was being "sandbagged," and that he had not been given the correct report by the prosecution.*

Feldman was not fazed by this. He argued that Gianelli was given the opportunity to talk to Dubey in advance of his testimony, or to have his expert talk to him. The Pistone affair had no apparent permanent effect upon the brazen prosecutor. From his point of view, James Diaz was receiving the fair trial to which he was entitled under the law. He would retain this air of self-righteousness even as he responded to the piercing examination of the State Commission of Investigation at its 1987 public hearing.

As sanctimonious as Feldman was in his quest for conviction of the "guilty," so was Ira Dubey unrelenting in his display of smugness and conceit. By 1985 he had hoodwinked the entire criminal bar and bench of Suffolk County, and by then he had expanded his horizons south to Maryland. Like my brethren, I too was impressed by his credentials and his ability to lull a jury of lay persons into true believers of his scientific word. Through our many cases together, we had developed a certain camaraderie, probably bred from our common Jewish heritage, and mutual love for travel. Although we never developed a social relationship, this limited friendship resulted in frequent whispered conversations at the bench about our travels to distant shores. So it was not unusual that my wife and I attended his farewell party given by members of the district attorney's office at a local country club earlier that year—B.C. (Before Corso). This was something that we rarely did, but Dubey seemed to be somebody special. Like in so many other respects, how wrong I turned out to be!

On the second day of his testimony, he suggested that we have lunch together to talk over old times. Both Gianelli and Feldman agreed that they had no problem with our lunch so long as it was at a place which would not be frequented by any of the jurors. Dubey drove me to a small restaurant in Westhampton, several miles from the courthouse in his Jaguar XJ-12 complete with personalized nameplate on the dashboard. I was appropriately impressed and the lunch, in the context of future events, turned out to be somewhat unusual.

After a brief friendly discussion about his new position and the house that he was building, he shifted the conversation to the real subject of our meeting—my open and very notorious problems with the district attorney's office. He volunteered that he was happy to have left Suffolk County, and happy that he no longer had to deal with that office. Without defining what he had seen, he claimed that he was uncomfortable with the way cases were being handled by the major offense bureau. I was really on to something, he said, and it was important that I continue to pursue my close scrutiny of the various homicide cases on my docket. Irony or chutzpah? Less than two years later, Ira Dubey was indicted for perjury for falsifying his credentials in several of the most important Suffolk County criminal cases.

****

The SIC was not kind to Ira Dubey in its final report:

> In another instance of false testimony by the People's witnesses in the Diaz case, Deputy Director of the County Crime Laboratory Ira Dubey, who was later to plead guilty to giving false testimony about his credentials in more than 20 serious felony trials in Suffolk County, testified falsely about his academic credentials (Public Hearing, 1987, pp. 602-610). Diaz prosecutor Barry Feldman, a personal friend of Dubey, had played the key role in failing to properly investigate, or to tell the District Attorney, information told to Feldman in 1983 by Dubey's supervisor revealing that Dubey was testifying falsely about his credentials in criminal cases. Despite his having been previously provided this information, Feldman allowed Dubey to again testify falsely about his credentials in the 1985 Diaz trial. Feldman's explanation for allowing Dubey to so testify was that he presumed Dubey had obtained the missing academic degree since the 1983 allegations (Public Hearing, 1987, p. 610).[11]

****

Hubris, arrogance, conceit, self-righteousness and perjury were the prosecution's formula for what they believed would be a swift and certain conviction in the trial of James Diaz. The prosecutor and his cohorts were convinced that their cause was just and that the certain conviction of the accused would do justice to the memory of Maureen Negus. But the jury, mercifully, had other ideas. They had not been asleep during the weeks of trial, and they would have the final word on the subject of conviction.

THIRTEEN

"We Were Afraid That We Were Letting a Murderer and a Rapist Go."**

I N 1956 I GRADUATED FROM THE U.S. ARMY RANGER SCHOOL at Fort Benning, Georgia. The goal of the school was to graduate officers and non-commissioned officers who would be able to exercise leadership under the most adverse combat conditions. They taught me to expect almost anything in a hostile situation. Twenty-nine years later, I was engaged in unexpected, undeserved and unsolicited daily combat with certain members of the Suffolk County Police Department and district attorney's office. I had been trained to be prepared for any eventuality, but the bizarre events which occurred during the trials of Peter Corso and James Diaz left this old "Ranger" overwhelmed and unprepared for the everyday events.

On September 6, after Pistone's emergence as a witness was reported in the news media, my law secretary, Bob Meguin, took a telephone call from a "male individual who identified himself as Jack the Ripper." The self-proclaimed "Jack" claimed that he'd had conversations with Joseph Pistone "about what kind of deal he should try to make with the DA." He also claimed that Pistone was "lying about the statements attributed to Diaz by him." He bragged that he had been an informant in the past and professed to be credible. According to the caller, who was obviously an inmate in the

---

** Anonymous member of Diaz jury. See "Jury: Not Guilty," Susan McGinn, *Port Jefferson Record*, October 31, 1985.

county jail, he was to meet with Thomas Maier of *Newsday* that afternoon. Bob correctly suggested that he contact either Feldman or Gianelli.[1] Our "Jack the Ripper" was not heard from again until December 9 of that year when calls were received by a court clerk and a court officer who were assigned to my courtroom. I wasn't available when he called, and even if I were I would not have spoken to him. The phone call went as follows:

"Hello, Judge Namm's chambers."

"I would like to speak to Judge Namm."

"Who's calling?"

"I can't give my name. I want to talk to the Judge."

"You would have to make an appointment to see or talk to the Judge."

"Tell him its 'Jack the Ripper' and I have a recorded message for him."

"The Judge is not available right now. Can you give me your phone number and I'll get back to you?"

"I don't have a phone, and my friend wouldn't like me to give his number."

"Why don't you call back in an hour at about 11:30 A.M. He should be available at that time."

"Alright, I'll call back in an hour."[2]

"Jack" called again during the lunch recess, and he was not heard from again. Unfortunately the bizarre events did not end with this self-styled "Jack the Ripper." Such happenings would not only take place on the telephone. They would extend to the courthouse and its immediate environs as well.

****

Feldman concluded the prosecution case in a defensive mode. He called Bill Keahon, the prosecutor in the Pius murder trials, to the stand to directly confront the "two knife" issue. Keahon left the district attorney's office in January to enter private practice, but prosecutor's blood was still running through his veins. He told the jury of an alleged informal meeting in the summer of 1984 between Rafferty, Wilutis and himself. "Rafferty," he proclaimed, "didn't believe that either of the knives was the murder weapon."* A second knife had been recovered from a creek which flowed into the Long Island Sound in Port Jefferson.

On cross-examination Gianelli went directly for Keahon's jugular. He was forced to admit that he usually became so emotionally involved in his cases as a prosecutor that he had once been angry enough to punch a hole in a picture in his office when he lost a case. But in this case he claimed he had no "personal emotional ties." He "would not lie at this time." Presumably that disclaimer extended also to his gratuitous statement from out of left field that, "Feldman is the best in the office."*

What better way for a prosecutor to convince a wary jury that only the "best" in the office was good enough to prosecute the likes of James Diaz, a despicable character who was unquestionably guilty of this dastardly deed? The "best" would certainly never mislead them into an unjust conviction. Four years later, Feldman and Keahon formed a business association for the practice of law. The deep bonds formed in their prosecutorial years helped to seal their professional future together.

But even the best of prosecutors could not make K. James McCready credible when he was deeply and emotionally involved in his witness routine. McCready and Keahon were called back-to-back to lend firm support and credence to the prosecution's case which was fast becoming more and more unhinged with each passing day. McCready not only told of his meetings with the railroad workers and his conversation with the accused. He also told of his brief discussion with Steven Walker, the deceased's brother-in-law. Steven Walker, in his expert opinion, was a "kook" who believed that he could communicate with the dead.

McCready's opinion notwithstanding, this so-called "kook" was a general contractor who employed fifty people in a construction company that grossed $3,000,000 a year. He had been deeply affected by Maureen's death. So he decided to do some investigating of his own after her funeral motorcade was disturbed by a motorcyclist with what he described as "hatred and violence in his voice." The biker called out to the bereaved friends and family, "All you mother fuckers..."* In Walker's unprofessional opinion, the mysterious stranger fit the published early description of the perpetrator. He turned out to be one Joseph Caligiuri, a chef in a local restaurant, who was somehow connected with United Cerebral Palsy, a charity in which Maureen had a limited involvement. But the police would have none of this, especially the information he had gathered by searching through Caligiuri's trash, a tactic used frequently by Suffolk County detectives.

"I went through a bag of garbage," Walker told the investigating detectives.

"We don't need your evidence," was their response.

Bluntly, he was told to "mind his own business," and he had not even told them that he had sensed Maureen's presence on three separate occasions after her death. In his vision, she had offered words of comfort for her husband and expressed concern for her two children. She had given him "inspiration." Despite incredulous badgering by Feldman on cross-examination, in an attempt to ridicule the witness, he could not get Walker to say that the deceased had accused Caligiuri of her murder. This, Walker said, "would be a lie."* Even so, Feldman callously pressed on. It could not hurt to heap ridicule upon an innocent defense witness in a case which was long since shattered by the prosecution's own witnesses, and where it seemed that any ridicule was previously reserved for the people's witnesses.

As an anti-climax, the jury was treated to two long days of verbal battle between the defendant's handwriting expert and a handwriting expert from the district attorney's office. It was the defense expert's opinion that Jimmy Diaz hadn't initialed any of the photographs, and certainly not with his right hand. Jean Berrie, who in the past was used by the Suffolk County district attorney's office as their expert, had obtained right-handed samples from Diaz. It was her opinion that "all known writings [the Diaz exemplars] were authored by a different person than the questioned writings [the initialed evidentiary photographs]."

Her testimony was the icing on the defense case, and Barry Feldman never succeeded in shaking her. Though she could not say with any degree of scientific certainty that all of the initials were penned by one person, she was certain that if Diaz had initialed the photographs with his right hand there would be, what she called, "a tremor of fraud."* She could find none. She was an extremely convincing witness.

On the other hand, Robert Jameson, an expert in the district attorney's office believed that it was "highly probable that the questioned writings and standards were written by the same person," but his opinion could not be "conclusive, because there are only two characters" (J and D). But he was convinced that Diaz "is capable of signing with either hand."

The testimony of the experts was a legal wash. A juror could believe what he or she wanted to believe. At long last, and not one minute too soon as far as I was concerned, the case was given to the jury. They were sequestered in a local hotel during the entire period of deliberations. Under New York law, the twelve jurors were rendered incommunicado—no outside contacts, no newspapers and no radio or television news—until they reached a verdict.

This jury was handed a monumental task by Barry Feldman. He told them in summation, over Gianelli's objection, that in order to find Jimmy Diaz not guilty of the charges, they'd have to characterize the police witnesses as "liars." In his hubris, he was attempting to convince them that no decent law abiding Suffolk County jury would ever place such a label upon members of its elite homicide squad. It was a shrewd strategy, given the circumstances of the Diaz case. But even this strategy was doomed to failure. The torturous and painstaking deliberations ultimately took a full four days, from Wednesday, October 22 until Saturday, October 25. Each juror gave a full pound of flesh to the ends of justice.

But deliberations or not, the bizarre occurrences of the Diaz trial were not yet destined to conclude. An unsuspecting jury was tussling with each other and the mountain of evidence while the trial judge was continuing to do battle with an angry prosecutor and some never-to-be-identified phantoms shouting expletives at him from the prosecutor's open office window on the fourth floor of the Criminal Courts Building. The camel's back was finally shattered, and life would never again be the same for this beleaguered and exhausted member of the judiciary.

Sixteen jurors heard the Diaz case. The twelve regular jurors ranged in age from twenty-eight to sixty-five, and the average juror was forty-five years of age. All were white and none was Hispanic. Five were women, including the forelady of the jury. Except for the number of women, it was a typical Suffolk County jury, although it did not represent a true cross-section of the community. Given the nature of the case and the charges faced by James Diaz, this jury should have leaned squarely on the side of the prosecutor. The odds were surely stacked against the defendant. Yet it was readily apparent to me, given the content of their questions and notes during the deliberations, that they were having real problems with the People's presentation.

But other persons involved in the trial were apparently not getting the same message. The prosecution team was becoming more and more confident of a guilty verdict. For them the verdict would be a welcome repudiation of me and my trial tactics designed, they must have believed, to insure the acquittal of a despicable murderer.

As I was exiting the courthouse building at about 5:00 pm of October 22nd to go home after sending out the jury for the evening, I'd gotten about thirty feet from the security area when I heard a male voice barking like a dog. There were sounds of male laughter and the shout of a voice which bellowed from the almost empty building. Some words were inaudible, but the words "You lose, Stu!" echoed clearly through the open space.

There was no one else in the immediate vicinity and there certainly was no other "Stu" in the area. The message was clearly meant to harass and intimidate me. I turned towards the building, a modern mass of steel, concrete and glass whose windows are usually sealed shut. My line of sight moved upwards toward a large open window on the fourth floor. I could see several unrecognizable male figures, including the male from whom the shouts had emanated. I knew only that the offices of the district attorney were located on that floor, and I instinctively decided to ignore what had just transpired. I turned away and continued towards my car, which was parked in that area of the lot closest to the back door.

My 1984 compact Toyota Tercel was personally washed and polished by me frequently during that summer and fall. It featured low mileage and the original paint was highly shined and unmarred except for an occasional supermarket dent. As I reached the bottom of the courthouse steps, closer to the side of my car which was adjacent to the nearest curb, I couldn't help but notice some long scratches in the paint which were obviously man-made, and which weren't there just three hours before. I had been the victim of vandalism before, and I knew what damage a key can inflict upon the outer skin of a defenseless automobile. I felt the blood rush from my head as I wheeled back towards the courthouse. I sensed a connection with what had just occurred. I now intended to confront the issue head-on. In my mind, the shouts and the vandalism were directly related. It was no mere coincidence. I intended to return to the building to confront the brave men, or man, whom I could see hastily exiting from the open window area as I bounded up the courthouse steps.

The events of 1985 raced through my mind as I awaited the arrival of the slowly descending elevator. Anyone, I thought, who was brazen enough to attempt to harass and intimidate a sitting criminal court judge in the midst of jury deliberations in an important homicide case was capable of almost anything. They had to be stopped now. I had swallowed enough. I had turned my cheek once too often. It was now my turn to take control of events before they were completely out of hand. It was time to directly confront Barry Feldman to determine who was responsible for the unhappy events of that day.

The court clerk was still in the building as I returned to my darkened chambers. I directed him to contact Barry Feldman immediately. He was to report to me forthwith. He would know whose office was the headquarters for a cowardly verbal attack upon an incensed judge. The prosecutor, I was certain, would surely want to help me get to the bottom of this mindless act of hostility.

In a matter of moments, a puzzled and sheepish looking Feldman was seated in a defensive posture just a few feet away from me staring directly into a pair of hardened and angry eyes.

"Whose office has an open window on the southeast corner of the fourth floor?" I asked.

"The only office with an open window on the fourth floor is mine," he responded. "It was just painted, and I've been letting fresh air into the room."

This was no mere coincidence. It could've been anyone's window. Why did it have to be the window of the chief of the trial bureau, the prosecutor of James Diaz? I knew from experience that the homicide detectives responsible for a case on trial spent their time in the district attorney's office to assist in trial preparation and procedure. The culprits were now identified in my mind. My next questions were rhetorical. They required no answer. There would be no presumption of innocence in this investigation. But my hostility wouldn't permit me to end it at that. I pressed on.

"What's going on here? Who was in your office just a few minutes ago?"

"Judge, I don't know. I wasn't in my office," he shot back.

But he'd been in his office less than five minutes later when he responded to the clerk's telephone call. I was convinced that he was lying, and his transparent false air of innocence only made me more furious.

"Who was that brave person that shouted at me as I left the building?

How dare anyone in that office refer to me as "Stu"? To you and your office, I'm 'Judge,' I'm 'Your Honor,' and I'm 'Sir.'"

A now worried Feldman angrily responded again: "I don't know who was in my office five minutes ago. I was down the hall."

"Mr. Feldman, I will get to the bottom of this. This is not going to end this afternoon."

In frustration, I dismissed the chief of the district attorney's felony trial bureau and left for the night. Tomorrow would be another day. I spent the entire night thrashing about in my bed. Some of Suffolk's "finest" had deprived me of a much needed night of sleep. But they couldn't steal my dignity or the dignity of my office. Nor would I permit them to soon forget what transpired that day or on so many other days in my courtroom. An idea which was only a seed in the deepest recesses of my mind now became a firmly planted resolve. I would ask Governor Mario Cuomo to appoint a Special Prosecutor to investigate what happened that afternoon, and the misconduct I believed that I'd witnessed in the Corso and Diaz trials-perjury, subornation of perjury and outright contempt for the justice system from those at the highest level of Suffolk law enforcement who were sworn to preserve and protect the law and the constitution.

Upon my return to court the next morning, I was still seething over the events of the previous day. Before doing anything else, I intended to confront Barry Feldman again—in open court—and this time on the record. Hopefully his memory had improved. Perhaps he had experienced a change of heart. Perhaps he would turn over the culprit or culprits, or admit his own involvement in the sordid affair. It was highly improbable, but I needed to vent my innermost feelings. In an effort to avoid confrontation with a trial prosecutor, I had suppressed my true feelings throughout the Diaz trial. It was time, I believed, to bare these pent up emotions. There was no longer any possibility of prejudicing the jury. They were sequestered and incommunicado except for their notes to the court and the responses which I gave to them in open court. The Diaz verdict couldn't possibly be affected by the events taking place during their deliberations.

"....I'm telling you now that this will not end today, and the Suffolk County Police Department will know today that if there is no investigation of what took place yesterday—because what took place yesterday transcends Judge Stuart Namm," I began. "It transcends the Suffolk County District Attorney's Office. It shows an absolute and utter contempt for the law. Nobody, Mr. Feldman, not I, not you, not the people who were in your office yesterday afternoon, are above the law. The greatest tragedy that may befall is—in this particular case, the greatest tragedy may be...that a guilty person may walk free because of prosecutorial misconduct...A perjurer was brought before this Court, open-eyed by the District Attorney's Office. There's been other perjury in this courtroom...I will not be harassed. I will not be intimidated...."[3]

In my anger, I rambled on as I vented all of the indignation and anger that had festered within me since the July 4th weekend. To my way of thinking, all of these events were interconnected. It was no mere coincidence. I was convinced that I had become the unwilling target of those persons in the highest echelons of law enforcement who could not accept that there were legal limits and rules which bound even them, and that there was at least one judge who was willing to speak out publicly in condemning their violation of individual rights. They had been exposed and they could not, or would not, accept the proposition that, under our system of justice, the end which they sought did not justify any and every means available to them.

I ended my speech by saying, "I'm going to request that an investigation be made to determine whether anybody is attempting to harass me or intimidate me in any way...."[4]

On the following day, a picture of my less than luxurious 1982 Toyota Tercel appeared in *Newsday* in an article captioned "'Intimidation' Alleged by Judge."[5]

An angry district attorney's office was quick to respond to my allegations. The article reported: "'We are astonished and disappointed by these allegations and innuendos, and we categorically deny these outrageous allegations,'" said Steven Wilutis, the county's chief trial prosecutor. "In the entire history of the Suffolk District Attorney's Office, there have never been any allegations as ludicrous as this. Police and prosecutors said they were particularly upset by Namm's assertion that he had been harassed and intimidated by them."[6]

By that time the twelve citizens deliberating behind closed doors were being upstaged by the confrontation between the trial judge and the enraged hierarchy of the district attorney's office. Fortunately, the extra-curricular activities and media coverage had no effect upon the back-room consideration of a verdict in an important murder trial. But they did have an immediate impact upon my closest superiors, the two administrative judges, Justice Stark and the county administrative judge, Arthur Cromarty. The first to express concern was Tom Stark whom I had avoided since our run-in before the commencement of the Diaz trial. At a meeting which he requested, he expressed his concern and the concern of Justice Cromarty "about what appeared to be statements which I was making which were biased against the prosecution."[7] (He was still playing the role of prosecution judge.)

I had to suppress my outrage when he expressed no concern about my recent difficulties, but was more concerned with protecting the honor of the district attorney's office. He made no attempt to ascertain first-hand what took place in my courtroom. To Thomas Stark, I was presumed guilty of prosecutor baiting. There was to be no presumption of innocence, and no effort to determine the truth. This unhappy meeting was cut short by a telephone call from Justice Cromarty. He was being inundated by calls from the media asking whether he was going to conduct an investigation, and he was not certain what kind of an investigation he should conduct. I told him that this was a matter for the police commissioner, and that "if an investigation were not conducted to my satisfaction, it was my intention to take this matter up with the governor."[8] Justice Cromarty wanted to resolve the problem quickly. He suggested a meeting with the district attorney. In his paternalistic way, he believed that he was reassuring me when he said that he would "vouch" for me.

"I don't need anyone to vouch for me," I snapped. I wasn't concerned about possible vulnerability as a result of my actions and statements. "I was simply doing my job as I saw it, and I will continue to call them as I see them!"[9]

Arthur Cromarty, former county Republican chairman and former presiding officer of the now defunct Board of Supervisors, was proposing a political solution to a non-political situation. It was his way of doing things. He wasn't programmed to understand that any intimidation directed at me in my capacity as a judge was an attack upon the entire system.

The chief administrator of all of the courts of Suffolk County had a reputation for having very little understanding of the dynamics of the criminal justice system. Both he and Patrick Henry came from the small town of Babylon. Both were long-time active members of the Republican Party. Patrick Henry's father was the district attorney before Arthur Cromarty traded his political post for the black robes of a justice of the Supreme Court. This confrontation between one of his judges and the DA could potentially tarnish the public image of an individual whom he had helped to nurture through the county's political vineyard.

Our conversation went nowhere. I was in no mood for compromise and I certainly was not about to sit down in the same room with the district attorney. Cromarty had been thwarted in his efforts to extinguish what was threatening to become a conflagration which could engulf many of his political cohorts. In his way of thinking, it was simply not possible that the purveyors of justice in Suffolk County could be snubbing their noses at the constitution, the law and the canons of ethics. And if they were, why could not we just sit down and talk about it in the spirit of gentlemen of good will?

By this time the jury was in its fourth full day of deliberations. Judging from the periodic shouts penetrating the jury room walls, one did not have to be overly perceptive to know that they were having great trouble with the case. By the third day, they were suffering from a type of claustrophobia experienced by many a sequestered juror. They sought permission "to go outside for fresh air."[10] That was the least that I could do for them. To serve as a juror in the Diaz case was to give of one's self above and beyond the call of duty. A little fresh air was not too much to ask.

The pressure was mounting. A short walk in the afternoon sun would not be enough to ease the tension being felt by all. By noon of the fourth day, Friday, October 25, 1985, one of the five female jurors wanted out. She'd locked herself in the toilet before sending out a tersely written note: "Your Honor, I wish to leave the jury room."[11] That request just couldn't be accommodated. The entire jury panel was returned to the courtroom. The note writer and another female juror were openly hysterical, tears flowing freely down their cheeks. After asking for cooler heads to prevail, I directed that lunch be served in a segregated area on the courthouse patio. We had all come too far for it to end that way. A verdict required unanimity of the remaining twelve deliberating jurors. The last thing I wanted was a mistrial. I wanted this case over and done with!

At 4:18 pm, another note was sent from the jury room. The forelady reported some progress. They'd moved from "9-3 to 11-1," but she noted "a decision cannot be made." We were teetering on the brink of the dreaded mistrial—a hung jury.

Judging from the content of their numerous notes, most courthouse observers presumed that the eleven were in favor of conviction. But I knew otherwise. Once again the walls had spoken. Eleven were in favor of acquittal, and only one person was still convinced that James Diaz was proven guilty beyond a reasonable doubt. On the Saturday morning of the fifth day of deliberations, Paul Gianelli was so convinced that the vote was heavily in favor of conviction that he objected to my continuation of the deliberations. He insisted upon the declaration of a mistrial. His client might have a better chance with a new trial. But the district attorney's office, sensing imminent victory, argued for continuation of deliberations. Two hours after the decision to continue, during the noon hour, the jury reached a verdict.

Twelve weary and disheveled citizens filed into a crowded and tension filled courtroom. It was the judicial moment of truth. Several jurors were openly weeping. A second group of twelve ordinary citizens of Suffolk County, like the Corso jury before them, had to know that their verdict would be an indictment of the homicide squad. In his summation, which seemed like eons ago, Feldman had much as told them so.

The grim faced forelady was so shaken that she asked whether she would have to announce the verdict in open court. This could not be avoided. The court clerk was instructed to take the verdict. One by one, the counts of the indictment were read aloud, and one by one, the forelady responded in a barely audible voice: "Count 1, murder in the second degree. Not guilty! Count 2, burglary in the first degree. Not guilty! Count 3, rape in the first degree. Not guilty! Count 4, murder in the second degree. Not guilty!" The numerous police and prosecutors in attendance, on a Saturday afternoon, sunk into a collective state of deep shock. But they were no more shocked than James Diaz and his court appointed attorney, who had worked so hard to achieve this victory.

Twelve typical, conservative, middle class, white, middle aged members of a law and order oriented community had acquitted a young Hispanic homeless drifter of the brutal rape and murder of one of their own—a mother and a nurse. In doing so, by the very standard established by the prosecutor in his closing argument to them, they had found the police witnesses guilty of perjury. They could not know it then, but by their verdict, they had shortened the long, illustrious careers of detectives Rafferty, Cassidy and McCready as members of the homicide squad.

The front page of *Sunday Newsday* announced the verdict to a stunned county: "Diaz Acquitted in Slaying Judge, Jurors Criticize Handling of Case by Police and DA."[12]

Thomas J. Maier of *Newsday* reported the following:

> (T)he jurors said they came to disbelieve the charges of murder, rape and burglary against Diaz presented by several homicide detectives and the prosecutor, Barry Feldman. Immediately after the verdict, juror Timothy Harris, voicing the consensus of the jury, told Feldman: "If someone close to me was murdered, I'd rather have a small-town police department investigate it than have the Suffolk homicide squad with all its resources."
>
> Family and friends of Negus, some of whom wept bitterly as the verdict was announced in the Riverhead courtroom, were upset by the way her death was investigated and prosecuted. "I just hope something good comes out of Maureen's death, which means an investigation of those detectives," said Negus' best friend, Terry Murphy. "It's a disgrace if this guy is free because of their screw-ups."

It was now clear why the jurors were openly weeping as the verdict was announced by their forelady. An anonymous member of the jury complained: "No one in the jury room thought he was innocent. But our job was to decide if they proved beyond a doubt that he was guilty. They didn't."[13] The jury had acquitted a person that they truly believed was guilty of the rape and murder of an innocent woman in the safety of her own home, but their collective conscience and their respect for the rule of law wouldn't permit them to utter the word: "Guilty!"

The greatest tragedy of *The People of the State of New York v. James Diaz* was that a person accused of the most brutal form of rape and murder may have gone free because of sloppy police work, thinly veiled perjury and an arrogance of power which was rooted in the institutional belief that once a suspect was targeted by Suffolk's elite homicide squad, his confession or the testimony of an informant, no matter how questionable, was sufficient to assure a conviction in the courts of Suffolk County. After three murder acquittals in less than ten months, that mythical bubble was burst in 1985. With the adverse publicity, it became progressively more and more difficult in the county to obtain a conviction without hard evidence to corroborate the confession or the testimony of the ever present police informant. It required drastic changes to produce a corps of homicide investigators whose feet were not mired in the muck of past abuses. In October 1985, those changes were just around the corner.

Judge Stuart Namm, District Court of Suffolk County, New York, circa 1977.

Suffolk County Court Judge Stuart Namm is proclaimed "Judge of the Year" by the
Suffolk County Court Officers Association, circa 1984.

Retired Judge Stuart Namm questions retired Suffolk County Detective K. James McCready in a Wilmington, North Carolina courtroom for the documentary, "A Question of Guilt: The Martin Tankleff Story," produced by Stuart and Nancy Namm, and Frazer Ashford of the Unted Kingdom, circa 1998.

Stuart with underwater video camera at Hanauma Bay, Oahu, Hawaii (*top*), and on board Holland America Lines cruise ship, 15 days, from San Diego to the Hawaiian Islands and return, circa 2000.

Retired Judge Stuart Namm, age 72, playing tennis almost daily in North Carolina, circa 2005.

Stuart with a group of Masai crafts women viewing themselves on his video camera. Taken during a photo and video safari to Kenya and Tanzania, first of three such trips to Africa, 2006.

Stuart and Nancy Namm married on January 3, 1997, after both were widowed in early 1996. Photo taken circa 2005.

FOURTEEN

The Investigation Begins

THROUGHOUT THE COURSE OF MY PROFESSIONAL CAREER, whenever the pressure was almost unbearable, a vacation always seemed imminent to ease the burden. The fall of 1985 was no different. Lenore and I had long since planned a trip to Chile, Argentina and Brazil, courtesy of Pan American Airlines' Advantage program. It was scheduled for the beginning of November, and it couldn't have come at a better time. However, before we left there was some unfinished business to attend to.

On October 29, 1985, I addressed a four page letter to Governor Mario Cuomo to request the "appointment of a special prosecutor." I'd taken the final plunge. There could be no turning back. By this one precipitous act, for better or for worse, I sealed the fate of the criminal justice system in Suffolk County, my own fate, and the fate of numerous other persons who toiled within that system. I hoped that it would be for the better. I was still idealistic and naive enough in the fall of 1985 to believe that it could make a difference.

I had been accused of playing politics, with the implication that it had been my intention to adversely affect the political future of the incumbent district attorney. If this letter became a matter of public knowledge, with the election only days away, I'd certainly be accused once again of being politically motivated. So, I wrote:

> When you receive this letter, my wife and I will be on vacation
> in South America—a vacation which was planned many months

ago. We will be returning to our home on November 17, 1985. Such vacation could not have come at a better time, because it is important that any investigation not be commenced until the election of 1985 is part of Suffolk County history. Since none of my actions as a judge have been politically motivated, it is important that this investigation not be perceived as being motivated by politics. However, political considerations aside, I cannot over emphasize my concern that action must be taken by you, before the situation has gotten out of hand, to restore public confidence in the criminal justice system in this county. The citizens of Suffolk County are deserving of nothing less than this by you, the one person who has the authority to ensure that an independent investigation is conducted into the activities of those persons who have abused the public trust which has been bestowed upon them.[1]

It had taken several days to draft this letter. It was important to convey a sense of urgency to Governor Cuomo, but at the same time it was important not to make accusations which could not be supported by fact. While contemplating the content of this important communication, the winds of turmoil were blowing through the county. I had hoped in vain that the police commissioner, a professional with a reputation for decency, would see fit to intercede and put an end to the gamesmanship which threatened the very fabric of law enforcement in the county. Not only would he not intercede, but it would be days before I could even reach him by telephone. He had been called away "on personal business."[2]

When he finally returned my call on the following Monday, he reported that the unnamed persons in Feldman's office denied any involvement in my allegations. Commissioner Treder professed the greatest respect for the judiciary, and a desire to cooperate "one hundred percent." He asked if I'd meet with his chief of detectives, John Gallagher. He was deeply concerned "because at one time the Suffolk County Homicide Squad was the most respected squad in the country, and that its image was now being tarnished."

I agreed to meet with Chief Gallagher, although I had already resolved not to reveal anything to the police department, and to only disclose what

I had observed during the Corso and Diaz trials to an independent investigative body. How could I trust a commissioner who would never even disclose to a judge the names of the shadows in Feldman's open window?

The national media was expressing an interest in the story. A representative of 20/20, a production of ABC News, conveyed an unsolicited offer to do the story on television. He expressed the opinion that this was part of a pattern of abuse which they were seeing throughout the country. I turned him down because, as I told him, I was not in a position to speak to the media at that time. I was not going to sensationalize the story. He believed that I couldn't get a "fair shake," but I wouldn't be persuaded.

I looked forward with great anticipation to my meeting with the chief of detectives. But I was intent on being prepared. We were to meet in my court chambers in Riverhead. I arranged for the presence of my law secretary and a court stenographer. This conversation was going to be memorialized by an accurate transcript. In my new-found paranoia, I had no intention of meeting with them alone, and what was said at the meeting was not to be misquoted.

The meeting with Chief John Gallagher and his assistant chief of detectives, Arthur Feldman (Gallagher also had a witness at his side), proved to be a brief lesson in basic Suffolk County police philosophy. It was made clear to me, in no uncertain terms, that an attack against one cop was an attack against all. I had vowed not to get involved in the specifics of Corso and Diaz, so I had to suppress my natural verbosity as I vented my frustration and anger towards those persons who had been making life very difficult for me since July 4th weekend.

I attempted to make it clear to all who cared to listen that I was not attacking the entire police department. "....anything I am saying to you is not directed at the Suffolk County Police Department," I told them. "It is not directed at—it is directed at a few individuals." While Chief Gallagher had little to say in response to my rambling narratives, Chief Feldman proved to be the outspoken member of the team.[3]

"What is happening is directed at the Suffolk County Police Department," he said. "I am thirty years, and John is equally thirty years in this business, and it is a personal affront to us and every man who wears that uniform. Make no bones about it. Everyone understands that. You know, you—like you say, why are people attacking my record with no facts at all? It just seems to be innuendoes, statements made with nothing specific. You know, it just sort of raises a cloud over everybody with nothing to attack."

I was being asked to understand that a legitimate charge leveled against one cop for misconduct placed a cloud over all of Suffolk's finest. Although I wasn't in the mood for a debate with a police professional with an obvious mission, I could not let it go at that.

"But, Detective, there were things specific said during the course of the trial," I responded. "There are very specific things in the record. All I am saying to you at this moment today is I don't think it would be appropriate for me to go over all those things, but I tell you right now there are specific things in the record. There are no innuendoes in that record. There are specifics...if you look at what certain witnesses said under oath, that is not innuendo. That is black and white, and that's fact."

In sharp contrast to his assistant, Chief Gallagher played the role of diplomat. After about thirty minutes, he felt it was time to draw the unsuccessful meeting to a close.

"We appreciate your talking with us...we look forward to looking at that record, and seeing, as you point out, certain failings, see what we can do, too," he said. "We don't want to continue this way. We can guarantee you that...insofar as the matter concerning the window incident, I can't comment, and I certainly will relay the message. I am sure he [Commissioner Treder] will be in touch with you as to what he found out...Enjoy your vacation. Thanks for your candor."

We did enjoy our vacation, but the commissioner never saw fit to divulge anything about the unsettling events of the previous week. Less than six months later, Chief Gallagher and the chief of the department's internal affairs bureau were placed on indefinite leave at the direction of the Republican County Executive, Peter Fox Cohalan, under the cloud of a federal investigation into the alleged tampering of a narcotics case involving Gallagher's son.[4]

Some six weeks later, in the last week of April, 1986, Gallagher filed his retirement papers. In the spring of 1988, a Suffolk County grand jury handed up an indictment brought by a special prosecutor charging the former chief with conspiring to falsify police records to assist his son avoid a jail sentence for the sale of cocaine. The indictment came just about one year after the retirement under fire of the police commissioner. Gallagher's resignation which was "encouraged and recommended"[5] by the acting County Executive, Michael LoGrande, came as the police department was being simultaneously investigated by the state commission of investigations, the county legislature and the United States Attorney's office.

The investigation and prosecution of a chief of detectives, especially in the County of Suffolk, is not like the prosecution of any other citizen. The prosecution of Gallagher developed a life of its own, necessitating the appointment of two special prosecutors, before he was finally tried and convicted by a Suffolk County jury late in the summer of 1990. A cloud of controversy would forever swirl about this case, with the central characters heaping verbal assaults upon each other.

The initial investigation was carried out by the office of the United States Attorney for the Eastern District of New York. They were looking into allegations of corruption in the police department. Having discovered no violations of federal law, the case was turned over by the feds to the Suffolk County district attorney whose office was itself then under investigation. Patrick Henry decided that he could not, or should not, involve himself in the investigation and prosecution of a high ranking police official.

He turned to Tom Stark, the administrator of the criminal courts, for the appointment of a special prosecutor. It was then that the controversy began, a controversy which involved the state commission of investigations, the court appointed prosecutor and another Supreme Court justice, Kenneth Rohl, Patrick Henry's neighbor and sometime rowing partner from the small village of Babylon.

Tom Stark appointed a fellow Riverhead attorney as special prosecutor, Harvey Arnoff, a former assistant district attorney. Arnoff had a minor role as a special prosecutor in the battle in the 1970s between the former district attorney, Democrat Henry O'Brien, and the former police commissioner, Eugene Kelly.

The commission of investigations, which had developed a file of its own on Chief Gallagher, was concerned that Arnoff was not sufficiently experienced in criminal matters to handle this important corruption investigation. The commissioners were also concerned that Arnoff saw fit to choose a Suffolk County police detective to supervise the Gallagher investigation.[6]

Publicly, the commission expressed concern at Arnoff's "intemperate and injudicious statements" at a press conference which was called by him to castigate the commission for what he claimed was obstruction of his investigation when they refused to turn over evidence and testimony of commission witnesses to him. Privately, however, it was clear from a telephone conversation between myself and the commission's counsel, John Kennedy, that they were concerned that there would be a whitewash of the Gallagher case. The commission was so insecure and unsure of the special prosecutor that they sought his removal by Judge Stark who had appointed him some three months earlier.

Within two weeks after his press conference, Arnoff was fired by Tom Stark. Stephen P. Scaring, a prominent criminal defense attorney and former Nassau County assistant district attorney, was appointed as special prosecutor. Scaring had served two years as chief of Nassau County's homicide bureau. The commission was now satisfied that a properly experienced prosecutor was appointed by Judge Stark to undertake this important investigation. As for me, I was surprised that Stark would choose such a well qualified person to prosecute a high ranking police official, but I was also concerned that at the same time Scaring was representing a Suffolk County police captain on corruption charges alleging that he had been shaking down local restaurant owners in Huntington. My concerns proved to be misplaced as Scaring pursued the investigation with vigor and expertise. The investigation and prosecution culminated in a felony conviction in 1990.

But from the very outset the path to conviction was paved with legal obstacles which threatened a just resolution of this very important prosecution. The criminal justice system can at times be very efficient when it involves the prosecution of a common criminal. Unfortunately, the reverse is often true when the target of an indictment is an important public official. The Gallagher case was no exception to the rule.

Chief Gallagher was represented by the law firm of David Clayton and Peter Mayer, who, but for the Corso case, surfaced often in cases involving police officials and persons connected in some way with the police or district attorney's office. I have always considered it highly ironic that Peter Mayer was the lawyer who first alerted me to acts of police misconduct in the Corso case. In later years I would learn that he had come to regret his role in precipitating an act of whistle blowing which alienated many of his former associates in the district attorney's office and the police department. But his actions were forgivable because they began and ended with the Corso trial. I, on the other hand, would forever be the one who was responsible for bringing in an outside agency, and I would never be forgiven by him or his compatriots.

After the meeting with the commissioner's representatives I was more than ready for Santiago, Buenos Aires and Rio. But the district attorney was not about to let up on his attacks against me. It was getting too close to the election and the county's chief prosecutor, whose office was on the line, was really feeling the heat. Patrick Henry was videotaped on a local television news program. He told the newscaster from Long Island Cablevision that I had been the cause of the acquittals in the Corso and Diaz cases. I had biased the juries against the prosecution in both of these cases. The station sought a response from me, but I was not about to get into that debate despite the absurdity of such a statement. I would bide my time and present the entire ugly truth to an appropriate investigating body. Unlike the district attorney, it was seven years before I would go before the electorate again. Time and truth were both on my side.

Even the sight of the magnificent Andes Mountains and trips to Copacabana Beach and the Argentine pampas were not enough to free our minds of the turmoil that we had left behind. My thoughts would often drift to the local elections. But those thoughts seemed grossly irrelevant as the city of Santiago fell under siege from local insurrectionists seeking the removal of the dictatorial Pinochet government. It was almost a relief to return to the Long Island battleground, after we were forced to speed away from our hotel in an unmarked taxi via back streets and alleyways to an awaiting Pan American Airlines 747 at the Santiago International Airport.

We returned to no surprises. Patrick Henry retained his public office. The electorate had been true to form. The Democrat, Robert Gottlieb, made the margin of victory closer than it should have been, but that was little consolation. He'd run a bruising independent campaign with little help from the county Democratic organization, which, under the long term leadership of Dominic Baranello, always seemed inept and unconcerned in political races which have no impact upon patronage. Independent minded prosecutors and judges, while good for society, create no new jobs for the party faithful.

There had been no response from the governor to my letter, and this was particularly disappointing. But almost immediately upon our return, I received a telephone call from Thomas F. Staffa. He identified himself as chief counsel to the New York State Commission of Investigations, an organization which was entirely unfamiliar to me. He wanted to meet to discuss the events of the last several months. He seemed to be very familiar with the Corso and Diaz trials. I mistakenly assumed that this call was a response to my letter to Governor Cuomo. It was not. The commission's investigators were apparently following the various stories in the news media. The commission had decided to act under its own broad investigative powers.

A meeting was scheduled for November 19 at my Stony Brook chambers. I gathered my notes and memoranda in the hope that at long last something might be done to correct a criminal justice system which, in my estimation, was running wild. I met for the first time with Tom Staffa and Tom Higgins, a retired New York City detective, the commission's chief investigator, in my Stony Brook chambers, some thirty miles west of the courthouse. We were far removed from the enemy camp and those persons who felt that I carried a grudge against Suffolk law enforcement. It was then that I learned that the commission staff had been following the stories in the media for several months. This precipitated the commissioners' decision to open an investigation. The meeting was to determine whether there was a real basis, beneath the media stories, for an investigation. After several hours of frank and open conversation, Staffa was convinced. I agreed to turn over my notes and the names of the jurors in the Corso and Diaz trials. I was going to cooperate to whatever extent the commission felt necessary.

Staffa was a young, well dressed, aggressive attorney who had been an assistant district attorney in Brooklyn at the same time that Barry Feldman worked in that office before his foray into Suffolk County. But Staffa's days as counsel to the commission were rapidly drawing to a close. He had higher aspirations. By July he was replaced by Susan Shepard, the wife of a former United States Attorney and now a Federal District Court judge.

Higgins was gray haired, hardened, and experienced. A former New York City detective, he made no bones about his dislike for the reputation of the Suffolk County homicide squad. But the actual investigation was to be conducted by Bob Frank and Joe Lyons, also veterans of the New York homicide squad, who likewise expressed no great love for Suffolk County's finest.

The commission was politically bi-partisan. Its members were appointed by both Democrats and Republicans. They were chosen by the governor and the presiding officers of the two houses of the legislature. It was chaired by David Trager, a Democrat who was a former United States Attorney and now the dean of Brooklyn Law School, my alma mater. A former Republican district attorney of Suffolk County and former state senator, Bernard Smith, was appointed by the senate majority leader. Another former United States attorney, Edward Korman, soon to become a federal judge, was a Democrat, as was Thomas Culhane, an attorney and former New York City police detective. The fifth member was a Republican from Buffalo, Earl W. Brydges, a former state senator. It appeared like an impressive group to me, but I was unaware of their work, and I remained disappointed that the governor had not seen fit to appoint an independent prosecutor with less ties to politics.

Tom Stark, like Patrick Henry, wasn't about to let me off the hook. In his view, I'd unjustly injured the reputation of the district attorney and the police department. In early December, he came shuffling into my chambers, cane in hand, smiling like the proverbial cat that had swallowed the canary. *Newsday* was reporting that James Diaz was arrested over the weekend by the Suffolk County police. He was being charged with attempted rape and burglary in Mount Sinai, a small residential community bordering Port Jefferson Station where Maureen Negus had been found brutally raped and murdered.[7]

Diaz was free after his family posted $10,000 cash bail on the sex abuse charge which was still pending on my calendar. He denied any involvement in the new case and claimed once again that he'd been framed. Diaz was now living in Queens with his grandmother. His story was that he had been in Queens on the day of the alleged burglary and attempted rape—November 1, 1985. According to the police, they had become suspicious of him because of the similarity of his appearance to a composite sketch drawn by a police artist with the assistance of the victims.

"What do you think about the article in *Newsday*?" Tom Stark asked, obviously referring to the article about James Diaz. "Do you still think that he is innocent?"

"I really don't know anything about that case. I only know what I read in the newspaper," I responded in an attempt to display annoyance with his unfair inquiry.

"I'm getting calls from the news media inquiring whether you will be handling the new Diaz case, and I don't know how to answer them." He was obviously looking for me to walk away from the Diaz case. I reminded him that I had another indictment pending which was going to be tried in January. He also needed to be reminded of the court policy to direct any new indictment to a judge who had a pending indictment involving the same accused.

Stark expressed concern that I was in an adversarial position with the district attorney's office, which I denied. "If I'm an adversary of the district attorney," I said, "then I shouldn't be handling any criminal case in Suffolk County. If so, I'll make the decision to recuse myself, not you for me!"

"Not only am I considering not assigning the new indictment to you," he said, "but I'm considering a transfer of the pending Diaz case to another judge."

My blood was beginning to boil. "If you do so, you'll be subject to criticism for singling out this case in moving it to another judge." I repeated that I was the only appropriate person to make the decision to recuse myself.

"I'm concerned that things will get out of hand, that stories will appear in the newspaper, and that things will be stirred up once again." He was going to get no sympathy or agreement from me. We had long since stopped seeing eye to eye. I just stared at him in an openly hostile manner. He got the message!

Judge Stark shrugged his shoulders and shuffled slowly out of the room. No sooner was he out of the door, then I called the counsel to the commission.

I wanted to immediately report this conversation. This was a practice which I would follow throughout the period of the investigation. Perhaps it was because besides my wife and kids, I no longer trusted anyone. For the next two years, my closest confidants were the attorneys and investigators of the SIC who kept the criminal justice system of Suffolk County under a magnifying glass. Occasionally, one local attorney or another, with a modicum of courage, would comment to me about the situation, or express some muted encouragement or empathy. But for the most part, in the eyes of the organized bar and bench, I was a pariah, a turncoat, a snitch, no better than a jailhouse squealer, who was not to be trusted to even pass the time of day. But for the love and support of my family, my staff and my few close friends, I would feel very alone and vulnerable to the sharks who were constantly circling the local waters in what often seemed like a feeding frenzy.

Paranoia, tempered somewhat by the verbal encouragement of countless unknown strangers, almost on a daily basis, became a way of life. I saw danger and enemies lurking behind every corner and in every confrontation. I stopped carrying my stainless steel .38 caliber Charter Arms Special for fear that I would be placed in a situation where it could be claimed that I had provoked a deadly incident which resulted in my demise. There was always the possibility of attack by a disgruntled defendant or his cohort, but I was now more concerned with the possible dangerous overreaction of police whose lives would be forever affected by the investigation than the criminals with whom I came into contact on a daily basis.

Among those who continued to communicate with me was Paul Gianelli, the attorney for James Diaz in the homicide acquittal. He continued to have strong feelings about the actions of the homicide detectives involved in Diaz and in other cases in which he had been involved as defense counsel. Ultimately, he turned out to be one of a handful of Suffolk lawyers who cooperated fully with the commission in its investigation. Shortly after the investigation began, but before it became public knowledge, he visited me in my chambers suggesting that I make a trip to the toilet facilities in a local Riverhead tavern called Esposito's. He thought that I'd find the visit enlightening.

Esposito's was located around the corner from the Supreme Court building and about a quarter mile from the Criminal Courts Building. It was a typical local watering hole which smelled of stale tap beer, cigarette smoke and oily french fried potatoes. Because of its convenient location and inexpensive lunch menu, it was frequented by many lawyers, assistant district attorneys, detectives and an occasional judge. The attorneys of Siben and Siben, with whom I'd worked for a few months in 1982, who were in and out of all the courts each day, would congregate for lunch at a long table to discuss business or simply to unwind at the expense of the wealthy Siben brothers. Their long table was opposite the dart board and just a few short steps from the backroom kitchen. In 1982, I too partook of the daily luncheon ritual. By the time Gianelli visited me in 1985, I had long since stopped frequenting Esposito's. I knew that some of its best customers were the detectives of the homicide squad and senior ranking assistant district attorneys, including Barry Feldman. I had also heard through the courthouse grapevine that he and some of the detectives on Diaz were seen unwinding in Esposito's on the afternoon in October shortly before I heard the shouts from the open courthouse window and found the scratches on my car door. Gianelli's visit had piqued my curiosity enough to make a short visit to Esposito's for lunch on November 20.

As always, the Siben crew was seated around their personal table. The bar was abuzz with courthouse conversation. Holding court was bespectacled, grey haired and very Jewish Bernie Leopold, Siben's chief negligence negotiator. He was puffing on his ever present cigarette while picking at an oversized chef's salad, as he pontificated in his best New Yorkese to the younger lawyers who seemed to be hanging on his every word. Bernie was a great role model. He made lots of money for the Siben's, and he drove a big, black Cadillac.

My former associates seemed genuinely happy to see me, so I decided to join them for a free lunch courtesy of the Siben brothers. I didn't think that it would be appropriate to enter the friendly confines of Esposito's just to visit the men's room. I decided to be more discreet. When the moment was right, I left the table for a trip to the windowless 3'x4' room which serviced the needs of the many customers of this well-worn establishment. It was probably my first visit, but very definitely my last to that facility. Along with the sort of homosexual and heterosexual graffiti one becomes accustomed to seeing in well used public restrooms were the following choice inscriptions featured prominently on the toilet walls:

"Impeach Stuey"
"Namm (expletive deleted) Sucks"
"Stuey (expletive deleted) sucks off little boys"

There may have been other "Stueys" in Riverhead, but, to my knowledge, I was the only Namm in town, and the messages of the authors were crystal clear. Esposito's was not being visited by criminal defendants; McDonald's and Burger King was their fare. It was the feeding trough and watering hole of prosecutors, detectives and lawyers. I had become their target—the "Ayatollah of Riverhead" so to speak. My detractors didn't have the guts to confront me directly or to mount my photograph, like the Iranian leader, on the dart board. They would simply attack me verbally through open windows and toilet wall graffiti. I had become a local celebrity of sorts, and the investigation was not yet a matter of public knowledge.

I made another visit that morning—to the chambers of a fellow judge who was one of my few friends on the bench. Harry Seidell, a Democrat from the town of Babylon, had served with me on the District Court. Harry was liked by all. His friendly, smiling face disguised a tough, no nonsense judicial demeanor. A hard working trial judge, he took his job very seriously. He would be paid for his dedicated years of service by losing a reelection bid at the end of his ten year term on the County Court bench. But he was later on the Supreme Court bench after a few years in private practice and working as a law secretary for a court of claims judge, who himself had lost a bid for reelection after twenty-six years on the bench before being appointed by Governor Cuomo to the Court of Claims.

The political system in Suffolk County had an unusual way of rewarding otherwise well qualified and experienced judges who run for reelection only under the symbol of the Democratic party. Harry, a Roman Catholic, was in the Supreme Court because he was able to garner the support of the minority Conservative and Right-To-Life parties.

Tom Staffa had asked me whether any other judge might be willing to talk to representatives of the commission. I could think of no one other than Harry who might be inclined to do so. He, like myself, was one of the three judges handling homicide trials. Only he had been doing so for a longer period of time. The same prosecutors and detectives were appearing before him on a regular basis. What I had witnessed couldn't have been unique. Perhaps he too would be willing to come forward.

"You know that I am going to continue to pursue what I saw in the Diaz and Corso trials," I said, without revealing how I was going to do this.

"I know you are," Harry responded in his even more than usual friendly tone. I became brazen.

"You've probably seen the same things that I've seen in my cases." He appeared to be barely nodding in the affirmative, but I seemed to be making headway with my friend.

Without being specific, I said: "I've been speaking to certain people who are anxious to talk to other judges who might have relevant information."

Harry hesitated for a moment to think before he replied: "Stu, for several reasons, I just can't get involved."

Disappointed and disgusted, I simply shrugged my shoulders and left him to deal with his conscience.[8] We never talked about the investigation again, nor would I ever broach the subject with any other judge.

Although I couldn't look to a friend for support or assistance, new "friends" would literally fall out of the woodwork. Two days later, I received a telephone call from Sam Markowitz who worked as a public relations officer in the office of Arthur Cromarty, the district administrative judge. It was his responsibility, among other loosely defined functions, to act as liaison with visiting school classes. My only contact with Markowitz was through that program.

"Judge, I'm calling as a friend. Perhaps with all of the news of recent months, the best thing for you would be to get back to business as usual," he suggested in a friendly tone. "You really ought to start another trial."

"You should be aware that I'm already involved in the jury selection process in a murder trial," I responded, wondering why he would be calling me on a personal basis. So I asked: "Why should you be concerned about me?"

"This is strictly personal and unofficial. I felt like you probably needed somebody to talk to at this time, and that in order to give the appearance of continuity, a trial would probably be appropriate at this time."

He continued with his explanation: "Now that the election is over, there are people looking for blood [presumably mine], and since you and I move in different political circles [I presumed he was a card carrying Republican, and I was a political eunuch], I'm probably hearing things that you don't hear."

I'd heard enough from this political hack! "I don't move in any political circles," I angrily shot back. The conversation was brought to an abrupt ending as the telephone was silent.[9]

I'd been so disturbed by that call that I decided to call Markowitz the next day to continue our conversation. Once again he reassured me that his motivation had been purely friendly. He claimed he was using his public relations background to give me some friendly advice. He did, however, define who was out for my blood. The remarks were coming from certain unidentified persons within the office of the district attorney "who were not happy with the recent turn of events." He thought that it might be good to talk these matters over with a friendly ear, since, in his opinion, there was no one in the courthouse in whom I could confide.

Three days later, I decided to call him again. I needed to know who my enemies were. Now the friendly tones were noticeably missing. He was sorry that he had ever made the original friendly call. That was our last real conversation of any consequence. I remain convinced that his call was precipitated by his boss, the administrative judge. Why did he choose Markowitz of all people to carry his message? Perhaps it would simply be accepted as the friendly message of one Jew to another. Although I was known to number none of my fellow judges as brethren, in Cromarty's eyes I probably wouldn't deny the brotherhood of a fellow Hebrew bearing good tidings and brotherly advice.[10]

Less than two weeks later another "friend" surfaced. Bill Keahon, the prosecutor in the Pius murder trials, a prosecution witness in Diaz, and one of the prosecutors called in the Waters hearing, but now in private practice, unexpectedly asked to speak to me in chambers. Without further explanation, he wanted to know whether we were still friends. I no longer knew who my friends were, but I was beginning to identify my enemies, and Keahon had toiled long and hard in their camp. Whether or not he was being sincere, he offered the unsolicited opinion that I was doing the right thing. First Dubey, and now Bill Keahon!

"It is amazing how many people out there support you," he said. He told me of a recent meeting of the Suffolk County Criminal Bar Association where some persons brought up the subject in an apparent effort to criticize my actions, but the majority of those present, he said, including two former presidents, were privately supportive of the stance that I'd taken. He was glad, he said, to have left the district attorney's office where many changes were taking place. David Freundlich, the former bureau chief of rackets was appointed chief assistant to Patrick Henry, and he, according to Keahon, was anxious to talk to me about what I had seen. I put him off in no uncertain terms with a few abrupt words. I wasn't about to talk to anyone except the appropriate authorities, and Patrick Henry's chief assistant certainly didn't fit in that category. Additionally, I could not be convinced that there was a silent majority which supported my actions. There was just too much hostility which I sensed and too much silence which I was encountering from the organized bar.

As he left, I was firmly convinced that Bill, in his own inimitable fashion, was trying to pump me for information. No one yet knew my intentions, and no one was yet aware of the pending investigation. In their eyes I was much like a loose cannon which was about to explode. Perhaps they felt that I could be defused before a catastrophe struck the county. I had considered my actions carefully, and I was not about to be detoured from my new crusade to rid the criminal justice system of the scoundrels.[11]

Little more than one month later, I received another visitor in my Riverhead chambers. This time the friendly advice was to come from the former president of the Suffolk County Criminal Bar Association and prominent criminal lawyer, Eric Naiburg, who went on to represent Amy Fisher, television's favorite "Long Island Lolita." By this visit, in the latter part of January, 1986, the investigation was a matter of common knowledge. He also asked to speak to me in private, but I asked my law secretary to sit in.

He expressed deep concern over what was taking place in the county, and wondered whether there was anything he could do to rectify the situation between myself and the district attorney's office. "There is nothing to rectify," I responded, somewhat taken aback by this solicitous and gratuitous offer. "What was done has been done, and there is now, as you know, an investigation pending over which I have no control."

Naiburg then became embarrassingly patronizing. "I'm really concerned about how this all looks to the public, and I really feel bad that the person whom I feel may be the best judge in the county is being subjected to this ordeal."

I couldn't believe that he was taking this approach. "I too am concerned," I replied, "concerned about the effect that this was having upon my life. What I saw actually happened, perjury and subornation of perjury, and I am deeply distressed that I am not getting support from any other judge or from the organized bar. I feel all alone on this, and I am being looked upon as a 'kook' for speaking out about things which other persons have to have seen over the years."

Naiburg agreed. "The problem is that most lawyers, including myself, were afraid to speak out and were basically cowards. But," he said, "some were now speaking to *Newsday's* reporters Tom Maier and Rex Smith, who are currently assigned to do a major story involving the last sixteen years of homicide investigations in Suffolk County." This was news to me! I'd talked to Maier on numerous occasions about his desire to do a hard-hitting story, but he had been put off and frustrated by his editor's refusal. I hoped that Naiburg was correct.

Then he hit me with a bombshell. He asked whether I would be willing to excuse myself from any pending Diaz cases if the district attorney's office were willing to state publicly that I was a "fair judge" in order to "save face." That was the beginning of the end of this conversation.

"I will continue to do whatever I feel I have to do," I said, "and I don't care whether I have anyone's support so long as my conscience is clear that I'm doing the right thing." With those words, I abruptly terminated an unsolicited and very disturbing meeting which lasted no more than twenty minutes. I could never have any real respect for Naiburg again whatever his accomplishments, and they would be many. Why, I thought, had he chosen my shoulder upon which to vent his own inner weakness? Was this his outward expression of the guilt which weighs heavily upon all Jewish males, or was he being less than sincere? My experience has led me to believe that he probably needed to feel a sense of expiation for his failure as a leader in the Bar to take a position in the fray.

If I had agreed to meet with the district attorney's messengers and the entire matter could be resolved and forgotten without further investigation, Eric and others like him could live with their collective guilt. If the situation, however, continued to fester, and the public became aware of what they had known and accepted for years, it would bring discredit and shame upon Suffolk's criminal defense bar which should have been in the fore of the battle against systemic corruption in the system. Ultimately, it could even affect their pocketbooks, for who, but a desperate person, would seek the assistance of a criminal lawyer unwilling or unable to take on a corrupt prosecutor? Fortunately, I was not burdened by such "weighty" choices. I would only have to answer to my own conscience.[12]

Meanwhile, as weeks passed and the investigation dragged forward, I obtained no direct response from the governor. In fact, the governor, even as he appointed special prosecutors in the Tawana Brawley affair and the Howard Beach incident, never directly responded to the problems in the Suffolk County criminal justice system.

The response to my first letter came after I was already aware of the commission's investigation, and after I'd had mailed a second letter on November 25 expressing my concern at not having received even an acknowledgment that my letter was received. The response, which crossed my second letter in the mail, was a terse statement from the governor's director of criminal justice, Lawrence T. Kurlander: "It is my understanding that an independent agency has undertaken an investigation of the allegations you raised. Accordingly, no further action will be taken by our office at this time."[13]

On December 9, Kurlander responded to my second communication. Obviously, the governor and his advisors didn't feel that an allegation of systemic corruption in a county's criminal justice system warranted the early appointment of a special prosecutor. He would ultimately do so years later after publication of the commission's final report, but the jurisdiction of the independent prosecutor would be limited to issues which bore no relation to the actions of the homicide squad about which I had complained. The letter read, in part:

> I regret any anxiety on your part that may have arisen awaiting a response to your letter of October 29, 1985. However, I am sure you can understand the need for us to give due consideration to the nature of your concerns and the appropriate role of other agencies before determining whether to initiate any direct action in this matter.
>
> I assume that you now have received my correspondence of November 25 and are aware that we do not contemplate an investigation of our own at this time.[14]

As the investigation dragged on for more than two years before the publication of a final report, even as the commission findings corroborated my worst concerns and more, and as Governor Cuomo quickly intervened in the Brawley and Howard Beach affairs, I became more and more bitter and cynical. It was readily apparent that Tawana Brawley and Howard Beach had the potential to impact upon gubernatorial votes, especially among black voters who were the governor's strongest supporters, but systemic corruption in Republican Suffolk County would have little or no impact upon Mario Cuomo and his future. So, there was no need to take any action, no matter how long the investigation dragged on. Homicide detectives, public officials and assistant district attorneys under investigative scrutiny were permitted to resign, retire and transfer while the commission searched every nook and cranny in the county, far beyond the boundaries of my complaint. Not one indictment would be the direct product of this investigation. The final report, even the interim statements, were an indictment of the system as it functioned under Patrick Henry. But the indictment of a system did not translate into the indictment of the culpable individuals. The commission's targets could continue to publicly profess their innocence, heap verbal abuse upon the commission and its investigators, complain of partisan politics and almost on a daily basis nauseatingly proclaim total vindication.

FIFTEEN

"I'm Giving This Case to Another Judge!"

—Judge Tom Stark

B y the winter of 1985 the fact that the criminal justice system was under investigation by the state was no longer a secret. Many were aware that *Newsday* intended to do a major series about homicide investigations in Suffolk County. The district attorney's office and the police homicide squad were literally operating under a microscope. But old habits die hard when you are confident of the legitimacy and righteousness of your cause. The targets of the state's investigation and *Newsday's* scrutiny were firmly convinced that they had done no wrong. Ultimately, their every action, they believed, would be vindicated. They would continue, without so much as a minor detour, in their quest to keep the county safe from those they saw as the culprits, including me whom they saw as seeking to interfere in the accomplishment of that lofty goal.

James Diaz, the acquitted rapist and murderer, still had a sex abuse charge pending on my calendar. The trial was scheduled for the early part of 1986. He was still being represented by Paul Gianelli. But the murder trial had taken a lot out of him, and he was receiving unbelievable pressure from his neighbors in Mount Sinai who were unhappy with his representation of a "murderer" who had plied his brutal trade just a few short miles away from their home. But he gathered together his barely five foot frame, ignored his neighbors and decided that he was obliged to continue to act as Diaz's trial counsel. Jimmy was free on bail and living with his grandmother in Queens some fifty miles east of Port Jefferson Station. On December 1 he was a dinner guest at Gianelli's Mount Sinai home. That visit created a real problem for Jimmy Diaz and his lawyer. On December 9, 1985, *Newsday's* front page headline announced: "Diaz Charged With Burglary, October Murder Acquittal Ignited Political Furor."

Jimmy Diaz was all over the local television news programs, seated in a sheriff's van, telling all who cared to listen that he was innocent of these new charges, and that he had been "framed" by the police once again. Eventually he would have to appear before me again. Since I had the sex abuse indictment on my calendar awaiting trial, and as I was not about to remove myself from the Diaz case, the new indictment would have to be placed on my calendar. The district attorney's office wasn't going to be able to avoid my courtroom. I'd rebuffed the initial attempt of Tom Stark to remove me from the Diaz indictments. As I read the lengthy *Newsday* story I couldn't wait to hear what was supposed to have taken place. I could not believe that James Diaz was that dumb.

I had agreed to release him on bail on the condition that he live in Queens during the pendency of the sex abuse case. He had just been acquitted of murder. The police and prosecutors were angry with the unhappy result. Why in heaven's name would he return to Suffolk to commit a burglary? It did not make sense. But criminal defendants are only presumed to be innocent. They are not presumed to be intelligent. Perhaps Diaz was truly an uncontrollable sociopath.

I no longer trusted Tom Stark. I was convinced that he would continue to make every effort to remove me from the Diaz indictments. I decided to meet with the court clerk who was involved in the assignment of new indictments. In the case of defendants charged with homicide, it was his practice to discuss every new assignment with Judge Stark who made the ultimate decision on judicial assignment. Though Diaz was only charged with a burglary, the clerk was directed to assign the new indictment to another judge because, according to Stark, I was probably going to be called as a witness in the trial of the new indictment. The hypothesis that I would be called as a witness was absolutely absurd. But if someone chose to eliminate me as the trial judge, it was a stroke of evil genius. Once again, I was seething! I couldn't wait for Tom Stark to arrive the next morning. Pacing the hall between his chambers and mine, my mind was transfixed on the Diaz case. I could think of nothing else, even though he did not arrive at work arrive until 10:30 am.

"I hear that I'm not going to get the new Diaz indictment," I said.

"I'm giving this case to another judge," he responded.

"Tom, you're making a real mistake, because you're violating a standing policy of the court. You know that any new indictment is supposed to be assigned to a judge who has a pending indictment involving the same defendant."

"I'm sorry. We've decided!"

"You're making a mistake. There is an investigation taking place, and I'm going to take this up with the people with whom I am talking."

"Stu, I don't know what you're talking about." He was getting angry with me and his voice reflected that he was losing patience with me.

"There is a state investigation under way, and I am talking to people who are concerned about Corso and Diaz."

He did not so much as flinch. Tom may have been physically debilitated, but he was still tough. He made it abundantly clear that another judge was going to handle the Diaz indictments. There was no way that I was going to change his mind. Frustrated, I turned and left his chambers. I decide to go over his head.

Before speaking to Justice Cromarty, I called Tom Staffa in New York City. He was very interested in what had just occurred. He was beginning to get a flavor of what I was experiencing in Suffolk. But the chief administrative judge was not immediately available. I finally reached him about one hour later. I filled him, in on my conversation with Stark. Stark had already spoken to Arthur Cromarty.

"Stu, he spoke to me yesterday afternoon, and I said: 'Tom, do what you usually do in these things.' He tells me that in this instance the fellow was found innocent, and then he goes and gets himself in additional trouble. Maybe I shouldn't put it that way. At least he is accused of getting himself in additional trouble. And that it's a whole new indictment, and therefore goes through the random system."

"That's not true," I told him. "He's not leveling with you. What he hasn't told you is that there's an indictment pending before me, and according to court policy, which can be verified by anyone in the court, any new indictment is to come to me. There are people who don't want me to handle this case, but I don't know why. What's being done here is improper. This is a calculated decision to move this case away from me, and that's wrong."

Like Stark, I told him that I have been talking to people. He was apparently already aware of this. I revealed that I had alerted them to the fact that a new indictment was forthcoming on James Diaz, and that I wasn't going to get the case despite a long standing court policy.

"Arthur, I don't know why Tom is doing this," I said, "but I'm talking to you because I like you." I was trying to strike a responsive chord. "If you don't intervene, I'm going to take this matter up with Bob Sise." Robert Sise was the state's administrative judge for all courts outside of the City of New York. "I don't think that the decision to move the indictment from me or to place the new indictment before another judge is being made by Tom Stark. I'm not going to sit by and see these things happen and keep quiet about it."

I was beginning to get to Arthur. "You indicate that you're talking to people. I assume it's the people...." Interrupting, I confirmed what must have been his worst fear. "I'm talking to a state agency which is investigating the Corso and Diaz matters, and other matters with which they were involved even before I asked for a state investigation. I'm talking to them on a regular basis, and that's no longer a secret."

"Excuse me, Stu, but shouldn't either a plaintiff or a defendant, or the prosecutor make an application for you to recuse yourself?" He had seen the light. There were no obscure principles of law involved. It didn't require the wisdom of a Solomon to see what was going on.

"If Tom Stark is allowing the DA's office to decide whether or not I should handle the new indictment, that would be a clear breach of ethics."

"Stu, I'll call you right back!"

Twenty minutes later, while on the bench, I received a call from Arthur Cromarty. "I finally caught up with Tom, and he is going to tell the clerk that the new case should be assigned to you." I had won the battle. But at what cost? That remained to be seen.

On December 16, James Diaz was brought before me in handcuffs to be arraigned on the new indictment. He was being charged with burglary and assault. The people were now represented by the always fastidious, prematurely grey, somewhat foppish and ever ambitious prosecutor, Timothy Mazzei. An ever-present gold chain and key dangled freely from his closely fitted vest. Diaz was now being represented by Marty Efman, the law partner of Eric Naiburg. Gianelli had apparently succumbed to community and family pressure. He wasn't going to represent him on the new charges. The crime was too close to home.

Mazzei argued vigorously for high bail after Efman entered a formal plea of "not guilty" to the indictment. The people, Mazzei stated, have a very strong case. Diaz was allegedly identified by two eyewitnesses, and his sneaker print was found at the scene. Mazzei smelled blood as he laid out his case: "This defendant broke into a woman's home, attacked her with a steak knife that was in the kitchen of the home, and he has been identified by the two girls, the two women who were in the home at that time. Because of the serious nature of the crime, because of the fact that in my opinion were it not for the fact that two girls were there would...we could have another murder here, or we could have a murder here, I should say."

Efman countered: "I think in a sense, from Mr. Mazzei's remarks, in a sense the People are trying to retry a case where the jury reached a verdict....I don't want to retry a murder case where he was found not guilty."[1]

Efman then proceeded to ask me to excuse myself from the case because of the "controversy" between me and Suffolk law enforcement. According to him, it might be too much pressure for me. There would be lots of pressure, but I was not about to step down—even at Diaz's request.

Despite my skepticism about the People's claims, I set bail at $100,000, an amount which was somewhat high under the circumstances, and which I knew Diaz could never make. Perhaps they were right. Maybe, he was a dangerous rapist and murderer. There was no doubt that he was capable of house burglary. He had admitted as much. But I asked to immediately see the grand jury minutes, as I set the matter down for a further bail hearing the next day.

The events of the next day would show that the district attorney's office had not yet learned the lessons of the Corso and Diaz trials. While Mazzei argued that the People had a strong case, the written statements of the two female complainants would prove otherwise. Both had described their assailant as a white man, twenty-five to thirty years of age, about 5'7", medium build, with wavy brown hair. Both had picked out James Diaz during a police lineup. Yet, both young women signed statements prepared by the investigating detective that they had not seen the face of their attacker. Said one: "I never saw his face and neither did Karen."[2]

But to a *Newsday* reporter, the same woman said, "I'm positive he's the man who came into my house. I saw his face several times." In reference to the police statement, she proclaimed: "I never really said that, that's completely untrue. They [the police] said please sign it while I was groggy. I signed it without reading it."

Efman announced plans to immediately move to dismiss the new charges based on the written statements given to the police. Over Mazzei's objection, he moved for a reduction in bail. Bail was reduced to $10,000, and despite the protestations of the district attorney's office that Diaz "is a threat to the community and should not be out on the streets," within a few short days bail was posted on his behalf and he was released to his grandmother in Queens once again.

As the district attorney saw it, this was the final straw. A biased judge had to be removed from the Diaz cases. The prosecution could no longer get a fair hearing in my courtroom. It was time for formal drastic action before the situation was out of control. The record, they believed, would strongly support the hypothesis that Judge Namm could not be fair, and that he was prejudiced against Suffolk County law enforcement, especially in their zeal to convict James Diaz of serious crimes. It was important to remove this continuing menace from society. Judge Stark was no longer the only person openly anxious to get another judge on the Diaz cases. As I saw it, it was clear that he was now part of a team with one obvious objective—remove me from Diaz, and, ultimately, from all criminal cases. In their eyes, I must have represented a clear and present danger to Suffolk law enforcement.

Timothy Mazzei, heir apparent of Spota, Keahon, Wilutis and Feldman, had taken up the cudgel. Spota and Keahon were gone. Feldman was about to be transferred to the East End bureau (Suffolk's version of Siberia), a prelude to his future resignation under fire. Wilutis had been elevated to the position of chief trial prosecutor—advisor to the district attorney. Mazzei had rapidly risen through the ranks after a short stint in the law offices of Sullivan and Spota, two former predecessors. He had been promoted under combat-like conditions. This was war! The enemy—Jimmy Diaz and Judge Namm—needed to be dealt with swiftly before the damage was out of control. The district attorney's office could not afford many more hits to its flanks.

On December 23, less than a week after his appearance in the new Diaz indictment, Mazzei, in a sworn affidavit to be submitted in support of a formal motion for my recusal from the Diaz case, stated their case:

> ...this Court has...formally requested an "independent inquiry" and thereby caused the institution of an investigation by the New York State Commission of Investigation into "allegations of wrongdoing by Suffolk Police and prosecutors into their handling of two recent murder cases" [one case involving this very defendant]. These allegations...involve claims of police and prosecutorial misfeasance or nonfeasance, harassment and intimidation of witnesses and the court, and subornation of perjury....
>
> We respectfully maintain that a pattern of conduct of this Court in these cases [Corso and Diaz], as well as in other recent matters [unnamed], has established a bias or animosity such that this Court's impartiality might reasonably be questioned which thus necessitates this Court's disqualification from the above captioned cases.[3]

In page after page of supporting affidavits, transcripts and newspaper clippings, the office of the district attorney laid out its case for recusal in the hope that I'd be legally or ethically persuaded to excuse myself from further involvement in the James Diaz cases.

In conclusion, it set forth the following: "The undersigned previously has had many cases before this Court and has never even questioned the Court's utmost fairness and impartiality in any regard. Indeed, notwithstanding those Court decisions reached during the course of these proceedings which were against the People, your deponent has never doubted the Court's sincerity or objectivity in reaching its determinations. However, in light of the facts outlined herein, we simply, and most respectfully, ask this Court to look to its personal conscience and the interests of justice and grant this application in these two cases only."

If you can't wear your opponent down with the continuous blows of a heavy stick, the carrot was always in order, especially if you might have to continue to do battle on a field of combat controlled by your self created adversary. Neither the carrot nor the stick proved to be convincing. On the contrary, the application only served to strengthen my resolve to continue to preside over the pending Diaz indictments. The application was being made by Mazzei, but there was no doubt that the wording had been carefully crafted by those in positions of higher authority. This had all the earmarks of a calculated move which was only the first formal step intended to remove an immovable and recalcitrant object. The next step was already in the making. They had to know that I was not about to recuse myself. But the voluminous application was worthy of a response-in writing.

"Perhaps, another judge, given the same set of facts and circumstances would opt for recusal and self disqualification in an effort to avoid an unpleasant confrontation," I wrote. "However, the question of when a judge should disqualify himself is generally a matter of personal conscience...since only the individual judge knows fully his own thoughts and feelings....While the option of recusal is indeed a tantalizing morsel available for the taking, this court's own conscience and sense of justice will not permit the first tempting bite."[4]

I had reached back into history for legal precedent. I was in the very position that Judge John Sirica had found himself in when being challenged in the Watergate cases by the Attorney General of the United States. But I was far from that important, and this was only the Suffolk County Court. I continued:

> While the issues before this court pale by comparison to those which confronted Judge Sirica in Watergate, a criminal case

which has been called "one of the most important cases in American judicial history," ...nonetheless, the principle that a judge is under an obligation to deny a groundless application for recusal transcends the magnitude of those issues.

The easiest course of action which this court could take in these matters would be to recuse itself. This court would then be free of the albatross which has weighed heavily upon it for the last several months. Presumably for now, the fires which have been fueled by the charges of animus, hostility, bias and prejudice will be dampened, and the court would be free and unfettered to deal with the many other matters pending before it.

I turned to the very words of Judge Sirica in denying the application of John Mitchell: "...the court cannot overlook the fact that it has an obligation to deny insufficient recusal motions. There is as much obligation upon a judge not to recuse himself when there is no occasion as there is for him to do so when there is....After such study as I could give the matter, I reached the conclusion that whether a judge should recuse himself in a particular case depends not so much on his personal preference or individual views as it does on the law, and that under the law, I have no choice in this case...In the absence of a valid legal reason, I have no right to disqualify myself and must sit."[5]

They weren't going to be happy with this decision in the office of the district attorney. Nor would Tom Stark rejoice in this decision. His emissary, in the person of his confidential law clerk, the peripatetic Malcolm Rogers, who normally spent every working day behind a desk thumbing through *The New York Law Journal* or voluminous case files, was by now nosing around my courtroom on an almost daily basis, in an effort to ascertain the outcome of the battle.

They might have been unhappy, but the result could not have been unexpected. No one could have realistically believed that I would take the bait. They would have to make a stronger case in a higher forum. In their eyes, that opportunity would shortly present itself. No matter what I decided, they were not going to allow this battle to end on my turf. They had lost the battle, but they were not prepared to lose the war. The stakes were too high!

Ceremonial formalities, although a long-time tradition of the judiciary, had long since been minimized in my courtroom. In an era where respect for institutions such as family, church, school, court and government seemed to be dwindling more and more each day, I saw these formalities as anachronistic, a throwback to times when judges and judicial office were truly deserving of the highest respect. I could not help but feel uncomfortable when lawyers and public alike shuffled to their feet, usually grumbling and smirking, as my black robed presence was announced in loud and intrusive tones by a clerk or a court officer. So when my daily calendar business was concluded, there would be no formal pronouncement, no call to attention to an empty courtroom. I usually remained seated behind the bench making notes on a desk calendar as I passed the remaining time in quiet conversation with the court personnel.[6]

****

January 7, 1986 was just another day in Suffolk County Court, except that on that day *Newsday* reported the senseless knife slaying of a man and woman in the bathtub of their Southampton home. No one had yet been apprehended and charged with the murders. It was still under intense investigation. In my courtroom, it had been a short and routinely uneventful day. There was no trial scheduled. I was busily bringing my desk calendar up to date. The court reporter was closing down his machine for the day. The court clerk was completing her daily paperwork. Our friendly conversation somehow turned from the Luciano Pavarotti show on public television to the Southampton murders. The assistant district attorney assigned to my part, Jeffrey Weeks, whom I had known for several years, was gathering his files together. The court officers were congregated in the well of the courtroom. They are responsible for courtroom security, and they can't leave until the judge clears the bench.

"Did you hear about those horrible murders in Southampton yesterday?" someone asked.

Jokingly, but perhaps in bad taste, and within earshot of the assistant district attorney, I sarcastically, and perhaps thoughtlessly, responded: "I guess I ought to look in tomorrow's newspaper because Diaz will probably be charged with the Southampton murders. They involve a stabbing, and Diaz was in this court yesterday." (The County Court lies physically within the geographical limits of the town of Southampton).

That was it! I had done it! Out of my mouth had sarcastically come the words which, to my detractors, surely displayed the animus, bias and prejudice which I must have held against Suffolk law enforcement. Without so much as a word, Weeks hurried out of the courtroom, files in hand, to report this tawdry conversation which he had overheard to his supervisors. By then, they must have been champing at the bit to get me out of their way. Even more damning! According to the young assistant, "Judge Namm appeared to be smirking or smiling."[7]

The full force of the district attorney's office was immediately mobilized to prove their presumption of bias. Joan Irwin, the court clerk who was present, was summoned to the fourth floor where she was confronted by senior detective investigator, Eugene Canale, whose usual duties were to assist in the preparation of homicide cases.

An affidavit was demanded from her which would corroborate the conversation which was heard by Weeks and repeated in a written report to his superiors and in a formal deposition. Corroboration from an independent source would strengthen their case against me. But they had not bargained for this feisty clerk. Irwin, a woman in her fifties, is an experienced, pugnacious, opinionated product of the streets of the Bronx. She was not intimidated by their tactics and she could see right through this thinly veiled charade intended to tarnish the reputation of a judge whom they saw as their enemy, but whom she liked and respected. Joan Irwin and I, both products of New York City's tenements, saw eye to eye on many subjects.

"This," she told Canale indignantly, "is a subject not even worthy of discussion. The judge is a man of integrity, and the entire conversation was had in a flippant manner." Quickly realizing that she would not cooperate, the detective asked her not to tell anyone about her visit to the district attorney's office and their "conversation." That afternoon, Irwin called me at my Stony Brook chambers to relate what had taken place in the district attorney's office. As tough as she was, she had been so shaken by the confrontation that she was calling from an outside line, out of fear that the courtroom telephone line was being tapped.[8]

The district attorney's office had that kind of reputation amongst experienced court personnel in the winter of 1986.

The experienced, but always nervous and sometimes sickly, court reporter, George DeFoto, was likewise summoned to the fourth floor. He was so shaken by that meeting, and his involvement in a meaningless, frivolous conversation, which was being turned into a cause celebre which he wanted no part of, that he decided to call in sick the next day. But he was not the only person missing from my courtroom on January 8. I would not see Jeffrey Weeks again for months. He had been permanently transferred to another part to avoid a confrontation with me. The fact that he had cases pending on my calendar for trial was removed to the back burner. Those cases would be sacrificed in the battle with a hostile judge. He was replaced by the deputy trial bureau chief, the district attorney's pit bull, Kerry Trainor, who knew nothing about the cases, including cases which were ready for trial.[9]

For the next several weeks and months, I would be entangled in explosive daily confrontations with senior members of the district attorney's office who were obviously placed in my courtroom to simply verbally bait me into making statements on the record which they hoped would strengthen their case for recusal. Bizarre events became the daily bill of fare in my courtroom. Jokingly, it would be referred to by the court officers as a "battle zone," for which they should receive "combat pay." But for the combatants themselves, and the people of Suffolk County, it was no joking matter. This was deadly serious business!

Two days after the Weeks episode, I received a telephone call from Robert Frank, one of the commission's investigators. He was seeking copies of Joseph Pistone's jail records, which I kept locked up in my desk file drawer. But to my dismay, the wood around the drawer lock was splintered into small pieces. It appeared to my untrained eyes that someone had obviously attempted to break the lock. He suggested that I report the incident to the police. I chose not to do so. I no longer trusted the police, especially since this involved the security of my files and notes concerning the investigation. I chose instead to file a report with courthouse security.

On January 13, I was visited by Frank and Joe Lyons, the two former detectives. They examined the file drawer and came to the conclusion that somebody had definitely attempted to break into the drawer. But there was no evidence left behind to support an accusation. We could only speculate as to who at that time would have reason to obtain my files and personal memoranda, but this was no time for useless speculation and meaningless suspicion. There was no proof.

Meanwhile, preparations were continuing apace in the appeals bureau of the district attorney's office to remove me from the Diaz indictments. The matter was no longer in the hands of Mazzei, then merely a rising trial assistant. No less than the district attorney's chief law assistant and chief of the appeals bureau, the highly intelligent but unctuous, Mark Cohen, undertook the responsibility to move the matter into the appellate division. James Diaz and Judge Namm were now the most important matter on the district attorney's docket. There was an enormous amount of principle involved.

It seemed to matter not that James Diaz was no longer charged with murder. The degree and nature of the pending charges bore little relation to the effort being made to remove the trial judge from his cases. They were going to prevail no matter what price was paid in time and resources.

On January 21, 1986, one day after I read my decision into the record denying the recusal application, I received an early morning telephone call from Justice Lawrence Bracken, a Republican member of the appellate division and former assistant district attorney in Suffolk County. He informed me that on the day before he had signed an order staying the trial of the Diaz indictments pending a hearing before the full court in one week. His call came as no great surprise. I had been waiting for the other shoe to fall! Although my jurisdiction as a judge had been temporarily swept out from under me, I would not be a party to the proceedings in the appellate court. By moving to transfer jurisdiction from the County Court to the Supreme Court instead of moving for a writ of prohibition to enjoin me from acting in my judicial capacity, Mark Cohen and his staff of legal assistants had shrewdly and effectively ensured that I would not have an opportunity to defend my actions in the appellate division. I wouldn't be given the opportunity to expose their naked attempt to divest jurisdiction from a judge who was not to their liking and who was poised to once again reveal questionable prosecutorial activity. They would prefer to take their chances with another judge in another court. Anyone but me would be acceptable! But I was not about to cave in to this tactic. I decided to contact the office of the attorney general of the State of New York whose function it was to represent state judges in litigation involving their judicial duties.

There was a local office of the attorney general in Hauppauge, the de facto county seat, located in the most populous part of the county. But I was immediately referred to the New York City office where I was shuffled back and forth between the chief of the litigation bureau and the deputy solicitor general, a Peter Sherwood, who was to call me back. Not receiving such a call, I took it upon myself to call the chief of the Hauppauge office, Ann Horowitz. She was already on the telephone discussing the matter with Patricia Murphy of the district attorney's office who was assisting Cohen in the application to the appellate division. Horowitz seemed to be more interested in what Murphy had to say about the case than what I was telling her. Without ever having seen the papers which I had received as a "courtesy" from Murphy, she had already concluded that the attorney general could not assist me in my effort to intervene as a party in the higher court. She said I would have an answer by Friday. She would have to discuss the matter with her superiors in New York. But I didn't have to wait until Friday. Her message was loud and clear! I was on my own.

Bob Meguin, my law secretary, and I began the preparation of a formal application to intervene in the higher court proceedings. I could not permit their trumped-up charges of "demonstrated predisposition, animosity and bias" to go unanswered. I would never allow myself to be intimidated into submission.[10]

I was not about to be divested of my criminal jurisdiction in any respect simply because I had sought a formal investigation of blatant prosecutorial and police misconduct which was probably still going on unchecked.

So, with the assistance of my law secretary, I took the unprecedented step, but in my view, a necessary one, of filing an Order to Show Cause to intervene in the pending appellate division proceeding which sought to move the Diaz indictments before another judge. I did not believe that there was any other judge who would be willing to publicly expose what I had seen in the past Diaz case and what I believed I was continuing to see in the new burglary indictment.

On February 3rd, Justice Bracken, reluctantly, signed the order on my behalf. Larry Bracken had, himself, been an appeals assistant in the district attorney's office before being elected to the Supreme Court. He was a Republican who had been appointed to the appellate division by a Democrat governor, Mario Cuomo, to the chagrin of Suffolk Democrats, at a time when many believed Cuomo was punishing Suffolk Democrats for Dominic Baranello's open support of New York City Mayor Ed Koch in his primary battle against Cuomo for the gubernatorial nomination.

In my moving papers I chose not to address the merits of the district attorney's application. I felt that I had done so adequately in my decision to deny the recusal application. Instead I challenged the back door procedure which was being employed to effectively deprive me of counsel and the opportunity to defend my actions. I was also fuming over Cohen's decision to allude in his court papers to a recent murder case which was handled by me.

In that case I suppressed another alleged oral admission on the grounds that the defendant's constitutional rights were violated by the police.[11]

Thus I wrote in my moving papers: "It is the height of presumptuous audacity to argue that the same constitutes another example of...alleged bias and prejudice without submitting a transcript of the hearing which was conducted and the decision which was placed on the record for this Court to consider. Such conduct exemplifies an attitude on the part of the prosecutor that any adverse judicial ruling must be the result of bias or prejudice, rather than the failure of the people to meet their burden required by law. Certainly, if this Court were to lend credence to such a flawed posture, the same would have a 'chilling effect' upon the entire judiciary."[12]

Without so much as a short comment about the merits of the district attorney's application, the appellate division, in early March, denied the application to divest me of jurisdiction in the Diaz cases. At the same time the panel of justices, without so much as a comment, denied my application to intervene in the proceedings. It mattered not. I had achieved the desired result. I knew that they had read my papers, and that was all that I wanted, in spite of their decision which denied me the opportunity to intervene. But this was a bitter-sweet victory. There had been a caustic exchange of vituperative comments between a prosecutor's office and a sitting judge whom they could not now avoid in Diaz or any other case which was assigned to his court unless I was totally divested of my criminal jurisdiction. This, I began to fear, with the help of the county's politically oriented judicial hierarchy, was going to happen sooner or later.

SIXTEEN

"Stuart, Keep
Your Powder Dry."

—Judge Robert J. Sise

A LTHOUGH THE AFTERMATH OF THE DIAZ ACQUITTAL was a continuing front page story in *Newsday* and local weeklies such as *The Port Jefferson Record*, the "battle" between the prosecutors and the judge spread to the New York City media. Under the caption, "Case of the Judge vs. Prosecutors," John Rather of *The New York Times* wrote:

> A dispute that could have broad implications for the criminal justice system in Suffolk County has embroiled a County Court judge and the Suffolk County District Attorney's office.
>
> An investigation into the dispute may shed light on purported techniques employed by homicide detectives in Suffolk County to gain confessions and statements from witnesses, techniques that have long been protested by attorneys for the accused.[1]

But it wasn't only the news media that was being awakened to the happenings in Suffolk County. On the very day that Justice Bracken called to say that he had stayed the Diaz proceedings, my secretary received the first of many telephone calls from a Dr. Ruth Littman, an apparently disabled and aged, heavily accented, self-proclaimed Ph.D. from Huntington, who was distressed that Justice Bracken was now involved in the Diaz matters. She claimed to have been in communication, and to be working, with the commission's chief investigator. According to her, Justice Bracken was elevated to the appellate division, not because of Dominic Baranello, but because of a "potential scandal" purportedly "uncovered" during a medical malpractice case in which she was involved. She claimed that it had been discovered that certain judges were hearing those types of cases while, at the same time, sitting on hospital boards thereby creating a "conflict of interest." Justice Cromarty, according to her, was "on his way out."[2] She couldn't have been more wrong about the county's administrative judge. He was destined to serve out his term through 1991. Dr. Littman continued to communicate with my office until the spring of 1988, always expressing concern for my safety and well-being. But we never heard anything again about the festering malpractice scandal.

The extensive media coverage wasn't only reaching persons with an axe to grind against the justice system, many of whom saw my problem as symptomatic of all that was wrong in the system. It was also penetrating the highest echelons of the judicial hierarchy in the state. These powerful judges could not have been happy with what was being written about the county's justice system. It wasn't long before I would receive a visit from their messenger, in the form of Judge Robert J. Sise of rural Montgomery County in upstate New York.

Robert J. Sise, prior to his retirement in December, 1990, served as the state's chief administrative judge under Governor Hugh Carey for eighteen months in 1983 and 1984. After the appointment of a new chief judge of the Court of Appeals, Sol Wachtler of Nassau County, Long Island, by Governor Cuomo in 1984, he was replaced and reduced in rank to deputy chief administrator for all of the courts outside of the City of New York. The father of nine sons, he had begun his judicial career as a judge of the Children's Court in 1960. Judge Sise cast an imposing figure with his booming voice and his better than six foot frame. The *New York Law Journal*, in a profile at the time of his retirement, referred to the judge as a "Master of Friendly Persuasion."[3] By the winter of 1986, although I had been on the bench for almost ten years, I did not know the judge at all, except by reputation. We had never met. I had heard him speak about his penchant for horses and racing at annual judicial seminars, and I knew of his reputation for jocularity and the sometimes use of crude street talk to emphasize a point.

On the very day that the appellate division was considering the district attorney's application to remove me from the Diaz indictments, I received a previously unannounced visit by the "friendly persuader" at 9:20 am, just as I was about to take the bench. He wanted to talk, he said, about my correspondence with the Office of Court Administration concerning the under representation of blacks in Suffolk jury panels. But this was old news! He attempted to explain that there were severe budgetary considerations, but he assured me that every effort was being made to reach out to minority groups. He said that he had run into similar problems years before in the Bronx where it had become "fashionable" to challenge the jury array by certain liberal attorneys. It would be difficult, he believed, to obtain a true cross-section of the population since the poorer members of minority groups would probably never be represented in the county jury pools. But, this I thought, could not have been the real purpose of his visit. What, I thought, was the real reason behind it?

It did not take long before he changed the subject to James Diaz. He had recently received a copy of my decision in the application for recusal. Not even attempting to conceal his patronizing and condescending manner, he said he was keeping a copy of it on his desk as a "treatise on the subject of disqualification." He was very aware of the problems which I had been facing and the existence of the state investigation. He made no attempt to conceal his disdain for investigating commissions, making specific reference to the state commission on judicial conduct.

He received, he said, many complaints against judges, but because of his personal strong feelings about that commission, he rarely forwarded the complaints to them. The judge was of the opinion that I had been dealing with a group of individuals who lacked "professionalism," and he was in agreement, he said, with my attempt to intervene in the proceedings in the appellate division. I did not believe a word he was saying!

But then he sounded an ominous note by referring to the many problems of Justice James Leff, a Supreme Court Justice in Manhattan, who had been publicly battling with court administrators for years in their efforts to transfer him from criminal to civil jurisdiction. He made a point of saying that there had been a terrible waste of money during a period of six months when neither the judge nor his staff were accomplishing any fruitful work. I got the thinly veiled message! His allusion to Jim Leff was meant to be a clear reference to my battle with the Suffolk County court's administrators.

He abruptly closed the nearly thirty minute meeting, which ran well into my court time, by warning me to be especially leery of the news media. I told him of the many unsolicited media contacts, and the fact that I had chosen not to accept invitations to appear on network television. With that, he raised his imposing figure (most figures are imposing to one who stands barely 5' 7") from his seat in front of my desk. Framed by the inner doorway, he cautioned, "Stuart, keep your powder dry!" I wondered what he meant by that. Against whom would I have to defend myself in the future? Had he been, I wondered, a messenger from my many enemies, both in politics and the courts?[4]

****

There was no meeting with the "friendly persuader" again until December 20, 1988, when I was in the midst of a heated battle with Arthur Cromarty, the county's administrative judge, to be returned to the County Court and criminal jurisdiction. It was after an eight month "elevation" to the Supreme Court in civil isolation against my will. I had been publicly exposing the county's increasing backlog of criminal cases to the county legislature, both in the news media. by appearances before the county legislature and on television. The backlog of criminal cases and the resultant increase in county jail population which was leading to dangerously overcrowded conditions was becoming a matter of great public concern. As a result of this exposure, Justice Arthur Cromarty, the county's chief administrative judge, was placed under intense public pressure to return four judges to the County Court, including myself, who had been temporarily transferred to the Supreme Court. In fact, three of the four were about to be returned to criminal jurisdiction. The fourth, who was not to be returned, was, not surprisingly, me. I and many others in the system and in the media were already convinced that the decision to mire me in the civil court was retaliation for the state investigation which I had instigated. The commission's final report, I was being told, was imminent, and it wasn't going to be flattering to the district attorney's office or the police department.

I had not sought this second meeting with Judge Sise. It was the result of a telephone call which I had made to Albert Rosenblatt, the then chief administrative judge of the state. It was he who suggested that I meet with Sise since Rosenblatt was going to leave that position in March. I was astonished, that after three years of investigation, he didn't seem to have any awareness of the activities of the State Commission of Investigations in Suffolk County. He became immediately concerned, he said, with these developments when I inferred that the investigation could spread to the question of whether I was being held in the Supreme Court in retaliation for the investigation. His greatest concern at that time seemed to be the public dialogue which was taking place about judicial assignments. Bob Sise was Arthur Cromarty's direct superior in the administrative hierarchy, and Rosenblatt wanted me to talk to him first. The meeting was to take place over morning coffee at a diner in Hauppauge, many miles west of the Riverhead courts.

This time, cordialities were short and perfunctory. It didn't take long to get down to the unhappy business at hand. Sise had obviously been well briefed by Rosenblatt about the possible unhappy turn of events. After impatiently listening to my grievance that I believed that I was being singled out by Judge Cromarty, he erupted with the comment that Arthur Cromarty was too much of a gentleman, and that had he been in his position, he would have "blown me out of the water." He would have told the public that I was no "white knight in shining armor on a white horse." I was shocked, but not surprised, by his openly hostile attitude.

The "friendly persuader" was wasting little time being friendly. He made it clear that I was no friend of his, nor of the judiciary. Still his greatest animosity was directed against the state's investigators. He boasted that he was not concerned with any state investigation of the assignment of judges in the courts of Suffolk County. He welcomed such an investigation. Sise was clearly dropping the gauntlet on that issue. It would not be manly to display any fear of investigation to a person that he considered to be his subordinate, even though that subordinate was a duly elected public official. In contrast, he served in this position of authority by virtue of political appointment.

I knew that Bob Sise was a renowned storyteller. I had heard some of his "horse tales" at judicial conferences. As if to make a point, he offered a parable for my consideration. This time, it was not a horse story. His was not a joking mood. This story, he said, was told to him twenty-five years before by his law partner: "If you ever find yourself walking on one side of the street, and everyone else is walking on the other side of the street, you should look around to see whether you are on the wrong side of the street."

The message was clear and obvious. He said that I had angered the other judges of the county by my public actions. I responded that I was not concerned about what the other judges thought about my statements and actions. Unlike some of them, my conscience was clear!

For some unknown reason, out of the blue, he then asked me whether I thought that Tom Stark was corrupt. I did not know whether Tom Stark was or was not corrupt, nor had I ever given that any thought, and I told him so. But I did point out that for years homicide cases were being assigned by Judge Stark to judges selected by the district attorney's office. Sise said that he did not approve of this practice, but he alluded to the practices in his home county of Montgomery, in a rural part of upper New York State. There, he said, traditionally the district attorney went on to become county judge, and the chief assistant district attorney would then be elected to the DA's office. So, he said, there ends up being much discussion between the court and the district attorney about pending criminal cases outside the presence of defense counsel. If that was so, I thought, it would be a clear violation of the canons of ethics. If Judge Stark were guilty of this practice, he said, he could not have known that he was doing anything illegal or immoral. I was truly shocked by his attitude of nonchalance over possible legal and ethical violations.

The meeting ended unresolved. I was given the clear message that Judge Rosenblatt was not about to intervene. Nothing, he said, could be done at this time. The decision had been made to keep me in a civil part of the Supreme Court. But, "If I rolled over and played dead," (my words) and I "knocked them dead" (his words) in Supreme Court, at the end of seven or eight months, if, and only if, there was an opening of additional criminal parts, I would be considered for one of those parts. But, he made it clear, he was making no promises![5] Ultimately, I was returned to criminal court in January 1990, after intense media pressure, thirteen months after this unfriendly meeting with the "friendly persuader."

SEVENTEEN

"His Eyes Had a Crazy, Wild Look About Them."

-Barmaid at the Nightlife Pub and Tavern
describing James Diaz

BACK IN 1986, THERE WAS STILL JAMES DIAZ TO CONTEND WITH. It was becoming increasingly more and more difficult to concentrate on the task at hand. The pending indictments were rapidly becoming a subplot in the larger story, the fallout from the continuing investigation of Suffolk law enforcement. Shortly after the decision of the Appellate Division, I was prepared to turn my attention to the pending sex abuse indictment, a charge which dated back to June 1984. Diaz was still being represented by Paul Gianelli who had opted out of the new burglary and assault charges.

After more than three days of questioning prospective jurors, Gianelli was "surprised," he said, "with the number of people in the panel who were familiar with the homicide case."[1] A tactical decision was made by Gianelli and Diaz to forgo a jury trial. They wanted me to decide the question of guilt. I was convinced that this decision was based not only upon their apparent inability to quickly obtain a fair and impartial jury, but upon their belief that I was so embroiled in my battle with the prosecutors that I would bend over backwards to make things difficult for the police and prosecutor. If so, they were wrong! As difficult as it was under the circumstances, I was resolute in my fervor to show that I was still able to give both sides a fair hearing.[2]

This time the people were represented by William Ferris, a tall, thin, soft-spoken, experienced prosecutor and administrator. Ferris was a high ranking reserve naval officer who always maintained a somber and appropriately professional decorum in the courtroom. But the trial was about to begin in an extremely tense atmosphere, and I am sure that he was convinced that the odds were stacked against the prosecution.

Diaz was charged with physically assaulting and sexually abusing a thirty-year-old woman just four days before the rape and murder of Maureen Negus. The attack allegedly took place in an underground "fort" occupied by Diaz in the woods not far from the empty cars in Port Jefferson railroad station. She was a married woman, but she appeared to be mildly retarded. Like James Diaz, in her youth she had been a student at Maryhaven School for "exceptional persons." Still, she had not previously known him.[3]

Innocently, she had agreed to go with him for a ride in her own car after he picked her up at a bar and promised her free marijuana and wine. Diaz led her to an underground fort littered with old furniture in the Port Jefferson woods where he said he lived. After she shared some wine and marijuana with the man who called himself "Jim," he put his outstretched arms around her neck in a stranglehold while attempting to grab at her right breast.

She said she thought she was going to die. He was sweating profusely and breathing heavily like an animal as he punched her about the head. She begged him, "Please stop." She tried to calm him down, but he ordered her to "shut up." Finally, he relented and abruptly left the shelter with a final fearful warning: "I've got a gun!"

This time, the police had a living victim who had survived her attack to tell about it and to identify her assailant. Still they had even more! Three latent finger impressions—fingerprints—were discerned on the left corner of the passenger window of the victim's 1970 Chevrolet Impala. However, only one of the latent prints was suitable for comparison with the known left ring fingerprint of James Diaz. There was a match! Both the known and unknown prints came from the same source according to the undisputed and uncontradicted testimony of a retired detective of the identification section of the Suffolk County police department.

The victim had driven her assailant, who was seated in the front passenger seat, to a dirt road adjacent to the wooded area which surrounded the fort. He had led her to the shelter in the woods. She had never been in that area before, and she had left in such haste, with her chest in pain, her neck burning, and her head swollen from pressure, that she had left her purse and one shoe behind. They were recovered from the woods by Detective Dennis Gannon that same evening after he took her statement at the emergency room of Mather Memorial Hospital in Port Jefferson.

There was also the prosecution testimony of the barmaid at the Nightlife Pub and Tavern where James Diaz had first encountered his victim who was a regular daytime customer at the neighborhood tavern. Still the barmaid said that she had never seen the man who was drinking Budweiser and talking to Kim (the victim) before. She remembered his eyes which had a "crazy, wild look about them." They were, she insisted, "vicious eyes." Still what would have been very damaging testimony was somewhat neutralized by her admission that she knew that the man whom she was identifying in court, James Diaz, was the same man who had been charged with the rape and murder of Maureen Negus in that very neighborhood. Was she picking out Kim's assailant, or was she simply selecting the most obvious candidate to fit the crime?

The owner of Plaza Wine and Spirits, from whom the cheapest bottle of wine, ninety-nine cent Soave Bolla, had been purchased, was also produced to identify the 5'7", brown-haired young man who had accompanied Kim into his store that afternoon. Yet he could not be sure whether the young man was in the courtroom that morning, although James Diaz was seated right alongside Gianelli at counsel table about fifteen feet away from the witness. Yet, two years before, he had picked Diaz out of two police lineups.

There was additional forensic evidence to link Diaz to the attack in the woods. According to Paul Hojnacki, a forensic serologist of the Suffolk County crime laboratory, the defendant's known head hair samples exhibited the same characteristics as some of the hairs which were recovered from the victim's blouse and from a pair of green pants which were found inside the fort. Although he could not say for certain that the hairs came the head of Diaz, they clearly fell within the full range of physical characteristics of the known Diaz hair. This time, for James Diaz, the noose was tightening and he was rapidly moving ever closer to a long stay in a cell at a state correctional facility.

Paul Gianelli chose not to put his client on the stand. He was content to call three witnesses, two of whom played prominent roles in the murder trial: William Dobbeck and Richard Tiedemann. I needed no introduction to them. I was not about to buy the tales which they wove on behalf of their friend. I was being asked to believe the testimony of an admitted "acid" user, Dobbek, that Diaz's fingerprint was probably left on the victim's car by chance, on some unknown day when they might have been hanging out in a shopping center parking lot, sitting around on the trunks of cars.

From a convicted house burglar, Tiedemann, I was expected to give credence to his assessment of Diaz, also a convicted house burglar, as a "nonviolent" thief." It wasn't even a close call!

In the final analysis, as I announced in open court on April 9, 1986, it was the "totality of the evidence" that sealed the fate of James Diaz. I simply was not about to speculate, in the light of the unshakeable testimony of Kim, that some time during his sojourn in the Port Jefferson Station community, the defendant, by fortuitous happenstance, or even by design, leaned against the victim's vehicle, which also by chance happened to be at the same place at the same time.

Yet the print was left in a downward facing position. I was convinced that at his height, he would have to have been in a completely distorted position. A more palatable and likely explanation, which was consistent with his guilt of these crimes, was that he had used his left hand to close the passenger door on one of the occasions that he had exited the vehicle on June 5, 1984. I announced the verdict: guilty as charged! To the relief of many in the community, once again, James Diaz was remanded to the custody of the sheriff. This time, there would be no bail. He was now being held to await sentencing. He was no longer presumed innocent!

The judge who, according to the office of the district attorney, was biased and prejudiced against them, had reached a verdict which, I am certain, was totally unexpected in many quarters. I am sure that it was expected that I would breach my oath of office and violate my own conscience in order to achieve some hidden, but clearly defined, agenda—the destruction of Patrick Henry and his prosecutorial associates. However, there was a much more appropriate agenda—the conviction and removal, at least temporarily, from society of a dangerous sociopath who might have been acquitted of the most heinous of crimes by virtue of unmistakable police and prosecutorial misconduct. The district attorney and his cohorts within the office and the police department were going to be, I hoped, appropriately dealt with by the State Commission of Investigations. Meanwhile, I would continue to attempt to function as a criminal court judge, if I would be permitted to do so. It was not going to be easy![4]

The district attorney had been totally unsuccessful in his efforts to remove me from the pending Diaz indictments. One of these indictments had now blossomed into an unexpected conviction. But the more difficult indictment was still outstanding. It was this indictment which was suspect from day one. It was this indictment which provoked the various applications for recusal. It was this indictment which could absolve the district attorney's office and the homicide squad. And, absolution in the form of public vindication was now their primary goal. In fact, it became almost an obsession. "Vindication" became a word which was used often by the district attorney and the police department in the media.

But there had been no vindication in the sex abuse conviction of James Diaz. The underlying incident took place before the brutal murder and rape of Maureen Negus. This pending burglary and assault, which some theorized was an attempted rape gone awry, was another story. The public was being led to believe that it had been a brazen act by a proven sociopath on the heels of a controversial acquittal, committed as he was awaiting trial on another serious felony. It was a crime committed by a dangerous criminal under a spotlight while he was still the target of Suffolk law enforcement. A conviction flowing from this indictment would be a certain vindication of their actions in the murder trial. That was why it was so important to find another judge—any judge but Stuart Namm!

That is why James Diaz would not only be arrested by regular cops this time, but the arrest also involved detectives assigned to the rackets bureau of the district attorney's office—an elite and highly loyal cadre under the direct control of David Freundlich, the chief assistant to Patrick Henry. There were many who believed that he actually ran the day-to-day affairs of that office. That had to be why Freundlich, himself, and Mark Cohen, chief of the appeals bureau and Patrick Henry's closest legal advisor, were present at the lineups. That had to be also why Steve Wilutis, the district attorney's chief trial prosecutor, and Ed Jablonski, chief of the major crime bureau, were standing by within the precinct. That was unquestionably why Timothy Mazzei, Barry Feldman's protege, who was also in attendance at the lineups, was selected to prosecute this indictment of Suffolk County's public enemy number one. Only Patrick Henry was absent from this party. They were not about to let him slip through their fingers this time.

April 21, 1986 was a red letter day in Suffolk law enforcement. It was the day that the preliminary hearings were scheduled to begin under the latest and final outstanding indictment. The assistant district attorney strongly objected to the hearings. Gianelli, Jimmy's previous attorney, Mazzei argued, had been present at the lineups. The arrest, Mazzei argued, did not flow from the lineups, but from the victims' signed statements and their subsequent identification of the perpetrator from carousels of mug slides at the police identification bureau. Marty Efman, on the other hand, contended that there had been no probable cause to arrest James Diaz or to search his home in Queens. The identification procedures, lineups and photo spread alike, he protested, were tainted by police misconduct. How, he argued, could the victims identify their perpetrator if neither could see his face? The decision whether or not to conduct these hearings was easy. Hearings were ordered to begin on April 23.

The district attorney had an interesting, but not unexpected, strategy. He was going to call only police witnesses to prove that Diaz's constitutional rights had not been violated. It would be, what is known in the law, as a bifurcated hearing. He didn't plan to call either of the victims, nor did he plan to call Detective Elfers who'd taken the first written statements from the young women at the scene of the crimes. In the light of what had already been revealed in this case, that strategy was understandable. He was not about to expose the strengths and weaknesses of his case before the actual trial. However, as the testimony and evidence would evolve in this almost two week hearing, that strategy would prove unacceptable to me as the hearing judge. I had strong suspicions that this case against James Diaz had been manufactured for the purpose of vindication, and, once again, I had no intention of leaving any stone unturned. If I had anything to say about it, the truth would come out. Yet I hoped that I was wrong about what I perceived to be the truth. It was hard to accept the thesis that the police would attempt to manufacture a case at the very time that their entire department was suffering under the glare of a state investigation and the most intense media coverage. Yet there was always the possibility that they believed that the investigation would go nowhere- that it could continue to be business as usual in Suffolk County. It was critically essential to quickly achieve public vindication in order to restore their credibility with the media and the local citizenry. These hearings would prove otherwise. Once again, there would be no vindication!

Detective after detective was called to the stand, six in all, to justify the police activity which resulted in the indictment of James Diaz for the Mount Sinai burglary. But none could satisfactorily explain how it was that Diaz had even become a suspect in this crime, or why the investigating detectives saw fit to have the victims view the carousels of slides at police headquarters—carousels which contained three separate photographs of James Diaz.

Detective John French of "Special Operations" could not satisfactorily explain why he had responded to the home of one of the victims with only one photograph in his case folder—a photograph of Diaz. I was no longer naive enough to accept his insistence that he was "carrying the photo in case he was seen in the street." "I would have arrested him," he said, "if I came across him." I was too skeptical to accept his explanation that when one of the victims, a Miss Hobert, rejected the likeness on the police artist's composite which was prepared with her assistance, she was shown only the top of the Diaz photograph, his hairline, a hairline which prompted her to proclaim, "That's the same type of hair." However, the composite depicted a fluffy and full hairline, and the Diaz mug photo displayed a clear and unmistakable center part. The police artist, Detective John Delgaves, just one hour before, testified that neither woman told him that the attacker's hair was parted down the middle. The fact was, that if James Diaz had any prominent facial feature, it was the manner in which he always parted his hair straight down the middle of his head.

As Mazzei's parade of detectives concluded, I could not help but wonder when he would decide to call Detective Elfers, the first detective on the scene. The People's case was getting weaker with each witness, and only Elfers could explain what had really been said to him by the two victims immediately after they had chased their attacker from the Collucci residence.

There was a simple question to be answered: Had they, or had they not, seen the face of their attacker? If so, why had they given him written statements saying that they had not? If he wasn't called in this case, there could only be one conclusion to draw from his unexplained absence—they could not describe the early morning intruder. Like the decision by Feldman never to call Detective Miller in the first Diaz trial, Detective Elfers was never called in the last Diaz trial. The parallel conclusion was inescapable. A skeptical hearing judge was once again being insulated from the truth!

The prosecutor had not met his legal burden in the bifurcated hearing. He had not proven, through the testimony of his police witnesses, that the slideshow and subsequent lineups had not been unduly suggestive in violation of Diaz's constitutional rights. There was no way he could avoid the inevitable. Unlike Detective Elfers, he'd have to produce Karen Hobert and Jami Collucci, the two victims in this case. Through their testimony he would have to convince me that there had been an independent source for their identification of James Diaz as the early morning intruder—a source independent of the suggestiveness created by the display of the suspected perpetrator's hairline. And possibly more!

Unfortunately, neither young woman, each of whom was an articulate college student, added any strength to the People's case. Although Karen testified that she had looked at the intruder's face for "five to ten seconds," she could never satisfactorily explain why she had told the police that she "never really got a look at his face." Nor could she explain under intense cross-examination why, according to her, she had allegedly told the police artist that the perpetrator's hair was "parted down the middle," but felt that Diaz's composite, which wasn't even close as to the hairline, should be used by the police in their investigation.

Still even more troublesome was her firm belief that the perpetrator had a distinct accent—an accent which her friend described to the police "9-1-1" operator as an "English-British accent." This almost illiterate and virtually unschooled street person, James Diaz, who, according to the police, lived between a fort in the woods and empty railroad cars, could barely speak appropriate New Yorkese English. His accent was a far cry from the "King's English." He sounded like a street tough.

Jami Collucci did very little to add credibility to the People's case. In the margin of my trial notes, as I listened intently to her words, I wrote: "(bull****)" alongside the notation of Jami's incredible testimony that she was sleeping while she was giving a written statement to Detective Elfers— that the police kept waking her up. She and her friend had been accosted and almost raped, or worse, in her home by a stranger, but she wanted us to believe that she did not want to be bothered by them. She was sleeping, but there was no doubt in her mind that she never told the detective that she did not see his face. I found this testimony absolutely unworthy of belief!

On this note, the People rested their case. There was no reason to believe that Karen Hobert and Jamie Collucci, innocent victims of an unprovoked intrusion into their home in the middle of the night, were part of a giant police conspiracy to pin the rap on James Diaz. Yet there was a more plausible explanation. In Port Jefferson Station and adjacent Mt. Sinai, for many months James Diaz was the devil incarnate—an evil demon. For months his face had been plastered all over *Newsday* and the local weeklies. He had been acquitted of the brutal rape and murder of Maureen Negus, and still most in the community were convinced that he had been the murderer and that he should have been convicted. It would not have been difficult for an experienced detective, suspicious that Diaz was the intruder and seeking to pin the burglary on him for purposes of police vindication, to successfully plant the suggestion that Diaz was the faceless night intruder. I was becoming more and more convinced that this had been the case.

Yet I was still not satisfied with what I'd heard. I wanted to hear more about this arrest. To my way of thinking, a trial, and no less a preliminary hearing, represented a search for the truth. If there was probable cause to arrest James Diaz and an appropriate basis for an in-court identification by the two young ladies, I wanted to be certain that he stood trial for committing these offenses. He could have been a dangerous sociopathic predator of women who needed to be taken off the streets for a long time. These new charges were about to disappear. Suppression of his identification by the young women would certainly destroy the People's case. There would be no evidence upon which to go to trial.

So, with the consent of the prosecutor and defense counsel, I told Mazzei to produce the first uniformed police officer on the scene and the civilian "911" operator. I also intended to call Detective Elfers who was still numbered among the missing. Unfortunately, I'd never get to hear the testimony of Elfers. Diaz's lawyer was not going to be that cooperative. He had heard enough, and he sensed victory. He was not about to permit the hearing judge to make the People's case for them.

Police officer Ronald Aimes could have added much to the search for the truth. Still, for some unexplained reason, he had destroyed the original notes which he had taken at the Collucci residence. They had been thrown, he said, into a wastepaper basket. In an effort to bolster Jami's testimony, he recalled that she had told him that the perpetrator had "brown eyes." Diaz had brown eyes. Even so, when he had broadcast a description of the perpetrator over the police network, he had made no mention of such an important physical characteristic. He had also been told that the intruder had an accent, and his field report contained no description of the perpetrator. Neither woman could provide him with any, just five minutes after a very traumatic incident. I was now, more than ever, eager to hear from Detective Elfers.

The following is an exchange between Marty Efman, defense counsel, and Tim Mazzei, the prosecutor regarding who they would and would not be calling to take the stand:

MR. EFMAN: Judge, I've considered this over the luncheon recess and in all due respect, I would be opposed to having the

Court call Det. Elfers. On this hearing, we're really looking into the question of a tainted identification. And I intend, after the hearing, to make a motion to dismiss, in the interest of justice, on the grounds of police misconduct or potential police misconduct in the way this case was handled and the way they singled out the defendant. But I think in order to allow anybody, other than the district attorney, to prove his burden of proof here...would be a detriment to the defendant.

The court, in its inquiry, is in effect, giving the people an opportunity to have their witnesses justify what appeared to be glaring inconsistencies in the paperwork that exists. And as well intended as this Court is, your Honor, I feel that it might be unfair to allow them to take the stand as a Court witness and explain these errors.

If anybody should have the burden of explaining it, it's the prosecutor. And I think he's conveniently chosen not to call them and not to make them his witness so that he could also be in the position of cross examining people that were called to the stand by the Court...."

MR. MAZZEI: I...certainly, it's true, Judge, that I have attempted to limit, initially, the hearings with respect to the witnesses called by the People. Certainly I have. Quite frankly, if there were no other reasons not superficial, most of the witnesses that could be called in hearings are possibly not material.

Tactically, certainly I didn't want to call the two girls to the stand in the hearings. As I would in any case -as I would not in any case. When your Honor indicated to me that you felt that you wanted to hear those witnesses testify, I did not question the Court, I brought them in.

I have objected a couple of times, but certainly not very much. I've encouraged the Court to ask questions. I hate to be redundant, to go back to aren't we here to find the truth and find the facts in this case....you have to make some very difficult decisions in this case, Judge, I recognize that, it's certainly easier for me to have explanations given. I mean that's no secret.

It's obvious it's easy for me if I cross examine someone, somebody to lead questions and to get what I believe to be the truth, to make it more clear on the record, to allow you to make a decision, I mean, I don't think that's any secret. I don't think I'm kidding anybody....why can't I cross examine a witness? It's for that purpose....I'm not putting anything over on anybody. It's very obvious what I'm doing.

As far as your wanting to call witnesses, Judge, you want any witness here, I'll have him here. I...I would never object to that. I have nothing to hide.

I don't believe there was police misconduct here. I believe there were many mistakes made...And I'll be the first to admit it. To show a photograph of a defendant, even if it was only the hair, I don't think it's good police work. I'm not satisfied with that. I had to put it on direct. I had no choice. That's the way it happened. I'm not happy with it. I'd like to...I wish it never happened, but it did.

If you, because you have to make the decisions in this case, and granted, very difficult decisions, and in your mind, I believe, in your mind, you're trying to be fair here, and I believe that in your mind, that you are calling these other witnesses to base your decision upon the truth and upon the facts as they existed. And if you have questions in your mind that still exist after certain witnesses have testified, I'm going to be the last guy to object to other witnesses being called...I've seen you do it before on other occasions. Not only in this case...Any witness you want, I'll have here...."[5]

Marty Efman was absolutely correct. There was no arguing with the position he was taking on behalf of his client. In my zeal to search for the truth, as ugly as it might turn out to be, I could be stepping on the rights of James Diaz. Tim Mazzei, who by his own admission, had chosen this tactical strategy, was simply pandering and being overly solicitous towards me. He had been hoisted on his own petard, and I was thoughtlessly opening an escape hatch for the prosecutor from his own choice of strategy.

Suddenly, the trial judge who had been accused of open bias and prejudice against the police and district attorney in their prosecution of James Diaz was "trying to be fair," to base his "decision upon the truth." Shameless and unsolicited words of spurious adulation intended only to move me to his position literally oozed from the prosecutor's lips. I was unmoved! He had known exactly what he was doing in this case, and he would have to lie in the bed which he had made for himself. No amount of trial strategy could camouflage a case against James Diaz which was built on a foundation of shifting sand. Little wonder that Mazzei chose not to put Detective Elfers on the stand. The war against Diaz was over. There would be no vindication of Suffolk law enforcement in May 1986!

In retrospect, I would have been forced to accept most, if not all, of the following absurd propositions in order to sustain the people's contentions:

1. That two young college women both signed written statements prepared by an experienced detective, within eight hours after the incident, that they had not seen the face of the perpetrator, although both testified that virtually all of the lights were on, and they had a clear view of the intruder for several minutes.

2. That they were subsequently able to identify James Diaz as the perpetrator without undue suggestion by the police.

3. That Jami Collucci signed and swore to her statement while she was asleep, and that her statement was prepared by the detective while she was asleep.

4. That the second written statement was read by the same detective to Karen Hobert, and she signed and swore to it, though it stated that she had not seen the face of the perpetrator, after having told the detective that if she ever saw the man again she would be able to identify him.

5. That Detective Elfers, who took these statements and who

was the detective assigned to investigate the burglary and assault, was not called as a witness for the prosecution for tactical reasons, and for all intents and purposes played no further role in this investigation, although this was his case.

6. That Karen Hobert has no recollection of the details of a thirty to forty-five minute conversation on December 5, 1985 with Detective French, although she had a very specific recollection that he only showed her the forehead and hairline of a mug photograph of James Diaz.

7. That Detective French showed Karen Hobert a picture of the defendant's hair because she was not satisfied with the hairline depicted in the composite which was printed in a local newspaper, even though she testified that she had not seen the local paper which carried the sketch.

8. That the detective was carrying the Diaz photograph in his case file when he visited the Collucci residence to interview Karen Hobert so that he could place Diaz under arrest for this crime if he fortuitously ran into him in the street, although the police would not have had an iota of probable cause to arrest him at that time.

9. That Jami Collucci, immediately after the incident, told the police "911" operator that the perpetrator had an English or British accent, and that Karen Hobert reported that he had some type of accent, although James Diaz spoke with no discernible accent, and his speaking voice could best be described as unremarkable and uneducated.

10. That the first police officer on the scene, Officer Aimes, who obtained a physical description of the perpetrator from the two women, was initially given no facial features by them, and reported none on his Field Report. And whatever notes might have been taken by him were inexplicably discarded.

11. That the one facial feature which the officer claims he was subsequently given—brown eyes—was never reported over his police radio, nor reported in his Field Report, although the

original description, as limited as it was, was called in and contained in his report.

12. That neither woman could describe the length of the perpetrator's hair to the officer, and it is not contained in any report as "shoulder length" until after Karen Hobert viewed a police slide carousel containing three separate photographs of James Diaz with shoulder length hair, and Jami Collucci viewed a photospread of six individuals, including the defendant wearing shoulder length hair.

13. That the composite prepared with the assistance of, and agreed upon by, the two women depicted a white male with hair below his ears, but well above his shoulders, although on the date of his arrest, December 6, 1985, Diaz's hair was cut to a length above his ears.

Immediately after my decision to suppress any in-court identification of James Diaz as the perpetrator was announced in open court, I turned to Mazzei and asked if he planned to go forward with the case. An angry prosecutor fumed: "You've suppressed all the evidence. The People cannot go forward." But there was still a piece of open business involving Jimmy Diaz. He wasn't going to be a free man! Later that week, I sentenced him to the maximum term of incarceration allowable by law, three and a half to seven years, for sexually abusing and physically assaulting the young woman in his Port Jefferson Station underground "fort."[6]

Looking at him for what might have been the last time, I could not help but quip, "Our names will probably be forever linked in Suffolk County. I am not sentencing you because of the murder. I don't think you were guilty of that murder. You were acquitted of that charge. However, I have no doubt that you are guilty in this case." An unremorseful James Diaz looking me straight in the eye, responded cooly, "I'm a changed person. I never did any of these crimes I was blamed for."[7]

For the next two and a half years, James Diaz's home was to be the Clinton State Correctional Facility in Dannemora, New York. He was released on parole in the summer of 1989 after serving the maximum time allowable by law with credit for "good time" served by the Department of Corrections. He was also given credit for the time he spent in jail awaiting trial.

The People don't usually have a right to appeal an adverse ruling in a criminal case. Yet where a ruling by the court has so weakened their prosecution that they can not proceed to trial, there is a right to appeal to the appellate division. Although the People were visibly shaken by my ruling which crippled their ability to go forward with this very important prosecution, no appeal was ever finalized after my devastating ruling even though a Notice of Appeal was actually filed at one point with the higher court. The intention to file an appeal was memorialized in a letter from Mark Cohen to the chief clerk of the County Court. But their failure to prosecute the appeal spoke volumes about the nature of their case against Diaz for the burglary and attempted rapes in Mount Sinai.[8]

In 1987, while still in prison, Diaz filed a $30,000,000 Civil Rights lawsuit in the United States District Court against Suffolk County and several former members of the homicide squad. He alleged that Suffolk police had manufactured a false written confession in the Negus murder; that they conspired to use perjured testimony; that they tampered with physical evidence and knowingly used perjured testimony from witnesses, including the inmate, Joseph Pistone.

That lawsuit was pending until the spring of 1992. Diaz refused an offer of settlement of $23,500 by the county, although he was willing to accept $24,900, which Tom Boyle, the county attorney, was not willing to recommend to the legislature. The prosecution of the Civil Rights suit was delayed by the chronic illness of his civil attorney, Stanley Shapiro, who suffered from Chronic Fatigue Syndrome. I was told that I was going to be subpoenaed to testify as a witness on behalf of Diaz when that case came to trial. I had already been subjected to extensive pre-trial examination by the various attorneys in this case. I was not looking forward to being used as a weapon by a convicted criminal and probable sociopath. But I would have no choice in the matter, and I would have been sworn to tell the truth—the whole ugly and sordid truth. Perhaps that is why the county decided not to go trial. In May 1992, the case was settled for $95,000. Stanley Shapiro called me to advise me of the settlement. I wondered whether the police and prosecutors involved in the Diaz debacle still felt vindicated. Maureen Negus was no longer the only victim in this case. The innocent taxpayers of Suffolk County who had never even heard about this settlement had also been victimized.

EIGHTEEN

"There Is a Time to Clean Up Your House."

—David J. Wilmott, editor/publisher
Suffolk Life *newspapers*

J AMES DIAZ AND PETER CORSO, AT LEAST FOR THE TIME BEING, were out of the way. Despite the continuing state investigation, it was important to attempt to continue to function normally on a day-to-day basis. But this was virtually impossible. By February 1986, I knew that an effort was afoot by Arthur Cromarty to move county court judges to the Supreme Court to handle civil cases exclusively. My office received a call from the Suffolk County Bar Association. They had been directed by the administrative judge to screen every county court judge for possible appointment as acting supreme court justice. My worst fears were about to be realized. I was not about to be transferred out of the criminal court at that time. In no uncertain terms, I absolutely refused their invitation for judicial screening. It did not matter! I was ultimately transferred to the supreme court in 1988 without ever having my qualifications considered by the screening committee. This was a clear violation of the understanding between the bench and the Bar concerning the assignment of judges. It was apparently that important to some people to remove me from my criminal jurisdiction.

The fallout from the investigation was beginning to be felt in the county. On January 24, 1986, the State Commission of Investigations served a very broad subpoena for police and court records and other documents relating to the murder trials of Peter Corso and James Diaz and the subsequent police investigation of these cases. The commission also sought the complete records concerning the three trials of the defendants in the murder of Johnny Pius. But the police and the county were not going to turn over these records without a long court battle. According to papers filed in the Supreme Court by the county attorney, Martin Bradley Ashare, the commission was on a "fishing expedition." He argued: "The operation of a police department should not be impaired by unfounded and unsubstantiated opinions of a few individuals." The Suffolk County Detectives Association, on behalf of the homicide detectives under investigation, opposed release of "internal-affairs" documents relating to police investigations of the manner in which these cases were handled by the homicide squad. Of course the detectives were represented by Gerry Sullivan of Sullivan and Spota, former chiefs of the district attorney's homicide bureau.

Patrick Henry claimed that he, too, "had asked for the state probe." He welcomed the investigation "to clear the air." For his part, the police commissioner, DeWitt Treder, "was concerned about the probe's affecting continuing police investigations." "When the time comes," he said, "everything will be ironed out, and the commission will get the information that it needs. I just don't want them coming in with fishhooks and picking up everything that is under every rock."[1] What he failed to publicly explain was why the county and the police would fight every commission subpoena tooth and nail. There would be no meaningful cooperation with the investigation until Treder and the County Executive, Peter Fox Cohalan, now a Supreme Court Justice along with Patrick Henry, the former district attorney, finally resigned from their positions of authority.

Fearing that their efforts would be thwarted in the "bizarre" courtroom of Suffolk Justice George F. X. McInerney, and not trusting the Suffolk judiciary, the attorneys for the commission sought a removal of the proceedings to a Manhattan court, far away from the Long Island battleground. Meanwhile, the department's only Hispanic female police officer, Rebecca Bernard, who had been acquitted of drug charges in 1984, but who still faced departmental proceedings, made allegations to the SIC of "drug use by Suffolk narcotics officers, illegal wiretaps and an alleged cover-up of a narcotics case involving the son of a high-ranking Suffolk police officer [Chief Gallagher]."[2] Two undercover narcotics officers who were now the center of an FBI probe as well as the state investigation, James R. Kuhn and Raymond Gutkowski, checked themselves into a psychiatric hospital at the advice of the PBA lawyer, to avoid having to talk to the various investigators.

At a meeting with *Newsday's* investigative reporters, on March 7, 1986, accompanied by a psychiatrist and a psychiatric attendant, Kuhn told of a meeting with Ray Perini, the assistant district attorney in charge of narcotics investigations.

According to *Newsday*, "At that meeting, at Suffolk police headquarters in Yaphank, Kuhn said Perini told him that he 'wants to clean house before the SIC did it for him.'....Early Feb. 22, Kuhn said, he was taken back home and contemplated suicide. 'I thought about eating my gun...'"[3]

At the same time, the department's Internal Affairs division was under fire. Its commanding officer, Inspector Donald Jeffers, denied that his officers, who had accompanied Kuhn and Gutkowski to the Perini meeting, ever directed the officers not to cooperate with the SIC. Even as his office was investigating alleged falsification of records in the prosecution of Chief Gallagher's son in a narcotics case, he and the commissioner had to fend off charges that there had been a massive cover-up of illegalities in narcotics enforcement, including the diversion of as much as $250,000 worth of government bought cocaine to personal police use. Commissioner Treder's reaction: "I really don't think there's going to be anything where there's a conspiracy. I think we just have a few foolish people."[4]

On March 13, after a meeting between the county executive, Peter Cohalan, and the police commissioner, both Gallagher and Jeffers were removed from their posts. Chief Gallagher was placed on indefinite leave and replaced by deputy chief Arthur Feldman. Inspector Jeffers was transferred to the department's patrol division. At the same time as the transfers were taking place, Cohalan expressed "complete confidence" in the commissioner. But that confidence, even if it was sincere, was not shared by others. In little more than a year, Treder was gone and replaced by an interim commissioner. But that did not happen until Cohalan himself resigned from office under the double edged pressure of an impending election and a Republican leadership anticipating a future political holocaust. But in the interim, Cohalan vowed to cooperate fully with the federal and state investigators and to "let the chips fall where they may." In an interview, he said: "The integrity and proper functioning of the police department is paramount. It's what the people of Suffolk want, that the department have the highest integrity. It must be beyond reproach."[5]

Dean David Trager, chairman of the SIC was furious. He announced that Cohalan's claim that he was welcoming a full and complete investigation was "outrageous." According to Trager, the county attorney was vigorously opposing the SIC's subpoena for court records and internal affairs documents. The county attorney, who represented the position of the county executive, was of the opinion that the SIC "is on a fishing expedition that lacks an articulate basis and focus." Their investigation, he said, was "based not on reliable and specific allegations but on notoriety generated by extensive, sensational media coverage." Responded chairman Trager: "In light of what has already happened this week, it's hard to call this a fishing expedition."[6]

Even the local weeklies were beginning to get into the debate. The gadfly publisher and editor, David J. Wilmott, whose weekly *Suffolk Life* newspapers were widely read throughout the county, called for the appointment of an "outside prosecutor":

> There is a time to clean up your house from within and that time has come and gone for Suffolk County....The time for shoving the dirt under the rug is past. A full-scale investigation by outside, independent sources is badly needed. Without such an investigation and review, who can have faith in Suffolk County government, the police department or the district attorney's office?...Let's get the investigation underway now so that we can put what appears to be a sordid blemish on Suffolk behind us as fast as we can.[7]

Newsday, which was closely following the day-to-day activities of the homicide squad, continued to report about almost daily personnel changes in the squad which were rapidly taking shape despite claims that this was all a "tempest in a teapot."[8] Detective Lt. Robert Dunn, who'd been relieved as commander of the squad and transferred to chief of investigations, announced his retirement. Dennis Rafferty, the senior member of the squad, "requested" a transfer to the robbery squad.

An untarnished detective sergeant, Kevin Cronin, was transferred into the squad in an administrative role. Detective Sgt. Kenneth McGuire elected to retire after being transferred to a precinct squad. Three other detectives retired or were about to retire. The squad was now under the command of a deputy inspector, Thomas Murphy.[9] In June, during a lull in a hearing in a homicide trial, homicide detective Leon McKenna whispered to me that he, detective Jack Miller and sergeant Richard Jensen were retiring. They were going to operate a travel agency in Lindenhurst. I had already learned through the grapevine of the retirements of detectives Louis Rodriguez and Anthony Palumbo, who had taken the surreptitiously taped Quartararo confession. The ranks of the "confession takers" were being decimated piece by piece. Outwardly, the entire fabric of the squad was beginning to take on a new face under new leadership. To Joe Lyons of the SIC, these retirements would make the conduct of the investigation "somewhat less difficult."[10]

But simultaneous investigations by both the state and federal governments were apparently not sufficient, or speedy enough, for some members of the county legislature who were beginning to feel the political fallout. It was time to share some of the glory! Its public safety committee which was charged with the oversight of county law enforcement summoned both the district attorney and the police commissioner to respond to questions about the alleged illegal activities. Treder reassured them that "This whole thing probably involved five police officers....We are cleaning our own house." He would welcome, he said, even the appointment of a special prosecutor "to clear the air here."

On the other hand, District Attorney Henry felt that a special prosecutor was unnecessary. The sharpest questioning was directed towards the district attorney. Commented one angry legislator: "The police department is almost out of control and the district attorney has a laissez-faire attitude." He felt that it may be time for the county legislature to consider the issue of a special prosecutor. But the majority was "content to wait for the completion of the state and federal probes before recommending further action by the Legislature."[11]

On April 23, 1986, Chief Gallagher announced his retirement after thirty-four years of police service. He had been chief of detectives since January 1984. When he was placed on involuntary leave just one month before, he had vowed to stay on to fight the allegations against him. He did not, he said, intend to leave under a cloud. Apparently, that cloud suddenly became too heavy a burden when both the commissioner and the district attorney publicly informed the legislative committee that police documents had, in fact, been altered in the case of the chief's son, Timothy. He now faced almost certain indictment.

This former chief of the homicide squad was scheduled to leave the department on May 12. It was almost two years before the axe would finally fall in the form of an indictment charging him with falsifying police records to help his son escape a jail sentence for dealing in cocaine.

Contemporaneously with these events, the media was beginning to convey the impression that there was a maverick judge in Suffolk County who was doing battle with the district attorney's office and the police department, who was willing to expose abuses in the system and who had broken the code of silence. Some persons were getting the erroneous message that this maverick judge could help them in their own battles within the criminal justice system. They attempted to reach out to me in the hope that somehow I could miraculously solve their problems—problems which sometimes had festered for many, many years. They claimed to be victims of police abuse, prosecutorial misconduct, collusive judges and a conspiracy of silence designed to foster these abuses.

In 1986, I became their conduit to the state probers. Although there was nothing that I could personally do for them, even if I privately sympathized with their cause, letters and telephone calls began to stream into my chambers. Despite my own experiences and observations, and the strong feelings which I had formulated, I could not bring myself to accept that all, or even most, of these people had truly been aggrieved. Still it was not for me to pass judgement, nor did I have the means or even the jurisdiction to investigate their complaints. It was my hope and expectation that the SIC would delve into each of these matters. I came to learn that the commission did not have the manpower, and in some cases, the inclination to conduct a full-fledged investigation of every complaint.

It was during this period that I received correspondence from the Quartararo brothers professing their innocence and the innocence of their cohorts, two of whom I had already sentenced to maximum terms of life in prison. At that time I was convinced that none of them was innocent of the death of Johnny Pius. Nothing which they wrote, no matter how well phrased, could dissuade me from that belief. Yet even their letters were referred to the commission. However, usually, the communications were from people whose cases were not familiar to me, and whose names I had never even heard.

In early February, we received a mysterious telephone call from a man who wouldn't give his name until he talked to me directly. Steven DeLise's son had been tried for rape in 1985, and there had been a mistrial—a hung jury. His son later pled guilty to sexual misconduct without ever admitting his guilt. In New York state, this is known as a "Serrano plea." However, according to the father, he was guilty of nothing, and both the grand and trial juries had received perjured testimony from the police and the victim. The assistant district attorney who handled the prosecution, he said, had to be aware of this perjury. The father visited the office of Barry Feldman, the bureau chief, to bring this matter to his attention. He left, he said, "after receiving the impression that he would do nothing to help him and that he was just like the rest of them." He was scared "because this DA would do anything to protect the record and to obtain a conviction.[12] Within one week, after a telephone call from me, Stephen DeLise met for three hours with a representative of the State Commission of Investigations.

Within that same week, my law secretary, Bob Meguin received a call from a member of the Islip Town auxiliary police. He was seeking the address and telephone number of the SIC. He and others, he said, "were tired of the Suffolk County Police Department falsifying police reports about several incidents."[13] He did not provide us with, and we weren't interested in, any details about his problems with the police. It was for the SIC to sort out his grievances.

NINETEEN

"All They Need is a
Dead Body and a Confession."

–Former District Attorney Henry O'Brien

G REEENHAVEN IS AN IMPOSING MAXIMUM SECURITY correctional facility in Stormville, New York, built around the time of the Civil War, behind huge grey walls intended to discourage its inmates from even considering the possibility of escape. Its prison population includes many career criminals and those convicted of the most heinous violent crimes— murderers, robbers and rapists. The last inmate sentenced to death in New York state, Lemuel Smith, was one of its residents. Vincenzo Rao is likewise a long term resident of Greenhaven. I have never met, nor even talked to, this man. I knew nothing about his case, but he was convicted of the murder of one Harold Gillard in Suffolk County. Rao was alleged to have hired an Edward Jordan to murder the deceased. Both Jordan and Rao were convicted after a joint trial in December 1982. For that crime, Rao is serving a sentence of twenty-five-years-to-life behind the walls of Greenhaven Correctional Facility.

In a letter to me seeking to "find some help in exposing certain corrupt dealing in Suffolk County homicide and district attorney's office," Vincenzo Rao claimed that he never knew and never did any business with his co-defendant:

Mr. Gillard was shot and killed sometime in early November of 1981. I learned at the trial...where it was rumored that Mr. Gillard owed me money. Although Mr. Jordan was arrested shortly after the killing, I was not arrested and charged with this crime until April 29, 1982. By that time (and I have strong reason to believe that homicide detective's Miller, Leonard, Sievers, and Sgt. Jensen had conspired to frame me by suborning perjure and perjuring their own testimony), the only evidence offered against me at the trial was the testimony of Detective Miller and one Joseph Warshawski. Mr. Warshawski an admitted con-man and perjurer testified that I told him (in the Suffolk County jail) that I ordered "someone" to kill Gillard. Also he admitted that someone with the district attorney's [sic] promised him less of one year in county jail. Detective Miller testified that he saw me and Mr. Jordan in conversation "two or three days after Gillard was shot." Both of these testimonies are complete and total lies. I have good reason to believe that either Mr. Miller or one of his partners (Leonard, Sievers, and Sgt. Jensen) conspired with Warshawski to commit perjury under oath and frame me for this crime...Please provide me with some assistance. This rape of justice should not be allowed to go uncorrected. If you cannot help, others may fall prey to these criminals...I am not looking for mercy but I am looking for justice.[1]

****

On November 18, 1982, Joseph Warshawski was being cross-examined by Rao's defense lawyer. The police informant claimed that Rao had told him in the Suffolk County Correctional Facility that he had ordered the murder of Harold Gillard. The "snitch" was awaiting trial for grand larceny and extortion.

> Q:...most of your life you spent your life earning your living as a con artist in one way or another?
> A: I would say so, yes.
> Q: And that's true of today...your lifestyle today, until today?

Still true you make your life as a con artist?

A: Yes. I don't hurt people....

Q: Mr. Warshawski, you lied in the past to help yourself, is that right?

A: That's true.

Q: Okay. And you will lie in the future to help yourself if that is necessary?

A: That's true.

Q: Okay. And if it were to help you to lie here, you would lie right now?

A: No."[2]

Although Joseph Warshawski claimed he didn't hurt people in the past, he certainly succeeded in hurting Vincenzo Rao who continues to profess his innocence. The admitted "con artist" was believed and used by a willing prosecution team in order to secure a conviction in a difficult case. More importantly, he was apparently believed by a cooperative jury of Suffolk citizens. As I perused Rao's unsolicited correspondence, I couldn't help but recall that the very same detective, Jack Miller, was the link between the perjurer Joseph Pistone and the prosecutor Barry Feldman in the Diaz fiasco.

****

Omie Saunders, prisoner #78 A 2121, like Vincenzo Rao, is serving a life sentence in Greenhaven for the murder of one Alfred Kirshner in 1977. He was tried by my one-time "mentor" and immediate superior, Thomas Stark. Like, Vincenzo Rao, I'd never heard of Saunders until he chose to write to me on three separate occasions in 1987 and 1988. He wrote to me, he said, because: "I am a poor black man, and could not afford to retain a lawyer whom (sic) would bring the misconduct out on my appeal, so I had to prosecute my appeal Pro se. The main issue raised on my appeal is that the prosecutor knowingly used false evidence, and perjured testimony at my trial."[3]

The prosecutor had been my sometimes "friend" Billy Keahon, and he was being accused, albeit by a convicted murderer, of "conspiring to frame the Complainant of a murder charge...." The alleged co-conspirators were the trial judge; Saunders' court appointed attorney; the arresting officer, Sgt. William O'Kula; the medical examiner; Suffolk County's ballistics expert, Sgt. Alfred DellaPenna; and Robert Genna of the Suffolk County Crime lab.

"I do not know who to turn to for assistance," wrote Saunders, "and Judge Stark's misconduct should be exposed to the public, because other people will become vulnerable to his techniques in court procedures....I am innocent of this crime, and I have evidence to prove that I was indeed framed."

In the summer of 1993, long after my early retirement to North Carolina, I received a fourth letter from Omie Saunders begging for my assistance in his cause. He will probably profess his innocence until the day he dies, or until someone in a position to help reaches out to him. There is nothing that I can do for him, and I have no idea whether his grievance is legitimate.

Not everyone who communicated with me was so directly and personally involved in the criminal justice system with an obvious axe to grind. Some were merely concerned citizens who were so openly distressed that they literally "gave up on our so-called men in blue." I received a letter from a resident of Bay Shore, a one-time peaceful south shore community which was now plagued by drugs and crimes. The letter read in part:

> Maybe our problems are not as serious as Diaz & Corso, but if our requests were heard, we may not have to see that in our neighborhood. A young man was found dead at 1327 Lombardy Blvd. a short time ago and the incident, according to the newspaper, he was a drunk who had fallen. The way he was found surely should call for a full investigation of why, where, how & possibly Who. This occurred in Nov. 86. Diane Schmidt was found hanging, according to Suffolk County Police, in Hauppauge jail, on October 12, 1986. Her mother and her husband have never been told the truth concerning the incident, that caused Diane's death. I do not accept this as a suicide, since I have known Diane for many years. Whatever happened from Brentwood to Hauppauge jail will never be honestly told....How many other parents and friends will have to live with the same

situation?....(The Kuhn-Gallagher mess happened on our corner) I have a file on our drug and youth problem, from 10-31-82 up to and including 4-7-86. Names, dates plate numbers and police officers who were here. We had Lt. Stores here from Internal Affairs, which was a joke. He told us this is not T.V.[4]

What I'd seen and what I was hearing was having a profound effect upon my view of the criminal justice system. But I needed to retain my objectivity. I simply couldn't allow my inner feelings to interfere with my continuing mission to objectively and impartially preside over felony criminal trials. It was not easy, since almost every day I was forced to confront belligerent prosecutors in whose view I was now the enemy. I began to look upon the courthouse as the "enemy camp," and I dreaded the work days of openly hostile verbal battles and unbridled belligerence. I wanted the investigation to come to a rapid conclusion. I was rapidly losing patience with what I perceived as the turtle-like progress of the SIC. I spent many hours on the telephone expressing those frustrations and concerns with the staff attorney who was responsible for the conduct of the investigation, John Kennedy.

Thomas Staffa had resigned his post to become chief of the criminal division in the office of the special state prosecutor for nursing homes, health and social services. He was immediately replaced by Ms. Susan E. Shepard, a former assistant United States Attorney in Brooklyn. She was also the wife of her former supervisor, now a federal judge, Raymond J. Dearie.[5] Despite this change in leadership, which came early in the investigation, there was no change in the slow progress of the investigation. Not long after her appointment, I met with Ms. Shepard and her chief deputy, Patrick Lupinetti. They were completely noncommittal about their progress, but they did indicate that they were experiencing difficulty in obtaining witnesses in Suffolk County who were willing to discuss the problems in the criminal justice system. It was clear that they were looking for names of potential witnesses and that they were focusing their attention on the area of "police brutality," although that had not been the focus of my complaint.

Although the SIC was moving at what seemed like a snail's pace in the conduct of its investigation, *Newsday's* team of investigative reporters was rapidly advancing their study of ten years of Suffolk County homicide cases. To that end, Tom Maier, the lead investigative reporter, met with me in my Stony Brook chambers on July 30, 1986. He was interested in learning about how homicide cases were assigned to judges. Although I would have liked to speak freely on the subject, I chose instead to listen to what he was willing to tell me about what they were discovering in their inquiry. Actually, I was somewhat surprised that *Newsday* was finally going to publish this story.

For months, Maier had been telling me that his superiors at *Newsday* just would not accept that there were real problems in Suffolk law enforcement. Most, he said, believed that Stuart Namm was operating "with less than a full deck." It could not be as bad as I was making it out to be—a mountain was being made out of the proverbial molehill. Maier had been aching to write this story, which he considered to be of the utmost importance, but he was concerned about his security and the security of his family. He knew that he would have to continue to live with these people. Apparently, he'd overcome those fears because the story was imminent.

The *Newsday* story was to run for one week during the month of September. Much of the story was being developed from computer studies of Suffolk homicide statistics. He was interested in one particular statistical finding, which had been a great surprise to him. Surprising to him, but not to me! Among Suffolk judges who had handled ten or more homicide cases, I had, on average, doled out, without question, the longest sentences. Maier was looking for a verbal reaction from me, but he got none. This statistic was far from surprising in the light of my judicial philosophy. I was more aroused when he advised me that he had spoken to attorneys and others concerning the abuses I had found in the Corso and Diaz cases. He said that his story would virtually corroborate what I had seen in those trials. He had even found a "prisoner up state who had provided vivid details about a meeting" with a highly placed Suffolk assistant district attorney, at which this inmate, who had been a police informant in a murder trial, "had been coached...about his testimony in court."[6.] He had also learned that Ira Dubey, the county's chief forensic serologist, did not have a Master's degree in forensic science, although he would testify under oath in homicide cases that he had, in fact, obtained such a degree. Maier's source was one of

Dubey's teachers at John Jay College of Criminal Justice in New York City.

He had also interviewed detective Dennis Rafferty, formerly of the homicide squad, the lead detective in Corso. Rafferty, he said, was surprisingly frank with him. In Maier's opinion, Rafferty believed that he was doing "God's work."

On the very next day, after meeting with Tom Maier, I happened to run into a rumpled Harry O'Brien, Patrick Henry's predecessor, at a local Centereach luncheonette where the former district attorney was nursing a cup of coffee while slumped over a copy of *The New York Times*.

He had been subpoenaed to testify before the SIC. The commission was looking into a possible cover-up of a drug case involving one of Patrick Henry's children. My interest, however, was more piqued by O'Brien's characterization of detective Rafferty as a person who thought that he was "doing God's work." In less than twenty-four hours, two very responsible persons, under uniquely different circumstances, had proffered the same opinion of a senior homicide detective. Their independent assessments were indeed frightening and it did nothing to restore my confidence in Suffolk law enforcement despite commissioner Treder's public assurances "that the outside investigators will find little the department has not discovered and already remedied by itself."[7]

*****

The former district attorney was always ready to offer an opinion about someone connected with Suffolk law enforcement. In April 1991, K. James McCready, who retired from the police department for more than a year, along with two others, was being investigated for the brutal and senseless beating of a petty thief who had stolen a flag banner from a bar that McCready had contributed to the annual St. Patrick's Day parade. At a conference in my chambers concerning an unrelated matter, O'Brien expressed shock at the allegations, although he said that he was not surprised. McCready, he said, had a serious drinking problem, which when coupled with his other unspecified personal problems, with which O'Brien seemed to be familiar, made him a very "angry man." What remained unstated, however, was how long he knew McCready was an angry man, or whether he was an angry man when good old congenial Harry had the helm of the district attorney's office and McCready was a highly decorated detective handling serious homicides.

Was he angry and capable of uncontrollable violence, I wondered to myself, when he was investigating the Catone and O'Toole cases? Both had accused him of physically abusing them behind the closed door of the homicide squad "interview" room? This was a question which was ripe for conjecture, but one which would probably never be answered. Still in 1993, he was found not guilty by one of the judges who had replaced me on the bench. McCready was represented by Tom Spota and Billy Keahon, the reformed alcoholic, who himself was arrested for driving while intoxicated during the trial. They had chosen not to take the case before a Suffolk jury. The judge's acquittal was no surprise and swift. There was no need for deliberations in that case.

****

It was clear that Maier was serious about this investigation. Our many conversations over the past several months were going to finally pay off. He had obviously overcome his previously expressed reluctance to dig too deep. He had also apparently convinced his faceless editorial superiors at *Newsday* that Judge Namm was not crazy and these abuses by the homicide squad could be documented and were truly systemic. They had not been the figment of an hysterical imagination. You could see in his eyes that his adrenaline was flowing. Suffolk County was an investigative reporter's dream. It was the kind of story of which Pulitzer prizes were made. Now that Maier had the ball, it was clear that he was going to run with it. But it was several months before the series finally broke as the headline story in a Sunday edition.

December 7, 1986 was forty-five years to the day after Japan destroyed the U.S. Pacific fleet at Pearl Harbor. Once again it fell on a Sunday morning, but this time it was the Suffolk County Police Department which was the target of a five day verbal bombardment which left the homicide squad—"The Confession Takers"—literally dead in the waters of the Long Island Sound. Although the revelations of recent years had rendered the squad virtually comatose and ineffectual, this was the final blow. With the following prefatory words, Tom Maier, Rex Smith and a team of *Newsday* reporters and photographers unleashed their relentless barrage of facts and anecdotal evidence to support their thesis that the squad's reliance upon obtaining confessions was inextricably tied to abuses of the system and weakened homicide cases:

> For more than a decade, Suffolk County's system of investigating murder cases has been marked by an extraordinary reliance on gaining confessions—a practice that has contributed to claims of civil-rights abuses, mishandling of evidence and repeated questions about the validity of police testimony.
>
> A year-long *Newsday* study has found that police and suspects made incriminating statements in 94 percent of the more than 300 murder cases since 1975—a rate that experts believe is without parallel in the country. Prosecutors and police say this is evidence of superior police work. "We are the best," said former homicide squad commander Al Holdorff.
>
> But others, including former prosecutors, say the high rate reflects a system based more on interrogation than on investigation. At its worst, the Suffolk system has depended upon confessions that violate the rights of suspects, substitute for extensive detective work, conflict with other evidence and strain the credibility of the county's cases in court. At times, the confession—normally the strongest piece of evidence available in a murder case—has become the weakest link.
>
> In fact, *Newsday* found, accused killers in Suffolk are less likely to be convicted of the top murder charge than in other suburban areas, and, if convicted, are given shorter sentences.[8]

For one year, *Newsday*'s reporters did a review and computer analysis of 361 Suffolk homicide cases between 1975 and 1985. They'd also examined 700 other homicide cases from six other jurisdictions and five states. Of the 361 Suffolk cases, there were 348 reported confessions—a staggering 94%.

By comparison, in the other large suburban counties which they studied, the confession rate ranged from a low of 54% to a high of 73.5%.

Jailhouse "snitches" were used against thirty-two defendants accused of murder—twenty-eight between 1980 and 1985 alone. Most of these informants received lighter sentences in exchange for their testimony, and "several committed felony crimes during the time they would have been imprisoned." According to Joseph A. Ball, a lawyer from California involved in drafting ethical standards for the American Bar Association: "It seems to me a bargain being made in return for perjury." (How perceptive and how prophetic!)

They reported that forty-seven murder suspects claimed to have been beaten by Suffolk homicide detectives, but "Suffolk criminal court judges have given little credence to the brutality allegations, and only once has a civil jury found that homicide detectives beat a suspect. The detectives were not disciplined in that case." Since the final report of the SIC which has been used often by plaintiffs in federal litigation in Suffolk brutality cases, that number has increased dramatically. Yet it can't be said with any degree of certainty that Suffolk judges have given any greater credence to claims of brutality which, though seemingly less frequent, continue to plague the "new" homicide squad.

For five full days, *Newsday's* readers were treated to a portrait of a group of "elite" detectives who had been on a mission of justice, but who were out of control in their willingness and zeal to test the bounds of legal and constitutional limitations in order to accomplish that mission.

The following quotes appeared in the *Newsday* articles:

> "In my mind, the end justifies the means. Now as far as anybody else knowing what I did? Not really. Because I kept most of my stuff to myself." —*Richard Zito, retired homicide detective*
>
> "My concern is that it seems that it's bad if you got 94%. I think its fantastic. I am disappointed personally that we got a six percent failure rate." —*Sgt. Robert Misegades, homicide detective*
>
> "If I was the police commissioner and there was a 94%

confession rate, I'd get the internal affairs department to see what's wrong." —*Gerald M. Caplan, former director, National Institute of Justice*

"The less you take, the better off you are." —*Robert Amato, retired homicide detective speaking about investigative notes*

"Could you, in clear conscience...expect a homicide detective or a guy who has dedicated his life to police work itself, could you expect them, after busting their ass to bring a guy in, to let a case go down? No way. They'd fight tooth and nail. They'd shoot it out with you....Why should I take notes? So that somebody can look at it and find something wrong...." —*Richard Zito, retired homicide detective*

"All they need is a dead body and a confession. Everything is geared toward confessions and admissions....They don't want to do the work on the harder cases." —*Henry O'Brien, former district attorney*

"When you rely on oral statements or jailhouse confessions over a period of time, your investigative skills atrophy- you lose the other skills." —*Charles Peterson former Suffolk deputy police commissioner*

[On the tail wagging the dog]: "As prosecutors, we were not the ones calling the shots. You couldn't express dissatisfaction with a cop's work. The climate was such that you couldn't do that." —*John Buonora, former chief felony prosecutor*

"...the homicide squad worked to such a status that everyone became subservient to them, even the DA's office." —*Salvatore Alamia, former assistant district attorney*

"It is difficult for a judge to question a police officer. You assume you have a law-enforcement official whose sole purpose is to protect the community from offenders, and you assume he did an honest and competent job...and you hesitate in questioning his tactics or his motives." —*Ernest Signorelli, Suffolk surrogate and former county court judge*

[On the perception that as a trial judge he was pro-prosecution]: "I don't honestly believe that I've ever indicated to juries anything like that, but I've been accused of it." —*Thomas M. Stark, Administrative Judge, superior criminal courts*

"We have safeguards against that—pre-trial hearings and cross-examination. And if a defense attorney is worth his salt, he's going to make sure police did what they said they did. Police wrongdoing in all jurisdictions has been exposed by these hearings." —*Arthur Cromarty, district administrative judge*

"We're willing to proceed with prosecution, perhaps sometimes where other people would be a little more hesitant or reluctant or timid." —*District Attorney Patrick Henry*

To those who toiled within the bowels of the Suffolk County criminal justice system, these daily revelations, though sometimes shocking, should not have come as any great surprise. What *Newsday* exposed to the light of day was accepted in Suffolk courtrooms for years by judges, including me until my eyes were opened, and attorneys who donned invisible blinders each day. There was no need for a knowing wink and a nod, only a convenient deaf ear.

Perhaps the most shocking revelation to some was the revelation that Ira Dubey, Suffolk's favorite forensic scientist and expert witness, had falsified his professional credentials in several important homicide cases. But this could not have come as a surprise to two of the highest ranking prosecutors in the district attorney's office, Steve Wilutis and my old nemesis, Barry Feldman. As early as 1983, they had been tipped off about Dubey and his perjury by the chief medical examiner, Dr. Sidney Weinberg, who got his information from Dubey's superior in the crime lab.

Wilutis and Feldman claimed that they had checked certain available transcripts at the time of this revelation, but they had found no discrepancy. This damning information remained their secret until the *Newsday* revelation.

Ira Dubey wrote: "If you don't maximize your credentials, I think you're not being in the real world if you say that. You're always trying to maximize yourself. Doesn't everybody try and do that?"

The state probers of the SIC likewise should not have been shocked by these daily disclosures. To them, some of this had to be old news. Their investigation was now more than a year old, and despite the resistance they had encountered, they had already interviewed scores of witnesses who had to be giving them some of the same information. John Kennedy informed me that they were now aware that Pistone had perjured himself at the Diaz trial when he swore that he had been offered no deal by Barry Feldman in exchange for his testimony. This too was exposed in the *Newsday* series. A state commission had been scooped by the efforts of two investigative reporters with a small supporting staff. It was time to go public to maintain the credibility of an investigation which was already taking too long as far as many were concerned.

TWENTY

"More Than One Has Referred to Suffolk as the 'Wild West' and Has Despaired of Meaningful Reform."

—SIC Commission Chairman David Trager

I T WAS ANNOUNCED THAT TWO DAYS OF PUBLIC HEARINGS would be conducted in Hauppauge in January. Yet Kennedy made it clear that there would be no findings or report at the conclusion of these hearings. The sole purpose of the hearings was to take testimony of witnesses under oath in public. The State Commission of Investigations was finally coming out from behind its closed doors. None too soon, as far as I was concerned. It would turn out to be, according to their many critics, a "media circus" to justify their existence. If so, I was slated to perform in the center ring. However, before I was asked to testify, I was invited to meet with the full commission at its offices in New York City. They apparently wanted to eyeball their lead witness before the tapes began to roll. They did not know me, and I certainly was anxious to meet with them. I had vociferously aired my frustration with the snail-like pace of the commission's probe at a meeting with Kennedy and his chief investigator at a Lake Grove ice cream shop in late December. I sincerely believed that, because of the political structure of the SIC, nothing positive would ever come out of this investigation. Kennedy tried to reassure me that the members of the commission were very concerned with what they had seen in Suffolk, but I was far from convinced. Cynicism was now firmly implanted in my psyche. It would take more than verbal reassurances to convince me that anyone really cared.

I was far from relaxed as I drove the more than fifty miles to 270 Broadway in Manhattan for a three o'clock meeting on January 15, 1987. Moral support, in the form of Lenore, was at my side. I was driving to the city of my birth, and the home of my youth, but it was a trip to uncharted territory to meet the unknown persons who were probably itching to scrutinize first-hand a judge whose actions had surely left some of them puzzled. Why not? There were days when my actions even left me puzzled. All too often, when I couldn't sleep at night, I'd ask myself the rhetorical question: "Why bother?" Nobody else seems to care!

There were some familiar faces around the conference table. The presence of Susan Shepard and John Kennedy made me feel more comfortable, and the commission chairman, David Trager, the dean of my alma mater where I had spent four long years at night, Brooklyn Law School, seemed to be extremely receptive to what I had to say in response to their many questions about Suffolk County justice. But one member, Thomas Culhane, appeared to be extremely skeptical as he pressed me for nothing but "facts." In fact, he seemed almost hostile in the manner in which he posed his questions.

Former Republican State Senator Earl W. Brydges, Jr. was interested in my background and experience as a lawyer as well as a judge. Although I had been told by Kennedy that they would not put me on the spot this way, I was asked some very pointed questions about what I had observed in the Diaz case. Without the availability of notes, I had to discuss the testimony of Joseph Pistone and Detective Rafferty, as well as the so-called "two knife theory" of the prosecution. Commissioner Culhane didn't seem to be happy with my presentation, although Commissioners Trager, Sheridan and Bridges gave the appearance of objectivity, sincerity and a willingness to listen. Dean Trager, the only real scholar among them, was most interested in my findings in the Waters case concerning the dearth of black jurors in Suffolk County.

The meeting lasted for about an hour, but it seemed like an eternity. I was only too happy to leave, especially after Dean Trager, chairman of a powerful investigative commission and former U.S. Attorney, asked for my advice as to what they could do to rectify the situation in Suffolk justice. To me, the answer was as obvious as the nose on his face. If they had found corruption in the system, then immediately recommend the appointment of a special prosecutor. The governor had done just that in the Howard Beach affair in less than three weeks!

It was a frustrated and somewhat less than upbeat judge who suffered the slow-moving expressway rush hour traffic back to the "friendly" confines of Suffolk County. I was quickly losing confidence in the ability or willingness of this group to act.

Although I had not expressed my frustration to John Kennedy that afternoon, I was on the phone the following Monday to complain about the brusque treatment by Commissioner Culhane. Culhane, he attempted to explain, was a former New York City police officer and state assemblyman, and that simply was his style. He reassured me that the commission was favorably impressed with my presentation. It was their intention to call me as the lead witness in the two days of hearings scheduled for the following week. There would be many public questions asked of me about the Diaz, Corso and Waters cases involving areas which the commission felt could be proven by independent corroborative evidence.

I had been under the lights and in front of television cameras before, but I was completely taken aback by the scene that I encountered at the county legislature's meeting room as I arrived for my formal appearance before the commission. The print, television and radio media were all represented, from local cable to network. The hearings were to be referred to as a "media circus" by the commission's critics, and judging from the apparent coverage it would be difficult to disagree. It reminded me of the scenes of the McCarthy and Watergate hearings!

The commissioners were obviously prepared for their first public confrontation with the Suffolk County criminal justice establishment, which was well represented in the audience. Dean David Trager had a prepared opening statement as a preface to the two full days of sometimes fiery testimony and debate:

The Commission began this investigation approximately twelve months ago in response to allegations that certain police assigned to the Homicide and Narcotics Squads had engaged in misconduct.

As the Commission's investigation has progressed- and the investigation is continuing- its scope, regrettably, has had to be widened to include other police officers and the District Attorney's Office.

In the course of its investigation, the Commission has found evidence that police officers committed perjury and fabricated evidence. More disturbing, though, the Police Department and the District Attorney's Office declined to investigate...." [I was now beginning to feel more comfortable.]

Further, in cases the Commission has examined, failure to follow even basic principles of investigation, documentation and case management demonstrates a startling lack of professionalism in the Suffolk County Police Department and shamefully tolerated by the District Attorney's Office.

Indeed, management's tolerance for misconduct has been a hallmark of this investigation. The Commission faults supervisory personnel in the Police Department and the District Attorney's Office for treating charges of misconduct primarily as problems of public relations or civil liability, and not as occasions to set and improve disciplinary standards for their organizations. An accusation results in a "circle the wagons" mentality in which the accuser becomes the enemy. [I was wrong! It was not going to be a whitewash.]

The legitimate desire of law enforcement officials for convictions cannot be a substitute for their true goal- the conviction of the guilty and the exoneration of the innocent. ...Not only have innocent people suffered, but the guilty have gone free.

Moreover, the rationalization that the end justifies the means seems to be infecting portions of Suffolk's criminal justice system. Unchecked, it may undermine the County's entire criminal justice system. The people of Suffolk County deserve better...

While several individuals, including Suffolk County Court Judge Stuart Namm, and a number of citizens and members of the Bar have in some instances courageously provided information and evidence, on the whole the Commission has been disappointed that others in a position to assist this investigation have not come forward....[What courage? Why was courage necessary to expose systemic injustice, I asked myself?]

The Commission has heard time and again from people in Suffolk County that they are afraid to cooperate due to fear of retaliation, particularly to their livelihoods or careers. More than one has referred to Suffolk as the "Wild West" and has despaired of meaningful reform.[1]

****

In my mind it seemed as though the words of Chief Counsel Susan Shepard echoed throughout the room as she softly called out, "Judge Stuart Namm." I was beyond nervous! I felt my pulse quicken momentarily as I heard the loud beat of my heart. My palms were slippery with perspiration, but I no longer felt alone in the wilderness. Dean Trager's remarks were couched in stronger terms than I could ever have anticipated. While I was now more comfortable with my role, the representatives of the police department and district attorney's office who were scattered throughout the auditorium had to be feeling more and more uneasy and ill at ease. Some were visibly squirming in their seats, as they sneered and were taken aback by the caustic tone of the chairman's opening remarks.

Tomorrow's headlines and the evening news reports were not going to help the public image of Suffolk law enforcement. I had come to this hearing anticipating a media show—which it certainly was—and expecting a whitewash of the district attorney's involvement in prosecutorial misconduct. For the moment, I could not have been more pleasantly surprised.

For about an hour, counsel and each of the commissioners walked me step by step through my many experiences as a judge with particular emphasis upon the Waters, Corso and Diaz cases. A commissioner who was new to the SIC and whom I had never seen before, Alton R. Waldon, an African-American, was particularly interested in my statistical survey of Suffolk County juries as it related to blacks. I was also given the opportunity to publicly discuss, for the first time, the courthouse window fiasco, and to vent my outrage over the accusations that my actions were politically motivated.

It was clear from the outset that each of the commissioners was very knowledgeable about the cases in question, and that they were distressed by what they had found during the course of their lengthy investigation. I no longer sensed an air of hostility. Even Commissioner Culhane, who had given me such a difficult time in the New York City meeting, seemed to be in agreement with my conclusions.

Yet, what I had to say was nothing new. In fact, it was old news. It was so old that I was champing at the bit for immediate action. It was time to publicly goad the commissioners into acting with some finality! The following is a portion of my testimony:

> Gentlemen, in October 1985 I asked Governor Cuomo to appoint a Special Prosecutor...the governor would not act because he was aware that this Commission was conducting investigations.
>
> This investigation, as much as I support it, leaves a cloud over this county. There are many thousands of fine police officers in Suffolk County.
>
> There are many fine, hard-working district attorneys in the District Attorney's Office of Suffolk County.
>
> I have never accused them of doing so, nor have I ever said that the Suffolk County Police Department is corrupt, that it is full of bad people or that the District Attorney's Office is corrupt.
>
> If you people have found it—and I believe that you found the same things that I found during the course of my trial...and the chairman said it today, you are expanding your investigation

beyond that which I found. All I would ask you is, please, don't hold the Diaz case and the Corso case until you conclude your investigation.

It is time for this county, for those people who may have not done the right thing, to be punished, to be called to answer, and for those people who are decent police officers and those people who are decent prosecutors not to have to operate with a cloud over them.

It makes the entire system difficult and it is difficult enough.[2]

As I took my seat without making eye contact with anyone in the audience, many of whom were applauding my presentation, once again my heart seemed to be palpitating rapidly. Perhaps I should have left at that time, but my feet would not move my body towards the back doors. I wanted to experience, once again, this time vicariously, the testimony of Joseph Pistone, Detective Rafferty and Detective Sgt. McGuire who were scheduled to appear before the Commission. I'd been told that Diaz's attorney, Paul Gianelli, was scheduled to testify that morning as well. He was one of the few lawyers who had been willing to come forward (one of the courageous ones). In any event, I needed the time to come back to earth.

But we were all cheated out of the live appearance of Joseph Pistone, my "pathological liar." Special agent Robert Frank testified that Pistone, who at that time was incarcerated at Riker's Island for crimes committed in New York City, refused to appear at this hearing because he "was in fear that the publicity generated by this hearing might cause his life to be in danger from his fellow prisoners at Riker's Island." Instead, he was there in the form of a sworn statement which was read into the record through the commission's questioning of Robert Frank under oath. The Commission had granted Pistone immunity from prosecution with regard to his testimony in the Diaz trial, and he had finally come clean.

Robert Frank's testimony went as follows:

> *Commission*: In your discussions with Mr. Pistone prior to that sworn statement...did Mr. Pistone discuss the fact that he had met with Detective Miller and Detective McKenna and Barry

Feldman in regard to his testimony at the Diaz trial?

Frank: Yes, sir, he did.

Commission: Did he state that there were a number of different meetings with regard to his testimony at that trial?

Frank: Yes.

Commission: I call your attention now...to...that hearing testimony: "...This sworn testimony is under oath taken at the State Investigation Commission offices [testimony is read]:

Question: At any time during the first meeting, did they provide you with any details about the Diaz case that you didn't know about yourself?

Answer: On the first meeting, no.

Question: Did there come a time when you met with McKenna and Miller at Feldman's office when they discussed the other facts about the Diaz case?

Answer: Yes.....

Question: When was that?

Answer: Late June 1985.

Question: Tell us, at this first meeting were they actually telling you additional facts about the case which you had not gotten from Diaz? Tell us what they told you. And when I say "they," I want you to be specific as to who said what, if you can recall.

Answer: Detective Miller showed me Diaz' statement on several different occasions, and he would ask me what happened and I would tell him and he would say "No, this is the way it happened," and hand me the statement to look at, which is Diaz' statement. [The commission had hit pay dirt!]

Question: How do you know that that was Diaz' statement?

Answer: Detective Miller and Detective McKenna told me that was Diaz' statement and it had Diaz' signature on it.

Question: Did you read it at their direction, did they tell you to read it?

Answer: Right.

Question: When they gave you the statement to read, did

they tell you that that's what they wanted you to say, and Diaz said to them?

Answer: Yes.

Question: Who told you that?

Answer: Detective Miller.

Question: When he asked you to say that, did you ever ask him, you know, what you were going to get out of all this?

Answer: They told me that my case will be taken care of after this was over. It wouldn't look good now if a deal was made in front of the judge.

Question: It wouldn't look good if you testified on the stand that they had made a deal with you?

Answer: Right.

Question: Who specifically said that to you about the deal?

Answer: Detective Miller, Detective McKenna and ADA Barry Feldman.

Question: During the time when you were shown the written Diaz statement or told by Detective Miller that they would like you to testify to the facts in the statement, who was present when that piece of paper was shown to you?

Answer: Detective Miller and Detective McKenna.

Question: Was ADA Feldman present when the statement was handed to you?

Answer: While the statement was being handed to me, they asked ADA Feldman to leave the room.

Question: When you say while it was handed to you, exactly the time the piece of paper was handed to you, was Feldman in the room when it was handed to you?

Answer: No, sir.

Question: Was he ever present when you were being questioned by Miller and McKenna and you told Miller and McKenna only the things that Diaz really said to you, was Feldman ever present for that?

Answer: Yes, sir.

Question: And was that in the early meetings?

Answer: Yes.

Question: So what I am trying to get to, so you understand it, I am trying to figure out what Feldman knew about what the information was that Diaz actually gave to you. So what I am trying to do is figure out if he was present when you told him the truth about what Diaz said and was he also present later on when you told the additional facts that were supplied to you by Miller?

Answer: Yes, he was. The facts that Mr. Miller and Mr. McKenna gave me were the facts that I told Barry Feldman after it was given to me by them. But Mr. Feldman had only known what I told the detectives until they gave me the other information, and then we went in with all that information.

Question: Just so that the record is clear, when you first went to Feldman, he knew the truth about what Diaz really told you, and later on he knew that there were additional facts that you testified to?

Answer: Right.

Question: Later on did he ever ask you how come the confession was larger or had more information on it?

Answer: That I got additional information from Diaz.

Question: You told him that?

Answer: Right.

Question: Did you just decide to tell him that on your own, or did Miller or McKenna say that you should say that to Feldman?

Answer: Detective Miller and Detective McKenna said I should say that to Feldman."

Question: Did there come a time when Feldman or anybody from the DA's office talked to you about any future deals on your pending criminal cases?

Answer: Just that it wouldn't look good in front of the judge if I were to go up there and say deals were made, but something would be done for me after the testimony was over with.

Question: Who said that to you?

Answer: ADA Barry Feldman.

Question: Did he say that you would probably be asked questions at trial by the defense lawyer about these things?

Answer: Yes, he did.

Question: What did he say you should say?

Answer: No deals were made and no promises were made.

Question: Feldman said that to you?

Answer: Right.[3]

I'd been wrong in my assessment of Pistone. He wasn't necessarily a pathological liar. He'd been a well coached liar for an undisclosed price!

Frank was then taken, question by question, through Pistone's statement concerning his testimony at the Diaz trial, as he recounted each of the times that he had perjured himself under oath by embellishing his testimony using material provided to him by the homicide detectives. His statement included the shocking revelation that he had been visited on two occasions at Riker's Island by Miller and McKenna, accompanied by their lawyer, Thomas Spota.

According to Pistone: "...Mr. Spota took a statement from me what was going on between me and Mr. Frank pertaining to this here case, and I informed them that I was going to take a lie detector test about this case, and he tried to discourage me, not to believe Frank, any promises that he would make...."

On the second day of the public hearings, Spota, who was apparently also representing Barry Feldman, got involved in a heated verbal battle with the members of the Commission. Feldman had been under intense and openly hostile examination from various members of the commission and counsel with Spota seated at his side. The questioners had grown tired of Feldman's lengthy commentaries in response to every query. Nothing was ever answered with a simple "yes" or "no." Commissioner Brydges sought to determine whether Spota's representation of the various police witnesses spilled over into representation of an assistant district attorney. Tom Spota (the current District Attorney of Suffolk County), who is reputed to have a short fuse, was incensed. He was also playing to the audience of police observers.

Commissioner Brydges to Feldman: In your opinion as an experienced prosecutor, what do good police procedures require, a spread or a single mug shot?

Spota: Mr. Commissioner, I think the witness needs more than a yes or no, and I don't—in that question you just asked, how can anybody answer that yes or no? Be that as it may, why don't we at least give the witness the courtesy of answering fully and completely?

Commissioner Sheridan: Answer honestly.

Spota: He is answering your questions honestly. Mr. Chairman.

Commissioner Sheridan: You made your speech.

The police supporters in the audience broke into a sustained round of applause drawing a mild rebuke from the chairman. Spota was there to represent Dennis Rafferty and Lt. Dunn of the homicide squad as well as Barry Feldman.

From the police point of view, he represented the side of truth and justice, and he was standing up to the evil commissioners. Up to now, the hearings had given them little to cheer about. They were obviously itching to publicly demonstrate the solidarity and brotherhood of Suffolk law enforcement. They were living proof that an attack against one of the brothers was an attack against all!

Commissioner Brydges: Has he retained you as his lawyer? "

Spota: I'm not going to answer that.

Commissioner Brydges: Mr. Spota, what I am trying to get at, and Mr. Feldman, what I am trying to get at, because I am not a member or resident of Suffolk County; I am from the other end of the state...I am trying to understand what your relationship is with a member of the police department of Suffolk County and the District Attorney's Office of Suffolk County...And I inquired of the relationship to see whether or not the District Attorney's Office is also part of an association with the police.

Spota: No. If that is what your questioning was, I'm absolutely sorry. I didn't understand that.
Commissioner Brydges: You should be.
Spota: I am sorry.

****

Although there was a media show taking place under the lights inside the auditorium, there was another media show being orchestrated by the police union outside of the building. For an hour, in the chilly winter temperatures, with mounds of snow piled along their route, a picket line of about 250, of a force of 2,500, "young police officers, veteran detectives and even an inspector or two"[4] dressed in civilian clothes snaked around the parking lot of the county complex until the television cameras were finally packed away. Some wore signs draped around their necks or carried placards reading:

"State Investigation Circus"
"Why Public Hearings? Trial by Media."

Their leadership was unanimous in the belief that the hearings were a disgrace—an affront to their integrity. But to some young cops who were not really sure why they'd had come to Hauppauge, there was concern about the impact of the hearings upon police morale. One seventeen year veteran, who was more accustomed to patrolling the streets of Bay Shore in his dress blues, echoed my own sentiments: "The general attitude of the officer on the street is, 'Let's get on with it.' In other words if anyone's guilty, let's get it out, have them take their punishment, and put an end to it once and for all. It's gone on long enough."

Still the SIC was in no particular hurry, and much to my chagrin, their agenda didn't seem to contain a timetable. Circus atmosphere or no, Suffolk law enforcement had to be bending under the pressure of the morning headlines and the many stories detailing the sordid public testimony. The damage to morale and department reputation had to be painfully deep and was excruciatingly slow in execution. No demonstration put together for the benefit of the television audience could overcome the words being uttered under oath by the many witnesses being paraded in front of the cameras. The truth, like cream, has a way of ultimately rising to the surface, although sometimes the truth takes a little longer!

The front page of *Newsday* carried a photo of Dean Trager with the headline: "Blast at Suffolk Cops, DA: Chief of State Investigation Commission Charges Perjury, Fabrication of Evidence By Police Were Ignored by DA's Office." The *Daily News* carried pictures of the chairman and myself with the headline: "Suffolk Police Probed."

Even the usually staid, stodgy and effetely snobbish *New York Times*, which carries very little Suffolk County news, despite its claim to publish "all the news that's fit to print," carried this story on the front page of its Metropolitan News with the headline: "Suffolk Police Are Described As Deficient"

The two days of public hearings concluded with a slow verbal waltz featuring Police Commissioner Treder and the members of the Commission on the subject of note-taking, and the proper supervision and training of police personnel. The charges of perjury, subornation of perjury and police misconduct seemed to have been buried under a host of boring, inane and irrelevant questions and answers about budgets, management and the writing of reports, as illustrated by the following:

> Q: And are you satisfied that the supervision in the Homicide Squad is adequate?
> A: At this time, yes, very satisfied...I spoke to Inspector Murphy no more than three or four weeks ago. He is now the Bureau Commander, and homicide comes under him. He said everything is working fine....

For the time being, everybody seemed to be satisfied—Commissioner DeWitt Treder with the operation of the Suffolk County Police Department, and the commissioners with the vague, indirect and rambling answers of the police commissioner and the publicity which the hearings had engendered. But yesterday's headlines, like yesterday's catch from the sea, rapidly grows stale, and the newspaper whose words have carried a sometimes deadly sting becomes nothing more than a wrapping for stale fish.

After forty-eight hours, the "media circus" was old news and it would be more than two years before the State Commission of Investigations published its final report. Two more years of dark clouds hovering over Suffolk law enforcement, and two more years that I would have to suffer before hearing whether the Commission would recommend any action against persons whom they'd already openly labeled, condemned and ridiculed in a public forum. The "whistleblower" continued to be an easy target, especially as the perception grew, with the passage of time, that nothing positive, in the form of bringing the culprits to justice, would ever result from this three year investigation. The slight feeling of satisfaction that I had experienced after two days of hearings which had largely corroborated my worst suspicions was to be short lived. For my part, there would never be any true feeling of vindication.

By the time their final report was published in 1989, I was toiling in the paper-filled civil vineyards of the Supreme Court, divested of my criminal jurisdiction. I was effectively removed from my elected office without the Commission so much as raising a finger, or even a faint voice, to defend the rights of their "star" witness—the raison d'etre for the investigation which had carried the SIC to the front page of every local newspaper, and to a feature roll on every television evening news program.

TWENTY-ONE

"...We've Had Everybody and His Brother Looking at Us."

—Police Commissioner DeWitt C. Treder

T HE COMMISSION'S PUBLIC HEARINGS IN JANUARY had truly been staged for the media. They were obviously intended to be a holding action to placate the public and the media- to keep everybody informed that the SIC was still actively working in Suffolk County despite the snail-like pace of its investigation. However, the hearings were largely anti-climactic. *Newsday* had preempted the state agency which was empowered and structured to weed out corruption in government. By the early part of 1987, the Commission's findings seemed to be old news, and the most shocking revelations had already taken place. Two more years of investigation would only serve to reinforce the local conviction that most of the true culprits in law enforcement would escape the investigation unscathed, although it might mean resignation, retirement, transfer or a move from the public to the private sector.

The little guy in private life may often experience the full wrath of the justice system for even an act of petty thievery, but those who are responsible for the enforcement of the law, and who may be responsible for the long term incarceration of an innocent person, if they carry a policeman's badge or the title of "prosecutor," simply turn in their papers and head for greener pastures like the private practice of the law, private investigation or the Florida sunshine.

Yet for at least one career cop under the cloud of this investigation, there would be no resignation, transfer or reassignment. He would suffer the ultimate penalty with one short squeeze of his own trigger finger. Certainly the most shocking and tragic result of the investigation might have occurred just two weeks before the public hearings. Detective Lt. John Gaggin, the fifty-seven-year-old chief of the robbery squad and thirty year veteran of the department, was subpoenaed to testify before the SIC's investigators about allegations that members of his squad had beaten and terrorized a teenage robbery suspect, Joseph Skorupski of Medford.

On the morning of January 14, 1987, Gaggin was found dead in his Sayville apartment. He had apparently shot himself once through the heart with his .38 caliber service revolver. His death was listed by the medical examiner as a suicide. Gaggin was scheduled to testify privately before the Commission later that day.

The Skorupski arrest turned out to be a case of mistaken identity, but the arresting detectives were accused of beating Skorupski, and terrorizing him by firing a weapon to frighten him, putting a service revolver in his mouth while threatening to kill him. Skorupski filed a $3,000,000 federal lawsuit against the county. Lieutenant Gaggin was not even named as a defendant but he had given an affidavit denying any police brutality. He had also apparently failed to call for an internal affairs investigation after he had received a brutality complaint from Skorupski's independent attending physician at Brookhaven Memorial Hospital. The Skorupski case was to be a subject of the second hearing day. Despite Gaggin's past unblemished record and noninvolvement in any brutality, according to a long-time friend, "He felt he wasn't prepared to go in—he felt confused." Commissioner Treder couldn't explain why Lt. Gaggin would take his own life, but he felt the subpoena "had to have something to do with it...." According to Treder, "The whole department has been operating under a lot of pressure and stress for the past year because we've had everybody and his brother looking at us...."[1] The Commission's investigators weren't surprised by the shocking turn of events. According to one, there always seemed to be at least one suicide connected to a major investigation. And this major investigation had generated a good deal of pressure on many persons, no less on this whistle blower.

No amount of weekly reassurance by John Kennedy of the SIC that the investigation was progressing in an orderly fashion could detract me from the sense of gloom which set in shortly after the euphoria of the hearings had faded into history. In March, Kennedy seemed to be satisfied with the changes taking place in the office of the district attorney. Barry Feldman was reassigned from his position as bureau chief of the Felony Trial Bureau to the East End Bureau, the "Siberia" of the district attorney's office. The Major Offense Bureau was restructured into the newly formed Homicide Bureau, whose mission was to work closely with the newly constituted homicide squad of the police department.[2]

But no amount of restructuring or reassignment under the administration of Patrick Henry as district attorney would change the manner in which his highest assistants dealt with me in my courtroom in the important cases which were still pending on my calendar. I was still a dangerous enemy! One of these cases resulted from the indictment of John Taylor, the son of a Suffolk County supervising probation officer, who was charged with the forcible rape and sodomy of a local Southold High School acquaintance. He was represented by the firm of Clayton, Miller and Mayer, the same attorneys who'd represented Peter Corso in 1985. Peter Mayer, who by now truly regretted the complaints which he had made about the police in the Corso case, had been telling the members of the Bar Association that I had been overzealous in my highly publicized comments about the homicide squad. He was temporarily smarting from the reaction of his friends in the law enforcement community. It had the potential of affecting his business, much of which evolved from those relationships.

Mayer sought my removal from the Taylor case in 1986 with the lame excuse that I should recuse myself because my wife was a probation officer working in the same department as Thomas Taylor, the defendant's father. My wife did not even recognize the name of the father, much less have any relationship with him. She had been mired in Hauppauge in the Juvenile Bureau because of my involvement in adult criminal cases, according to her supervisors, a potential conflict of interest. The father worked within the adult criminal system in the Riverhead office. In fact, I did not even recognize his name at that time. Still they badly wanted me off the case. They must have believed, that if John Taylor was convicted, my sentence would probably exceed that of any of the other judges. Or, perhaps, Mayer was aware that I knew what he was saying about me at meetings of the Bar Association, and thought that I was small enough to take it out on his client.

In a lengthy opinion, which was featured on the front page of the *New York Law Journal*, I refused to remove myself from the Taylor case. In the summer of 1986, the first Taylor trial resulted in a mistrial—a hung jury (six for conviction and six for acquittal). The retrial was scheduled for January 1987, coincidentally the month of the first public SIC hearings.

Once again, Mayer moved for my recusal. But this time, in December of 1986, he took a different approach. He sought to have the appellate division in Brooklyn remove the case to another jurisdiction on the basis of "actual bias" on the part of the trial court, which was allegedly displayed during the course of the first trial.

The district attorney's office, again represented by Mark Cohen, the chief assistant and counsel to Patrick Henry, apparently saw this as an excellent opportunity to publicly embarrass the person whom they saw as their chief protagonist. He wrote to the appellate division that the district attorney opposed my "unseemly" application to intervene while curiously taking no position on the defense application to move the case out of Suffolk County. Once again, I could see through this charade, and I vowed to fight as hard as I had done in the Diaz case, any effort to find a more favorable judge.

It was peculiarly coincidental that on December 15, 1986, Cohen reported to the appellate division that an investigation recently revealed that "...a tape recorded conversation, heretofore unknown, between the victim in this case and the initial Southold Town Police Department officer at the scene was apparently made and destroyed by that officer."[3]

Shades of Corso! The letter was written only two days before Cohen's affidavit to the appellate division. Could it be that, once again, the Suffolk County district attorney's office would be happy with any judge, in any jurisdiction, so long as his name was not Namm? Certainly, Mayer wanted nothing more to do with me. If he was going to do battle with the police over a missing tape which was vital to his defense, he wanted it to end right there in the courtroom. To him, it was simply a matter of damage control and professional self-preservation. The obvious purpose was to keep any allegation of misconduct within the confines of the Taylor case. It was not intended to reflect unfavorably upon his relationship with the law enforcement community.

One might ask why I would once again take the unprecedented action of attempting to intervene in a proceeding which normally only involved the defendant and the prosecutor? Things were simply not normal in Suffolk County justice! Under normal circumstances, a district attorney's office does not consent to a change of jurisdiction. Prosecutors do not relish trying their cases in a foreign jurisdiction, especially away from the friendly Riverhead confines. However, if in 1986 the district attorney of Suffolk County could succeed in removing an important and highly publicized case which could present a problem to the prosecution from my courtroom, it was apparent that he'd make every effort to do so. So the office made such attempts in Diaz, Brensic and Taylor.

It was not that I didn't trust any other judge to do the right thing. It was simply my view that no other judge had so far shown a willingness to embroil himself in a potential controversy with the office of the district attorney on the important issue of prosecutorial misconduct. On the contrary, the attitude of my superiors reinforced my belief that there was a double standard in the administration of justice—one for the law enforcement community and another for an ordinary citizen ensnared in the web of prosecution. Mistress Justice was only truly blind when she peered down upon misconduct in Suffolk law enforcement. Usually her blindfold slipped just enough to provide a small peek at the weak and powerless lying prostrate at the alter of her law.

So when I learned that Mayer had hired a former Suffolk County homicide detective to investigate my alleged bias against his client, my resolve to remain on the Taylor case was firmly fixed. Anthony Palumbo was the detective who had surreptitiously recorded the confession of fifteen-year-old Peter Quartararo in violation of his constitutional rights—a confession which I had suppressed in the trials of Robert Brensic and Thomas Ryan.

He, like so many of his brethren, resigned early under the cloud of a state investigation which I had precipitated, but still he had been chosen by Mayer to make a case against me as a trial judge with a bias against his "innocent" client.

How sweet it must have been for the detective to interview two alternate jurors who did not deliberate at the first trial, and four of the six jurors who'd voted for the acquittal of John Taylor and who believed that Judge Namm "would not be fair with Taylor or his lawyer." How could a trial judge who, according to Palumbo, "put scotch tape on his forehead" and "was constantly looking through books, moving around in his chair or staring at the floor"; "ate pistachio nuts"; "prevent[ed] Mr. Mayer from asking questions"; "pick[ed] his ear with a toothpick"; and "[cut] different pieces of paper..." be fair and unbiased to a defendant in a serious criminal prosecution?[4]

The application was absurd on its face, but it was apparently sufficient enough for both a Suffolk County Supreme Court justice and an appellate division justice to grant a stay of the trial pending a hearing by the full appellate court for a change of venue. In my application to intervene in the appellate division I wrote the words which apparently stuck in the craws at the highest echelons of the district attorney's office:

> ...What is at stake in these proceedings is not so much the question of whether your affirmant can sit as a fair and impartial arbiter of the issues before him. Your affirmant's record as a judge for the past ten years speaks to that question. What is at issue is whether that trial will be conducted by an independent member of the judiciary, free from the pressures of defense counsel and prosecutor who threaten that independence by viewing judicial action which may be unfavorable to them as being the result of undue bias and prejudice; and whether the defendant and/or prosecutor have the right, under the law, to avoid a particular judge by seeking removal to another court without meeting the requirements of the law. The true measure of a judge's bias, hostility or prejudice are the decisions which he or she has rendered in regard to the party alleged to be the target of such bias and prejudice.[5]

Citing my decision not to recuse myself in the Diaz case, I forwarded a complete transcript of the first Taylor trial. I'd let the justices judge my actions for themselves. I had no doubt about the fairness of the trial, and I was confident of the result.

But my words that drew the angriest response from Patrick Henry's chief assistant and legal advisor were directed towards the prosecutor: "It is indeed unfortunate that the posture of the district attorney, who is responsible for the indictment of this defendant, is presently such that no one appears to be representing the interests of the People...it has become readily apparent that the prosecutor, who should be pressing this matter for trial, has become very comfortable with the steps being taken by the defendant to ensure that this case is not tried by this judge."

The words of my application to intervene were seen by Mark Cohen, in his response to the appellate division, as "untoward, injudicious and wholly unfounded," and an example of "the type of bias and partiality maintained by..." me as alleged by the defendant. His argument in support of Mayer's application, though couched in impressive legalistic syntax, typical of Cohen's style of writing, was summarily dismissed by the appeals court. On March 6, 1986, the trial of John Taylor for rape was ordered to proceed in Suffolk County before the assigned trial judge, me, who sometimes foolishly picked his ear with a paperclip and occasionally munched on a pistachio nut.

The second trial proved to be surprisingly uneventful. Once again the serious question of guilt or innocence of a heinous crime was overshadowed by extraneous matters. These distractions were either intended to intimidate and publicly embarrass the trial judge, so as to provoke a public response from me which would achieve the desired result (i.e., any other judge, anywhere!). This time there would be no hung jury. It wasn't the trial judge who would find Taylor guilty as charged, but a jury of Suffolk County citizens, with no axe to grind, who were apparently not influenced by a "biased" judge.

The missing tape recording of a police officer's three minute conversation with the teenage victim in his police cruiser proved to be a non-issue, although it took a special hearing to sort out the facts. The defense argued that this missing tape would have clearly revealed that the complaining witness had reacted inappropriately to the alleged rape—proof that, in fact, there had been no rape at all. The tape was recorded over by accident. There had been gross negligence, but no apparent police misconduct. A second tape recording was also made by the lead detective at police headquarters when he questioned the victim about the events of July 29, 1984, a date which will be indelibly imprinted in her psyche.

A young woman doesn't easily suppress the trauma of forcible sexual assault, especially where the assailant is armed with a handgun. The second tape was intact and available to be played at the trial.

However, the question of the victim's early reaction to the alleged forcible rape and sodomy became a real issue at the trial. Thus the emphasis by the defense on the missing tape with its assumed verbal nuances and inappropriate nonverbal responses. How should she have acted when she revealed the horror of her story to the police for the first time? Should she have been hysterical? Shouldn't she have been quaking with fear, rather than sounding like she was laughing and smiling "inappropriately" although she'd suffered a most humiliating and degrading experience at the hands of the perpetrator?

> *Victim*: ...All of a sudden this guy like bumped hard in to the door almost like from the movies, you know like bumping against it, opening it and then getting in and shutting the door and just sat there like this and said....
>
> *Detective*: (Interrupts her) Where, (pause) now just a minute. But...
>
> *Victim*: (Laughs)...And he had this gun...it looked huge to me....He was being very, I guess you could say very kind, and I was standing there with no clothes on, and the mosquitos were biting me....'cause it was all, stuck to my hair and under my fa...my chin and (pause)...
>
> *Detective*: O.K. Don't wipe on it. O.K. (pause)
>
> *Victim*: (Chuckles)...It was probably, oh, and my legs, I'm sure

it's all over my legs....Because I wouldn't swallow it and it was just gushing out of my mouth and I had saliva coming all out of my mouth as if, it was like I was foaming at the mouth there was so much saliva. And it was like all over so I'm sure my legs are covered.

Detective:...You're doing very well.

Victim: (Laughs)[6]

How could a young woman who claimed to have been brutally raped and sodomized, while looking down the barrel of a gun, laugh and chuckle while recounting a terrifying experience? Perhaps her story was fabricated or exaggerated. Or perhaps she was suffering from what has come to be known as "rape trauma syndrome." These were all questions with which the jury would have to grapple in determining the guilt or innocence of the defendant. For the first time in New York State, I permitted an expert to testify about this newly documented syndrome, an outgrowth of the "post-traumatic stress disorder," which was well documented after the Vietnam War.

Professor Eileen Treacy, an expert in the field of sex abuse victimization, teaches graduate students at the City University of New York. She was called by the prosecution, but she wasn't permitted to offer the ultimate opinion in this case because it was for the jury to decide whether the young lady had actually been raped and sodomized. But she was permitted to enlighten the jury about the diverse and multitude of reactions of female victims to forcible rape and sodomy.

Why did the victim, who knew her assailant, not immediately tell the police that John Taylor was her assailant? Simply put, it was clear that she was suffering from "rape trauma syndrome," and so there was no necessarily predictable response. Failure to immediately identify the known assailant and to respond with hysteria was perfectly consistent with having been the victim of rape. It is not even unusual, Treacy testified, for a rape victim to smile and laugh inappropriately under the cloud of recent trauma.

To this very damaging testimony, the defense could provide no rebuttal. Despite the attempt at an alibi defense through the testimony of his parents, which apparently fell upon deaf ears in the jury, he was found guilty of attempted rape and sodomy in the first degree. John Taylor was sentenced to seven to twenty-one years in a state correctional facility. His name will forever be linked in New York State to the Court of Appeals decision permitting expert testimony on the issue of "rape trauma syndrome."

****

But in 1987, the outside distractions resulting from the continuing state investigation were having more impact upon my life than the criminal trials which were my real mission. It was becoming more and more difficult to work. Each trip to the courthouse in the morning was like a new foray into the enemy camp. It was only a matter of time, I believed, before I would be transferred out of the criminal court. There were just too many powerful forces in the county who wanted me out of the way—in every sense of the word. At long last, the shoe was dropped in the spring of that year. But, to my astonishment, when the administrative judge could get no volunteers, he selected four other judges with the least seniority to work as acting Supreme Court justices trying civil cases exclusively. I was sure that I was still not out of the woods. Time was not on my side. It was just not propitious, I believed, for them to take such precipitous action in the midst of the investigation. It would have been too obvious, and the media would have been all over them. I was convinced that my days as a criminal court judge were numbered.

One of the most serious problems in society in 1987, and no less so in Suffolk County, was the growth of drug related arrests and the increase in crime. It was the cause of a spiraling increase in criminal case backlog. Yet, in June, five criminal court judges were transferred to the civil part of the Supreme Court.

But the confusion and chaos being created in the Suffolk court system by thoughtless decision-making paled by comparison to the chaos generated by the many investigations of the justice system which were taking place at that time. On April 1, 1987, Police Commissioner DeWitt Treder announced his retirement after a thirty-one-year career in the police and forty-three months as commissioner. His resignation was requested by the acting county executive, Michael LoGrande, under the pressure of state and federal investigations. In support of his action, he told the media: "I believe that change is necessary, and I also believe a change wouldn't be bad for the police department at this time, to have a new image."[7] LoGrande vowed to conduct a national search for a new commissioner, but in the interim the job was given to James Caples, a twenty-seven year veteran of the department, and the permanent choice of the conservative members of the Legislature who had publicly condemned the various investigations. According to one, Caples, a local high school graduate, had a Ph.D. in legitimate police work and "pride, honor and dedication to duty." To the leaders of the various police associations, Treder's removal was "a grave injustice," a "bum rap." He was "the fall guy and the scapegoat," the "sacrificial lamb." To the district attorney, Patrick Henry, himself operating under a cloud, he was "a good man who has done his very best." The police unions were happy, and they would have been more than satisfied with the permanent appointment of Caples. He was one of their own, and not likely to undertake any meaningful changes.

But the media, especially *Newsday*, was not about to allow the acting county executive off the hook. Names of known whistle-blowers in the police community were hoisted as trial balloons. This included David Durk of the New York City Police Department whose name was put forth by Sidney Schanberg, the Pulitzer prize winning author who was now a *Newsday* syndicated columnist. Durk, along with Frank Serpico, had blown the whistle on New York city police corruption. There was no way that such a commissioner would be appointed in Suffolk County in 1987.

It was not until after the inauguration of a new county executive in 1988 that action would be taken to appoint a police commissioner. On March 1, 1988, Patrick Halpin, a former Democratic state assemblyman who had been elected in November, announced the appointment of Daniel Guido, the controversial chief of the Stamford, Connecticut Police as his choice to run the beleaguered department.

While a new police commissioner was being considered for the county, and the local newspapers rang with headlines and stories about the potential candidates, the lines of communication between Tom Stark, my former mentor and friend, and myself were being melted by hostile, sarcastically phrased letters intended to sting the recipient. It was no coincidence that on the day that the overdue shoe—my transfer to a civil court—finally fell, he decidedly changed his tone. It was no longer necessary to kick Stuart Namm around the courthouse. Arthur Cromarty had accomplished that by formal order of reassignment.

"I would like very much to resume a friendly and professional relationship with you," Stark wrote. "We have both said and written things which we would not have under the circumstances.

"When you first came to the County Court, you demonstrated, to my satisfaction and admiration, your competence to preside over criminal matters. Because of such competence I was pleased when you accepted assignment to one of the Major Offense Bureau trial parts. Your ability and competence in handling criminal matters has in no way been changed or diminished over the past several years."[8] I was in no mood for insincere and empty praise. They had been so anxious to get me into a civil part that I was moved out of my courtroom in the midst of a highly publicized rape trial which was being covered daily by the local and national print and television media. It was the trial of the Scott Carroll, the so-called "South Shore Rapist," a serial rapist who'd left a wake of no fewer than thirteen victims. My new civil courtroom didn't even have enough seats for the jurors, let alone representatives of the media. I was fuming. In my anger, I sarcastically responded to Tom Stark: "I was heartened to read your expression of satisfaction and admiration as to my purported competency to preside over criminal matters. However, in the light of what has recently transpired, this would seem to be more lip service, since apparently what seems to be more important is that certain people may not have appreciated what has taken place for the last two years, and may have been adversely affected by the current investigation. Thus, persons like myself, who possess a certain degree of competence and ability, are transferred, against their will, to conduct civil trials, qualifications notwithstanding."[9]

It was a long time before I'd communicate in any form with Tom Stark again. On that occasion, it would be I who would initiate the conversation by telephone. The communications from his office to mine ended with my transfer. Almost one year later, on January 30, 1989, I decided to swallow my pride. I was beginning to feel brain dead in the Supreme Court from trying automobile accident cases, and I was getting tired of battling Arthur Cromarty, Bob Sise, Tom Stark and their appellate division cronies in Brooklyn. He agreed to meet with me.

Practically groveling, I told him how badly I wanted to return to the County Court. He claimed that he had asked for my return, but Sise, Cromarty and the chief justice of the appellate division, Milton Mollen, were angered over my letter writing campaign, and the "people in Brooklyn" were incensed over my well publicized attempt to intervene in the application to remove the Brensic retrial from Suffolk.

The criminal courts were going to be rid of a troublesome gnat for at least another year. They would make sure of that! There was no longer any need to keep open the lines of communication. The battle lines were now firmly drawn. I'd have to scratch and claw my way back to my elected office, and I was not going to rest until I accomplished that goal!

But the visit to Stark's chambers was not a total loss. Probably in an effort to renew an old friendship, he volunteered some startling information about some old news. It had been rumored for some time that one of the county court judges, Al Tisch, had his eyes on the Republican nomination for district attorney. Tom confirmed that Al was actively seeking the blessings of the Republican leadership. Tisch had told him so! Stark said that he told Tisch that he had to do something soon, because ethically he couldn't continue in his judicial office if he was a political candidate. But that was not the shocker.

Al Tisch had come to him for his help as administrative judge—the person who doled out the homicide cases to judges. He wanted to be assigned some high publicity homicide trials so that he could keep his name on the front burner in the media. Stark, with apparently no thought given to the ethics involved, agreed to assign him the two most highly publicized murder cases in the county. He'd be the judge in the trial of Richard Angelo, the nurse dubbed "the Angel of Death" in the media because of his senseless slaughter of innocent elderly patients, and Martin Tankleff, a teen charged with the murder of his wealthy adoptive parents.[10]

****

It was almost two years in exile before I was finally returned to the County Court in February 1990. In the interim, I would spend week after week, day and night, battling the administrative judges before the county Legislature, on television and in the newspapers. I was the last county court judge to remain involuntarily in the supreme court. I had been banished to a civil form of purgatory! The history of my civil exile was well documented in the media, at the same time that one of my brethren was likewise appearing on an almost daily basis on television and in the newspapers. But he was basking in the glow of two gruesome murder cases, while I was simply trying to do the job for which I had been elected in 1982.

It will be a cold day in hell before any other judge even thinks about blowing the whistle on corruption in Long Island! Even the American Civil Liberties Union, whose assistance I sought, was helpless in this battle. Not only had I angered the police and the district attorney, but I had publicly challenged and defamed the administration of the courts by the untouchable guardians of justice in black robes. When I returned in 1990, I knew full well that I'd be gone at the end of my term in December 1992!

Still there was some comfort in knowing that I was not the only elected official to be expelled, and my expulsion could only be de facto until the end of my term. By 1989, Patrick Henry had become such a liability to the powerful Republican party as district attorney that he was denied renomination. He was replaced by the acerbic-tongued and politically well connected James Catterson of Port Jefferson, like myself a former U.S. Army Ranger. Catterson defeated Robert Gottlieb in November by the narrowest of margins, but enough to ensure that the Republican organization would continue to control the office of the district attorney. One year later, Patrick Henry was elected to the Supreme Court.

TWENTY-TWO

"He Should've Been a Basket Case."

—Detective McCready

A S ALWAYS, THE MASSIVE INCANDESCENT CRUCIFIX of St. Charles Hospital, rising high above the waters of Port Jefferson, New York, offered safe haven to the pleasure boats arriving by dawn's first light of September 7, 1988. The fleet of tethered sailboats, masts sealed in canvas, quietly rocked on their moorings to the ebb and flow of the undulating tides and cross wakes created by an occasional late night cruiser or early morning fishing boat. The murky waters of the harbor slapped quietly against the rocky shoreline beneath the sandy cliffs. They form the foundation of the Incorporated Village of Belle Terre, home to many of Suffolk County's wealthiest citizens. The magnificent estates, built upon mammoth dunes carved by millennia of glacial and tidal forces which created the eastern shore of the harbor, play counterpoint to the imposing utility company smokestacks of LILCO, which dominate the western shore of the harbor.

Death was in the harbor air, however. Gruesome, bloody, premeditated, premature and homicidal. But to the prominent local Port Jefferson citizenry who ambled slowly one-by-one out of the sprawling Tankleff home, peering out over the dark waters of the Long Island Sound, Seymour Tankleff and his fellow high stakes poker players were going to be around for a long time to come—certainly until the next poker game.

His deep pockets and gambling instincts made him a necessary and regular part of the game. How could they have know that in a few short hours their gambling buddy would be slumped, barely alive, behind his desk, blood gushing from a gaping slit in his severed throat, the victim of a merciless assailant who had also left his second wife, Arlene, bludgeoned and slashed to death in a pool of blood in her own bedroom?

By 7:30 am, the ultimate survivor and premier "confession taker," Detective K. James McCready of the Suffolk homicide squad, was on the scene. Within a few short hours, and before noon, according to him and his cohorts, he'd extract a complete oral confession from the only survivor of the slaughter at 33 Seaside Drive; the cool, calm, seemingly passionless seventeen-year-old adopted son, Martin "Marty" Tankleff. This time, the detective was accompanied and supported by a new partner. Detective Norman Rein was quiet, unassuming and very believable. Together they made up the quintessential "good cop-bad cop" investigative team, in which McCready always seemed to be the heavy. But once again the police version of a vile homicide would became the center of a stormy controversy which threatened to boil over into the 1989 race for district attorney.

Patrick Henry, the incumbent, was out of the picture. He had decided not to run for reelection—or so he claimed in public. Most believed that he had been denied renomination by a worried Republican party, still reeling from the many investigations of the criminal justice system. On the other hand, Robert Gottlieb overcame a group of announced opponents and emerged once again as the candidate of the Democratic party. He had been hired by the survivors of the Tankleff family to represent Marty, in whose innocence they believed despite police claims that he had confessed to two brutal murders. Complicating the whole issue, and adding an unusual ingredient into the already turbid mix, was the fact that the presiding County Court judge, Alfred C. Tisch, a former assistant district attorney, had, himself, considered entering the Republican primary, even as he was presiding over the preliminary hearings in the Tankleff case.

The controversy began almost as soon as McCready arrived on the murder scene, while Seymour Tankleff lay comatose in a hospital intensive care unit, life slowly exiting his battered and trauma-ridden body. McCready, the lead detective and the last survivor of the "confession takers," had a tailor-made prime suspect. It takes no great investigative genius to hypothesize that if three members of a family are at home, and two are brutally attacked and murdered, while the third is left unscathed, claiming never to have heard or seen anything, he must be considered an important target of the homicide investigation.

In the case of a teenage suspect, just keep him away from any intrusive adults and avoid inquisitive legal counsel—the Quartararo technique—and the investigating detective is almost home free.

At 8:00 am, as the trauma team was working feverishly over the near lifeless body of Seymour Tankleff, his adopted son, Martin, was sitting on an unmarked police vehicle in the street outside the murder scene calmly discussing the events of that morning with Detective McCready. One would assume that compassion and humanity would dictate that Seymour's only son would have been transported to the hospital to be at his father's side as he prepared to leave this mortal coil. However, compassion was not K. James McCready's strong suit, and he had other plans for Marty Tankleff. If he was going anywhere, it was to the "interview" room at the Yaphank headquarters of the homicide squad to continue what was turning out to be a fruitful conversation.

It hadn't taken much to further stimulate the already aroused suspicions of McCready as Marty openly accused his father's business partner, the self-proclaimed "bagel king" Jerry Steuerman, of the crimes. According to the detective, the conduct of the bereaved teenager and "his emotional response to what was going on, what had happened in that house...was totally, totally inappropriate."[1] He was too cool and unaffected by the tragic events of that morning. In McCready's opinion, he should have been a basket case—"a box of rocks." Instead, he appeared devoid of normal human emotion—as cool as a block of ice.

At about 8:05, the Tankleff family lawyer, Myron Fox, appeared on the crime scene. He was more than just a lawyer to the family. He and the dying Seymour "were as close as two men can get." To Marty, he was simply "Uncle Mike." He had come directly from John T. Mather Memorial Hospital, because Seymour's oldest child, Shari Rother, asked him to go to the house to get Marty. She feared for the safety of her brother because he was still at the house where her mother had just been slain. What happened after that depends upon whom you believe—the lawyer, with no apparent motive to perjure himself, unless one believes that he was lying to cover his professional behind, or the various police witnesses who told a very different story.

Fox claimed that when he arrived at the house, he never saw Marty, who was sitting on the police car with detective Rein about sixty yards away from the point where Fox was engaged in a conversation by McCready. McCready told him that Marty was not with him, after Fox identified himself as the family attorney. According to the lawyer, he had given McCready his business card.

"I'm the Tankleff family attorney. I'm here to represent Martin Tankleff. I don't want him questioned except in my presence and I'd like to see him now," Fox told McCready.

"That's fine, but we don't have Marty," replied McCready. "He told us everything he knew…and we sent him over to the hospital with his father."[2]

According to the man known to the family as Uncle Mike, he returned to the hospital shortly thereafter to find Marty, drove back to the house again—found no detective McCready—and drove to the hospital for a third time. There he met a detective who was questioning other family members. He was informed that Marty was now in Yaphank, and the attorney became very upset by the turn of events.

"What the hell is he doing in Yaphank?" Fox asked.

"Well, he's not being questioned, he's volunteering information…and as soon as he's debriefed, he'll be brought over to the hospital."

At about 12:30 pm, for some unexplained reason Fox was driving back to his office in Garden City, some forty to fifty miles away in Nassau County. One would assume that instead he would have been speeding to Yaphank to insulate his "client." Over his car radio, he heard a news report that Marty was being held for questioning in connection with the brutal assaults on his parents. Upon arrival at his office, he called headquarters, represented himself as the attorney for Martin Tankleff and ordered that all further questioning cease. It was too late! McCready already had his alleged oral confession. According to police records, that call was received at 1:22 pm, and all police questioning was concluded at that time.

But to McCready, Myron Fox was a liar. It was a bald face lie—perjury—

when he testified that he had put police on notice on two occasions that he represented Marty Tankleff. A very confident McCready told Tankleff's defense attorney, Bob Gottlieb, about two weeks after the murder: "If you want to allow Fox to come into court and perjure himself, that's your business, but no judge in the world is going to believe that he put us on notice at eight in the morning and then called us again at 1:22 and put us on notice."

The feisty detective had thrown down the gauntlet, and he was at least partly right! That's all that was necessary. The trial judge, Al Tisch, had not bought the Fox story. If he had, he would have been compelled to suppress the confession. He did not! It was heard by the jury, through the words of Rein and McCready, with all its gory details.

What the judge did buy was the homicide detectives' version of the events of September 7, 1988. Fox, McCready claimed, walked up to him and Marty in the street. He talked to Marty for a bit, gave McCready his business card, and introduced himself as "Seymour's business partner for thirty years".

"How's it going?" asked Fox.

"The kid's talking to us and telling us everything he knows," responded McCready.

Within minutes, it was a quick trip to Yaphank for Marty, and his introduction to the "interview room" which had been frequented by so many unfortunates before him, both innocent and guilty. Yet there was no mention of Myron Fox in McCready's investigative notes that described the events of that morning. After reading newspaper accounts that detailed the lawyer's claim that Marty had been questioned in violation of his constitutional rights, the detective claimed that he placed the business card in his file and, one week later, prepared a supplemental report with his best recollection of the street encounter.

As usual, at the pre-trial hearings, McCready put on his best courtroom face. He was in his element. There was no jury trial yet—that would be a long time coming. But he was playing to a mostly appreciative, overcrowded and cramped courtroom audience, including this acting supreme court justice, which snickered and laughed to the cutting cadence of his deprecating verbiage when recounting his conversation with Marty's defense lawyer, Bob Gottlieb. I was in the audience because I was becoming brain dead in the civil part, and because I wanted to experience once again the inimitable style of prosecution witness K. James McCready. Besides, the newspaper accounts of the Tankleff case whetted my curiosity. The cast of characters and the defenses being raised conjured up old ghosts in my memory.

I said, "Fox must be kicking himself in the ass because he fucked up!'"[3]

But Myron Fox was not the only problem with the Tankleff case. Suffolk County homicide cases do not shake out that painlessly. Perhaps the biggest problem was the Jerry Steuerman odyssey. It was this adventure, and the public police reaction to it, which finally drew my full attention to the Tankleff case. Until then it was just another Suffolk County homicide, albeit with McCready as the lead detective.

Fifty-year-old, New York City bred, street-wise Jerry Steuerman owed Seymour Tankleff $350,000. Steuerman had borrowed the money from Tankleff, who was his partner in the ownership of a "few" race horses. In late 1985, or early 1986, Steuerman needed financial help to build his $900,000 dream house in Belle Terre. As collateral to insure the weekly cash payments of $25,000, Tankleff insisted upon taking a one-half interest in Steuerman's two very popular and successful bagel bakeries in Setauket and Stony Brook, when Steuerman, in his words, "ran a little short."

Though Steuerman resented the "usurious" manner in which Tankleff dealt with him, he still considered Seymour to be his friend. They had a "beautiful" friendship, and "Seymour was a good businessman," who was like a father to him. He was entitled to be paid back. So said Jerry Steuerman, a man with many troubles, a modern day Job, if he is to be believed.

Their friendship was disintegrating because he was being squeezed financially by his good friend and father figure. Yet Steuerman was one of the late night poker players on that fateful night in the Tankleff home. In fact, he had been the last one to leave the house. Not only did he leave the Tankleff house that morning, but Steuerman, if he had his way, would have left his troubled life behind him by successfully staging his own disappearance about a week later. His life was in shambles when he abandoned his automobile at an airport after concocting a story that he had received death threats after the fatal attacks on the Tankleffs.

His wife had died within the past year; he was drowning in debt; one of his children was facing felony criminal charges; and his friend, the mayor of Belle Terre—another regular at the weekly poker game—told him that Marty was accusing him of the murders. In an effort to leave no trace, he traveled from hotel to hotel in Atlantic City, Los Angeles, Big Sur, Marina Del Rey and Redondo Beach, where he was found in seclusion by Suffolk police authorities. He said that he was deeply despondent over the death of his friends. That is why, he claimed, he traveled under the fictitious name of Winston—snatched from a limousine service owned by his closest boyhood friend and best man, another street-wise, self-made, Brooklyn bred local entrepreneur.

He left behind $2,000,000 in life insurance policies for the benefit of his girlfriend and his children—policies which, ironically, would have not been paid to the beneficiaries of a missing person. He vehemently professed his innocence to the police and the media. In no way was he involved in the Tankleff murders, although a person of an even normal suspicion could not be faulted for looking upon his very bizarre conduct as the actions of a person suffering from a "consciousness of guilt." Yet no such suspicions blossomed in the minds of Suffolk's homicide investigators. They had their oral confession from the targeted teenager. Case closed!

Steuerman was tracked to California by McCready and associates when he made the fatal mistake of placing a telephone call to his girlfriend in Suffolk County with a one word message—"pistachio." Steuerman, known for his love of pistachio nuts, intended to convey the message that he was alive and well. Within twenty-four hours, he had unexpected company at his southern California motel—Detective McCready, Detective Sgt. Robert Doyle (McCready's supervisor), and the chief of the district attorney's Homicide Bureau, Ed Jablonski (the Corso prosecutor). This was quite a distinguished group, which flew out to California at taxpayer expense to meet with a man, who, despite his very unusual behavior on the heels of the murder of his two friends, according to the police, had "absolutely no connection" to the homicides. "He's just a missing person," reported Doyle from Steuerman's motel room. "He's not wanted for any crime."[4] A Suffolk County prosecution team had once again rushed to judgement!

In the words of Peter L. Davis, professor of legal ethics and criminal procedure at Touro Law School who had served as special counsel to the Public Safety Committee of the Suffolk County Legislature in its investigation of Suffolk law enforcement in 1987:

"When he (Steuerman) resurfaced, his explanation for his bizarre and remarkably suspicious conduct was incoherent and unpersuasive. Any self-respecting viewer of TV police drama would have regarded this guy as almost too obvious a suspect. Yet the Suffolk County Police Department announced that it never considered him a suspect."[5]

Fortunately for Steuerman and for the unsuspecting police, the "bagel king" had an available alibi for his whereabouts in the early morning hours of September 7, 1988, after he left the final poker game. His daughter, Bari, who shared his Old Field home, was asleep when the doorbell rang that morning. It was her father. It was "3:17 am," she said and her father had once again forgotten his house key. It was something he usually did.

She next saw him after he went right up to bed, at 6:00 am, when he helped her start her car. Marty Tankleff said that he found his parents after awakening at 5:35 a.m., and that he called 911 at 6:10 am. For a self-proclaimed unlucky guy, it was indeed a stroke of good luck for Jerry Steuerman that he had forgotten his house key once again, and that his daughter could not get her car started the next morning. Otherwise, he would have had no witness to support his alibi. He would have had to depend upon the credibility of his own good word, or the good faith of Suffolk homicide detectives who never considered him to be a suspect—or so they said.

Why should Jerry Steuerman be suspected by McCready and his cohorts? They had their murderer! Did Martin Tankleff not confess to the crimes within a few hours after he frantically called police emergency services in an attempt to save his severed and battered father? Did he not, like Jerry Steuerman, have the motive and the opportunity to murder his parents? Why bother to consider anyone else when your investigation has been rendered virtually effortless by a cooperative suspect? Still, the Martin

Tankleff confession raised many questions in the minds of the skeptical—this observer included. It had too many of the earmarks of the Diaz-Corso syndrome, not the least of which was the unrecorded and unsigned oral confession obtained in the privacy of the Yaphank "interview room" attested to only by the police witnesses.

What of this confession? What manner of trickery, even by one as honed in the art of chicanery as Kevin James McCready, would possess a sixteen year old, who vehemently protests his innocence, to admit to the brutal slaying of the parents he claimed that he loved? Certainly, there have been other persons, both young and old, who have been confronted by a team of incredulous and persistent Suffolk homicide detectives in the Yaphank "interview room," who did not submit to their terror, inflicting suggestions and theories of guilty conduct.

Detective McCready clearly took great pride in the manner in which he broke the defense and spirit of the isolated teen even as he softened him with a cup of coffee, "light and sweet." Confessions to the Suffolk homicide squad were invariably lubricated by a pack of cigarettes, a cup of coffee or a can of Coke. It is a small price for the police investigator to pay to the confessor to lock up his case, a confessor whom he may claim to pity while he buries his true feeling of contempt.

The McCready-Rein team was certain from the outset that Marty Tankleff was responsible for the horrors of that morning. But how do you extract the truth from a son who persisted in protesting his innocence as he accused Jerry Steuerman of murdering his mother and mortally wounding his father?

The first confrontation came as the detectives would not accept Marty's story that he awoke at 5:35 am on what was the first day of the new school year to complete the installation of a stereo system in his car. Why was there no blood on his sweatshirt, they asked, though he claimed that he attempted to perform first aid on his dying father—stuffing a clean towel against the gaping wound in an attempt to stop the blood which was gushing from his father's neck? Why had he not carried out the instructions of the 911 operator in an effort to save his father's life? Why did he appear concerned when McCready stared at a patch of blood on his leg? Why was there a blood smear on the light switch in his bedroom? Why was there no blood on the light chain in the linen closet or on the kitchen closet or on the door leading to the garage, objects which he claimed he had touched after having aided his father? The questions by the incredulous detectives came fast and furious as McCready displayed his temper and moved himself closer to the seated suspect—knee to knee. For about two hours, the story of the cold and passionless teenager would not budge as the detectives became even more convinced that he was a murderer. There were too many inconsistencies in his story. It simply didn't add up!

It was time for K. James McCready to pull off the greatest trick of his illustrious investigative career—his final gambit. The kid had not responded to the McCready hard line: "You're a criminal, I'm going to lock you up!"

The detective left Marty alone with Rein in the interview room. Perhaps the "good guy" approach would melt this iceberg who was so adamant about his innocence that he was offering to take a polygraph test. But there would be no polygraph! Their investigative instincts were sufficient. In their minds, they had their perpetrator, although their verbal prodding and appeals to decency had not been enough to break him.

McCready decided to answer a fictitious call from a telephone which was situated about ten feet away, in the adjacent room, within earshot of Marty who was still alone with Rein in the interview room. The door was ajar. The detective answered the ringing telephone in a loud, clear voice, certain to be heard in the next room. He created the short, but very effective, conversation as he went along.

"Homicide, McCready. Yeah, John [apparently, Detective John Pfalzgraf. You're kidding! He came out?"

The telephone receiver was quickly returned to its cradle, and the detective re-entered the small room to continue the clever ruse in an effort to reap the results of his high stakes maneuver. He told Marty that his father, whom Marty knew was in a coma, had been "pumped full of adrenaline," and that he had come out of the coma. He then told the youth that his father was saying that his son had stabbed him. The trap was tightly set and it did not take long for the mouse to take the bait. A charade which had been conceived on the spur of the moment to entrap a young murderer was about to strike pay dirt. It was no longer any great task to wear down his defense.

"My father must be confused...I didn't do this. I'll even take a lie detector test...Whoever did this to my mother and father needs psychiatric help," Marty said.

"Could it be you that needs psychiatric help?" he was asked by the disbelieving detectives.

"Could it have been possible that I blacked out? Maybe it wasn't me but another Martin Tankleff that did this....Could I be possessed?"

"Why don't you tell us about it?"

It was time to give him his constitutional rights. Martin Tankleff was no longer simply a cooperative witness who just happened to be the prime suspect to the police. He was about to make their case for them. In homicide police parlance, he had "gone for it!" Of course he did not need or want any attorney present as he spent his innermost feelings and assuaged an overwhelmingly guilty conscience. He was about to admit to matricide and fratricide to two hardened homicide detectives that he had known for about five hours. Who would want a lawyer under those circumstances?

What would possess an otherwise normal teenager, who seemed to have everything that a teen would want, to wake up early on the first day of school for the express purpose of slaughtering his adoptive parents? There seemed to be no single reason. There rarely is! The problems of life are much too complex, even for a teenager--perhaps even more so for a sixteen year old. The final straw came when his mother forced him to set up the card table for his father's weekly poker game. Even worse, they were going to make him go to school in a "crummy old Lincoln." He wanted something more "sporty." That old Lincoln, which would have made the tongue hang out of most teenager's mouth, would not enhance Marty's image with the girls at Port Jefferson's Earl Vandermuelen High School. He would also become deeply distressed over the many verbal fights between his parents. Marty was afraid that they were going to break up. What would happen to him? The adopted prodigal son feared for his future and his financial security. His mother would not allow him to engage in "contact sports." He had been restricted in the use of the family boat and an all-terrain vehicle. They had hired a house sitter because they did not trust him to be alone in the house during a planned cruise. In short, his world was collapsing around him—according to the police!

For these less than earth shattering reasons, an overindulged, angry, egocentric teen had bludgeoned his parents with a body building dumbbell and slashed their throats with a knife that was used to cut watermelon. His murderous motivation seemed almost trivial by comparison to the problems which besieged the bagel king, Jerry Steuerman. But how do you account for the logic of a spoiled teenager?

McCready had his confession, and, according to him, they would have had it in writing if they had not received the 1:22 pm telephone call from "Uncle Mike" directing that they cease any further questioning of his client.

Still there were other doubts built into the case against Martin Tankleff. Fortuitously, there were two "power failures" at the Yaphank police headquarters on September 7, 1988. The first was between 6:40 and 6:48 am, and a second lasted for thirty-nine minutes from 7:27 am. Although there was a built-in emergency back-up system, that system had also malfunctioned that morning. As a result, all 911 telephone calls and radio transmissions between police, detectives and headquarters throughout the county, which were routinely recorded and preserved, were lost.

If, as he claimed, Myron Fox told McCready at about 8:05 am that he represented Marty, the detective would, in all likelihood, have conveyed this information to his commanding officer by radio transmission. With the loss of the back-up tapes, there was no way to confirm his claim. The judge and jury would have to rely upon the testimony of K. James McCready that he had never made such a call.

But long before the jury would have the opportunity to test the reliability of the detective's story, it was up to the trial judge to determine whether the teen's rights had been violated. To some observers, that presented a real ethical problem. Judge Tisch had inserted himself into the midst of the race for successor to Patrick Henry as district attorney. This was the most highly publicized homicide trial of the year, and any candidate for that office would need the support of the powerful police unions to insure his success. Their eyes had to be focused on the Tankleff trial—and Robert Gottlieb was to be the Democratic candidate once again.

He sensed the potential for conflict of interest, and he chose to meet the issue head on. *Newsday* reported that the Republican leaders voted to offer the nomination to Tisch while the judge was pondering his decision on the critical pre-trial issues. Gottlieb's law partner, Ron Sussman, citing the state's canons of judicial ethics forbidding a judge from seeking non-judicial elective office, immediately sought an answer from the judge whether he was, in fact, a candidate for that office.

"If the answer is yes" Sussman said, "I have no choice but to move for your recusal."

"I don't think there is any question to answer at this point," responded Tisch.

He claimed that he was not truly a candidate because his name had only been offered for nomination by the executive committee.[6] But what he did not say was that he, a sitting judge, was actively seeking the Republican nomination, and that he had solicited the Tankleff trial, a high profile case, from the administrative judge to help further his ambitions. Gottlieb was aware of this fact, but chose not to confront him with it. His source had been sheer hearsay-from Tom Stark through a conversation with me, and either he was too much the gentleman to embarrass his source, or he felt that he would never be able to prove what had been told to him in confidence.

It was common knowledge that the recommendation of the GOP executive committee was tantamount to nomination, and everyone in the courthouse who knew the judge, knew that he had been actively seeking the nomination for some time. He had made no secret of his desire to move on to other things. He believed that he was the logical choice for that office. At a time when he was formulating his critical opinion on the voluntariness of the Tankleff confession- whether his constitutional rights had been violated- the judge was quietly meeting with political leaders in an effort to wrest the nomination as the county's chief prosecutor. He was being assailed in the news media since "Tisch's apparent interest in being a prosecutor could taint the cases he currently presides over."[82]

Even the former county Republican leader, who had been relegated to authoring a part-time column in a local weekly newspaper, publicly criticized the judge for this obvious conflict of interest:

So, with Pat Henry leaving the doors open for a candidate for the Republican nomination for district attorney, lots of strange things started happening. Present Republican County Court Judge Al Tisch received the nod to be the candidate at an executive meeting of the Republican leaders a couple of weeks ago. This was rather strange in the fact that Tisch was not an announced candidate for the job. There are a number of reasons why Tisch isn't an announced candidate as #1. He is presently a sitting Judge and it's a no-no for a judge to be an announced candidate and still remain being a judge; #2. He is presently the sitting judge on a number of important cases and is already in hot water with defense attorneys, calling for him to rescue himself because of a possible conflict; #3. Tisch's possible adversary for the position of district attorney on the Democratic ticket is representing a defendant in one of these important trials in which Tisch is the judge. All of these reasons make the Buzz Saw believe that Tisch had better fish or cut bait soon as to whether or not he is a candidate. Less than that, and he might find himself out in the street not being the district attorney or a judge. He cannot ride all of the horses at the same time in this situation without being burned.[7]

On April 28, the Republican leaders had second thoughts about the Tisch candidacy from an ethical point of view. They had also become concerned that his interest in the chief prosecutor's office could taint the cases he was presiding over. They decided to re-evaluate the situation. Tisch's candidacy was now dead as a doornail! Less than two weeks later, he published his opinion on the voluntariness of the Tankleff confession. He had previously decided not to remove himself from the case. The judge would allow the jury to hear Marty's oral confession to McCready and Rein. As an outside observer, one can only speculate as to how much Tisch's burning desire to become Suffolk County's district attorney had weighed upon his decision, either consciously or unconsciously. You don't get elected as chief prosecutor unless you are perceived as tough by the public and the powerful police unions whose support you must have in order to be elected. I hoped that Al Tisch, who had been something of a friend, was too much the professional to knowingly permit politics to taint such a significant decision. Yet, that is precisely why the Canons of Judicial Ethics prohibit not only actual impropriety, but the appearance of impropriety as well.

Even with all of his other problems, the biggest problem that Marty Tankleff had to confront was Marty Tankleff himself. From the first moment that he met with the investigating detectives, and right up to the time that the twelve men and women of the jury returned to the courtroom to announce their verdict, he could not get out of the way of his own personality. Some said that he convicted himself. If Marty is innocent, as he protests so vehemently, then he has his own personality to blame for his conviction.

On the witness stand, he was no less cool, composed and compassion less then he appeared to the homicide detectives on the morning of the murders. He did not fit the jurors' image of the bereaved orphan whose parents had been brutally slaughtered in their own home by some unknown assailant. Whatever passion he could stir within his emotionless testimony was reserved for his description of the confrontation with his chief accuser, K. James McCready. Marty, who testified that he was "brought up always to trust and believe cops," was tricked into confessing to the murder of his parents by a cop whom he trusted. Even his cool and passionless disposition could not conceal his obvious contempt for McCready.

According to several of the jurors, who deliberated for eight days, it had been a tactical mistake for Marty to take the stand. In effect, he convicted himself, and his public lack of emotion played a significant role in that conviction. One juror, who preferred to remain anonymous in *Newsday*, said "the panel didn't understand how—based on testimony from police and the defendant himself—Tankleff could have such a lack of emotion on the day of his parents' murders..."[8]

Juror Peter Baczynski concurred. "I think it would have been a lot more difficult for us if he (hadn't) testified. I think it was a mistake that he went up there. None of us honestly believed him when he went up there. The lack of emotion and the way he acted, we said, 'This guy's lying.'"[9]

"Basically, it was his testimony that determined his guilt," was the judgement of juror Teresa Quigley. According to her, the jurors disregarded the oral confession, the purported confession which Judge Tisch refused to suppress. The jurors, unlike the judge, felt that the police violated Marty's constitutional rights. Be that as it may, it would have taken an almost superhuman group effort for a lay jury to totally disregard a confession which was presented in a murder trial involving the deaths of two people.

While the jury was convinced that Marty was guilty of both murders—depraved indifference murder of his mother and intentional murder of his father—the members of his family, but one, publicly stood behind him throughout the trial. They continued to believe in his innocence. The lone member of his family who, late in the game, became convinced of his guilt, is his only sister, Shari Rother, who stood to inherit the entire Tankleff estate if Marty's consecutive life sentences are upheld on appeal.

To her chagrin the bulk of the Tankleff estate was left to her adopted brother, and she, the natural child of his first marriage, has contested her father's will. It must be difficult to accept that your father would leave more of his estate to an adopted brother who is many years younger than you—a brother whom the police say has murdered your father and step-mother. She didn't always accept the guilt of her brother. Within days after his arraignment, she and four other members of the family, posted a bond in the amount of $1,000,000 to obtain his release pending trial. The family also offered a $25,000 cash reward for information leading to the arrest and conviction of the Tankleff murderer.

No sooner than the jury was sequestered in deliberation, K. James McCready, by then a private citizen and retired from the Suffolk County Police, and not under restraint as a public official, took it upon himself to proudly announce to the assembled courthouse press corps that Shari Rother and her husband, Ron, were "fully and totally behind the police."[10]

McCready had suffered days of intensive cross-examination by Bob Gottlieb. Whatever little was left of his personal integrity and credibility was publicly attacked in the trial which became a much watched daily television show from opening statements through the judge's sentence on NEWS 12 LONG ISLAND. He had been publicly humiliated while being subjected to heated and lengthy interrogation about his change of testimony in the Diaz murder trial. That was the testimony which caused the State Commission of Investigations to conclude that he had perjured himself at the trial. He had to be smarting from Gottlieb's unbridled barbs and the Tankleff family's public show of support for Marty and obvious distrust of him.

The detective's pride would not allow him to await the jury's final verdict for a judgement on his actions in this case. By telling the world that Shari Rother believed that her brother was guilty, he would be vindicated, no matter what the jury decided. So long as he was convinced of the rightness of his cause, Robert Gottlieb, Martin Tankleff and the State Commission of Investigations be damned! He had succeeded in convincing the defendant's unbelieving sister that he had solved her father's murder. This had to be very important to K. James McCready. If there were an acquittal, he could now rationalize that such an unjust result was the end product of a smart-ass, fancy-pants lawyer being paid a wad of money by a rich family to create a legal smokescreen to cloud the real issues. He knew that Marty Tankleff was guilty, and now, so too, did Marty's closest living relative.

As it turned out, the jury bought the prosecution's case built largely upon the testimony of detective McCready. For Shari Rother, the ends of justice had been served. Yet she refuted McCready's boast that she had been in the prosecution's corner from early in the investigation. As for the rest of the family, they had nothing but contempt and disdain for the lead detective on the case. But the talkative lead detective couldn't contain his jubilation with the verdict. Once again, he proudly announced, the actions of the homicide squad were vindicated. He was publicly chirping like a lark, and the media ate it up. He was a private citizen, free to speak his piece.

"We did everything up to Hoyle. We don't go into courtrooms and lie, cheat and steal to convict guilty people. He is guilty. He convicted himself....Martin Tankleff took the witness stand and obviously lied. From day one in this investigation, I said that if he came into this courtroom he could say any story he wanted but he couldn't tell the story that fit the physical evidence. I think his own testimony is what convicted him. I think my argument and the fine work of the Suffolk County Police Department has been borne out by the verdict in this case."[11]

But the Tankleff case would not go away. It would be many months before Al Tisch could impose two consecutive maximum life sentences. Like so many other homicide cases in Suffolk County, it developed a life of its own. Some said that it was because Marty's family was so wealthy that they could continue to foot his extraordinary legal expenses long after the jury had reached its verdict.

Others complained that Bob Gottlieb was milking the issues to ensure continued media exposure during the heat of the 1989 race for district attorney.

Yet there were serious issues which arose even during deliberations when the twelve members of the jury were sequestered for eight days at the Holiday Inn of Riverhead. Two members of the jury who had voted to convict Marty Tankleff, complained that the security of the jury had been breached. Once again, former detective K. James McCready was at the heart of the furor.

Juror Peter Baczynski, at a special hearing, testified that another juror, Frank Spindel, told him on the very first night of deliberations, after the jury was instructed by the judge that they could have no contact with anyone outside of their fellow jurors and court personnel, that he had been informed in a telephone call that "Shari Rother has been working with the prosecution since January and McCready called a press conference to say that today."[12]

Baczynski confessed that the information about Rother influenced his decision to convict Marty Tankleff, and that he had been troubled about his actions since the verdict. Still he had rationalized that "it's OK and even though you may have cheated and not played by the rules, he's still guilty." The juror admitted that he too had broken the rules by calling home during deliberations and listening to radio broadcasts about the case.

A second juror, Teresa Quigley, also heard Spindel say that Marty's sister was not "on his side." Spindel, she said, claimed to have inside information about the case. But she, unlike Baczynski, had not allowed this to affect her decision—so she said. Telephone company records revealed that eight calls were charged to Spindel's home telephone number on the very first night of deliberations—calls which were placed at the Riverhead Holiday Inn.

A third juror voluntarily testified, without subpoena, that he was unaware of the McCready press conference until after his release from jury service. But his testimony could not alleviate the taint. The damage, it seemed, was done! The security of the jury had been breached. But what it seemed like from the outside was meaningless. What counted was how this was perceived by the person who had the responsibility to decide whether Marty Tankleff had been deprived of his right to a fair trial—the trial judge. And Judge Tisch was getting testy. This couldn't help the defendant. It seemed like there was a new issue being raised by the defense every week.

Not only were jurors being accused of misconduct, but Gottlieb had the gall to accuse the trial judge of misconduct as well. It was claimed by the defense that Al Tisch had attended a Tankleff victory party with homicide detectives and prosecutors at the Port Jefferson Country Club, just a few miles from Tisch's home. The judge angrily denounced this allegation. In a written decision which he read from the bench in front of a bank of media microphones and cameras, he railed against "character assassination of the presiding judge based on specious if not ludicrous grounds...and a new and dangerous era, the era of jury bashing." He accused the defense of "apparently unlimited resources" and an "attempt to portray the defendant as the victim of the great 'Frame Up.'"[13]

Bob Gottlieb, in his zeal to defend his client, had probably made a serious tactical error in attacking this particular trial judge on a very sensitive personal level. For a second time, he had publicly asked Tisch to recuse himself. The attorney had succeeded in moving the judge away from the real damaging issue of juror misconduct, but Bob Gottlieb, who is a zealot on the issue of legal ethics, was offended by the judge's comments, and he was sincerely convinced that the judge apparently had "an unjustified objection to defense counsel doing everything possible pursuant to law to represent [his] client."

By the time Gottlieb accused the prosecution of anti-Semitism and called for the appointment of a special prosecutor, the judge had had enough. The alleged epiphytic comment had been gratuitously made to another attorney in a Riverhead restaurant by the assistant representing the district attorney at the juror misconduct hearing. In response to a question about the case, the assistant DA allegedly responded: "Great, we got the little Jew bastard

[Gottlieb] now....we've got him good, we're not the slightest bit worried about Tankleff, he's nothing now, we have Gottlieb...we'll finish that Jewish shyster, he's done for, he better have gotten enough money on this case to put in a Swiss account because he is finished practicing law in Suffolk County."[14]

The trial had been turned into a media circus from the opening bell, but the real question was who was responsible. The sharp tongued district attorney, James Catterson, who had defeated Gottlieb at the last election, lashed out against his former adversary: "This man has an exaggerated idea of his own importance. I've always maintained that he was the best weapon the district attorney's office ever had. I think it is ludicrous to be raising these spectres to bring attention to his own shortcomings. I've had it with this turkey."

These are strong words, even from one who is known to occasionally shoot from the hip in public. The accusation of anti-Semitism had been brought forward by an attorney who bore no relation to the Tankleff case or Robert Gottlieb, and who swore to what had been said to him in an affidavit. By doing so, the attorney had put his professional career and his livelihood on the line. Still, months later, a committee of the Suffolk County Bar Association found that the charges were unfounded. *Newsday* and others quickly came to the defense of the unsuccessful trial attorney:

> It wouldn't be surprising if a lot of people on Catterson's staff didn't like defense lawyer Robert Gottlieb. Gottlieb nearly beat their boss in a bitter election last fall and, in the murder trial of Martin Tankleff, has directly attacked the honesty of the prosecutors....Gottlieb, to be sure, has tested the limits of courtroom practices in his tenacious defense of Tankleff....He attacked the judge and challenged the objectivity of a juror and the ethics of the DA's office. But none of that would be adequate excuse for official bigotry.[15]

From Indiana to Washington, D.C., legal experts rushed to join the public verbal flagellation of Gottlieb, accusing him of creating a "circus" with irrelevant and meritless post-verdict motions. With all this piling on, it is time for someone to throw a flag. In their zeal to condemn Gottlieb, the media and their experts have missed the real meaning of the Tankleff case—and have forgotten or ignored fundamental facts about it, facts that suggest that Tankleff may be just another example of a continuing course of misconduct by law enforcement officials in Suffolk County....The real headline in the Tankleff "circus" is the persistent misconduct and impropriety in Suffolk law enforcement, not one defense attorney's attempts to expose it to secure a new trial for his client; Gottlieb did not create these problems, he merely brought them to light. The law enforcement community of Suffolk has bitterly attacked all of its critics, attempting to silence them—the county judge, the County Legislature and the SIC....Gottlieb is only the current messenger; shooting him will not change the message [Prof. Peter L. Davis].[16]

As this chapter is being written, Marty Tankleff, who is confined for life in a state correctional facility, has only his appeals lawyers to rely upon as they prepare briefs for their argument in the courts of appeal. The judges of those courts, which are far removed from the Riverhead battlefield, will have many burning and serious issues to consider. They will not be saddled with the problems which must have become a great burden to the trial judge who sought a high publicity case in his unsuccessful quest for the chief prosecutor's mantle. It is difficult to see how they will find a way to uphold the convictions. In this corner, Marty Tankleff seems destined for a new trial. But no matter what the result, the Tankleff case, like so many other Suffolk cases before it, will be remembered, unfortunately, not so much for the deaths of Seymour and Arlene Tankleff, but for the problematic issues which never seem to go away, no matter who is at the helm of Suffolk law enforcement!

****

Several years later, after becoming involved in the British television series, and before producing a video documentary about my unit, the 17th Infantry Regiment in the Korean War, Nancy and I decided, with our own funds, to produce a television series of documentaries about prisoners who claimed to be innocent. We retained the services of the British crew with whom I had previously worked, including my good friend, Frazer Ashford, who would come on as a full partner for his services as producer. It was to be a thirteen part series, called "A Question of Guilt!", made up of murder cases that I was personally either involved in, or was aware of in Suffolk County, as well as cases of persons on "death row" who had been communicating with me gratuitously from around the country. Marty Tankleff's case was to be the pilot for the series, and we visited him in Greenhaven Correctional Facility where his part of the story was put on tape. I also visited Robert Patterson in Clinton Correctional Facility on our way back from Plattsburgh when he begged me, on his knees, to do his story, as he still professed his innocence! As luck would have it, the series was never picked up by a television station or network, and we still have many of the unsold balance of the 1,000 copies which we had produced commercially, and which we have given gratis to libraries and persons who expressed interest in acquiring them. Although I truly believed in Marty's innocence, knowing as I did the cast of characters, it was our decision to let the audience decide, thus "A Question of Guilt!" The documentary closed as I stood at the gravesite of Marty's parents leaving open the question of guilt or innocence, which only his deceased parents could answer. With the help of his wealthy family who always believed in his innocence, pro bono attorneys, and two retired New York city homicide detectives, after several lost appeals and seventeen years in a maximum security prison, his conviction was thrown out by the Appellate Division, 2nd Dept. Marty's story had been true, and the names of the perpetrators had been turned over to the Suffolk County District Attorney, now Tom Spota, but no action has ever been taken against the real suspects. To do otherwise would be to admit that you were wrong, and Suffolk County justice is "never" wrong. As for Marty, he is now in his third year at Touro Law School, is married with a daughter, and upon graduation he will be engaged in the practice of helping others in the same predicament in which he had long found himself!**

**On January 7, 2014, Marty Tankleff settled his lawsuit against New York State for "false-imprisonment" in the Court of Claims for $3.37 million dollars, with another case still pending against the County of Suffolk and certain individuals in the United States District Court. (*Newsday*, January 8, 2014)

TWENTY-THREE

"Don't Worry About It, We Just Want to Talk to You."

—Detective Broesler

I T WAS GOING TO BE A BIG NIGHT ON THE TOWN for Jamaican-born Kenny McLaren. It was pay day, and he had just taken home $281.97. He was flush with cash, as much cash as one who worked as a supermarket maintenance man could have at one time. All decked out in a black leather jacket, his black baseball cap, heavy gold chains encircling his neck, he sported four glittering gold rings on his fingers. With his pockets full, he would find some lady. Who knew where that would take him?

Kenny was ready for action as he left the small room where he lived alone in the low rent district of Brentwood. The father of seven children, he was separated from their mother and alienated from his offspring. He enjoyed his drink, and he could be nasty when he had too much.

It was the night of December 14, 1990. By 8:30 pm, he was already feeling no pain from the bottle of malt liquor he'd stashed in a paper bag during the short visit with his store manager at the C-Town supermarket. He might have been ready to party, but he could not possibly have been ready for the fate that would befall him that night. How could he know that he would never see C-Town or his room again? Kenneth McLaren had picked up his last paycheck.

Kenny must have been thinking that he would have no problem scoring that night. His destination was RanJon's, the local watering hole in a nearby strip mall. The place would be teeming with the usual Friday night crowd of locals, hookers, Johns and crack heads. The little man had a fistful of money in his pockets, more then enough to buy a couple of hours of sexual pleasures. No sooner had he arrived at the bar, than he was in the right company—two ladies of the night, Annie and Angela. But even professional whores weren't interested in a sloppy, fall-down old Jamaican who was dropping his money all over the floor. He had been hitting on Annie all night, but he was offering only a solitary dollar bill in exchange for her sexual favors. There were too many cool, young, white customers cruising the streets of Central Islip and Brentwood in their racy automobiles ready to shell out a quick $20 bill for a few minutes of ecstasy with a willing black beauty. Who wanted to be bothered by a nasty, slobbering drunk when there was a ready supply of cheap crack to be smoked? The night was young, and turning just a couple of tricks would keep Annie and Angela in heaven all night.

Unlike Kenny, Anthony Atkinson, street name "Bosco," had no trouble connecting and scoring with those of the opposite gender. Although the police had him tabbed as gay or, worse yet, bisexual, according to his court-appointed lawyer, Kevin Fox, Bosco's biggest problem was staying away from the ladies!

He was living with Carol, with whom he fathered two children, and he was having an active affair with another woman. He had been out with his latest lady friend before he too arrived at RanJon's where providence, and a penchant for trouble, caused him to meet up with Kenny, Annie and Angela. At age twenty-eight, he had already served a state prison term for sodomy of a young boy, but he claimed that he was innocent. He was out on parole from that charge. For him, December 14, 1990 would turn out to be a very long Kafkaesque nightmare, ending days later with a very bizarre twist. For sure, his life would have been much less complicated had he simply gone home to face the music from Carol. Instead, as fools and rogues are wont to do, he too decided to drop in at the bar where he sipped rum and 7-Up from about 11:30 to 2:00 am.

By the time he stopped by, Kenny McLaren was feeling no pain. He had either lost or spent his entire paycheck. Meanwhile, Annie and Angela, who had spurned his drunken advances, high on crack, had been in at least one fight with some "white girls" at the bar. Bosco, who was vicariously taking it all in from a dimly lit booth, knew Annie from the neighborhood. For some unexplained reason, he decided to hook up with the unlikely la dolce vita troika of Angela, Annie and Kenny after they had all been tossed out of the bar by the bouncers. Even a place like RanJon's has some minimum standards of decorum!

Their mutual destination became the "7-11" twenty-four hour convenience store about one-half mile away on Carleton Avenue. But only two of the group made it to the "7-11." Annie split from the group when she was picked up by "John," a white man in a brown station wagon. She was more interested in the $20 bill which he exchanged for a quick trick at the East Islip marina overlooking the beautiful Great South Bay.

Angela, who was leisurely strolling with Kenny at her side, last saw him hanging onto a street light in front of a store with a very appropriate name— "We Are Nuts." A quick stop at the "7-11," which had lost its beer license, and Angela traded Bosco's company for another lonely "John" in a car. John was a very popular name on the streets of Central Islip that night! That was the last she saw of Anthony or Kenny that night.

If Bosco is to be believed, he then headed home alone. Along the way, he spotted a loud and belligerent Kenny shouting obscenities at some guy walking about ten yards behind him. Bosco was greeted at his door by his furious girlfriend. It was 3:50 am on his mother's clock.

Just a few short blocks from the Carleton Avenue "7-11," and not far from his empty room, at about 6:00 am, Kenneth McLaren was discovered unconscious, lying on the southwest corner of St. John's Street and Cordello Avenue in the fetal position. His pants and underwear were down around his ankles, he was wearing only one sneaker, and there were numerous contusions about his head and face. He appeared to be bleeding from his mouth, nose and eyes, and there seemed to be trauma in the vicinity of his distended rectum.

About one foot from where he was lying, in a pile of leaves, there was a beer bottle covered with fecal matter. He had been beaten and stomped unmercifully by an unknown assailant and left to die alone like an injured dog in the street.

Kenny was taken by ambulance to Community Hospital in Smithtown where he underwent emergency neurosurgery and was placed on a respirator. He never regained consciousness from a coma. He expired just a few days later, and the case was picked up by the Suffolk County homicide squad.

Enter detectives Lester "Rusty" Stevens and Douglas Morgan of the newly constituted homicide squad—the end product of years of controversy, investigation and reform. Still they were not assigned the case until detective John Broesler of the 3rd Squad had conducted five days of intensive investigation into the incident. Over six feet tall and about 250 pounds, in his blue uniform days, Broesler was known on the mean streets of Central Islip as "Salt," the tough white member of the blue and white "Salt and Pepper" team. By the time Morgan and Stevens arrived on the scene, Broesler had already reached certain conclusions—that Kenny had been beaten, robbed and sexually assaulted; that Anthony "Bosco" Atkinson, whom he had previously arrested for robbery, and who was the last person seen with the deceased, was the most likely suspect; that the beer bottle found at the crime scene covered with fecal matter was probably the instrument which caused the injury to Kenny's rectum; that the beer bottle was the same bottle that Bosco Atkinson allegedly had in his hand when he left the bar on his early morning trek to the "7-11;" and that Atkinson, who had been convicted of sodomy and sentenced to six years in prison, was more than capable of committing such a repulsive, despicable and abominable act.

Like Broesler, Doug Morgan and Rusty Stevens were typical Suffolk County detectives—white, forty-something, street-wise and tough talking. Morgan was balding, and Stevens' locks of curly red hair were thinning and prematurely mixed with white. Their physical appearances quickly revealed their years of police work on the streets. No sooner had they taken over the investigation, at 10:00 a.m. on December 20, 1990, then the two detectives were fully briefed by Broesler as to the direction of his investigation and his suspicions.

The first order of business was to conduct a mid-afternoon re-interview of Angela at the precinct to see if her story was still the same, or if it had changed. It was and it had not! It was then that the three detectives, at about

5:10 pm, decided to "verify the last known address of Anthony Atkinson, A/K/A Bosco."[1] Broesler would show them where his prime suspect hung his hat and parked his shoes at night.

If the detectives are to be believed, it was just by fortuitous circumstance, mere serendipity, that while "en route to that location Atkinson was seen walking in a southerly direction on the west side of Carleton Avenue...." So, according to the detectives, although they had not previously planned to do so, it was decided "on the spot" to "pick him up and question him." In Suffolk County homicide arrests, invariably the prime suspect, from whom the police sought to obtain a "voluntary" statement, was usually found, as if by chance, alone on the streets, like Robert Brensic and Tommy Ryan, or alone in a parking lot, like Timothy O'Toole. Rarely is a suspect asked to voluntarily accompany the detectives to the Yaphank interview room when he is in the presence of friends or family. So it was almost always the word of one man against the word of a team of detectives as to how their long encounter first began. From the outset, the odds were stacked against the accused. It was a very valuable and rewarding investigative technique which paid great dividends in Suffolk homicide investigations!

From this point, the stories of the detectives and Anthony Atkinson, as too often seemed be the case, vary greatly in the detail of what happened that night and into the next morning. Therein lies the real mystery of the murder of poor Kenneth McLaren, whose death has by now been sadly subjugated to the controversy which came to surround this otherwise routine murder case.

There is no dispute that an unmarked four-door burgundy sedan pulled up to Atkinson on the street. Three guys exited the vehicle, one of whom Bosco recognized as a cop. It was "Salt" and his two police cohorts. They said that they simply wanted to talk to him, but they slapped his hands onto the police vehicle, spread his legs, searched his person and placed him in the back seat of the car. According to Atkinson, Broesler did all the talking.

"Your parole officer sent us. We want to ask you some questions," Broesler said.

"Is this about the fight in RanJon's?" said Bosco.

"Don't worry about it. We just want to talk to you. Do you recognize me?"

"Yeah, you used to be in a blue and white."

But, according to detective Broesler, he did not know that Atkinson was on parole, and never mentioned his parole officer to him. By that time, he says, he had not "pulled up his record." Yet, Rusty Stevens, who came in on the heels of Broesler's investigation, testified that he knew Atkinson was on parole. He had been given this information by Broesler. According to him, they had simply introduced themselves to Atkinson, who after being patted down by the detectives, voluntarily agreed to accompany them to headquarters. The interview room in Yaphank was about to receive another cooperative visitor.

It was 8:30 pm on the squad room clock, but there was no clock in the interview room. The willing recipient of the police invitation for a visit to headquarters was stripped of his gold chains, earrings and rings. There is no need for the visitor to be decked out with jewelry or to keep track of time when he is alone in that room behind a closed door with a team of questioners. It is they who control both the time and the environment.

Once again, an all too familiar scene was about to be played out in the modern high-tech headquarters of the Suffolk County police department at Yaphank. Fully equipped with video cameras, cassette recorders, eavesdropping devices, none was used by the homicide detectives that night. Other than the three hardened veteran detectives, only the barren walls, some old file cabinets, a steel desk and a few well-used chairs would bear silent witness to the alleged confession of one overwrought and frightened human being.

Anthony Atkinson wanted to talk about the fight at RanJon's in which he had not been involved. That, he thought, was the purpose of his automobile trip through the dark streets of Suffolk County. But the detectives were not interested in that fight. They wanted to know about Kenny, and Atkinson's involvement in his death. According to Atkinson, the one he called the "blondish guy," Rusty Stevens, was coming on as the heavy. It was he who seated himself right in the suspect's face, challenging his every response, after they had left him alone in the room with his thoughts for about ten minutes, they returned:

"Did you have a fight?"

"No!"

"You had a fight with a guy at RanJon's," they insisted.

"I didn't have a fight."

For about fifteen minutes, the conversation went nowhere, although Atkinson told them about the fight between the girls. But they did not want to hear that. The questions were being fired at Atkinson by both detectives in shotgun-like fashion. They had a one-track mind, and they were being frustrated by his denials. He was left alone again for about five minutes, which must have seemed like an hour to a lonely and frightened suspect.

Once again, the door to the interview room opened. This time, three detectives entered the room. Morgan and Stevens were joined by Broesler who positioned himself behind Atkinson. The two homicide detectives moved their chairs "real close to him," and just stared right into his eyes.

"Come on, you had a fight with this guy Kenny." He knew who they meant by Kenny.

"Honest, I had no fight...I'm not lying." Atkinson wanted to go home.

"You had a fight...somebody provoked you." That said, and apparently dissatisfied with the responses they were getting, Rusty hit Atkinson hard in the chest, so hard, that he was knocked from his chair.

"Come on, if somebody provoked you, you're gonna fight." As Atkinson got back into his chair, he was pushed again by the soft-spoken, but angry, detective. Simultaneously, he was grabbed from behind by the neck. The questioning become more hostile and heated.

"Take a deep breath, and you're going to tell us what we want to hear! You're not going nowhere until you tell us what we want to hear. You better tell us what we want to hear, or you're going upstate forever. How would you like it if Kenny's brother put a bullet to your kid's head? You're not leaving. We'll tell them that you resisted arrest."

By now, even a street-wise, convicted felon like Anthony Atkinson was beginning to feel terrified and nervous. He believed that they meant business. He had seen the big guy (Broesler), he said, "beating people in the street." He'd tell them whatever they wanted to hear! He just wanted out of that room.

"You had a fight!"

"Yes," responded a compliant Atkinson. But just verbal assent was not enough to satisfy the inquisitors.

"Just sign that you had a fight with Kenny."

"I guess," were the strongest words Atkinson could muster from his quaking body.

He was then directed to remove all of his clothing. He was left alone and naked as the detectives left the room once again. In short order, they returned with a detective from the identification bureau, flash camera in hand. It was a degrading and humiliating experience for the man who was about to confess to robbery and murder. He was photographed head to feet, from the front, from behind, and from both sides, as naked as the day he was born.

According to the detectives, these "stand-up photos" were taken to "show wounds from a fight." The only flaw in that explanation was that Anthony Atkinson displayed no evidence of having been in a fight on his nude body. What they obtained were simply photographs of a fully developed, black male standing sheepishly in front of a group of fully clothed, white, male strangers, which conjures up the unhappy image of a antebellum black slave on an auction block being appraised by a group of white masters.

It was time to continue the "interview." Atkinson was still not being sufficiently cooperative. He wasn't giving them the answers that they needed, and that they wanted to hear. According to him, "The big officer" then came back into the room.

"We're going to pin stuff on you!" Threatening him with the back of his hand, Salt called him a "bastard."

"They're going to fuck you in the ass....They're going to kill you. You're going to go upstate...You're never going to see your kids!"

Detective Morgan—the one with the receding hairline—began to write. According to Atkinson, they never told him what exactly had happened to Kenny. The process continued until 4:00 in the morning.

"You had a fight with Kenny, and you beat him up," one of the officers said.

"Don't tell me you didn't do it," screamed the voice behind the finger that was pointed menacingly in his face.

"You're gonna sign this paper. Yeah, you did! You had a fight and you fucked him in his ass!"

Atkinson wanted desperately to be anywhere else in the world at that time. The outside world seemed to be slipping away from him. He must have wondered whether he would ever see his kids again. He so much wanted to leave—just to get out of that room, or at least to hear a friendly voice, any voice but the ones in that room. He asked to make a phone call.

"You're not leaving....You'll get your phone call, when you tell us what we want to hear....We can make this very bad for you. We'll beat the shit out of you and say you resisted arrest."

He thought to himself: "Instead of getting beat, I'll say I had a fight." But he continued to hedge on his answers. He was churning inside. One part of him was screaming at him to admit to anything to get out of that room, but, on the other hand, these guys had to have some real good reason for coming down this heavy on him. It was a lose-lose situation. The die had been cast. They put a paper in front of him which "he never read," and which was never read to him. One or the other would "point at places for him to sign."

"Just sign it right there! Don't give me that bullshit that you didn't do it....If you say you didn't do this, you're gonna get it. You did it! You're gonna sign this....We're gonna kick your ass....We'll beat the shit out of you right here!"

His body was quaking. The words on the paper were just a blur. But he did recognize the guy in the hospital picture that Salt held in front of him. It was Kenny. Salt directed him to write, and what to write. He wrote "the guy that got beat up." By now, he would write or say anything they wanted. They dictated and he wrote. He signed a little card. They even asked him to draw a map which they detailed for him, although he was familiar with the area of the map. After all, it was his neighborhood. The "blonde guy" (Stevens) told him to write on the map—"This is where I jumped the guy."

The detectives were placated. They had what they'd been looking for—a complete confession to what amounted to a felony murder. For the first time, he was told that he would be charged with murder. It was Salt who told him that the guy was dead. Atkinson was in deep shit! He had not only confessed to beating up somebody—he now knew that he had admitted to killing another human being. It was all beginning to sink in when the detectives left him alone in the room once again with his thoughts. He was visited by a detective sergeant whom he described as "overweight" and of "older age."

Veteran detective Sgt. William Pepper, the team supervisor, responded to headquarters at 10:30 pm. He was advised by telephone that his team had a suspect in custody who was admitting involvement in the McClaren murder. But he had not been in the interview room during the questioning. His first contact with Atkinson was at 11:00 pm when he checked on the prisoner's condition for the Prisoner Activity Log. Suffolk County homicide supervisors did not involve themselves in the give and take of the interview process. That was left in the hands of their subordinates.

After giving the detectives what they wanted, Atkinson was left alone in the interview room for about one and a half hours until 4:00 am, when Pepper claims that he sent Broesler into the room to discuss a sodomy case in the 3rd precinct. But neither Pepper nor Broesler knew any of the details of that case, nor was there a file at headquarters to which they could refer. Atkinson was allegedly questioned about a case which came to them by "word of mouth." Yet, that would be enough reason to place Broesler in the interview room although the McClaren investigation had long since ceased to be his case. Not only did they not get the confession they were looking for to the 3rd precinct sodomy, but, to their chagrin, Atkinson then recanted his written confession. He did not, he said, rob or assault Kenny, just as he hadn't sodomized a little girl in the 3rd precinct.

It was time for Sgt. Pepper to enter the room once again. He spent the next forty-five minutes alone with the admitted killer. According to Pepper, the conversation went like this:

"You're saying you're not involved. Why would you give a four page confession?"

"Because I was scared." He was not used to cops, he said. "I was scared—I didn't know what I was saying."

The theme was consistent. Anthony Atkinson insisted that he had no hand in the robbery and death of Kenneth McLaren, despite the written confession. He told the team supervisor that he had been forced to sign a confession. It mattered not. Sgt. Pepper was unfazed by this latest revelation. The lengthy conversation, alone with Atkinson, whatever its content, was not even sufficient cause to confront Morgan and Stevens about the manner in which the interview was conducted. After all, he said, they would simply deny any of Atkinson's accusations, so why bother. Although the sergeant took some notes for his own use, he did not think enough of the conversation to file a formal report. A confession to robbery and murder had been recanted less than two hours after it was obtained by his team, but he did not think it was important enough to memorialize the retraction in a written report.

According to Pepper, only the perpetrator would have known the details of what was contained in the confession. But he had to know that the investigating detectives had themselves theorized as to the grisly events which caused McLaren's demise. Even before talking to Anthony Atkinson, they had postulated a probable robbery, sodomy and murder scenario.

Earlier that night, assistant district attorney Matthew Parrella had also arrived at headquarters. He wanted to memorialize the confession on videotape after the fact, thus virtually assuring a conviction at trial. After being briefed by the detectives as to the details of the confession, he entered the interview room with Stevens who had been refused a videotaped interview after the alleged confession. According to the prosecutor, he was greeted by a smiling, "very relaxed and calm" suspect who simply didn't want to go on tape, but who, in any event, reaffirmed his guilt.

"I don't want to go on videotape. What do you need a video for? You have it all in my statement....I'll stand by my statement!"

"This is an opportunity to personalize your statement," Atkinson was told.

Atkinson was not buying the prosecutor's pitch. For some reason, the calm and relaxed person who was being accused of murder had ceased to be cooperative. He insisted upon making a telephone call. At 3:55 am, he finally got to call his mother. By that time, the detectives had, for all intents and purposes, made their case against him. But that was not enough!

Confessions, recantation and denials notwithstanding, the detectives had not finished with their charge. A pre-dawn trip was made to the crime scene. Atkinson, in handcuffs, was seated in the back of an unmarked police vehicle. Once again, the story of that trip is rife with controversy.

According to the detectives, it was Atkinson who directed them to the scene of his brutal assault of Kenneth McClaren. Not so, says Atkinson. He claims that it was the detectives who drove him to a wooded area where they told him that he had assaulted Kenny. Now, the previously cooperative suspect was in denial. For those denials he would pay a heavy price.

At about four o'clock in the morning, a time when most decent people are long since in their beds, they drove him to a wooded area off Cordello Avenue in Central Islip. With flashlights in hand, and Atkinson still in handcuffs, "the big guy" was punching him in his chest, and pounding him on his back.

"You told the sergeant you didn't do it, right?"

"But, I didn't do it!"

"You fuckin' liar, don't say you didn't do it. Show us where the spot is. Where did you stick the bottle in his ass?"

"Honest, I don't know where the spot is."

They were pulling him around in the dark, and banging him on his legs with a flashlight. His legs were getting weaker. He was tired. Didn't they ever get tired? He wanted to sleep. He couldn't stand. He just pointed to anywhere. Salt-the big guy- wanted to punish him right there for his transgressions.

"Let's just fuck him up a little bit," Salt said.

"No, we got to get him back."

"Don't you tell the judge that you didn't do this, or we're going to get you."

So, the compliant and confused accused said nothing at his arraignment later that day. Within a few short days he was indicted by the Suffolk County Grand Jury for the robbery and murder of Kenneth McClaren. But the grand jury would only hear about Atkinson's oral and written confession. They'd hear nothing about his denials. Although the assistant district attorney, Matthew Parrella, had allegedly been made aware of the subsequent denials by Sgt. Pepper, for some unknown reason, he chose not to present that information to the grand jury. At that point, no one on the prosecution team was buying the subsequent recantation. As far as they were concerned, the case was signed, sealed and delivered. So why confuse the grand jury with an irrelevant and incredible story? Since the district attorney was in complete control of the grand jury presentation, he did not see fit to clutter the record with such extraneous matter as the accused's denial of a murder. The question of the recantation would be left to the trial jury, if anyone ever learned about it!

Almost immediately after the case arrived on my calendar, I was advised by the prosecutor that he'd failed to notify the grand jury of the later denials. Despite the recantation, the prosecutor still had a complete confession to murder—in writing. So I set bail high enough to ensure that Anthony Atkinson would remain in custody while he awaited a trial. Since he couldn't afford to retain an attorney, Kevin Fox, a former assistant district attorney who had worked in my courtroom and was now in private practice, was assigned by me to represent Atkinson. I had great respect for Fox's integrity and his ability to represent an accused murderer.

When he agreed to accept this assignment, neither Fox nor I had any inkling of where this case was going to end. Although he gladly accepted the assignment, he was not particularly thrilled about being assigned a murder case where the people had a complete written confession. Anthony Atkinson's future seemed to be sealed by this document. It did not seem like anyone could help him. How wrong we both were in our assessment of this case!

In less than a week, the district attorney, James Catterson himself, supported by an entourage of assistants, was planted in my courtroom when the doors opened at 9:00 am. They had a real problem on their hands, and it was, they said, under investigation. Two teens, with no apparent connection to Anthony Atkinson, confessed on videotape to robbing and beating Kenneth McClaren on the very street where he had been found unconscious and dying the next morning. But unlike Atkinson, the two, Robert Sullivan and Raymond Martinez, were in possession of Kenny's jewelry. Anthony Atkinson might be innocent after all, but the district attorney was not ready to concede that possibility. From his point of view, such a concession was premature, especially since it probably meant that two homicide cops had coerced a confession from an innocent man. But he was graciously recommending that I release Atkinson on his own recognizance. Bail, even he felt, was no longer appropriate. Within a few short hours, Atkinson was a free man. But he still had the cloud of a felony murder charge over his head.

Kevin Fox lost no time in moving to dismiss the pending charge against his client after being provided with copies of the two videotapes by the prosecutor. Grudgingly, the district attorney conceded that the charge should be dismissed. It was left in my hands, but in order for a judge to dismiss an indictment without a hearing, both sides must agree to the facts. Kevin Fox argued that his client had been coerced by the investigating detectives. The district attorney consented to the dismissal, but he would not agree that the Atkinson confession was the result of police misconduct. Fox pulled no punches in his papers.

> The detectives approached the defendant, pushed him against their unmarked police car, searched him and then forced him into the back seat of the police vehicle....On 1/22/91 Mr. Atkinson submitted to a polygraph examination...and it was the examiner's opinion that he answered all questions truthfully. The only evidence connecting Mr. Atkinson to the crime is his "alleged" statement and that statement has been rendered completely incredible and unreliable in light of the written and video taped statements from Robert Sullivan and Juan Martinez....Mr. Atkinson allegedly told the police that he took four rings from the victims hands. However, the truth is that Robert Sullivan and Juan Martinez actually took the four rings from the victim's hands and at least three of those rings were recovered from Martinez, Sullivan and their girl friends....In sum it seems quite apparent that the "alleged" statements of Anthony Atkinson taken by the police contain gross fabrications and inconsistencies which render it completely worthless and devoid of any evidentiary value. None of the incriminating statements in Mr. Atkinson's "alleged" written statement are supported by any physical evidence and in fact are completely contradicted by all other evidence in the case...."[2]

But the district attorney 's office would accept none of this. "Initially, we would note our disagreement with defendant's recitation of the facts of the case at bar. We do not agree that defendant was 'pushed-up against' or 'forced into the back seat' of a police car...that he was 'interrogated over a prolonged [3 1/2 hour] period'...or that his statement contains 'apparent' and 'gross fabrications'...."[3]

Once again it was necessary to conduct a hearing which would expose blatant misconduct by members of the homicide squad. Again I was placed in the unfortunate position of having to publicly expose improper police conduct. It had been unusually peaceful for several months, but the lines were drawn anew. I privately dreaded the possibility of what was about to occur. It was my worst nightmare all over again! Once again, in the words of the new district attorney, if I did the right thing I would resume the roll of "cop basher." The district attorney wanted desperately to avoid this hearing. The outcome was predictable. He had to know that once again there had been the grossest form of police misconduct at the highest level of law enforcement, and that such misconduct, if it became a matter of public knowledge, would reignite the fires of controversy.

For two long weeks in June 1991, six months after the untimely death of Kenneth McLaren, I listened to the very believable, but uncorroborated, story of Anthony Atkinson, and the incredible and outrageous testimony of ADA Parrella, detectives Pepper, Morgan, Stevens and Broesler. Six years later, I was revisiting ancient history. It was Diaz and Corso all over again, but this time there was a smoking gun! We had the videotaped confessions of Sullivan and Martinez.

It was readily apparent that the case against Anthony Atkinson was built on sand. He had been anointed by the police as the culprit, and there were no other suspects to consider until Martinez and Sullivan happened along. Other than the police, only the murderer was aware of the gory details of the crime. In their eyes Atkinson had the motive, the opportunity and the appropriate sociopathic profile to commit this horrible murder.

Atkinson, they presumed, saw McLaren flashing his money in the bar. Both Annie and Angela were suspicious of him. He was on parole for the sodomy of two boys. He had been last seen with a brown beer bottle in his hand, and a brown beer bottle with fecal matter was recovered at the scene.

There was trauma to the victim's rectum. All they needed was a confession—oral, written or otherwise, and the case was closed. It was going to be that easy.

In the end, there was never any physical evidence to connect the defendant to the crime. The lab could not determine the origin of the fecal material. Angela denied that she had ever told the police that she had left Atkinson with a beer bottle in his hand. In fact, she testified that she was "high" when Broesler took a written statement from her. There was no evidence of human urine on Kenny when he had been removed to the hospital emergency room, although the detectives claimed that Atkinson had said that he had "pissed" on an unconscious McLaren!

During the hearing I learned for the first time that the Atkinson recantation and denials were never made public until five days after the police learned that Kenneth McLaren's gold nugget ring was given to a girl named Jessica by her boyfriend who had no connection to Anthony Atkinson. Sgt. Pepper, who had listened to Atkinson's denials, filed no written report, and there was no mention of it on the Prisoner Activity Report. But it was claimed that he had advised the assistant district attorney Parrella of the recantation by telephone on the day of Atkinson's arraignment. Yet there was no mention of it to the arraigning judge who set bail in the amount of $1,000,000 at the request of the prosecutor, nor was the grand jury told about his immediate denials.

The first mention of the recantation was made to me after the police and the district attorney were aware that they had a serious problem with this prosecution and the Atkinson confession. Two other persons might have committed that brutal assault, and they were probably in possession of the missing jewelry. The investigating detectives had been hoisted on their own petard. It was time to minimize the losses, if that was at all possible.

I could not accept the incredible testimony of Lester Stevens, the lead detective, that never in his "wildest imagination" did he believe that the victim had been sodomized, despite the fact that there'd been trauma to his rectum and a rape kit was turned over to the attending nurse by detective Broesler. It was also impossible to believe that Broesler didn't know that Atkinson was on parole, although he did know that he'd been sentenced to six years for sodomy. Nor would I buy the story that Broesler was not involved in the interrogation, although he remained in police headquarters from 8:30 pm until 5:30 the next morning, and traveled with them back to the scene in the pre-dawn hours of December 15. I would not be convinced that Broesler only went into the interview room for no more than five minutes to discuss a 3rd Squad sodomy investigation of which he had no details, and for which there was no file. I was also deeply troubled by the preparation of retroactive reports by Stevens and Morgan after the Sullivan and Martinez confessions to fill in gaps in their investigation concerning events and interviews which occurred prior to these confessions. They had been too busy in school!

But the proverbial smoking gun came in the form of the videotaped confession of Robert Sullivan. This was indisputable evidence of police misconduct. At 4:20 am, in the morning of January 15, 1991, one month to the day after the assault on Kenneth McLaren, Sullivan was confessing his mortal sins to an assistant district attorney.

"He's the guy we had the fight with," Sullivan said. "That's the ring that I took from the guy after we beat him up [being shown a photograph of Kenneth McLaren in his black baseball cap, smiling from behind a crystal champagne glass]. I walked up to him and we started fighting...we beat him up and we took his rings....We beat him up at the corner of St. John's and Cordello [where Kenny was found unconscious]. The guy got up and walked across the street....He pushed me so I hit him twice....I hit him in the jaw...twice....He fell to the ground....I started kicking him all around...in the stomach area...kicked him in the face...my cousin was kicking him in the chest, in the legs, in the head....He was groaning...ugh....We kicked him until we thought he had enough...until he was unconscious...we kept hitting him....I grabbed him by the back of his pants...and his pants came down so you could see half of his rear end....I moved him because he was in the middle of the road. I didn't want the guy to get hit by a car while he was unconscious....The guy got up and stumbled across the street...."

"You moved the body?" asked an incredulous assistant district attorney.

"We took off the rings...four. We each took two rings....We were giggling because we could see half his butt....We talked about what we just did...he got knocked down and we started stomping him...."[4]

In a twenty-one page decision on July 11, 1991, the case against Anthony Atkinson came to a crashing halt. I dismissed the indictment in a purposeful scathing verbal rebuke to the police and prosecution team. It gave me an opportunity to vent some of my pent-up feelings about certain Suffolk County homicide investigations:

> In short, the investigating detectives have woven an illusory web in which they themselves have become entangled, in an effort to ensnare Anthony Atkinson, the fabric of which is composed of conjured hypotheses, allegations and facts which cannot stand the test of objectivity, logic and common everyday experience. They have created an environment where lead balls bounce, elephants fly and fairies reign supreme. The case against Anthony Atkinson is not based upon reality and fact, and thus cannot be verified by truth and logic....It has been two years since the State Commission of Investigations rendered its final report in the investigation of the Suffolk County District Attorney's Office and Police Department. Two years is not very long when measured against a lifetime, and virtually microscopic when measured against the history of human experience. Thus, it is both profoundly disturbing and distressing that with the passage of such a short period of time, given the impact of that report upon the criminal justice system of this county, that there would be members of the police department and the district attorney's office who have either forgotten the lessons of that investigation, or who have ignored or failed to heed to them. It is even more distressing to realize that because of the manner in which this particular case has been handled by the investigating detectives, two persons, who may very well be guilty of felony murder, have yet to be indicted, or even arrested, despite their confessions, for the brutal assault and robbery of Kenneth McLaren. Justice demands more from those who are appointed to uphold and enforce the law.[5]

Needless to say, the district attorney was fuming over this decision. Once again, I was under attack by a district attorney who chose to publicly attack the messenger and blindly defend improper police conduct. Under a byline captioned "Suffolk police, DA faulted," *Newsday* reported, "Catterson said Namm is still fighting past battles, adding: 'He apparently wants to relive his role as the last honest man in Suffolk County, and I seriously dispute that.'"[6]

Despite the public protestations and mean-spirited personal attack of James Catterson, the police department began an internal affairs investigation of the circumstances surrounding the Atkinson affair. The commissioner selected his highly respected subordinate, chief inspector Joseph Monteith, to conduct the investigation. While his probe lasted for several months, and his findings will never be made public, what is known is that the three key homicide detectives, Pepper, Morgan and Stevens, were quietly transferred out of the homicide squad, and two of them, Sgt. Pepper and Det. Morgan, subsequently handed in their retirement papers.

But there was a much more disastrous result from the stiff-necked attitude which was adopted by the office of the district attorney. That office persisted in the public position that Anthony Atkinson was responsible for the death of Kenneth McLaren. Tragically, it took more than one year and much editorial pressure from the media before they took any action to indict either Sullivan or Martinez. For some unknown reason, a decision was made to only present the Sullivan confession to a grand jury, and to seek only an indictment for robbery. The presentation to the grand jury came more than one year after his confession to assault and robbery. There would be no felony murder presentation. To do so would be to admit that there had been police misconduct, or that the district attorney's theory as to how Kenny met his untimely fate was erroneous.

The grand jury which is the representative body of the people of Suffolk County was never advised that Kenneth McLaren did not survive the brutal beating which he sustained that fateful morning. It appears that the prosecution team bent over backwards to insure that no grand juror would even think to question what happened to him as a result of a merciless beating and stomping. So an obviously well-prepped uniformed police officer testified: "We observed a subject that we later identified as Kenneth McLaren, lying in a fetal position on his side, facing west on the southwest corner of Cordello Avenue and St. John Street. Upon closer looking at him we observed he had trauma and contusions to the head and face areas, including bleeding from his mouth and his nose and from the eye area, but he was breathing."[7]

After his indictment, Robert Sullivan was brought back from a state correctional facility to face the robbery charge. By the grace of the district attorney's office, while still out on the street after confessing to beating and robbing Kenneth McLaren and leaving him to die on a Central Islip street, he had been quietly convicted of stalking another RanJon's patron and robbing him. The county court judge before whom he took a plea to the robbery charge was never even made aware of Sullivan's known involvement in the Atkinson murder. There was no charge pending at that time despite his written and oral confession. Had the Suffolk County district attorney not been so involved in protecting the reputation of overzealous detectives, there would have been at least one less robbery on the streets of Central Islip in 1991, and someone would have paid for the senseless death of Kenneth McLaren. In 1991, protecting the reputation of the police by the office of the district attorney seemed to be more important than protecting the citizens of Central Islip!

TWENTY-FOUR

"This Is Not Your Year, Stuart."

—Dominic Baranello, County Democratic Chairman

S OMEWHERE IN A DARKENED HOUSE HUNDREDS of miles away from Suffolk County, in a place where people speak in slow drawls, well worn black judicial robes hang limply in a cedar storage closet alongside a rumpled set of outdated Army fatigues emblazoned with a Ranger insignia and cloth lieutenant's bars. They share the space with a threadbare City College varsity jacket with the word "LACROSSE" embroidered on the sleeve and a blue cotton softball uniform from a lost generation with the words "17th Infantry Regiment" across the chest. In the quiet darkness of that closet, hanging in a zippered plastic bag, is a never used, musty, well-pressed, midnight blue, wool worsted three-piece suit—the immediately recognizable uniform of an aging member of the legal profession.

The photographs of Roy Campanella, Pee Wee Reese, Dale Hunter, Colin Powell and other luminaries of recent past generations, together with the fading photos of a proud father and grandfather, a smiling mother and grandmother, and a happy family of children and grandchildren, no longer peer down from the antiseptic walls of the chambers behind Courtroom 19 of the Criminal Courts Building in Riverhead, New York.

In July 1992, six months before my term of office expired, my former partner and friend, the man whom I'd called "my brother," Dominic Baranello, county Democratic chairman, was party to a bi-partisan conspiracy to deprive

me of renomination. In a back room, far away from the public eye, after the
county committee members of both major political parties deferred to their
respective executive committees, the Republican party, with the assistance
of my friend, ensured that I would no longer be a thorn in the side of their
district attorney or their police commissioner. They would never again suffer
embarrassment at the hands of a maverick judge who did not play by the
rules as they understood them to be in Suffolk County. The "cop basher"
would be gone. The price the Republicans paid was a heavy one: three new
Democratic judges would be cross-endorsed for the County Court, and the
Republicans would give one Family Court position to a Democrat. As part
of the package, the Democratic supervisor of the town of Babylon, who was
initially found unqualified for the judiciary by the Bar Association's screening
committee, was to become a county court judge (my vacancy.)

It was so important to remove me from the bench and to return the
leadership of the town of Babylon to the Republican fold that the
Republicans, who in 1992 could easily have elected one of their own to each
of these judicial offices, gave away four county judgeships. It was a deal
which was unprecedented in Suffolk political history. In order to qualify one
of the keystones of the package, the Democratic supervisor of Babylon, a
group of judges and former judges, including now supreme court justice
and former district attorney Patrick Henry, was shamelessly paraded by the
two political parties before the judiciary committee on his behalf. The die
was cast, and the ambitious, but cowardly judiciary committee members
had to know that they had no choice. This package deal was very important
to the powerful political leaders. So, Arthur Pitts, previously found
unqualified, was thereafter found qualified to serve as a judge of the highest
felony court by the same group which only days earlier had found him
unqualified for that very office.

The people of Suffolk County who only gave lip service to caring about
the criminal justice system were effectively disenfranchised by arrogant
political leaders and gutless attorneys who had chosen to bite the bullet.
They were prepared to accept a few days of negative media attention and an
unfavorable editorial or two in order to achieve a result which probably had
its genesis on the first day that I began to publicly criticize the district

attorney and members of the homicide squad in 1985. It was, as one local newspaper stated in its lead editorial, "a black day for the judiciary."[1]

It had taken seven long and painful years to insure that Judge Stuart Namm did not fit "the package."[2] It was, as Dominic Baranello said to me, just not my year.

****

July 7, 1992 was a red-letter day for me. I'd been hearing rumors for weeks that the Democratic and Republican leadership were attempting to negotiate a cross-endorsement deal. I was realistic enough to know that the Republican leadership would never support my candidacy. But my former law partner was still the county Democratic leader. I hoped that some principled blood still flowed through his aging political arteries, but I wasn't optimistic. Although he and I had very little communication in recent months, I had formally advised him by mail of my desire to seek renomination.

When he failed to acknowledge receipt of that communication, I contacted Dominic by telephone. The county Bar Association suggested that I appear before their screening committee, a necessary formality prior to nomination. But I had already heard rumors that I was going to be dumped from the ticket. I knew that I would have to be found qualified for reelection by the bar association, and then suffer the public humiliation of not being renominated by my own party. I expressed these feelings to the leader, my friend, and I was told to do nothing. He said that no commitments had been made, and that I would hear from him on the following Monday.

Three weeks passed. I heard nothing but more courthouse rumors, and they were not good. The Republicans wanted to unseat the Democratic supervisor of the town of Babylon. The Democrats likewise wanted him out. He had not been cooperative in the patronage department. So they would make him a county court judge. But he was found unqualified by the screening committee of the bar association. There was a fly in the ointment! The political parties decided to pull out all the stops in order to cement the bi-partisan deal. Justice Patrick Henry, former district attorney, and Paul D'Amaro, former court of claims judge and very close personal friend of the Democrat's leader, appeared before the committee to seek a reversal of their original finding. The candidate was represented by Thomas Spota—attorney for the Suffolk County detectives association.

The political leaders got their wish. The deal was complete. Howard Pitts was now qualified to sit as a county court judge, and I would be a private citizen on January 1. The boys in the back room had to be elated. They had rid themselves of two unwanted albatrosses—Judge Namm and the Democratic supervisor of Babylon. When I got wind of the news I immediately called my former partner.

"Dominic, I've heard rumors that I have been dumped from the democratic ticket," I said. He replied: "This is not your year, Stuart."

"I want to thank you," I sarcastically responded. "I hope you want to thank me for the ten years which I gave you as a judge."

With those last words, the click of the receiver resonated in my ear. I immediately called again. I had more to say. He was not going to be allowed the final word!

"Dominic, we were partners for ten years, and I don't deserve this kind of shabby treatment. You should've called me to tell me what took place. I didn't have to hear about it through courthouse rumors." I was incensed by his lack of even minimal common decency.

"Goodbye, Stuart!" were the last two words that I heard from my friend of twenty-six years, the man who'd been like a brother to me. Political expediency had won out! (Dominic has been peacefully in his grave for several years now.)

With those last words uttered to me by my former law partner in angry and sarcastic exchange, sixteen stormy years as a judge were brought to an ignominious conclusion. I was receiving payment in full from the political system for having honestly carried out the job to which I had been elected by the people of Suffolk County. Yet the people could not care less. They did not know it, but in no small measure they too were being paid back by the political leaders for their apathy and ignorance.

To an irate media, Dominic gave the lame and disingenuous excuse that he thought that I was moving to North Carolina and that I was not interested in running for re-election. Privately, in an angry rage over their open support for my candidacy, he told Paul Gianelli, a former Democratic candidate for district attorney, and John Grossman, the former Southampton Democratic town leader, that Stuart Namm had "done shit for the Democratic party." The fact that a sitting judge is ethically bound to stay out of partisan politics was never even a consideration in the rush to terminate my judicial career, by a "great" political leader, who had even become the New York state Democratic chairman while I was still on the bench.

Postlogue

THE EARLY MORNING MIST HAS SETTLED OVER the Carolina coastal marsh. The rising sun is still hidden behind the morning clouds. A female river otter and her young brood slide gracefully through the dark, muddy waters. The belted kingfisher trills his familiar song as he dives into the schools of mud minnows and baby spot. The unmistakable whistles of a pair of ospreys hovering overhead compete with the sounds of the bob white quail and the Carolina wren. All is peaceful on the wetland which still teems with wildlife.

Almost due north, hundreds of miles away in Suffolk County, the massive white crucifix of St. Charles Hospital overlooking Port Jefferson harbor will soon be illuminated by the rays of the early morning sun. The first Port Jefferson-to-Bridgeport ferry will quietly glide out of its harbor slip towards the open sound past the spacious homes of Belle Terre and the shadows of the huge Lilco smokestacks.

Small children will again play and chase one another as they frolic innocently on the grounds of the Dogwood Elementary School in Smithtown. They are much too young to know that once, long before they were born, another happy little boy rode his bicycle to that school for the last time before suffering a gruesome death at the hands of four local teenagers, little different from their older brothers.

The first commuter train will once again roll out of the yard at Port Jefferson Station towards the manmade canyons of the Big Apple. Bleary eyed commuters, coffee container in hand and daily newspaper under arm, barely awake on the platform, unhappily await the arrival of another crowded commute at the beginning of a long day. Among their number may be a young man with the fading memory of a nightmarish scene in a basement just a few short blocks away which left him motherless and alone.

The daily stream of automobiles, headlights still brightening the early morning haze, is rapidly filling the asphalt lanes of the "Expressway" as it winds its way westward, past communities with names like Central Islip, Brentwood and Dix Hills. They travel from the bedroom communities of Suffolk County towards the modern industrial parks and office complexes that smother the once beautiful and pristine Long Island.

The small ferry from Sayville to the Fire Island National Seashore will once more be filled with casually dressed passengers breathing the fresh, saltwater air of the Great South Bay as they escape the crowded city streets.

Somewhere in this peaceful setting, in a still darkened bedroom, or on a littered lot overgrown with scrub oak and twisted pine trees, or on a quiet roadway, a once thinking and breathing human being may be lying lifeless, in a pool of blood, the violent victim of another, who was either uncontrollably angry, desperate, drug-crazed, insane or intoxicated.

In a few short minutes, the 911 emergency operator at police headquarters in Yaphank will be responding to the anguished voice of a person whose life will never be the same after happening upon that chilling and unforgettable scene.

Elsewhere in a typical upper middle class home in Suffolk, a person, almost always a man, who has been vested with great judicial power by the even more powerful back-room politicians, will soon be peering into a bathroom mirror as he shaves the early morning stubble from his droopy jowls. He will step into his trousers, one leg at a time, like his less powerful neighbors. But unlike the homicide detective who has been roused from his peaceful sleep by the annoying ring of a portable telephone, he will have the luxury of poring over the early morning edition of *The New York Times* or The *Wall Street Journal* at the breakfast table in the comfort of his upper middle class kitchen in the company of his wife who is probably also about to scurry off to her own mundane occupation.

There are fourteen or fifteen other citizens in the county, who, like the judge, are about to begin their daily routine. Most have never given any thought to the possibility that since they were registered to vote or licensed to drive, they too will soon be vested with judicial power of a sort. They will be called upon to judge another faceless person who even now may be spilling his guts over a cold cup of coffee, with the stub of a lighted cigarette in hand. More likely than not, he will be guilty of an unspeakably brutal act against one of their neighbors.

He will almost certainly be alone with two or three unshaven, rumpled, sometimes agitated, sometimes calm, but always accusative, hardened and experienced homicide detectives. They will be alone together for hours in the small 8 x 12 interview room at homicide squad headquarters in Yaphank.

Those citizens and their anointed judicial representative, who each morning must confront his conscience in a foggy bathroom mirror, will someday have to decide the fate of that wretched soul. But for now he finds himself, willingly or otherwise, behind closed doors, isolated, friendless, without counsel, fighting sleep, stomach empty and growling, lips parched, in a small barren room, devoid of furniture and telephone except for an old desk, a few gray metal chairs and some old file cabinets.

These citizens, like that sometimes imperious figure who each day must don black judicial robes before ascending to his official duties, will have to dispassionately and objectively decide whether the confession, which is almost always the product of that interview, often given orally without recorded verification, under circumstances that would break the resolve of even the strongest person, was given voluntarily to his captors. They will be bound to do so even though their experience, instincts, intuition and deepest human emotions tell them that they have been presented with a despicable person, undeserving of compassion or consideration—a James Diaz or a Peter Corso!

In their collective hearts they will want to believe that the police very rarely arrest an innocent person for homicide. But if they depend upon their emotions alone, their ultimate decision may turn out to be dreadfully wrong and a second human tragedy may compound the already completed and irreversible tragedy which has gathered them together in the foreign atmosphere of a stuffy jury room away from the routine of their everyday affairs.

Still the jurors will not be carrying the baggage of the professional to whom they must look for guidance and advice. Too often he will be looking over his shoulder at the persons who were responsible for his elevation to public office—the political leaders—who are responsible to nobody but the party faithful. And often, not even to them. The judge must also look ahead to the day when once again he will have to kowtow to them and pander to a weary electorate to ensure his return to his very comfortable, powerful office for another several years.

He too will be called upon to decide the fate of that pitiful soul, knowing full well that, unlike the nameless jurors, unless he maintains a low profile his every action will be taken in a fish bowl, in full view of the media, the survivors of the victim and an aroused community. Every one of his decisions will be closely followed by the police and the office of the district attorney. If those decisions do not conform to their concept of justice, he will be judged a renegade within the justice system. Like the common criminal, he will become the enemy!

Unlike the jurors, he is supposed to be the product of years of education and experience. He may have listened to thousands of hours of sworn testimony by police officers and ordinary persons. His powers of observation and ability to make the correct decision are presumed to have been honed to a fine edge by his experience and wisdom. But those powers will sadly be tempered by the desire to remain in public office, and on the side of the angels—the most vocal members of the criminal justice community. It may no less be tempered by the desire to curry favor with the members of the bar from whom, unless he is a person of substantial wealth, he will need to solicit financial support each time that he seeks re-election. Once those powers have been so tempered—or tampered with—the fate and rights of the accused person may be seriously affected, whether he is guilty or not.

An even more powerful and more political figure will shortly be driven to his Hauppauge headquarters by a well armed police officer in civilian clothes. The district attorney of Suffolk County, unless the victim was someone of prominence, will have enjoyed a full night's sleep before returning to his spacious office adorned with the photographs of his illustrious political career. Like most elected and politically appointed judges today, he is the product of a political system which rewards party loyalty and longevity more often then ability and principle. He is a political animal who depends upon the political system every four years for his very survival in public office. He must depend upon the support of the organized law enforcement community as well as the members of the legal profession to place his message of law and order before the electorate. He must retain that law and order image throughout the course of his administration, and an acquittal in a high profile criminal case, in these days of extensive media coverage of the courtroom, will serve to tarnish that image. This is especially true where that acquittal may be the result of police or prosecutorial misconduct. It is then that a real conflict will arise between the chief prosecutor's need to survive and the principles and laws which he is sworn to uphold.

In Suffolk County, New York, a microcosm of middle America, where the law enforcement community was out of control in the prosecution of high profile homicide cases, two successive district attorneys unashamedly publicly defended the actions of rogue cops who would undermine the very foundations upon which our system of justice has been built. To publicly criticize police and prosecutorial misconduct, where that was in order, was to invite the wrath of the people's elected representatives. In the words of the district attorney, it made me a "cop-basher." It made me a renegade judge, a lonesome maverick.

So long as one who is willing to take a stand and blow the whistle against injustice is treated within the system as a maverick and a renegade, and so long as the accuser becomes the accused, the system of "criminal injustice" will continue to flourish in this land, and no one of us will be safe from its accusatory finger!

Epilogue

DOES THE SYSTEM OF "CRIMINAL INJUSTICE" CONTINUE to function in Suffolk County? Has anything really changed in the place Dean Trager called the "Wild West?" Almost two years after I quietly retired to a place over 700 miles away from the chaos and turmoil of a Riverhead courtroom, I continued to receive mail and calls from people in Suffolk County who are desperately seeking my help-help which I am helpless to provide.

On July 25 and August 1, 1993, I received the following messages on my telephone answering machine from a local businessman whom I had not seen for many years. Whether they are the ramblings of a crazed and paranoid mind or the outcry of an ordinary citizen with legitimate grievances against a still corrupt system of justice, I will never know. For all intents and purposes, I have been rendered as impotent as a eunuch!

> JULY 25, 1993: Judge, this is_____in Lake Ronkonkoma again. I'm sorry to bother you. But I believe that I'm either going to be exterminated tonight or tomorrow before I can make another call simply because I have the police in a corner now, and there's two younger patrolmen and two senior officers that are in deep trouble and they're cornered like a rat, and all I have is...all the information. The only person that I have with any credibility...in other words, who will vouch for my credibility to any degree is you. My own wife is standing here and telling me...I need help! If you can call the Justice Department. I've tried to call [Congressman] George Hochbreuckner's number—two numbers. He doesn't have an answering machine. Please help me!

AUGUST 1, 1993: Judge Stuart Namm, I hate to bother you. This is_____in Lake Ronkonkoma again. I need your help! I have found the bottom. I've come to the conclusion on the corruption in Suffolk County. It's as big as Nathan Hale when he said....It's the biggest history story since Nathan Hale! I'm not looking for any credit or anything like that for this here. I may be shot tonight! I need the Justice Department! I need the F.B.I. and there'll probably have to be federal troops. I have found the corruption in Suffolk County after fourteen years of police brutality! I need to speak to someone. There's evidence spread out all over the place in case I'm shot. Somebody has to help! I wrote out a check to Ross Perot—United We Stand America—in the event of my death just so that somebody will investigate what I have discovered. Judge, I know that you had great faith in me at that time, and then maybe you investigated and found I was under indictment. That was a provoked incident to draw me out and to shame me. Those charges were dismissed for insufficiency after a policeman had witnessed the supposed incident. Please help! Please! Please! Please! For the sake of the United States and Old Glory and the constitution which doesn't operate in Suffolk County and doesn't function. Thank you. Thank you very much! I'm on the roof. I won't be able to respond to your calls. I didn't get the recorder hooked up. I've been harassed and I haven't been sleeping at all. Please help, Judge! I am one of those ordinary people that got stuck with an extraordinary thing!

In the solitude of my 10'x10' office, with only the sound of a computer purring in my ears, after conveying his message to the local F.B.I., I couldn't help but sympathize with his anguished cries for help. But I too am no more than an ordinary person, who, for some ungodly reason, God chose an extraordinary, but probably impossible, mission!

Conclusion

W HY PUBLISH A MANUSCRIPT WHICH WAS FIRST completed over twenty-five years ago? That is the question I have asked myself time and time again since leaving Suffolk County, New York, more that twenty years ago. Each time, the same answer comes back to me. Over the years since I left New York, I have received unsolicited messages from friends, from long-time supporters whom I have never met, members of the media seeking my opinion on matters that I have never been involved in; and each time, the message is clear: "Nothing has really changed in Suffolk County criminal justice. Only the faces have changed!"

Thus, if this continues to be so, as I have been told time and time again, the need to render my opinion based upon my experience in a place which I called my home for over twenty-five years is something which I am compelled to do.

I have concluded for years now that nothing will ever change in a court system which encourages turning the other cheek to prosecutorial corruption in places like Suffolk County until we change our method of selecting judges in places like New York state, which still relies on the election of most of the trial judges. It is politics and money that are the corrupting forces in our system of selecting judges, especially trial judges. When it is the political leaders who choose our judicial candidates, those prospective judges are rarely chosen on the basis of their legal experience and philosophies, but on what they have done for their political party and, by extension, its leader; and who can raise the most money to spend on campaign expenses. Thus, more often than not, the candidate is not beholden to the people and the law, as he or she has to look over his or her shoulder to the next election, and to the people who were responsible for getting them elected or reelected.

Many years ago, before I was a judge, an elected judge whom I had never met before, came up to me when I was running for a seat on the local Board of Education and asked me why he had never seen me at the meetings of the Republican Party. My simple answer was, "Because I am not a Republican." His instant retort was: "Well, none of us were Republicans before we came to Suffolk County!" There is a moral to that story, but I have yet to figure it out!

****

There have been several attempts to make changes in the manner that most trial judges are selected in New York State. One such attempt was by the New York State Commission on Government Integrity.

> From its inception on April 21, 1987, until the conclusion of its work on September 18, 1990, the New York State Commission on Government Integrity issued 20 reports recommending reforms in the areas of government ethics....[1]

In its introduction, the report entitled "Becoming a Judge: Report on the Failings of Judicial Elections in New York State" states the following: "The Commission has found that New York State fails to choose its judges in the manner that best fosters the presence of these attributes on the bench. Indeed, some methods of judicial selection-namely, judicial elections, are so captive to the interests of political party organizations that they clash with the ideal of an independent and non-partisan judiciary. By subordinating judicial values to political favoritism and party loyalty, judicial elections invite undue influence over judges and threaten public confidence in the integrity of the judicial system."[2]

Prior to the issuance of its report in book form, two prominent members of the committee on the judiciary, John D. Feerick, Chairman of the New York State Commission on Government Integrity and the then Dean of

Fordham Law School, and Cyrus Vance, then one of the commissioners of the Commission on Government Integrity, and secretary of state under President Jimmy Carter from 1977-1980, wrote a "Report" on the work of the Commission for the *Pace Law Review*, Spring 1989 edition, Volume 9, Number 2, where they listed on the final page all of the witnesses who had testified before the Commission on two days in March 1988. Among the fifteen witnesses from the judiciary, like myself, who were listed were Sol Wachtler, the then chief judge of the State of New York, Malcolm Wilson, former governor of the State of New York, and Robert Kaufman, then president of the Association of the Bar of the City of New York.[3]

They concluded, as did the Commission on Government Integrity, that there was a conflict between partisan politics and judicial values, and they concluded that "the selection of judges should be removed as much as possible from the control of political parties," and that "to achieve this result, judicial elections should be eliminated." They then went on to recommend "an appointive method for the selection of Supreme Court justices and judges of courts of limited jurisdiction," like the District and County Courts of Suffolk County, the two courts in which I served for almost seventeen years.[4]

Likewise, the Commission on Government Integrity, of which Dean John D. Feerick, was the chairman, and Secy. Cyrus Vance was one of the commissioners, in its report entitled "Becoming a Judge: Report on the Failings of Judicial Elections in New York State," recommended "amending the New York State Constitution to provide for an appointive system for the selection of all Supreme Court justices and judges of courts of limited jurisdiction."[5]

While there have been many suggestions to change the selection of judges from an elective system, dominated by the political parities and their bosses, there have been those like Judge Jonathan Lippman, the Chief Administrative Judge of all New York Courts in 2005 who, at the Public Policy Forum on "Court Reform in New York State," speaking before the Rockefeller Institute of Government, opined in the section entitled "Judicial Elections" that "My own view, to be quite direct, is that our mixed system of elected and appointed judges has served us well. It has produced a first-class judiciary-*aberrational conduct by a very few notwithstanding* [Italics added]. But what is unmistakably true, regardless of one's view, is that the endless debates do not offer the slightest promise of legislative willingness to change the State's method of selecting judges anytime soon."[6]

For me, it was interesting to note that Judge Lippman, as he spoke, held the title of Chief Administrative Judge of all of the New York State Courts, the title which Judge Robert J. Sise held for the courts outside of the City of New York when he recited his parable in my chambers of the judge who found himself "on the wrong side of the street," for my personal benefit! I ask myself: "Do we ever learn?" Some fifteen years after the fact, when naught had been accomplished in New York State about the selection of trial judges, when, according to Judge Lippman, forty-two other states had already gone to another system, other than the election of judges, John Feerick, the former Dean of Fordham Law School, and former chairman of the aforesaid Commission on Government Integrity and co-author of the article in the *Pace Law Review,* was appointed once again to chair a "Commission to Promote Public Confidence in Judicial Elections."

While a very distinguished group of citizens, including Patricia Salkin, Esq., the Associate Dean and Director of the Government Law Center of Albany Law School, as Vice Chair, no changes were recommended or made in the selection and election of judges, other than the system which was already in place when the commission began its work. The commission, after extensive research and hearings, found "that public confidence in judicial elections is foundering." It also found that "Testimony at the public hearings overwhelmingly expressed concern over the current judicial election system's effect on public confidence. The judicial survey and the public opinion poll revealed widespread concern regarding judges' impartiality and independence under the current system."[7]

While the Commission recommended many means to "promote ethical campaign activity," and recommended "retention elections," and many other well intentioned changes to the current system, and more importantly, the system that existed in Suffolk County when I was stripped of my robes for having done what any decent judge should have done, to my knowledge the method of selecting judges in most of the trial courts in the State of New

York, including Suffolk County, remains unchanged. Politics is the means by which one becomes a judge, and remains on the bench, until promotion or retirement.

Nothing will ever really change in the Suffolk County judiciary in Suffolk County, New York, or in any other place in New York State where judicial candidates are selected by the political parties, run by their respective political leaders, who seek out the lawyers who have done the most politically for his or her respective party, or who are willing to pay and spend the most to live out their working lives behind the bench in black robes. Prospective judicial candidates, be they local, county or statewide, need to be selected by the Governor, the County Executive or Mayor, with the support of a committee of distinguished lawyers, or perhaps even some lay persons, recommended by the respective professional bar associations, who will be required to pass on the candidate's real qualifications to don the black robes.

I have seen and lived through both of these systems, and I am living proof to the fact that this will be the closest way to achieve an independent judiciary free from political pressures, and free from fear that if he or she renders opinions which are antithetic to one or another of the political parties, or the powerful political forces, he or she will not have to pay a price at the next election day for doing the right thing. That judge should never again have to be beholden to a political party for reelection. In the last year of his or her term of office, his or her name should be put before the electorate unopposed, without identification of political affiliation, to be retained or removed from office. I could even see a system where there is no election, and that decision will be made once again by the commission which recommended the judge in the first instance.

I am convinced that if my now deceased law partner, the Democratic County chairman of the Suffolk County Democratic Party, and one time State Democratic chairman had even thought for a moment in 1975 that I could have been elected a Judge of the District Court of Suffolk County, I would never have been asked to run by his judicial selection committee for the District Court judgeship from the Town of Brookhaven, a known bastion of conservative voters who had always voted Republican. For this is the same shrewd politician, when he needed to elect a Democratic County

Executive while I was in the District Court, "accidentally" failed to give the names of prospective Supreme Court Justice candidates to the Board of Elections, so that the Democratic candidate for County Executive would then be at the top of the ticket, and be elected, as he was. Shrewd political leaders are not necessarily the best judges of who should don the black robes.

As he said to me often, as I sought to return to the bench after losing my bid for reelection, when a lawyer is elected to a judgeship, the party loses a worker, and there is always a long line of lawyers waiting to fill that vacancy. Under the system I propose, never again will a good judge say, "Stu, I can't get involved!" Why not, he tried to explain. He had to run again for reelection!

Chapter Notes

PROLOGUE

1. "My Hero May Be Your Stoolie," *The New York Times*, August 27, 1989

PREFACE

1. "Familiarity Breeds Mayhem," Richard Elman, *The New York Times*, October 8, 1989

CHAPTER FOUR

1. Letter of Michael Quartararo dated May 20, 1983
2. "Nine Years Later, a Confession," *Newsday*, May 19, 1988
3. In June 2003, Thomas (Tommy) Ryan pleaded guilty to attempted manslaughter for his role in the killing of John Pius. He had already served eighteen years in prison, and the sentencing was "little more than a formality" (*Newsday*, June 20, 2003). He was released almost immediately after taking the plea, having already served his time.

CHAPTER FIVE

1. I could find no publication of the reversal of the conviction of Phillip Wang. Perhaps he ultimately took a plea which would not be recorded. City attorneys representing Lai and Wang should ask me to disqualify myself as trial judge because the father of the eighteen-year-old college student killed in a gas station robbery served as the Republican Deputy Commissioner of Elections.
2. "Two Critically Wounded in Holdups: Three Are Held," Robert McFadden, *The New York Times*, March 21, 1982
3. See *State of New York v. Fabrizio Barbaran*, Mar. 3, 1986, 118 A.D. 2nd 578. P. 580 (1986), and *State of New York v. William Lai*, June 8, 1987, 131 A.D. 2nd 592 (1987) 10

CHAPTER SIX

1. *People v. Daniel Gallagher*, New York Court of Appeals
2. "Perjury Case Affects A Trial," *Newsday*, January 5, 1989

CHAPTER SEVEN

1. "MD Hurt, Lawyer Charged With DWI," *Newsday*, May 14, 1993
2. *People v. Vincent Waters*, County Court of Suffolk County
3. Statistical Data of Jury Survey conducted by Judge Stuart Namm
4. Letter dated May 10, 1984
5. Letter dated June 19, 1984
6. Recorded telephone conversation
7. Recorded telephone conversation
8. *People v. Vincent Waters*, Appellate Division, 2nd Dept., N.Y.

CHAPTER EIGHT

1. 1961 Yearbook, Patchogue High School, N.Y.

2. Ibid.

3. Testimony of William Patterson, trial notes

4. Testimony of Detective Robert Amato, trial notes

5. *People v. William Patterson*, County Court of Suffolk County, N.Y.

6. Affidavit of William Patterson

7. Ibid.

8. *People v. William Patterson*, County Court of Suffolk County, N.Y.

9. Official Court Record

CHAPTER NINE

1. "Prince of the City," Robert Daly

2. News Channel 12, Long Island, NY

3. News Channel 12, Long Island, NY

4. Final Report of the State Commission of Investigations

5. *Newsday* (date unknown)

6. *The New York Times* (date unknown)

7. Ibid.

8. Letter of James Corrigan

9. *Newsday* (date unknown)

10. Ibid.

11. Ibid.

12. *People v. Peter Corso*, County Court of Suffolk County

13. Supplementary Report of Det. Thomas Mongan

14. Memorandum of Lt. Dunn

15. Ibid.

16. Ibid.

17. Ibid.

18. Ibid.

19. *Newsday* (date unknown)

20. Official trial transcript

21. Ibid.

22. Ibid.

23. Ibid.

24. *Newsday* (date unknown)

25. Official court transcript

26. *Newsday* (date unknown)

27. Ibid.

28. Ibid.

29. Ibid.

30. Final Report, State Commission of Investigations

31. Letter of William Patterson

32. Final Report, State Commission of Investigations

33. Ibid.

CHAPTER TEN

1. "DA Questions Corso Probe," *Newsday*, July 4, 1985
2. Ibid.
3. Ibid.
4. Official transcript of hearing, July 10, 1985
5. Ibid.
6. Ibid.
7. Memorandum Decision, July 19, 1985
8. "Corso's Drug Charge Dismissed," *Newsday*, July 23, 1985
9. Ibid.
10. "Murder-Probe Rules Changing," *Newsday*, August 18, 1985
11. Ibid.
12. "Suffolk Homicide Chief Replaced After Criticism," September 10, 1985

CHAPTER ELEVEN

1. Pre-sentence report, Suffolk County Department of Probation, May 3, 1996

CHAPTER TWELVE

1. Letter of Judge Stuart Namm, dated August 5, 1985
2. Letter to the Hon. George F.X. McInerney, dated August 5, 1985
3. Letters of August 15, 1985
4. Pre-sentence report, Suffolk County Department of Probation
5. Ibid.
6. "Judge Calls Witness a Liar," *Newsday*, October 5, 1985
7. Ibid.
8. Ibid.
9. Final report, State of New York Commission of Investigations, April 1989
10. Ibid.

CHAPTER THIRTEEN

1. Memorandum of Robert R. Meguin, Esq, September 6 1985
2. Memorandum of Senior Court Officer Edward Dunseath, December 9, 1985
3. Excerpt from official trial transcript
4. Ibid.
5. "'Intimidation' Alleged by Judge," Thomas J. Maier, *Newsday*, October 24, 1985
6. Ibid.
7. Memorandum dated October 24, 1985
8. Ibid.
9. Ibid.
10. Court Exhibit #17
11. Court Exhibit #22
12. *Newsday*, October 27, 1985
13. Ibid.

CHAPTER FOURTEEN

1. Letter of October 29, 1985
2. Memorandum dated October 28, 1985
3. Official court transcript
4. See "Police Probing Plea by Son of Detectives Chief," Tom Demoretcky, *Newsday*, March 10 1986 and "Top Suffolk Police Officials Ousted in Corruption Probe," Tom Demoretcky and Thomas J. Maier, *Newsday*, March 13, 1986
5. "Treder, Bowing to Pressure, Quits as Police Commissioner," *Newsday*, April 12, 1987
6. "Cop Investigators at War," *Newsday*, December 9, 1985
7. See "Diaz Charged With Burglary," William Bunch, *Newsday*, December 9, 1985 and "Cleared, He's Held in Attack," Paul Meskil, *Daily News*, December 9, 1985
8. Memorandum dated November 21, 1985
9. Ibid.
10. Memorandum dated November 22, 1985
11. Memorandum dated December 2, 1985
12. Memorandum dated January 15, 1985
13. Letter dated November 25, 1985
14. Letter dated December 9, 1985

CHAPTER FIFTEEN

1. Official trial transcript
2. "Contradictions in Diaz Evidence," Thomas J. Maier, Newsday, December 18, 1985
3. *People v. James Diaz*, Corrected Notice of Motion, December 23, 1985
4. "Judge's Role in Dispute," Susan McGinn, *Port Jefferson Record*, January 9, 1986
5. *People v. James Diaz*, 130 Misc. 2nd 1024
6. "Case of the Judge vs. Prosecutors," John Rather, *The New York Times*, February 16, 1986
7. Affidavit of Jeffrey D. Weeks, January 7, 1986
8. Memorandum dated January 7, 1986
9. See "Diaz Case Judge Asked to Step Down," Bob Wacker, *Newsday*, January 7, 1986 and "Judge's Role in Dispute," Susan McGinn, *Port Jefferson Record*, January 9, 1986
10. Affidavit of Mark D. Cohen, January 21, 1986
11. *People v. Donald Kersch*
12. Affirmation of Judge Stuart Namm, dated February 3, 1986

CHAPTER SIXTEEN

1. *The New York Times*, February 16, 1986
2. Memorandum dated January 22, 1986
3. *New York Law Journal*, December 10, 1990
4. Memorandum dated January 29, 1986
5. Memorandum dated December 20, 1988

CHAPTER SEVENTEEN

1. "Diaz Will Forgo Jury, Face Judge," *Newsday*, November 28, 1986
2. "Diaz Will Forgo Jury, Face Judge," Bob Wacker, *Newsday*, March 28, 1986
3. "Woman Testifies at Diaz Trial," Bob Wacker, *Newsday*, April 2, 1986

4. "Diaz Guilty in Assault, Sex Abuse," Bob Wacker, *Newsday*, April 11, 1986
5. Official transcript of hearing
6. See "Judge Dismisses Diaz Indictment," Don Smith and Scott Minerbrook, *Newsday*, May 6, 1986 and "Drifter Sentenced to Prison," Salvatore Arena, *Daily News*, May 9, 1986
7. "Diaz is Given Maximum Term," *Newsday*, May 9, 1985
8. Letter dated May 20, 1986

CHAPTER EIGHTEEN

1. "State Subpoenas Suffolk Trial Records," *Newsday*, February 22, 1986
2. "Cop Fed Information to Probe," *Newsday*, March 9, 1986
3. "Cops in Drug Probe Dodge Investigation," *Newsday*, March 8, 1986
4. "Police Probing Plea by Son of Detective's Chief," *Newsday*, March 10, 1986
5. "Two Top Suffolk Police Officials Ousted in Corruption Probe," *Newsday*, March 13, 1986
6. "State: Suffolk Blocks Cop Probe," *Newsday*, March 14, 1986
7. "Outside Prosecutor Needed," *Suffolk Life* Newspapers, March 19, 1986
8. "Two Top Cops Say Copgate is No Big Scandal," *Daily News*, April 8, 1986
9. "Homicide Squad in Transition," *Newsday*, April 18, 1986
10. Memorandum dated February 13, 1986
11. "Three Probed in Faking Records for Cop's Son in Drug Case," *Newsday*, April 8, 1986
12. Memorandum dated February 6, 1986
13. Memorandum dated February 14, 1986

CHAPTER NINETEEN

1. "Letter dated July 8, 1987
2. Ibid
3. Letter dated July 8, 1987
4. Letter dated January 29, 1987
5. "Chief Counsel is Chosen at Investigation Agency," *The New York Times*, April 28, 1986
6. Memorandum dated July 30, 1986
7. "Suffolk Studying Changes in Police Force," *The New York Times*, September 14, 1986
8. "The Confession Takers," *Newsday*, December 7, 1986

CHAPTER TWENTY

1. Official transcript of hearing, January 28, 1987
2. Ibid.
3. Ibid.
4. "To Picketing Cops, a Day at the Circus, *Newsday*, January 30, 1987

CHAPTER TWENTY-ONE

1. "Suffolk Robbery Squad Chief, Set to Testify, Kills Himself," *Newsday*, January 15, 1987
2. Memorandum dated March 6, 1987
3. Letter dated December, 1986
4. Motion for Stay dated November 18, 1976
5. Affirmation dated December 15, 1976

6. Transcript of tape recorded statement of victim to Detective Burke at Southold Police Department
7. "Treder Bowing to Pressure, Quits as Police Commissioner," *Newsday*, April 2, 1987
8. Letter dated April 20, 1988
9. Letter dated April 27, 1988
10. Memorandum dated January 30, 1989

CHAPTER TWENTY-TWO

1. Official trial transcript
2. "Lawyer: I Told Detectives Not to Question Tankleff," *Newsday*, March 28, 1989
3. "Gottlieb Grills Homicide Detective," *Port Jefferson Record*, March 16, 1989
4. "Jittery, Agonized Flight from LI," *Newsday*, September 30, 1988
5. "Don't Attack Tankleff's Attorney: He Was Doing the Right Thing," *Newsday*, November 5, 1990
6."How Many In Court Running For DA?" *Newsday*, April 11, 1989
7. "DA Race Heats Up," *Pennysaver News of Brookhaven*, May 6, 1989
8. "Juror: Defendant Convicted Himself," *Newsday*, June 19, 1990
9. "Juror: Story Didn't Fit," *Port Jefferson Record*, July 5, 1990
10. "Sister Feels Tankleff Guilty, Ex-Cop Says," *Newsday*, June 22, 1990
11. Ibid.
12. "Marty Didn't Do It, Relatives Say," *Port Jefferson Record*, July 5, 1990
13. "Judge Blasts Tankleff Attorneys," *Newsday*, October 2, 1990
14. "Tankleff Defense: ADA Anti-Semitic," *Newsday*, October 6, 1990
15. "There's No Room for Bigotry in Suffolk DA's Office," *Newsday*, October 18, 1990
16. "Don't Attack Tankleff's Attorney: He Was Doing the Right Thing," *Newsday*, November 5, 1990

CHAPTER TWENTY-THREE

1. "Don't Attack Tankleff's Attorney: He Was Doing the Right Thing," *Newsday*, November 5, 1990
2. Affidavit of Kevin Fox, March 13, 1991
3. Affidavit of Asst. District Attorney Michael H. Ahearn, March 21, 1991
4. Videotaped confession of Robert Sullivan
5. *People v. Anthony Atkinson*, decision dated July 11, 1991
6. *Newsday*, July 12, 1991
7. Testimony of P.O. Stephen Jacobs before the Grand Jury, February 10, 1992

CHAPTER TWENTY-FOUR

1. *Three Village Herald*, July 15, 1992
2. Dominic J. Baranello, "Long Island Newsmakers," News 12, July 19, 1992

CONCLUSION

1. *Government Ethics Reform for the 1990s: The Collected Reports of the New York State Commission on Government Integrity*, Fordham University Press, New York, 1991
2. Ibid., p. 271-272
3. *Pace Law Review*, Volume 9, Spring 1989, Number 2
4. Ibid., p. 229

5. *Government Ethics Reform for the 1990s*, p. 299
6. *The Public Policy Forum, Court Reform in New York State*, p. 6
7. Final Report to the Chief Judge of the State of New York